**I LOVE GERMANY
WWW.MAMYWOTO.COM**

Für Amélie
To Amélie

**Publiziert in Zusammenarbeit
mit dem Deutschen Komitee für UNICEF
Published in cooperation
with the German Committee for UNICEF**

MAMYWOTO
I LOVE
GERMANY

nicolai

GRUSSWORT

Bei meinen vielen Reisen durch Deutschland war ich oft erstaunt über die vielen landschaftlichen und architektonischen Schönheiten in unseren 16 Bundesländern: beeindruckende Schlösser und Kirchen, gewaltige Berge, bunte Wälder und weite Küsten. Es lohnt sich sehr, unser Land zu entdecken – gemeinsam mit dem Gartenzwerg Mamywoto, der es einen Sommer lang erkundet hat.

Mit einem Blick für die Schönheit des Landes und mit Leidenschaft für skurrile Details präsentiert Mamywoto in über hundert Farbfotografien die ganze Vielfalt Deutschlands – von den Sylter Stränden über den Kölner Dom bis hin zum Königssee bei Berchtesgaden. In kurzweiligen Texten erzählt er uns zudem interessante Details aus Kultur, Geschichte und Politik. Ich bin zuversichtlich, dass die Bilder aus der Perspektive des kleinen Mamywoto Einheimischen wie Besuchern aus dem Ausland neue Blickwinkel auf das Land bieten. Besonders freue ich mich jedoch darüber, dass der Bildband Kindern in Not hilft. Denn zum 60. Geburtstag machen der Berliner Nicolai Verlag und Mamywoto UNICEF ein Geschenk: Von jedem verkauften Buch geht ein Anteil an UNICEF. Mit dem Erlös werden Hilfsprojekte in 160 Ländern unterstützt.

Ich hoffe, dass Mamywoto auch Sie neugierig darauf macht, Deutschland noch besser kennen zu lernen – und den nächsten Strandurlaub vielleicht an der Ostsee zu verbringen. Ich danke dem Verlag und Mamywoto für ihr großes Engagement.

Heide Simonis, Vorsitzende des Deutschen Komitees für UNICEF

GREETING

In all my many travels through Germany, I was often surprised by the many beautiful kinds of countryside and architecture that are on display in our 16 federal states: impressive castles and churches, huge mountains, colourful forests and far-flung coasts. Discovering our nation is well worth it – together with Mamywoto, the garden gnome, who explored it one summer long.

In over one hundred colour photographs and with an eye for the beauty of the country as well as a passion for bizarre details, Mamywoto presents Germany in its entire spectrum: from the beaches of Sylt, by way of Cologne Cathedral, to the Königssee near Berchtesgaden. In entertaining prose, he furthermore provides us with interesting details about its culture, history and politics. I am confident that the photos seen through the vantage point of little Mamywoto will offer the inhabitants as well as visitors from abroad a new slant on Germany. I am especially pleased by the fact that this book will help children in need. For, on its 60th anniversary, the Berlin Nicolai Verlag and Mamywoto are presenting UNICEF with a gift: a share of the proceeds of every book sold goes to UNICEF. The proceeds will support aid projects in 160 countries.

I hope that Mamywoto will make you curious enough to learn more about Germany – and perhaps prompt you to take your next beach holiday on the Baltic. I can only thank the publisher and Mamywoto for their grand commitment.

Heide Simonis, Chairperson of the German Committee for UNICEF

Nationalflagge Deutschlands und Flaggen der deutschen Bundesländer
National flag of Germany and flags of the German Federal States

Berlin
Berlin

Baden-Württemberg
Baden-Wurttemberg

Bayern
Bavaria

Brandenburg
Brandenburg

Bremen
Bremen

Hamburg
Hamburg

Hessen
Hesse

Mecklenburg-Vorpommern
Mecklenburg-West Pomerania

Niedersachsen
Lower Saxony

Nordrhein-Westfalen
North Rhine-Westphalia

Rheinland-Pfalz
Rhineland-Palatinate

Saarland
Saarland

Sachsen
Saxony

Sachsen-Anhalt
Saxony-Anhalt

Schleswig-Holstein
Schleswig-Holstein

Thüringen
Thuringia

LIEBE FREUNDE,

wie ihr ja schon lange wisst, habe ich mich vor einiger Zeit zum ersten Mal in meinem Leben zu einer richtig großen Reise aufgemacht. Ich war viele Monate in ganz Deutschland unterwegs, von Rügen bis zum Bodensee, von Görlitz bis nach Völklingen, von Passau bis zum Teufelsmoor, vom Watzmann bis nach Helgoland. Eigentlich ist unsereiner ja nicht grade besonders reiselustig, und es war natürlich sehr anstrengend für mich, aber ich habe wunderbare Orte gesehen und viele liebenswürdige Menschen kennen gelernt.

Auch das wisst ihr schon alles, ich habe euch in diesen Monaten ja immer wieder mal kurz davon berichtet. Und für meine Reise habe ich auch von euch viele schöne Tipps bekommen. Herzlichen Dank dafür. Ihr habt oft gefragt, ob ich nicht einmal ein bisschen ausführlicher erzählen könnte. Manche hätten gerne auch mal Bilder gesehen, andere wollten wissen, ob ich nicht ein Reisetagebuch geschrieben habe usw.

Ich habe lange überlegt, wie ich diese Wünsche am besten erfülle. Und eines Tages habe ich mit einem guten Freund vor meinem großen Haufen von Fotos und Notizen gesessen und versucht, sie zu sortieren. Plötzlich sagte er: »Warum machst du nicht einfach ein Buch draus?« Nun wisst ihr wahrscheinlich besser als ich, dass man ein Buch nicht mal einfach so machen kann, und einer wie ich schon gleich gar nicht. Aber der Gedanke hat sich doch irgendwie bei mir festgesetzt, und was daraus geworden ist, seht ihr nun ja. Die Bilder habe ich übrigens nach Bundesländern geordnet: Berlin als Bundesland und Bundeshauptstadt vorneweg, der Rest in alphabetischer Reihenfolge.

Ich hoffe, ihr habt Spaß daran. Vielleicht lasst ihr mich wissen, was ihr von meinem Werk haltet. Mailt einfach an mamywoto@mamywoto.com.

DEAR FRIENDS

As you've known for some time, a while ago I set off for the first time in my life on a really long and proper journey. I was on the road for many months travelling through Germany, from Rügen to Lake Constance, from Görlitz to Völklingen, from Passau to Teufelsmoor, from the Watzmann to Helgoland. Actually our sort is not particularly keen on travel, and it was naturally very strenuous for me, but I saw wonderful places and met many lovely people.

But then you already know that too; over the past months I have sent you short reports from time to time. And you have helped me out with many good travel tips, for which I heartily thank you. You have asked me again and again if I couldn't please report to you in more detail. Some of you would have liked photos, others wanted to know whether I have kept a travel journal, etc.

I thought a long time about how best to fulfil these wishes. And one day I was sitting with a good friend facing a large pile of photos and notes with the intention of sorting them out. Suddenly he said to me: »Why don't you simply make these into a book?« Now you probably know better than I do that it's not so simple to just make a book, and particularly not at all for someone like me. But the thought had somehow got fixed in my mind, so that what you see before you is the way it all turned out. I have, by the way, arranged the photos according to the federal states: Berlin as a city-state and the federal capital leading the way, and all the rest in alphabetical order.

I wish you pleasant browsing. And maybe you could let me know what you think of my work. Simply send an E-mail at mamywoto@mamywoto.com.

REICHSTAG, BERLIN

Der Berliner Reichstag ist Sitz des Deutschen Bundestages, des Parlaments der Bundesrepublik Deutschland. Er wurde 1884 bis 1894 gebaut, 1933 in Brand gesteckt, ist 12 Jahre später durch Bomben zerstört und nach dem Krieg vorläufig wieder instand gesetzt worden. Er stand 28 Jahre lang direkt an der Mauer, die Berlin in Ost und West teilte, und wurde 1995 bis 1999 um- und ausgebaut. Wie kaum ein anderes Gebäude ist er ein Symbol für die wechselvolle Geschichte Deutschlands vom späten 19. bis zum Ende des 20. Jahrhunderts: vom Kaiserreich über den Ersten Weltkrieg, die Weimarer Republik, die Nazi-Diktatur, den Zweiten Weltkrieg, die Gründung der BRD und der DDR, den Kalten Krieg, Bau und Fall der Mauer bis zur deutschen Wiedervereinigung und dem Umzug der Regierung von Bonn nach Berlin. Seit 1999 ist der Reichstag das Zentrum des neuen Regierungsviertels.

REICHSTAG, BERLIN

The Berlin Reichstag is the seat of the German Bundestag, the parliament of the Federal Republic of Germany. It was built from 1884 to 1894, set fire to in 1933, was destroyed 12 years later by bombs, and after the war, provisionally restored. It stood for 28 years directly next to the Wall which divided Berlin into East and West, and was thoroughly rebuilt and expanded from 1995 to 1999. Like hardly any other building, it is a symbol of the chequered history of Germany from the late 19th century to the end of the 20th century: from an Empire, via World War I, the Weimar Republic, the Nazi dictatorship, World War II, the founding of the FRG and the GDR, the Cold War, the building and the fall of the Wall, up to German reunification and the government's move from Bonn to Berlin. Since 1999, the Reichstag has been the centre of the new government quarter.

DIE MAUER, BERLIN

Der erste eiserne Vorhang der Weltgeschichte ist 1782 in der französischen Stadt Lyon in einem Theater heruntergegangen. Er sollte die Bühne vom Zuschauerraum trennen, falls es mal brannte. Damals gab es noch kein elektrisches Licht und keine Scheinwerfer, sondern nur Kerzen und Fackeln, und deswegen sind Theater immer wieder mal abgebrannt. Eiserne Vorhänge sind seitdem in die meisten Theater der Welt eingebaut worden, und wenn dann auf einer Bühne mal Feuer ausbrach, war's nicht mehr ganz so schlimm.

Am 5. März 1946 sagte der britische Premierminister Winston Churchill in einer Rede, dass über ganz Europa von Stettin bis nach Triest ein »Eiserner Vorhang« heruntergegangen sei, mit dem der Sowjetführer Stalin seinen Machtbereich vom Rest Europas abtrennen wollte. Davon war Deutschland ganz besonders betroffen, denn diese Grenze ging mitten durchs Land und trennte die drei westlichen Besatzungszonen, die spätere BRD, von der östlichen, der späteren DDR. Mitten in der DDR aber lag die ehemalige deutsche Hauptstadt Berlin, die auch in vier Zonen aufgeteilt war.

»Niemand hat die Absicht, eine Mauer zu errichten.« Mit diesen Worten hat der DDR-Staatsratsvorsitzende Walter Ulbricht am 15. Juni 1961 angekündigt, dass er vorhatte, West-Berlin einzumauern. Angefangen hat er damit knapp zwei Monate später, am 13. August. Die Mauer war ungefähr 160 Kilometer lang und ist im Laufe der Zeit zur bestbewachten Grenze der Welt ausgebaut worden: mit Beton, Stacheldraht, Flutlicht, Wachtürmen, Soldaten, Hunden, Minenfeldern und Selbstschussanlagen.

Heute gibt es nur noch Mauerreste, viele davon sind bemalt, das längste Stück ist 1,3 Kilometer lang. Hier begrüßt einer von Stalins Nachfolgern, der Herr Breschnew, den Nachfolger von Walter Ulbricht, den Herrn Honecker.

THE BERLIN WALL

The first iron curtain in world history was rung down in 1782 in a theatre in the French city of Lyon. It was meant to separate the stage from the audience in case fire broke out. At the time, there was no electric lighting and no spotlights, only candles and torches, for which reason theatres tended to burn down from time to time. Since then, iron curtains have been built into most of the theatres around the world, and so if a fire ever broke out on stage, it was no longer quite so bad.

On March 5, 1946, the British prime minister Winston Churchill stated in a speech that an »iron curtain« had been lowered over all of Europe, from Stettin to Trieste, which the Soviet leader Stalin meant to use to separate his power base from the rest of Europe. Germany was particularly affected by this, for the boundary line ran straight through the middle of the country and separated the three western zones of occupation (the future FRG) from the one eastern zone (the future GDR). However, right in the middle of the GDR lay the former German capital Berlin, which was also divided into four zones.

»No one has the intention of erecting a wall.« With these words on June 15, 1961, the GDR Chairman of the State Council, Walter Ulbricht, announced his plan to enclose West Berlin. Two months later on August 13, he began to do just that. The wall was about 160 km long and, over the course of time, was converted into the best-guarded frontier in the world: with concrete, barbed wire, floodlights, guard towers, soldiers, dogs, mine fields and automatic firing devices.

Today, only relics of it are left, all awash in graffiti; the longest segment runs for 1.3 km. Here you see one of Stalin's successors, Leonid Brezhnev, as he greets Walter Ulbricht's successor, Eric Honecker.

MARX-ENGELS-DENKMAL, BERLIN

Das Marx-Engels-Denkmal auf dem Marx-Engels-Forum im ehemaligen Ost-Berlin in der Nähe von Dom und Rotem Rathaus ist am 4. April 1986 eingeweiht worden. Anschließend hat die Deutsche Demokratische Republik nur noch dreieinhalb Jahre existiert; die Planungen und Vorbereitungen für den Platz und das Denkmal hatten mehr als doppelt so lange gedauert.

In der Zeit nach 1989, als der Eiserne Vorhang verschwunden war, sind in allen Ländern Osteuropas Hunderte von Denkmälern sozialistischer Staatsmänner und Helden abgebaut, versetzt oder eingeschmolzen worden. Auch für Karl Marx und Friedrich Engels, die Verfasser des »Kommunistischen Manifests« von 1848, hat es damals lange Zeit nicht sehr gut ausgesehen. Die einen wollten nach Möglichkeit alles, was an die DDR erinnerte, aus der Welt schaffen, die andern haben dagegen versucht, die Erinnerung an die jüngere deutsche Geschichte wach zu halten, und die haben sich schließlich durchgesetzt.

Jeden Tag kann man um das Denkmal herum Besucher beobachten, wie sie sich zusammen mit den beiden alten Herren fürs Album fotografieren lassen. Karl Marx hat davon schon ganz abgewetzte Knie bekommen.

MARX-ENGELS MONUMENT, BERLIN

The Marx-Engels Monument (on the Marx-Engels Forum in East Berlin near the Cathedral and the Red Rathaus, Berlin's city hall) was officially opened on April 4, 1986. Following this the GDR only existed for another three-and-a-half years. Just planning and preparing the ground for the monument had taken more than twice that long.

In the period following 1989 when the Iron Curtain was finally lifted, many hundreds of monuments to socialist statesmen and heroes were dismantled, moved or melted down in all East European countries. Even for the authors of the 1848 Communist Manifesto Karl Marx and Friedrich Engels, things didn't look too good for a long time. There were those who wanted to eliminate, as far as possible, anything that recalled the GDR, while others tried to hold onto the memory of recent German history, and they were the ones who finally prevailed.

Any day of the week, you can observe visitors at the monument having their photograph taken with the two elderly gentlemen for their album. Karl Marx's knees have already been worn smooth from all this attention.

POTSDAMER PLATZ, BERLIN

Was heute Potsdamer Platz heißt, war um 1830 bloß eine Kreuzung westlich von Berlin. Die hatte noch keinen richtigen Namen und hieß einfach »Platz vor dem Potsdamer Thor«. Dann hat man 1838 dort den Potsdamer Bahnhof gebaut, und aus der Kreuzung wurde allmählich ein richtiger Platz. 1890 sind hier im Jahr schon über 1,4 Millionen Menschen in die Züge gestiegen, weit mehr als auf den anderen Berliner Bahnhöfen. 1895 gab es in der Umgebung 92 Restaurants, 10 Destillen, 13 Cafés und 36 Schankwirtschaften.

In den »Goldenen Zwanzigern« wurde der Potsdamer Platz zum verkehrsreichsten in ganz Europa: 100.000 Menschen, 20.000 Autos und 30 Straßenbahnlinien haben ihn jeden Tag überquert.

Nach dem Zweiten Weltkrieg war vom Potsdamer Platz nicht mehr viel übrig. Nur das Weinhaus Huth stand noch und Teile vom Hotel Esplanade. Als die vier Besatzungsmächte die Stadt unter sich aufteilten, stießen hier drei Sektoren zusammen: der sowjetische, der britische und der amerikanische.

Nach dem Bau der Mauer war die Gegend um den Potsdamer Platz fast 30 Jahre lang ödes Niemandsland vor dem Todesstreifen. Am 9. November 1989 ist über Nacht alles anders geworden: Die Mauer war offen. Plötzlich lag der Potsdamer Platz wieder im Herzen von Berlin und sollte bald wieder zu dem werden, was er früher einmal gewesen war. Auch die alte U-Bahn-Station »Potsdamer Platz« ist wieder eröffnet worden; sie ist der älteste im Original (von 1907) erhaltene U-Bahnhof in Deutschland.

POTSDAMER PLATZ, BERLIN

Around 1830, the present Potsdamer Platz was merely an intersection west of Berlin. It had no real name and was simply called »Square at Potsdam Gate«. In 1838, the Potsdam Railway Station was built, and the intersection gradually turned into a proper square. By 1890, there were already more than 1.4 million people per year boarding trains here, far more than at the other Berlin railway stations. By 1895, there were 92 restaurants, 10 distilleries, 13 cafés and 36 bars in the immediate area.

In the Golden Twenties, Potsdamer Platz boasted more traffic than any other square in Europe: 100,000 people, 20,000 cars and 30 tram lines crossed it everyday.

In the wake of World War II, there was not much left of Potsdamer Platz. All that stood was Wine House Huth and parts of the Esplanade Hotel. When the four occupying forces divided up the city amongst them, three sectors bumped together here: the Soviet, the British and the American sectors.

After the building of the Wall, the area around Potsdamer Platz was a grim no-man's land along the death strip for almost 30 years. On November 9, 1989, everything changed overnight. Potsdamer Platz lay once again at the heart of Berlin and was soon to become what it once had been. The old underground station »Potsdamer Platz« has also been reopened; it is the oldest tube station in Germany still preserved in its original 1907 state.

POTSDAMER PLATZ, BERLIN

Die Firmen Sony und Daimler-Benz (inzwischen DaimlerChrysler) haben 1991 das über 50 Hektar große Gelände um den Potsdamer Platz herum gekauft, und bald darauf war hier die größte Baustelle in Europa: Die »Daimler-City« und das »Sony-Center« wurden gebaut, eine komplette Stadt in der Stadt, mit allem, was dazugehört und was nach Metropole aussieht: Bürohochhäuser, Nobelhotels, Firmenzentralen, Luxusapartments, Musicaltheater, Casino, Kinos, Discos, Bars, Restaurants, Fastfood-Läden und eine dreistöckige, 180 Meter lange Einkaufspassage. An manchen Tagen kommen 60.000 Menschen hierher.

Das »Lindenbräu« ist die nördlichste Weißbierbrauerei in Deutschland. Von der Terrasse hat man einen schönen Blick auf das »Forum«, den 4000 Quadratmeter großen Platz im Sony-Center. Obendrüber haben die Architekten einen riesigen Schirm aufgespannt, 40 Meter im Durchmesser, und es ist schwer zu sagen, ob man hier drinnen ist oder draußen.

POTSDAMER PLATZ, BERLIN

Sony and Daimler-Benz (now DaimlerChrysler) bought the more than 50-hectare plot around Potsdamer Platz in 1991 and soon after, at Europe's biggest building site, »Daimler City« and the »Sony Center« were built. An entire city within a city with everything that goes with it and which has a metropolitan air: high-rised offices, company headquarters, noble hotels, luxury apartments, musical theatres, a casino, cinemas, discos, bars, restaurants, fast food chains and a three-storey, 180-metre long shopping arcade. On some days, 60,000 people come here.

The »Lindenbräu« is the northernmost wheat beer brewery in Germany. From its terrace you get a good view of the »Forum«, the 4000 square-metre courtyard within the Sony Center. Over it all, the architects have spanned a giant umbrella, 40 metres in diameter and, once under it, it is difficult to tell if you are indoors or out.

NEUE NATIONALGALERIE, BERLIN

Anfang der 60er Jahre des vorigen Jahrhunderts meinten die West-Berliner, sie müssten sich unbedingt auch von dem berühmten Architekten Ludwig Mies van der Rohe etwas bauen lassen. Was das aber genau sein sollte, war anfangs noch nicht so ganz klar. Berlin war damals »Frontstadt« im Kalten Krieg und »Schaufenster des Westens« mitten im Feindesland, und da sollten eben auch besonders interessante Bauwerke zu sehen sein; damals wurde viel gebaut in Berlin. Von dem finnischem Architekten Alvar Aalto stand jedenfalls schon ein Gebäude, auch von dem französischen Baumeister Le Corbusier und von einer Reihe anderer bekannter Architekten.

Schließlich hat man sich darauf geeinigt, dass West-Berlin eine neue Nationalgalerie brauchte, die alte stand ja auf der Museumsinsel im Osten, und der »westliche« Teil der im Krieg ausgelagerten Sammlung war nur provisorisch untergebracht.

Mies van der Rohe nahm den Auftrag an und konnte planen, wie und was er wollte. Also hat er in der Nähe der neuen Philharmonie von Hans Scharoun die größte freitragende Stahlplatte der Welt zusammenschweißen lassen, 64,8 Meter im Quadrat und 1250 Tonnen schwer, hat sie hydraulisch in acht Meter vierzig Höhe heben und auf acht Stützen absetzen lassen. Den Raum darunter hat er rundum verglast, so dass eine große freie Halle für Wechselausstellungen entstand. Das eigentliche Museum hat er ins Untergeschoss verlegt.

1968 wurden dort die Gemälde aus der Alten Nationalgalerie und die der Galerie des 20. Jahrhunderts untergebracht. Nach der Wiedervereinigung kamen die Werke aus dem 19. Jahrhundert wieder zurück in den Tempel auf der Museumsinsel, und in der Neuen Nationalgalerie sind jetzt ausschließlich Bilder und Skulpturen aus dem 20. Jahrhundert zu sehen.

NEW NATIONAL GALLERY, BERLIN

At the beginning of the 1960s the people of West Berlin thought they just had to have the famous architect Ludwig Mies van der Rohe build something for them. But what that was to be precisely, they weren't at first quite clear about. Berlin was then a city on the frontline in the Cold War and a »showcase of the West« in the midst of enemy country, where interesting architecture was considered a visual must. At that time a lot of building was going on in Berlin. At any rate, one building by the Finnish architect Alvar Aalto was already standing, as was one by the French architect Le Corbusier and buildings by a series of other well-known architects.

It was finally agreed that West Berlin needed a new National Gallery; the old one stood on the Museumsinsel (Museum Island) in the East, whereas the »western« part of its collection, stored away for safety during the war, had only a provisional location.

Mies van der Rohe accepted the commission and was free to plan how and what he wanted. So, near Hans Scharoun's new, shiny gold Philharmonic Hall, he had the largest suspended steel plate in the world soldered together, 64.8 metres square and weighing 1250 tons. It was then lifted hydraulically to a height of 8.40 metres and set onto eight supports. The space underneath was completely glassed in so that a large free hall for changing exhibitions was created. The actual museum with its permanent collections he assigned to the lower floor.

In 1968, the paintings from the Old National Gallery and the Gallery of the 20th Century were installed there. After reunification, the works from the 19th century were taken back to the temple on the Museum Island, and the New National Gallery now houses exclusively paintings and sculptures from the 20th century.

INSEL MAINAU, BODENSEE

Wie wird bloß ein schwedischer Erbfürst Eigentümer einer Insel im Bodensee und der berühmteste Gärtner von Europa?

Ganz einfach: 1853 erwirbt der spätere Großherzog Friedrich I. von Baden die Mainau und fängt damit an, einen Park anzulegen. 1856 heiratet er die Tochter des späteren preußischen Kaisers Wilhelm I., Prinzessin Luise. 1907 stirbt der Großherzog, und die Mainau fällt an seinen Sohn, Großherzog Friedrich II. Der will seiner Schwester Viktoria, inzwischen Königin von Schweden, eine Freude machen und schenkt ihr die Insel, über 1400 Kilometer südlich von Stockholm. Der Sohn der Königin, Prinz Wilhelm von Schweden, heiratet die russische Großfürstin Maria Pawlowna, eine Enkelin von Zar Alexander II. 1909 kommt ihr Sohn zur Welt: Prinz Lennart Nicolaus Paul, Erbfürst von Schweden und Herzog von Smarland. 1930 stirbt Königin Viktoria, und ihr Sohn Prinz Wilhelm erbt die Mainau. 1932 überträgt der die Verwaltung der Insel an Prinz Lennart, einen studierten Land- und Forstwirt.

Der heiratet anschließend Karin Nissvandt, die Tochter eines Stockholmer Fabrikanten, verzichtet auf die Thronfolge und zieht sich auf die Mainau zurück, in ein feuchtes barockes Deutschordensschloss mitten in einem verwilderten Park. In den nächsten Jahrzehnten macht Graf Lennart Bernadotte, so nennt er sich jetzt, die Insel zum schönsten Park von Deutschland und zur größten touristischen Attraktion im und um den Bodensee. Und nebenher wird er Vater von neun Kindern.

Jedes Jahr kommen 1,7 Millionen Besucher aus aller Welt hierher, und 2005 hatten sie was ganz Besonderes zu bestaunen: einen Riesenzwerg – oder Zwergriesen? – aus 16.000 Pflanzen, 16 Meter lang, 6 Meter breit und 9 Meter hoch. Wir hatten uns sehr viel zu erzählen.

ISLE OF MAINAU, CONSTANCE

How did a Swedish crown prince ever become the owner of an island in Lake Constance and the most famous gardener in Europe?

Quite simple: in 1853, the future Grand Duke Friedrich I of Baden purchases Mainau and begins to lay out a park there. In 1856 he marries Princess Luise, the daughter of the future Emperor Wilhelm I of Prussia. In 1907, the Grand Duke dies and Mainau falls to his son, Grand Duke Friedrich II, who wants to please his sister Viktoria, now Queen of Sweden, with the gift of an isle more than 1400 kilometres south of Stockholm. The queen's son, Prince Wilhelm of Sweden, marries Maria Pavlovna, the Grand Duchess of Russia and a granddaughter of Czar Alexander II. In 1909, their son is born: Prince Lennart Nicolaus Paul, crown prince of Sweden and Duke of Smarland. In 1930, Queen Viktoria dies and her son Prince Wilhelm inherits Mainau. In 1932, the island's administrators confer the island upon Prince Lennart, who has a degree in agriculture and forestry.

The prince then subsequently marries Karin Nissvandt, the daughter of a Stockholm manufacturer, waives his right of succession to the Swedish throne and withdraws to Mainau to live in a damp, Baroque castle of the Teutonic Order in the midst of an untended park. Over the next decades, Count Lennart Bernadotte, as he now calls himself, transforms the isle into Germany's most beautiful park and the greatest tourist attraction in and around Lake Constance. And, in passing, he fathers nine children.

Every year, 1.7 million visitors from all over the world come here, and in 2005 they had something very special to marvel at: a giant dwarf – or dwarf-giant? – made up of 16,000 plants, 16 metres long, 6 metres wide and 9 metres high. We two had a lot to tell each other.

INTERNAT SCHLOSS SALEM, SALEM

Wenn ich mir eine Schule aussuchen dürfte, dann bräuchte ich nicht lange nachzudenken: Ich würde nach Salem gehen. Aber nicht etwa, weil in diesem Internat schon der Herzog von Edinburgh, die spanische Königin Sophia, der Historiker Golo Mann und viele andere berühmte Leute die Schulbank gedrückt haben. Sondern weil man viel mehr lernt als das, was in den meisten anderen Schulen auf dem Lehrplan steht. Am besten lässt sich das vielleicht so zusammenfassen: Verantwortung für andere und für die Gemeinschaft, Hilfsbereitschaft, soziales Denken und Handeln.

Die Internatsschule ist 1920, kurz nach dem Ersten Weltkrieg, von Maximilian von Baden und dem Reformpädagogen Kurt Hahn im ehemaligen Zisterzienserkloster Salem gegründet worden, nicht weit von Konstanz, ein paar Kilometer nördlich vom Bodensee. Heute sind alle neun Jahrgänge an drei verschiedenen Orten untergebracht: die Unterstufe in der Burg Hohenfels, die Mittelstufe im Schloss Salem und die Oberstufe im modernen Salem College.

Salem ist die einzige Schule in Deutschland mit einer eigenen Feuerwehr, einem Technischen Hilfswerk und einem Sanitätsdienst. In der zehnten Klasse muss sich jeder für einen dieser Dienste entscheiden. Im Notfall haben sie immer Vorrang, und alles andere muss warten. Außerdem bekommen die Schüler Einblick in verschiedene Handwerksberufe.

Für mich könnte das schwierig werden, denn bei der Feuerwehr, fürs THW und für den Sanitätsdienst wäre ich wahrscheinlich nicht so gut zu gebrauchen. Aber in den Salemer Gärten könnte ich mich ganz bestimmt nützlich machen.

BOARDING SCHOOL IN SCHLOSS SALEM, SALEM

If I were allowed to choose a school, I wouldn't have to think about it twice. I would go to Salem. But not because the Duke of Edinburgh and the Greek-born Queen Sophia of Spain, the historian Golo Mann and many other famous people once sat at these desks. But because you learn much more here than what most schools offer on their curriculum. Perhaps it's best summed up by the following: responsibility for others and for the common good, helpfulness, social values in thought and deed.

The boarding school was founded in 1920, shortly after World War I, by Maximilian von Baden and the reformist pedagogue Kurt Hahn, in the former Cistercian cloister Salem, not far from Constance, a few kilometres north of Lake Constance. Today, all nine school years are located on three different campuses: the lower school classes in Burg Hohenfels, the middle classes in Schloss Salem and the upper classes in modern Salem College.

Salem is the only school in Germany with its own fire brigade, a technical relief organization and a medical service. In 10th grade, everyone must decide which one to join. In any state of emergency, these services take absolute precedence, and everything else is put on hold. In addition, the students get a good look into different trades.

This could become very difficult for me; I would probably not be much use as a fireman, technician or paramedic. But in the Salem gardens I could quite certainly make myself useful.

INTERNAT SCHLOSS SALEM, SALEM

Auf der vorhergehenden Seite habt ihr mich gesehen, wie ich im Wohntrakt von Schloss Salem den Stundenplan studiere. Jetzt stehe ich im Speisesaal, und in ein paar Minuten beginnt der Ansturm auf das Mittagessen. Dann wollen die 240 Jungen und Mädchen der Mittelstufe satt werden. Für das Decken der Tische sind die Schülerinnen und Schüler zuständig; hier müssen alle ran.

BOARDING SCHOOL IN SCHLOSS SALEM, SALEM

On the previous page, you could see me in the residential wing of Schloss Salem, studying the timetable. Now I'm standing in the dining hall and in a few minutes the assault on lunch will begin, when 240 boys and girls from the middle school rush to still their hunger. The pupils are themselves responsible for setting the tables; no one is left out.

GASTHOF SOMMERAU, SCHWARZWALD

Am Südostrand des Schwarzwalds, an der Strecke von Schaffhausen nach Freiburg, liegt Bonndorf. Von hier aus fährt man über die L 170 nach Westen Richtung Schluchsee bis zur ersten Abzweigung in einer engen Linkskurve. Jetzt geht's ungefähr fünf Kilometer durch den Wald, und da sieht man sie auch schon liegen, in den sanft ansteigenden Wiesen des Steinatals: die Sommerau.

Von weitem sieht der Gasthof aus wie ein ganz normales, traditionelles Schwarzwaldhaus. Aber wenn man näher kommt, merkt man: Das ist doch bestimmt noch keine hundert Jahre alt. Das Walmdach hat die vertraute Form, aber die Giebelseite sieht aus, als wäre sie verspiegelt –: Solarzellen.

Tatsächlich hat hier einmal ein 400 Jahre altes Haus gestanden, aber das ist 1988 bis auf die Grundmauern abgebrannt. Der Wiederaufbau hat drei Jahre gedauert, und 1991 ist das neue Haus eröffnet worden. Das Hotel mit dem Restaurant und das Nebengebäude sind aus Holz gebaut, und zwar so schön, dass die Architekten 1992 dafür den »Deutschen Holzbaupreis« bekommen haben.

Bei der Sommerau ist die Straße zu Ende, hier gibt es keinen Durchgangsverkehr und auch sonst keine Hektik. Zum Ausruhen, zum Entspannen und um gut zu essen ist das genau der richtige Ort.

GASTHOF SOMMERAU IN THE BLACK FOREST

On the southeast perimeter of the Black Forest, on the road from Schaffhausen to Freiburg, lies Bonndorf. From here you drive along the country road 170 westwards in the direction of Schluchsee, until you get to the first turnoff in a narrow left bend. From here it's about five kilometres through the woods, and then you see it set in the gently rising meadows of the Steina Valley: the Sommerau.

From a distance the guesthouse looks like any normal traditional Black Forest residence. But on approaching it, you notice that it is most certainly not even a hundred years old. The hipped roof has the familiar shape, but the gable side looks as if it were covered in mirrors: solar cells!

And, in fact, a 400-year-old house did once stand here, but in 1988 it burned down to its foundation. Its reconstruction took three years, and in 1991 the new house was opened. The hotel, with the restaurant and annex, was built as a pure wood-frame construction, and its architects did it so beautifully that they received the »German Timber Construction Award« of 1992.

The road ends at the Sommerau; there is no through traffic here and no other hectic activity. It is just the right place to put your feet up, relax and enjoy good food.

FREIBURG IM BREISGAU

Wenn es jemand gern sonnig hat und Mallorca ihm zu weit weg ist, dann sollte er nach Freiburg ziehen. Nirgendwo sonst in Deutschland scheint die Sonne so oft und so schön wie hier im Breisgau auf dem 38. Breitengrad, und nirgendwo ist es wärmer.

Vielleicht ist das ja der Grund dafür, dass Freiburg als die »Öko-Hauptstadt« von Deutschland gilt. Das merkt man nicht zuletzt auch an den vielen Fahrrädern, und zum ersten Mal ist hier ein Politiker der ökologischen Partei »Die Grünen« Oberbürgermeister einer deutschen Großstadt geworden. Und ganz bestimmt kein Zufall ist es, dass das Fraunhofer-Institut für solare Energiesysteme in Freiburg sitzt.

Von den über 200.000 Einwohnern studieren ungefähr 20.000 an der Albert-Ludwigs-Universität und 10.000 an einer der anderen Hochschulen der Stadt.

Schwer zu sagen ist, ob es am Klima liegt, dass der SC Freiburg immer wieder mal in die Fußballbundesliga auf- und wieder absteigt.

FREIBURG IN BREISGAU

Whoever likes the sun (and thinks Majorca's too far off) should move to Freiburg. Nowhere else in Germany does the sun shine so often and so intensely as here in the Breisgau on the 38th parallel, and nowhere is it warmer.

Perhaps this is the reason that Freiburg is considered the eco-capital of Germany. This is not least of all noticeable from the many bicycles on the streets, and from the fact that for the first time a Green Party politician has become the mayor of a major German city. And it is quite certainly not by chance that the Fraunhofer Institute of Solar Energy Systems should be located here.

Around 20,000 of its over 200,000 inhabitants are students at the Albert Ludwig University, while 10,000 are enrolled at the city's other schools of higher education.

Hard to say if it is also the climate that is responsible for the fact that the FC Freiburg soccer team keeps getting promoted to the first league, only to be relegated again to the second.

EUROPA-PARK, RUST

Vor 50 oder 60 Jahren brauchten sich nur die wenigsten Menschen in Deutschland Sorgen um ihre Freizeit zu machen; davon gab es einfach noch nicht genug. Und wer mal ein paar Stunden übrig hatte, der musste selbst zusehen, wie er damit zurechtkam.

Seitdem hat sich allerdings eine ganze Menge geändert. Die Deutschen – und nicht nur sie – mussten immer weniger arbeiten, freie Zeit gibt's heute reichlich, und nicht jeder weiß, was er damit anfangen soll. So ist allmählich die Freizeitindustrie entstanden, inzwischen eine Branche mit beachtlichen Umsätzen.

Vor einigen Jahren soll ein bekannter Politiker die Bundesrepublik sogar einen »kollektiven Freizeitpark« genannt haben. Das war aber stark übertrieben, und ich kann mir nicht vorstellen, dass dieser Politiker zum Beispiel irgendwann einmal in Rust gewesen ist. Hier hätte er nämlich sehen können, wie ein moderner Freizeitpark in Wirklichkeit aussieht.

Der Freizeitpark Rust, nordwestlich von Freiburg im Breisgau, ganz nah am Rhein und an der französischen Grenze, ist der größte in Europa. Deswegen heißt er auch Europa-Park. Hier gibt's 700.000 Quadratmeter Freizeitvergnügen und nichts als Freizeitvergnügen für jeden Bedarf und jedes Temperament. Der Park ist aber nicht nur der größte in Europa: Er zählt zu den zehn schönsten in der Welt. Das haben jedenfalls die Amerikaner herausgefunden.

Die Arena gehört zu den besonderen Attraktionen. Sie ist zwar bescheidener als ihre antiken Vorbilder, und die Kämpfe sind heute harmloser als damals. Keiner wird mehr vom Dreizack durchbohrt oder von Löwen gefressen; alle gehen zum Schluss auf den eigenen Beinen aus der Arena. Aber ich hatte den Eindruck, dass die Begeisterung nicht sehr viel anders ist als vor 2000 Jahren.

EUROPA-PARK, RUST

Fifty or sixty years ago, only very few people in Germany gave much thought to their free time, for there was little enough to go around. And anyone who had a few hours to spare had to find out his own way of spending them.

Since then, however, quite a lot has changed. The Germans – and not only they – have had to work less and less; free time today is out there aplenty, and not everyone knows what to do with it. Thus, slowly but surely, the leisure industry has come into its own and has in the meantime become a business with a respectable turnover.

Several years ago, I happened to hear of a well-known politician who called the Federal Republic a »collective recreation park«. That was grossly exaggerated, and I can't imagine that this politician had, for instance, ever been to Rust. Here he would have seen what a modern leisure park really looked like.

The Rust leisure park, to the northwest of Freiburg in Breisgau, close to the Rhine and on the border with France, is the largest in Europe. Which is why it's called Europa Park. Here there are 700,000 square metres of recreational entertainment, and nothing but entertainment, for every need and every temperament. But the park is not only the biggest in Europe, it is among the ten most beautiful in the world. That, at least, is what the Americans have discovered.

The arena is one of the special attractions. It is, however, more modest than its ancient predecessors, and the battles that take place here are less harmful than they once were. No one is speared by a trident or eaten by lions. Everyone leaves the arena on his/her own feet. But I got the impression that today's enthusiasm is not all that different than it was 2000 years ago.

KASINO, BADEN-BADEN

»Das ist die schönste Spielbank der Welt!«, soll Marlene Dietrich ausgerufen haben, als sie zum ersten Mal durch die Säle im Baden-Badener Kurhaus ging. Und ob sie das nun wirklich gesagt hat oder nicht: Recht hat sie.

Verantwortlich für so viel Schönheit ist der Kasinodirektor Jacques Bénazet. Der kam 1838 aus Paris und hat die Lizenz von dem Bankier Antoine Chabert übernommen. Jacques Bénazet und vor allem sein Sohn Oscar Edouard haben aus der Spielbank das gemacht, was die Frau Dietrich ungefähr hundert Jahre später so begeistert hat. Und die Bürger haben Bénazet seinerzeit so geschätzt, dass sie ihn zum »Roi de Bade« ernannt haben.

Mendelssohn, Paganini, Liszt und viele andere sind hier aufgetreten, und jeder, der was auf sich hielt in der Belle Epoque, ist irgendwann mal hier gewesen: Könige, Dichter, Scheichs, Fürsten, Industriebarone, Künstler und Glücksritter aus der ganzen Welt.

1872 musste auch die Spielbank Baden-Baden auf Beschluss der Reichsregierung den Betrieb einstellen. Das war ein schwerer Schlag für die Stadt, denn die Betreiber haben mit ihren Überschüssen immer viele Vorhaben und Einrichtungen gefördert.

1933 machte das Kasino wieder auf, musste aber 1944 erneut schließen. Am 1. April 1950 wurde schließlich die »dritte« Baden-Badener Spielbank eröffnet, und seitdem rollt die Kugel hier ununterbrochen.

THE GAMBLING CASINO IN BADEN-BADEN

»It's the most beautiful casino in the world!« Marlene Dietrich was supposed to have cried when she entered the Baden-Baden gaming rooms. And whether she really said this or not: she is right.

And the man responsible for all this beauty was the casino director, Jacques Bénazet. He arrived in 1838 from Paris, having acquired the licence from the banker, Antoine Chabert. Jacques Bénazet and, above all, his son, Oscar Edouard, made the casino into what it was that, about one hundred years later, so enthused Ms. Dietrich. The town's citizens so appreciated Bénazet's feat at the time that they called him the »Roi de Bade«.

Mendelssohn, Paganini, Liszt and many others performed on its stage, and everybody who was anybody in the Belle Epoque came here at one time or other: kings, poets, sheiks, princes, barons of industry, artists and fortune seekers from the whole world.

In 1872, Baden-Baden's gambling casino was closed in accordance with the Reich government's resolution. This was a hard blow to the city, since the operators always used a part of their profits to sponsor many public projects and facilities.

In 1933, the casino was re-opened but had to close again in 1944. Finally, on April 1, 1950, the »third« Baden-Baden gambling casino was opened and, ever since, the ball has been rolling here without interruption.

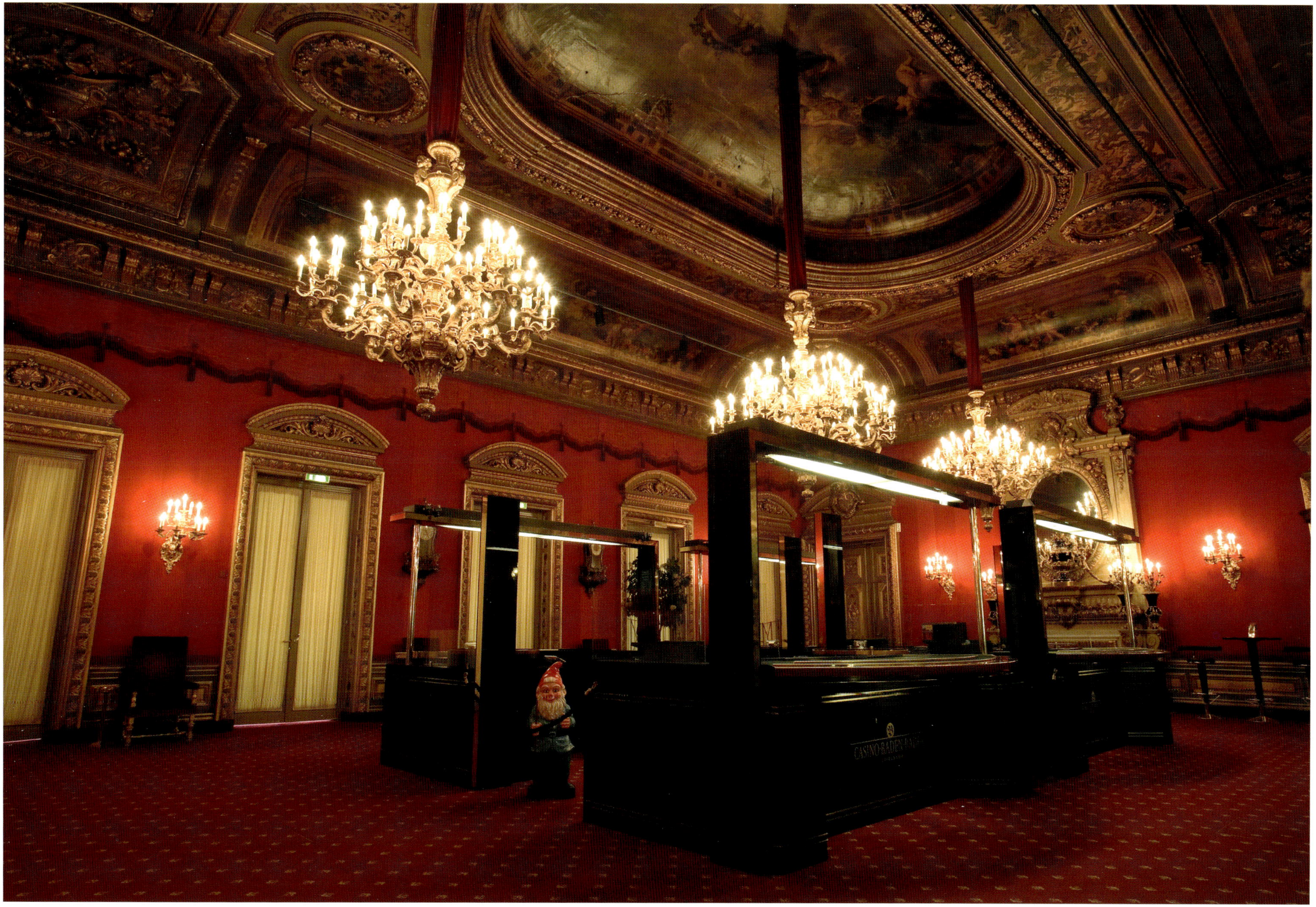

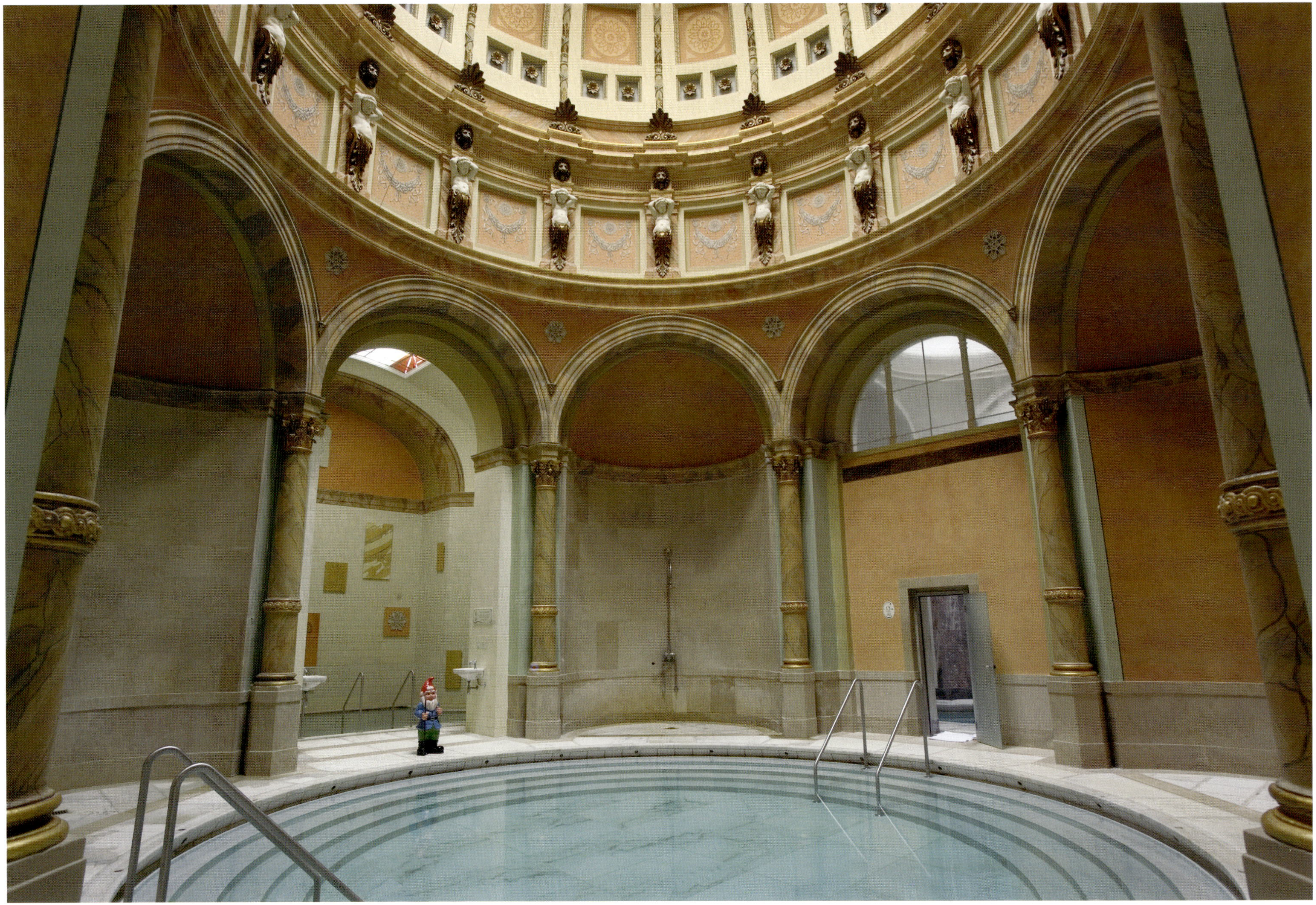

FRIEDRICHSBAD, BADEN-BADEN

Wenn die Römer vor 2000 Jahren irgendwo auf heiße Quellen gestoßen sind, haben sie fast immer eine Therme gebaut und eine Stadt drumherum; sie haben nämlich für ihr Leben gern gebadet. So war das auch am nordwestlichen Rand des Schwarzwalds, in der Gegend also, wo heute Baden-Baden liegt.

Die Alemannen haben vom Baden anscheinend nicht so viel gehalten. Warum sonst hätten sie im dritten Jahrhundert die schönen römischen Thermen zerstört?

Sie waren offenbar genau so wasserscheu wie die meisten anderen Völker in Europa, und die römisch-orientalische Badekultur hat sich nördlich der Alpen in den nächsten anderthalb Jahrtausenden nie so richtig verbreitet.

Erst im späten 19. Jahrhundert haben sich die Baden-Badener wieder an ihre römische Therme erinnert, und zwar hauptsächlich deswegen, weil die Reichsregierung in Berlin 1868 drohte, in ganz Deutschland die Spielbanken zu schließen, also auch die in Baden-Baden. Denn jetzt musste eine neue Attraktion her, um Besucher anzulocken, und die sollte natürlich etwas ganz Besonderes sein. 1872 wurde das Kasino geschlossen und 1877 das prachtvolle Friedrichsbad eröffnet. Die Vorbilder dafür standen in Rom, Budapest und – Irland.

Es ist nämlich ein römisch-irisches Bad, das heißt, man kann hier in heißem Wasser (römisch) und in heißer Luft (irisch) baden, und beides zusammen gibt's in keinem anderen Bad auf der Welt.

FRIEDRICHSBAD, BADEN-BADEN

Whenever and wherever the Romans came across hot springs, they almost always built a thermal bath and a town around it; they just adored taking baths. This was the case on the northwestern perimeter of the Black Forest, that is, in the region where today Baden-Baden lies.

The Alemanni were apparently not so taken with Baden. Why else would they have destroyed the lovely Roman spa in the 3rd century? As things go, they were just as hydrophobic as most of the other tribes in Europe, and over the next one-and-a-half millennia the Roman-Oriental bathing culture never really developed north of the Alps.

Not till the late 19th century did the citizens of Baden-Baden remember their Roman hot springs, even if it was mostly because the Reich government in Berlin threatened to close all the gambling casinos in Germany, which meant, also the one in Baden-Baden. Therefore, a new attraction was desperately needed to lure visitors, and it naturally had to be something very special. In 1872 the casino was shut down and in 1877 the magnificent Friedrichsbad was opened. The models for it can be found in Rome, Budapest and – Ireland.

It is, namely, a Roman-Irish spa, which means, you can bath in hot water (Roman) and in hot air (Irish), and this combination exists nowhere else in the world.

SCHLOSS, HEIDELBERG

Vor allem im 18. und 19. Jahrhundert waren Ruinen ganz groß in Mode. Sie waren so beliebt, dass die, die es gab, gar nicht ausreichten. Weil aber niemand intakte Schlösser oder andere Gebäude so einfach ruinieren konnte, hat man künstliche Ruinen errichtet, wenn man welche brauchte. Auf der Pfaueninsel in Berlin zum Beispiel, in Kassel, in Schwetzingen und anderswo. Auch in der Malerei waren Ruinen damals beliebt, und von Beethoven gibt es eine Schauspielmusik zu den »Ruinen von Athen«.

Das Heidelberger Schloss, die ehemalige Residenz der rheinpfälzischen Kurfürsten, ist eine echte Ruine. Dafür hat vor allem der »Sonnenkönig« Ludwig XIV. 1689 und 1693 mit seinen Truppen im Pfälzischen Erbfolgekrieg gesorgt. Und dann schlug 1764 während der Instandsetzung auch noch der Blitz ein. Danach hat man es so gelassen, wie es war.

Das Schloss wäre ja vielleicht auch nur halb so beliebt, wenn es keine Ruine wäre. Zur Zeit der Romantik war es eine regelrechte Pilgerstätte für Ruinenliebhaber aus ganz Europa, und bis heute zieht es jedes Jahr Hunderttausende Besucher aus aller Welt an. Das hat natürlich auch mit seiner Lage zu tun, über dem Neckar am Westhang des Odenwalds, und mit dem Blick, den man von hier in die Rheinebene hat. Ganz zu schweigen von Heidelberg selbst, wo die älteste deutsche Universität steht und sogar Elvis Presley sein Herz verloren hat.

Ganz besonders habe ich mich über die Begegnung mit einem entfernten Verwandten gefreut: dem Zwerg Perkeo, dem »Wächter des Großen Fasses«, den Kurfürst Karl Philipp nach Heidelberg geholt hatte. Er ist ein Vorfahre aus unserer Tiroler Linie, die aber nördlich der Alpen sonst keine Spuren hinterlassen hat. In das Heidelberger Fass sollen 221.726 Liter Wein hineinpassen, aber selbst Perkeo glaubt nicht, dass es jemals voll war.

HEIDELBERG CASTLE

Ruins were once the height of fashion, above all, in the 18th and 19th century. They were so popular that the authentic ones were quite insufficient. And because no one could simply wreck intact castles or other buildings, they built artificial ruins when the need arose: on the Pfaueninsel in Berlin, for example, in Kassel, Schwetzingen and other places. Ruins were also a popular motif in painting, and Beethoven composed the overture to »The Ruins of Athens«.

The Heidelberg Castle, the former residence of the Rhineland-Palatinate prince-electors, is a genuine ruin. For which, above all, the Sun King Louis XIV and his troops were responsible in 1689 and 1693, during the French-Palatinate War of Succession. And then in 1764, right in the midst of work to renovate it, lightning struck and brought it all to a standstill, and everything was left as it was.

The castle would probably be only half as popular if intact. At the time of Romanticism, it was a regular place of pilgrimage for aficionados from all over Europe. And still today it attracts over hundreds of thousands of visitors every year from all over the world. This naturally has to do with its site, which overlooks the Neckar from the west slope of the Odenwald, and the view it gives you across the Rhine Plateau. Not to mention Heidelberg itself, where the oldest university in Germany stands and where even Elvis Presley lost his heart.

I particularly enjoyed meeting a distant relative of mine there, the dwarf Perkeo »Guard of the Great Vat«, who was brought to Heidelberg by Prince-Elector Karl Philipp. Perkeo is a descendent of our Tyrolean line, which, however, left no other traces north of the Alps. The vat supposedly holds 221,726 litres of wine, but even Perkeo didn't believe it was ever full.

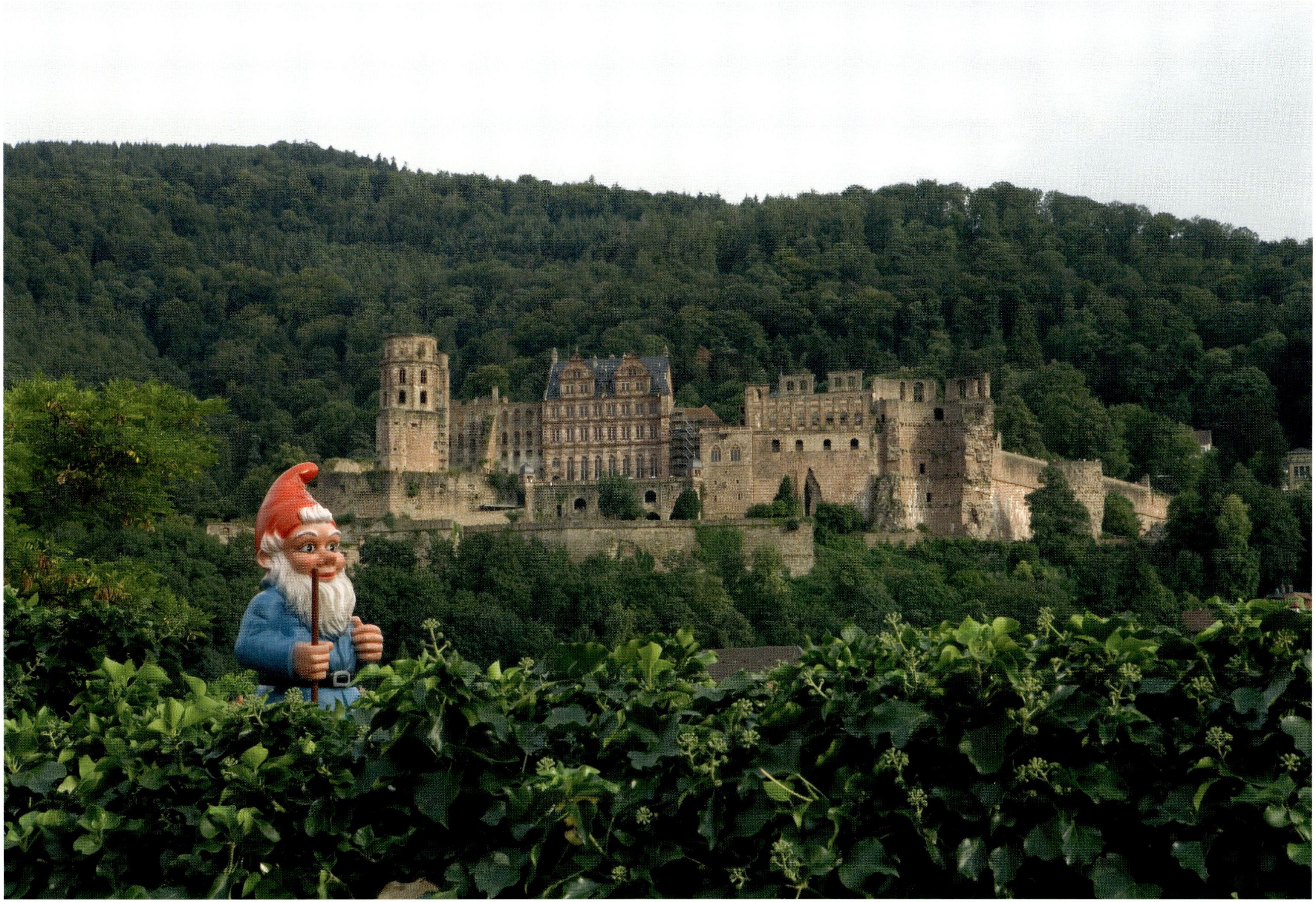

FERNSEHTURM, HAUS HAJEK, STUTTGART

Anfang der 50er Jahre des 20. Jahrhunderts brauchte der Süddeutsche Rundfunk in Stuttgart einen neuen Sendeturm. Es sollte ein 200 Meter hoher Stahlgittermast sein, auf dem »Hohen Bopser« am Südrand des Stuttgarter Kessels. Diese Vorstellung hat dem Stuttgarter Ingenieur Fritz Leonhardt, einem berühmten Brückenbauer, überhaupt nicht gefallen, und er hat darüber nachgedacht, wie er sich und den Stuttgartern so einen unerfreulichen Anblick ersparen könnte. Dabei kam er auf eine ganz einfache Idee: Wie wäre es denn, hat er sich gefragt, wenn man statt einer nüchternen Zweckkonstruktion aus Stahl eine elegante aus Stahlbeton bauen würde? Und er hat sich hingesetzt und den Fernsehturm erfunden, so wie wir ihn heute kennen: eine schlanke Röhre mit Aussichtsplattformen und einem Restaurant in 150 Metern Höhe und dem Sendemast auf der Spitze. Seitdem werden die Fernsehtürme in aller Welt nach diesem Vorbild gebaut.

Das Haus Hajek steht schräg gegenüber vom Fernsehturm im Südwesten von Stuttgart. Hier hat der berühmte Bildhauer und Kunstprofessor Otto Herbert Hajek bis zu seinem Tod im Frühjahr 2005 gelebt. »Stadt-Ikonograph« hat man ihn genannt, und seine farbenfrohen Plastiken aus Stahl oder Beton stehen in vielen Städten und haben ihn in vielen Teilen der Welt bekannt gemacht. Ich finde, was die Farben betrifft, passe ich doch ganz gut dazu.

TV TOWER, HOUSE HAJEK, STUTTGART

At the beginning of the 1950s, the South German Broadcasting Station needed a new broadcasting tower. It was to be a steel grid mast built 200 metres high on the »Hoher Bopser«, at the southern perimeter of the Stuttgart Hollow. This idea did not at all appeal to the Stuttgart engineer Fritz Leonhardt, a famous bridge builder. He thought hard about how he could spare himself and the Stuttgart people such an unpleasant sight. He then arrived at a very simple solution. How would it be, he wondered, if instead of a sober functional construction of steel, he built an elegant one of reinforced concrete? He then sat down and invented the TV tower as we know it today, a slim tube with viewing platforms and restaurant 150 metres above the ground and a transmitter mast on top. Ever since, TV towers throughout the world have been built after this model.

Haus Hajek is located diagonally across from the TV tower in southwest Stuttgart. It was here that the famous sculptor and art professor, Otto Herbert Hajek, lived up to his death in the spring of 2005. He was called the »city iconographer«, and his bright-coloured sculptures of steel or concrete can be found in many cities, and have made him famous in many parts of the world. I think, as far as the colours go, I fit in very well.

43

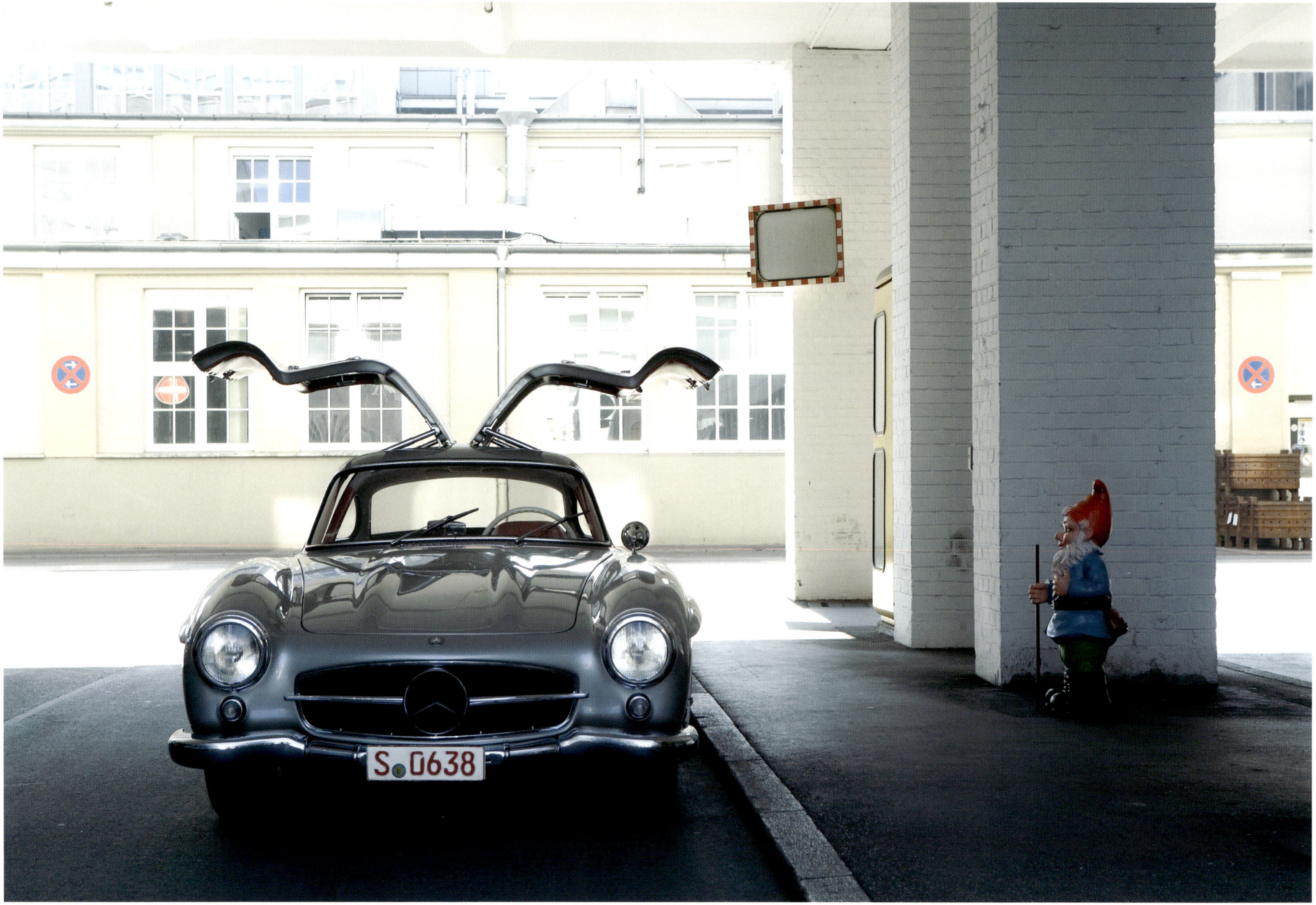
S 0638

DAIMLER-CHRYSLER-WERK, STUTTGART-UNTERTÜRKHEIM

Für viele Menschen ist er der schönste Sportwagen überhaupt: der Mercedes 300 SL (Sport leicht). Und, seitdem ich ihn in Untertürkheim aus der Nähe gesehen habe, für mich auch. Gut, dass ich keinen Führerschein habe, ich würde glatt einen Kredit aufnehmen, um einen zu kaufen. Aber ein Bankkonto hab' ich ja zum Glück auch nicht.

Als der 300 SL 1954 auf den Markt kam, war sich die Fachwelt, aber nicht nur die, sofort einig: »Besser kann man ein Auto heute nicht bauen.« Zwei Jahre zuvor hieß er noch W 194 und war eigentlich als reiner Rennwagen geplant. Dann ist er zum W 198 weiterentwickelt worden und hat als 300 SL Automobilgeschichte gemacht: 1400-mal in der Coupé-Version und danach 1858-mal als Roadster.

Zur Zeit des 300 SL war das Auto selbst schon fast 70 Jahre alt. Und es ist hier ganz in der Nähe erfunden worden. Das heißt, genau genommen ist es zweimal erfunden worden. Einmal von Gottlieb Daimler und einmal von Carl Friedrich Benz. Am Anfang hat man diese Vehikel mit Verbrennungsmotor »Automobile« genannt, das ist griechisch/lateinisch und bedeutet »Selbstbeweger«. Die ersten haben nämlich wirklich so ausgesehen, als hätte jemand von einer Pferdekutsche die Deichsel abgeschraubt.

1926 haben sich die Firmen Daimler und Benz zur Daimler-Benz AG zusammengetan, und seitdem ist der Mercedes-Stern eines der bekanntesten Markenzeichen der Welt. Nach dem Zusammenschluss mit der amerikanischen Firma Chrysler heißt der Konzern jetzt DaimlerChrysler AG.

DAIMLER-CHRYSLER FACTORY, STUTTGART-UNTERTÜRKHEIM

For many, it is the most beautiful sports car of all: the Mercedes 300 SL (sport light). And, ever since I was in Untertürkheim and saw it up close, for me, too. Good that I don't have a driver's licence; I would take out a loan at the drop of a hat and buy one. But, fortunately, I also don't have a bank account.

When the 300 SL was launched in 1954, the experts (but not only they) immediately agreed: »A better car than this cannot be built today.« Two years previously, it had been called the W 194 and had actually been planned solely as a racing car. It was then further developed to become the W 198 and made automobile history as the 300 SL: it was produced 1400 times in the coupé version and then 1858 times as the roadster.

At the time of the 300 SL, the automobile itself was already almost 70 years old. And it was invented quite close to here. That is, to be exact, it was invented twice. Once by Gottlieb Daimler and once by Carl Friedrich Benz. From the beginning this vehicle with an internal combustion engine was called an »automobile«, which comes from Greek/Latin and means »self-mover«. And the first models really did look as if someone had simply unscrewed the shaft from a horse-drawn carriage.

In 1926, the two firms Daimler and Benz merged into Daimler-Benz AG, and since then the Mercedes star has become one of the best-known trademarks in the world. Following the merger with the American firm Chrysler, its name is now DaimlerChrysler AG.

MEDIZINISCHER HÖRSAAL, TÜBINGEN

Jeder ausgewachsene Mensch hat mindestens 206 Knochen – manchmal sind es auch ein paar mehr –, die Hälfte davon allein in den Händen und den Füßen. (Ich komme mit viel weniger aus, aber gezählt hat bei mir natürlich noch niemand.) Über das Skelett und alles andere, was die Menschen unter der Haut haben, weiß man seit langer Zeit ganz gut Bescheid. Das verdanken wir vor allem den Anatomen, die sich schon seit Jahrtausenden damit beschäftigen. (»Anatomie« kommt vom griechischen »anatemnein«, und das heißt »aufschneiden«.)

Zu einer richtigen Wissenschaft ist die Anatomie aber erst in der Renaissance geworden, und in dieser Zeit, 1477, ist in Tübingen die Universität gegründet worden. Am Anfang gab es vier Fakultäten, eine davon war die Medizin. Inzwischen sind es siebzehn, und auf die verteilen sich über 20.000 Studentinnen und Studenten. Dabei hat die Stadt insgesamt nur gut 70.000 Einwohner. Der Hörsaal, in dem ich hier stehe, stammt zwar nicht aus dieser Zeit, aber ungefähr so kann man sich den von vor vier-, fünfhundert Jahren vorstellen.

Bis zum Jahr 1784 hatte das menschliche Skelett übrigens noch zwei Knochen weniger. Die Wissenschaft war damals überzeugt, dass ein wichtiger Unterschied zwischen Menschen und Tieren nämlich genau darin besteht, dass der Mensch keinen Zwischenkieferknochen hat (das ist der, in dem die oberen Schneidezähne sitzen). Dann hat Johann Wolfgang Goethe das Gegenteil bewiesen, und er war ja hauptberuflich eigentlich kein Anatom. Seitdem sind aber keine neuen Knochen mehr entdeckt worden. Auch nicht in Tübingen.

MEDICINE LECTURE HALL, TÜBINGEN

Every adult has at least 206 bones – sometimes there are a few more – half of them alone in the hands and feet. (I get by with quite a few less, but naturally no one has ever tried counting.) Quite a lot has been known for a long time about the skeleton and everything else that humans have underneath their skin. We have, above all, the anatomists to thank for this, who have been working on it for several thousands of years. (»Anatomy« comes from the Greek and means »dissection«.)

But anatomy first became a proper science in the Renaissance, and it was exactly at that time, 1477, that the University in Tübingen was founded. At first there were four faculties, one of which was medicine. In the meantime there are seventeen, and 20,000 students are spread among them. Whereby the town itself has only a good 70,000 inhabitants. The lecture hall in which I am standing does not go back to that time, but it gives you an approximate picture of the way it looked four or five hundred years ago.

Incidentally, up to 1784, the human skeleton had two bones fewer. Scientists were convinced at the time that an important difference between humans and animals was the very fact that humans had no auxiliary jaw bones (where the upper incisors are embedded). Then Johann Wolfgang Goethe proved the opposite, and he was actually not an anatomist by profession. Ever since then, though, no new bones have been discovered. Not even in Tübingen.

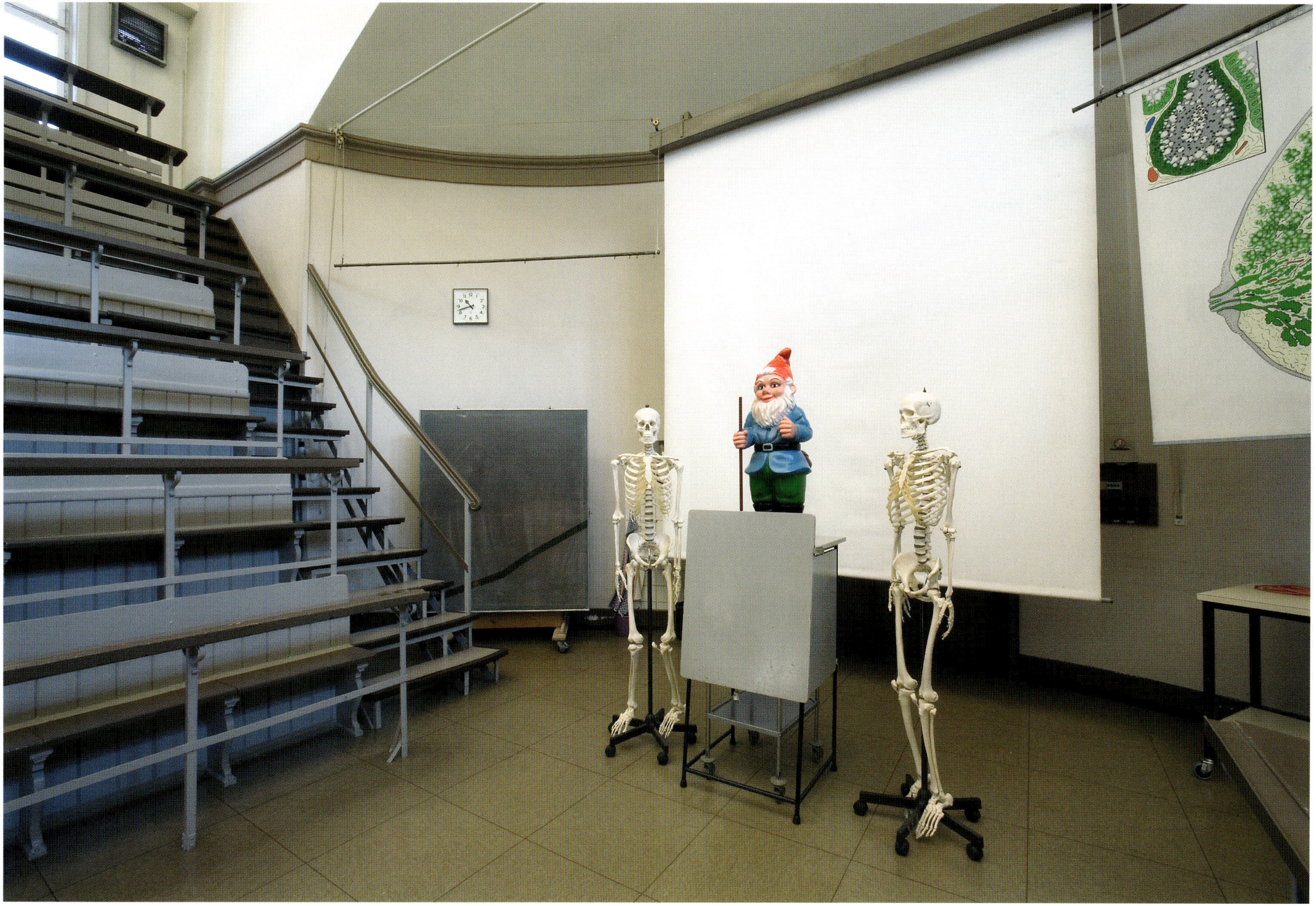

MÜNSTER, ULM

Das Ulmer Münster hat eine ähnliche Geschichte wie der Kölner Dom: Es ist zunächst einmal nicht fertig geworden. Die Arbeiten wurden 1543 eingestellt, 166 Jahre nach der Grundsteinlegung. Da war der Turm genauso hoch wie der in Köln: ungefähr 100 Meter. Aber es stand kein Baukran oben drauf, sondern der Stumpf bekam ein provisorisches Dach. Außerdem hatten sich die Ulmer 1531 der Reformation angeschlossen, die katholische Kathedrale war per Volksentscheid zu einer protestantischen geworden und ist seitdem die größte evangelische Kirche der Welt.

300 Jahre später, fast zur selben Zeit wie in Köln, sind auch in Ulm die Bauarbeiten wieder aufgenommen worden. Der Kölner Dom ist allerdings früher fertig geworden, obwohl hier zwei Türme gebaut werden mussten, und war deshalb zehn Jahre lang die höchste Kathedrale in Europa. 1890 wurde endlich auch in Ulm die letzte Kreuzblume aufgesetzt, und nun war das Ulmer Münster die höchste Kirche der Christenheit: 161,53 Meter. Das hat sicher auch einen elfjährigen Ulmer Jungen gefreut: Albert Einstein.

Über 768 Stufen kann man zur Aussichtsplattform in 141 Metern Höhe steigen. Bei gutem Wetter kann man im Süden die Alpen sehen, von der Zugspitze bis zum Schweizer Säntis.

Wie das Ulmer Münster die Bombardierung vom 17. Dezember 1944 fast unbeschädigt überstanden hat, kann niemand erklären, denn drum herum waren fast alle Gebäude schwer getroffen; auch darin ähneln sich die Dome von Köln und Ulm. Erst kurz vor Kriegsende ist im Chorgewölbe noch eine Sprengbombe explodiert.

Direkt neben dem Münster hat der amerikanische Architekt Richard Meier 1992 bis 1994 das Kulturzentrum Ulmer Stadthaus gebaut – ein Gegensatz, wie man ihn sich stärker kaum vorstellen kann.

MINSTER, ULM

Ulm Minster has a similar biography to that of Cologne Cathedral: it languished unfinished for ages. Work was stopped in 1543, 166 years after the laying of the cornerstone. The tower was then just as high as the one in Cologne: around 100 metres. But no building crane topped it, rather the stump was given a provisional roof. In addition, in 1531, Ulm's citizens had joined the Reformation; the Catholic cathedral had become Protestant per referendum and has been the world's largest Protestant church ever since.

And 300 years later in Ulm, almost at the same time as in Cologne, work was taken up again. However, Cologne Cathedral was finished sooner (although not just one tower, but two, needed to be built) and consequently, for ten years, was the highest cathedral in Europe. In 1890, though, Ulm finally made it; the last finial was put in place and the Ulm Minster then became the highest church in Christendom: 161.53 metres. A fact that surely also pleased an eleven-year old Ulm boy: Albert Einstein.

Over 768 steps must be mounted to reach the viewing platform at a height of 141 metres. Weather allowing, the view to the south takes in the Alps, from the Zugspitze to the Säntis in Switzerland.

How it was that the Ulm Minster survived the bombardment on December 17, 1944 almost intact is something no one can explain, for almost all the buildings around it were severely damaged. In this fact, too, the cathedrals of Cologne and Ulm resemble each other. Not until shortly before the end of the war did a demolition bomb explode in the choir vault.

Between 1992 and 1994, directly next to the minster, the American architect Richard Meier built the Ulm Town Hall cultural centre – an architectural contrast more striking than anyone could ever imagine.

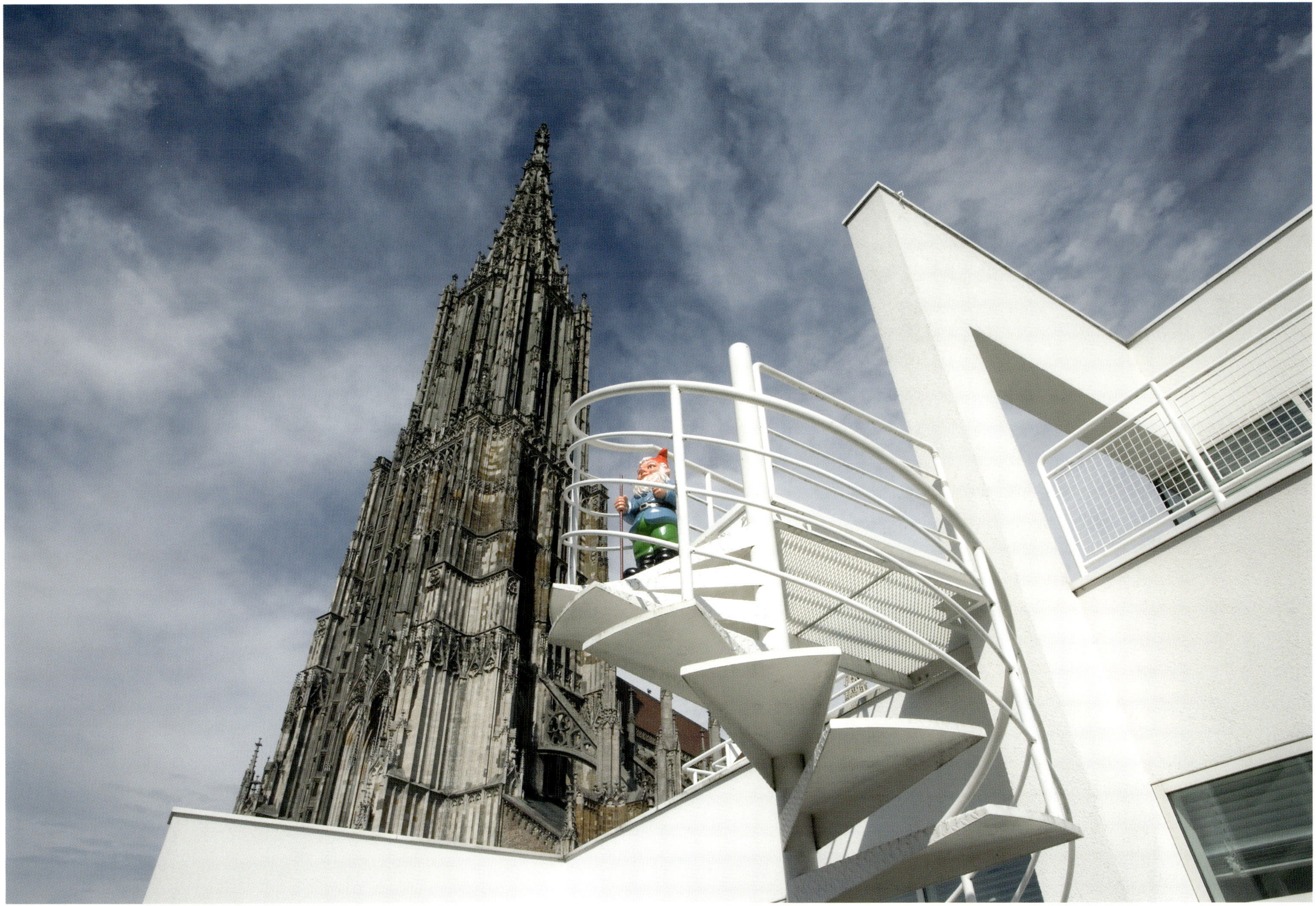

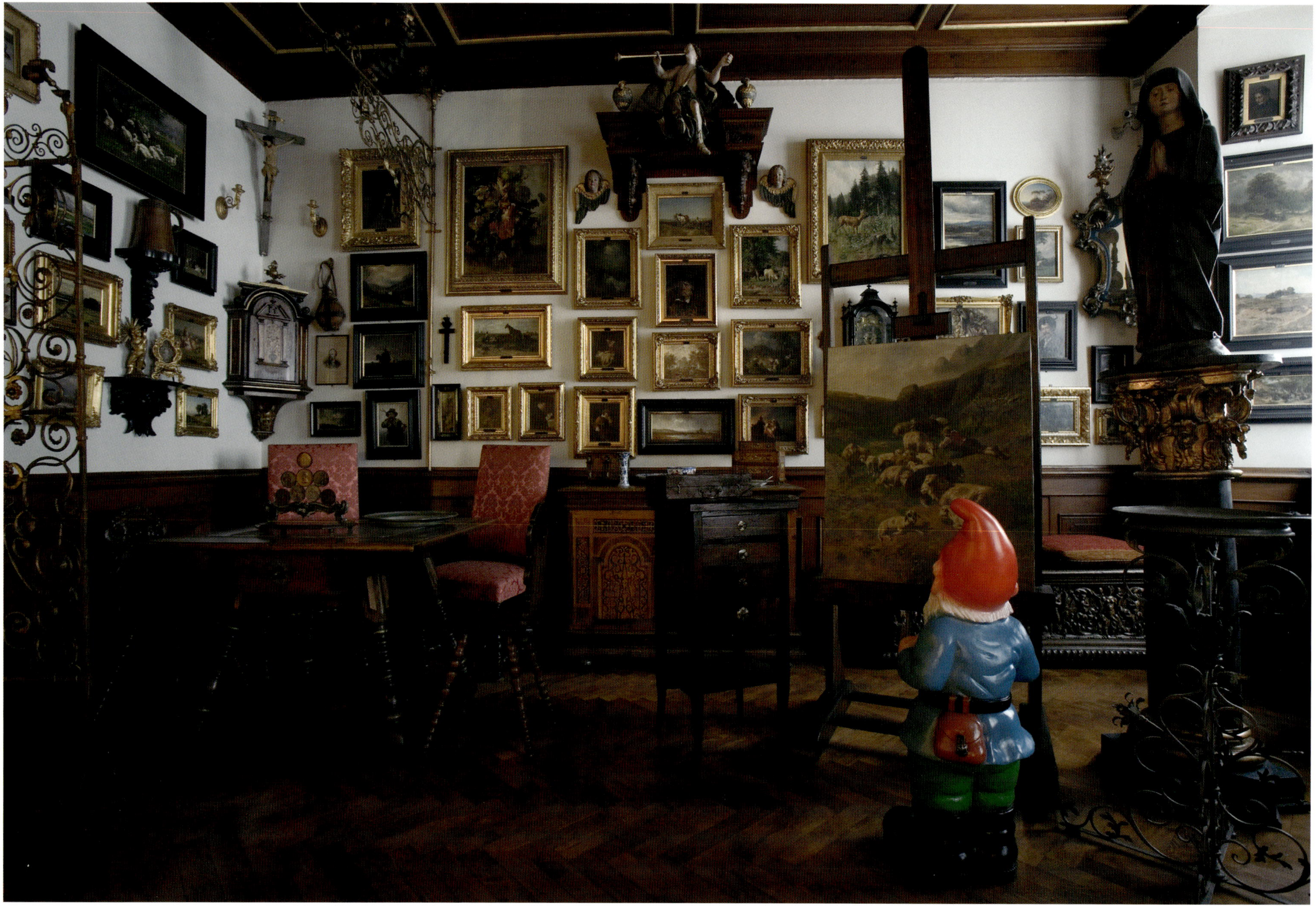

BRAITH-MALI-MUSEUM, BIBERACH AN DER RISS

Biberach an der Riß – von diesem Nebenfluss der Donau hat die Riß-Eiszeit ihren Namen, aber fragt mich nicht, warum – Biberach an der Riß ist eine glückliche Stadt mit zufriedenen Bewohnern.

Biberach ist eine Stadt wie aus dem Bilderbuch. Sie liegt zwischen der schwäbischen Alb und dem Allgäu, keine 50 Kilometer vom Bodensee entfernt, hat einen mittelalterlichen Stadtkern und ist eine Station an der Deutschen Fachwerkstraße und an der Barockstraße.

Der berühmteste Biberacher ist Christoph Martin Wieland, einer der fleißigsten deutschen Dichter. Nicht ganz so berühmt ist der Tier- und Landschaftsmaler Anton Braith. Anton Braith hat es vom Sohn eines Biberacher Tagelöhners zunächst in die Stuttgarter Kunstschule und von dort bis zum Kunstprofessor in München gebracht. Besonders die Kühe hatten's ihm angetan, einzeln, zu mehreren oder in ganzen Herden.

In München hat er den vier Jahre älteren holländischen Maler Christian Friedrich Mali kennen gelernt, mit dem er bis zu seinem Lebensende in gemeinsamen Ateliers gearbeitet hat. Auch Mali hat hauptsächlich Tiere und Landschaften gemalt.

Biberach hat beiden Malern ein eigenes Museum eingerichtet: das Braith-Mali-Museum. Es teilt sich in sieben Sparten: von der Naturkunde über Archäologie und Kunst bis zur Stadtgeschichte. Kern des Museums aber sind die Münchener Ateliers der beiden Malerfreunde. Sie sind die einzigen vollständig erhaltenen deutschen Malerateliers aus dem 19. Jahrhundert und stellen damit ein Kulturdenkmal von großem Seltenheitswert dar.

BRAITH-MALI MUSEUM, BIBERACH AN DER RISS

Biberach an der Riss – it was from this tributary of the Danube that the Riss Ice Age got its name, but don't ask me why. Biberach on the Riss is a happy town with happy inhabitants.

Biberach is a picture-book town. It lies between the Swabian Alb and the Allgäu, less than 50 kilometres from Lake Constance, has a medieval town centre and is a stop on the »German Framework Route« and on the »Baroque Route«.

The most famous son of Biberach was Christoph Martin Wieland, one of the most productive of German poets. Another not quite so famous son of the town was Anton Braith, an animal and landscape painter. As the son of a Biberach day labourer, he managed to make it, first of all, to the Stuttgart Art School and from there, to become an art professor in Munich. Cows turned out to be his speciality, singly, in groups or whole herds.

In Munich, he met the Dutch painter Christian Friedrich Mali, four years his senior, with whom he shared studios up to his death. Mali, too, painted mostly animals and landscapes.

Biberach has provided both painters with their very own museum: the Braith-Mali Museum. It is subdivided into seven sections: from natural history via archaeology and art, to the history of the town. However, it is the Munich studios of the two friends which form the heart of the museum. They are the only completely preserved, 19th century painters' studios in Germany and, for this reason, represent a cultural heritage of great rarity.

LINDAU, BODENSEE

Der Bodensee verteilt seine Ufer auf drei Länder: Österreich, Deutschland und die Schweiz, aber zwischen denen gibt es im See keinen festgelegten Grenzverlauf. Daran hat einfach keiner gedacht, als die Eidgenossen 1648 aus dem Verband des Heiligen Römischen Reiches ausgetreten sind. Deshalb ist der Bodensee ein »Kondominium«, das heißt, alle drei Anrainer sind gleichermaßen dafür verantwortlich und müssen sich immer wieder einigen, wer was zu tun hat. Der See ist immerhin der Wasserspeicher für viele Millionen Bewohner in der Umgebung.

Am Bodensee hat es den Menschen anscheinend schon vor Jahrtausenden gefallen, sie haben sich hier bereits in der Steinzeit angesiedelt. Wie das ungefähr ausgesehen hat, kann man an dem Pfahldorf in Unteruhldingen studieren, gegenüber der Mainau am westlichen Bodensee. Es ist – nach verschiedenen Funden in der Umgebung – in den 20er, den 30er und den 90er Jahren des vorigen Jahrhunderts in den See und ans Ufer gebaut worden. Die ältesten Vorbilder dafür stammen aus der Zeit um 4000 v. Chr.

Auch am östlichen Bodensee, in der Gegend von Lindau – das ist die Insel da links im Bild –, hat es vielleicht mal so ausgesehen, genau weiß man das nicht. Ziemlich genau weiß man aber, wie es hier im Mittelalter ausgesehen hat, nämlich ungefähr so wie heute: Der Stadtkern hat sich in den letzten fünf-, sechshundert Jahren nur wenig verändert.

LINDAU, LAKE CONSTANCE

The shores of Lake Constance are divided among three countries: Austria, Germany and Switzerland, but in the lake itself no hard and fast borderline has ever been defined between them. It was simply that no one had thought of this when the Swiss confederacy opted out of the Holy Roman Empire in 1648. Which is why Lake Constance is a so-called »condominium«, which means that all three riparian states have equal responsibility and must constantly agree on who is to do what. The lake is, after all, the water reservoir for many millions of people living in its environs.

Already thousands of years ago people were apparently attracted to Lake Constance and settled here as early as the Stone Age. What it once must have looked like can be seen at the pile-village of Unteruhldingen, across from Mainau at the western end of the Lake. In accordance with various finds made in the immediate area, it was built there in the lake and on the shore in the 1920s, 1930s and the 1990s. The oldest models for it stem from the time around 4000 B.C.

Also at the eastern end of Lake Constance, in the region of Lindau – which is the island on the left in the picture – it might once have looked like this, though one doesn't know this exactly. But one does know the way it looked here in the Middle Ages, namely, just about the way it looks today. The centre of the city has changed only slightly over the past five or six hundred years.

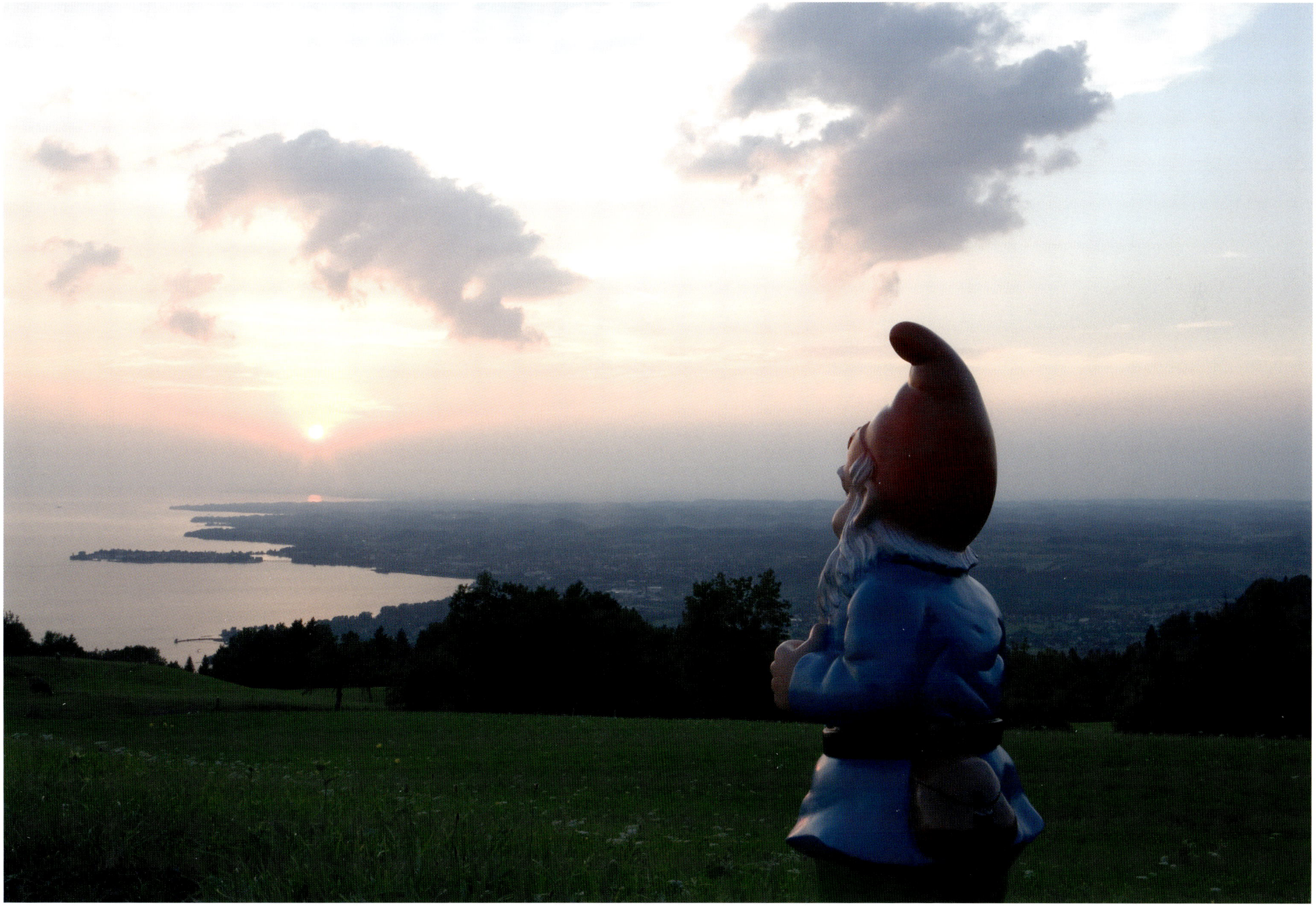

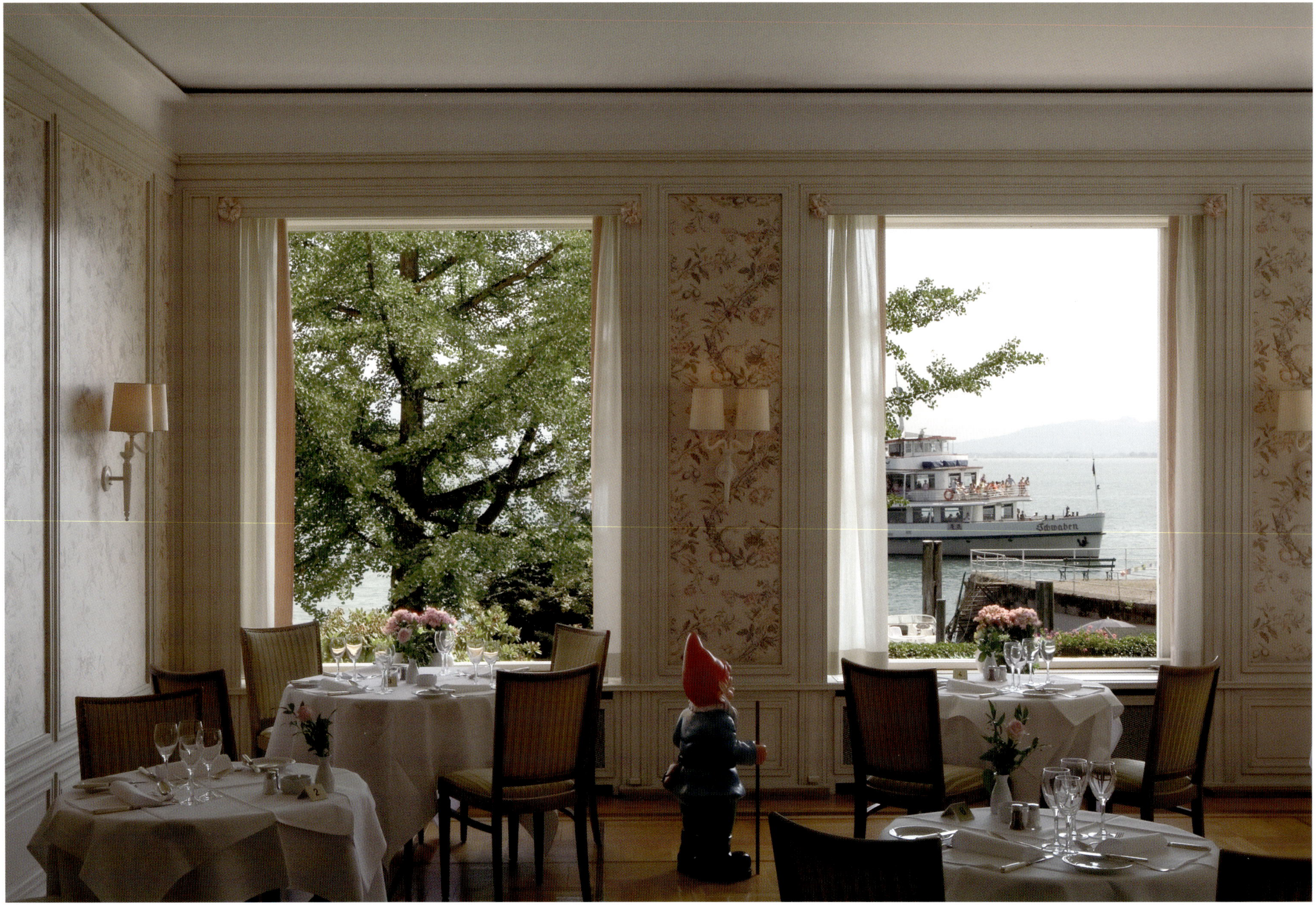
Schwaben

HOTEL BAD SCHACHEN, BODENSEE

Bad Schachen ist ein Stadtteil von Lindau und liegt gleich westlich davon am Seeufer. Wer will, kann sogar mit dem Schiff hierher kommen, denn Bad Schachen hat eine eigene Anlegestelle. Von da aus kann man zum Beispiel auch nach Bregenz zu den Festspielen fahren, falls man eine Karte bekommen hat.

Direkt an der Anlegestelle liegt das »Hotel Bad Schachen«, das traditionsreichste am ganzen Bodensee. Es hieß früher »Gasthaus zum weißen Schwanen« und ist seit vielen Generationen in Familienbesitz.

Für alle, die hier mal absteigen wollen, habe ich einen guten Rat. Am besten reist ihr nachts an und lasst die Vorhänge im Zimmer bis zum nächsten Morgen geschlossen. Wenn ihr sie dann aufzieht, werdet ihr mit einem unvergesslichen Blick belohnt: ein wunderbares Seepanorama – bis hinüber in den Schweizer Kanton Appenzell, wo im Jahr 1975 in einer Volksabstimmung das Wahlrecht für Frauen eingeführt worden ist.

Die Menschen, die in Bad Schachen Urlaub machen, haben mir gesagt, dass sie diese Gegend ein bisschen an die Riviera erinnert. Vielleicht sollte ich da auch mal hinfahren.

HOTEL BAD SCHACHEN, LAKE CONSTANCE

Bad Schachen is a district of Lindau and lies to the west of it on the lakeshore. Anyone who wishes to could even arrive by boat, for Bad Schachen has its own pier. From here you could, for example, get to Bregenz for the festival, if you managed to get hold of a ticket, that is.

The »Hotel Bad Schachen« lies directly at the landing and is the richest in tradition on the whole of Lake Constance. It used to be called »The White Swan Inn« and has been family-owned for many generations.

For all those who want to check in here, I have a word of advice. It is best to arrive at night and leave the drapes in the room closed till the next morning. When you then open them, you will be rewarded with an unforgettable view: a wonderful panorama of the lake that reaches all the way to the Swiss canton of Appenzell where, in a 1975 referendum, women's suffrage was introduced.

The people who go to Bad Schachen on holiday have told me that this region reminds them a bit of the Riviera. Now maybe that is a place I should try going to sometime.

SCHLOSS NEUSCHWANSTEIN

»Ich habe die Absicht, die alte Burgruine Hohenschwangau bei der Pöllatschlucht neu aufbauen zu lassen im echten Stil der alten deutschen Ritterburgen, und muss Ihnen gestehen, dass ich mich sehr darauf freue, dort einst (in 3 Jahren) zu hausen; mehrere Gastzimmer, von wo man eine herrliche Aussicht genießt auf den hehren Säuling, die Gebirge Tirols und weithin in die Ebene, sollen wohnlich und anheimelnd dort eingerichtet werden; Sie kennen Ihn, den angebeteten Gast, den ich dort beherbergen möchte; der Punkt ist einer der schönsten, die zu finden sind, heilig und unnahbar, ein würdiger Tempel für den göttlichen Freund, durch den einzig Heil und wahrer Segen der Welt erblühte. Auch Reminiszenzen aus ›Tannhäuser‹ (Sängersaal mit Aussicht auf die Burg im Hintergrunde), aus ›Lohengrin‹ (Burghof, offener Gang, Weg zur Kapelle) werden Sie dort finden; in jeder Beziehung schöner und wohnlicher wird diese Burg werden als das untere Hohenschwangau, das jährlich durch die Prosa meiner Mutter entweiht wird; sie werden sich rächen, die entweihten Götter, und oben weilen bei Uns auf steiler Höh, umweht von Himmelsluft.«

Das sind Sätze aus einem Brief von König Ludwig II. an den Komponisten Richard Wagner im Mai 1868, den »angebeteten Gast« und »göttlichen Freund«. Ein Jahr später legte der »Kini«, wie ihn seine bayrischen Untertanen nannten, den Grundstein für seine romantische Ritterburg. Die Terminplanung war allerdings zu optimistisch, Richtfest war erst 1880, und als Ludwig 1884 endlich einzog, war der Bau noch immer nicht fertig. Und anschließend hatte er nicht mehr lange Freude an seiner Burg: Zwei Jahre später ist er im Starnberger See ertrunken.

NEUSCHWANSTEIN CASTLE

»It is my intention to rebuild the old castle ruin of Hohenschwangau near the Pöllat Gorge in the authentic style of the old German knights' castles, and I must confess to you that I am very much looking forward to living there one day (in 3 years' time); there will be several cosy, homely guest rooms with a splendid view of the noble Säuling, the mountains of Tyrol and far across the plain; you know the revered guest I would like to accommodate there; the location is one of the most beautiful to be found, sacred and unapproachable, a worthy temple for the divine friend, who has brought salvation and true blessing to the world. It will also remind you of ›Tannhäuser‹ (Singers' Hall with a view of the castle in the background), ›Lohengrin‹ (castle courtyard, open passage, path to the chapel); this castle will be in every way more beautiful and homely than Hohenschwangau down below, which is desecrated every year by the prose of my mother; they will take revenge, the desecrated gods, and come to live with us on the lofty heights, breathing the air of heaven.«

This is an extract from a letter by King Ludwig II written in May 1868 to the composer Richard Wagner, who is the »revered guest« and »divine friend«. A year later, »Kini«, as his Bavarian subjects called him, had the foundation stone laid for his romantic knights' castle. His time schedule was, however, much too optimistic; the »Richtfest« ceremony (when the roof timbering is completed) did not take place till 1880, and in 1884, when Ludwig finally moved in, construction was still not complete. And subsequently he could take only brief pleasure in his castle: two years later he drowned in Lake Starnberg.

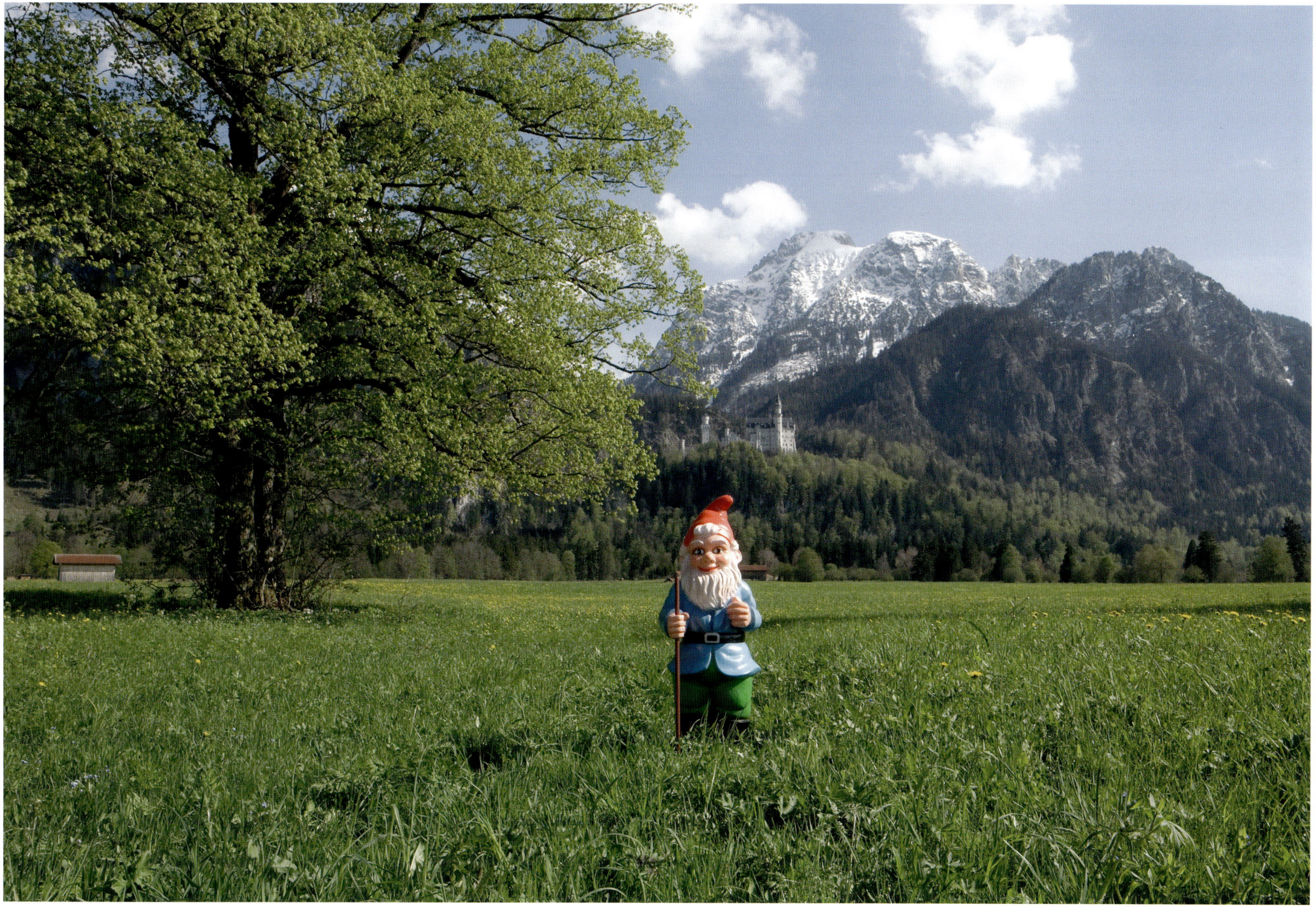

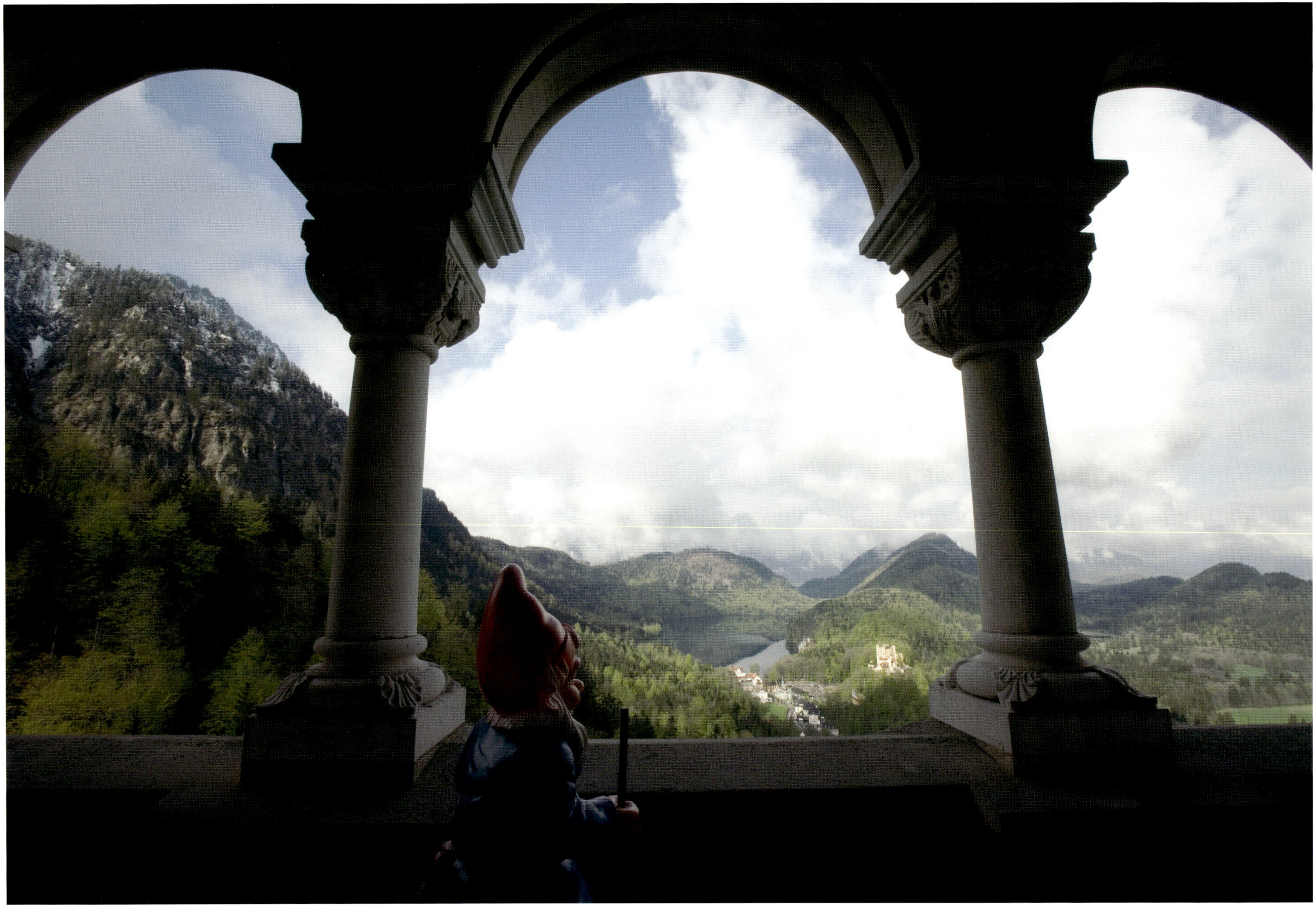

SCHLOSS NEUSCHWANSTEIN

Auch dieser geheimnisumwitterte Tod Ludwigs II. hat viel dazu beigetragen, dass Neuschwanstein zum berühmtesten Schloss der Welt geworden ist, auch wenn vom »echten Stil der alten deutschen Ritterburgen« nicht viel übrig geblieben ist. Fast jeder, der einen Blick auf das alte Europa werfen will, kommt hierher ins westliche Allgäu.

Und wenn man vom Balkon des Thronsaals nach Nordwesten schaut, dann sieht man in der Ferne das Schloss Hohenschwangau, wo Ludwig seine Kindheit verbracht hat und das seine Mutter jährlich »mit ihrer Prosa entweiht« hat.

NEUSCHWANSTEIN CASTLE

It is Ludwig II's mysterious death that also contributed a lot to the fact that Neuschwanstein became one of the world's most famous castles, even if not very much was left of the »genuine style of the old German knights' castles«. Almost anyone who wants to see something of old Europe comes here to west Allgäu.

And if you look from the throne room balcony towards the northwest, you see in the distance Castle Hohenschwangau, where Ludwig spent his childhood and which his mother »desecrated with her prose« year after year.

WIESKIRCHE, STEINGADEN

Ungefähr 25 Kilometer nördlich von Neuschwanstein steht eine schmucke kleine Kirche, die »Wallfahrtskirche zum Gegeißelten Heiland auf der Wies«. Dass sie zum Weltkulturerbe gehört, sieht man ihr von außen nicht direkt an. Das ändert sich aber schnell, wenn man hineingeht. »Ein schwingendes Oval, ein vom Himmel gefallenes Kleinod«, so hat sie einmal jemand beschrieben. (Nach dem Aachener und dem Speyerer Dom und der Würzburger Residenz kam sie 1983 als viertes Bauwerk in Deutschland auf die Unesco-Liste.)

1738 hat sich bei der Bäuerin Maria Lory auf dem Wieshof das »Tränenwunder« ereignet: Der Figur des »Gegeißelten Heilands« flossen Tränen aus den Augen. Das hat den Ort in ganz Europa schnell bekannt gemacht, und der Bauernhof konnte die Wallfahrer bald schon nicht mehr fassen. Also hat man beschlossen, für den »Gegeißelten Heiland« auf einer Waldwiese eine eigene Kirche zu bauen – die Wieskirche. 1754 ist sie geweiht worden, das war die Zeit des Rokoko.

Am Anfang des 19. Jahrhunderts, während der großen Säkularisation, sollte die Wieskirche eigentlich versteigert und abgerissen werden, da stand sie grade mal 50 Jahre. Die Bauern aus den umliegenden Ortschaften haben das nur mit Mühe verhindern können.

Eine Million Menschen kommen jedes Jahr aus aller Welt zur Wies im Allgäu, das sind am Tag mehr als zweieinhalbtausend. Es ist also fast unmöglich, dass man irgendwann einmal allein ist hier drin.

Deswegen hab ich mich ganz früh morgens aufgemacht, und tatsächlich, es war fast zwanzig Minuten lang ganz still im Raum.

WIESKIRCHE, STEINGADEN

About 25 kilometres north of Neuschwanstein there stands a trim little church, the »Wies Pilgrimage Church to the Scourged Saviour«. The fact that it is a world heritage site is not directly visible from the outside. However, this changes very quickly when you enter. »A swinging oval, a jewel fallen from heaven,« as someone once described it. (In 1983 it was put on the Unesco list as the fourth architectural building in Germany, after the cathedrals in Aachen and Speyer and the Residence in Würzburg.)

It was in 1738 at Maria Lory's Wieshof farmhouse that the »miracle of the tears« took place: tears flowed from the eyes of the statue of the »Scourged Saviour«. This very quickly made the place famous throughout Europe, and the farmhouse soon could not accommodate the number of pilgrims who came. It was then decided to build the »Scourged Saviour« its very own church in a meadow – the Wieskirche. It was consecrated in 1754, in the Rococo era.

At the beginning of the 19th century, during the great wave of secularisation, the church in the meadow was actually scheduled to be auctioned off and torn down; it had stood just 50 years. The farmers from the outlying villages only managed to prevent this with great difficulty.

One million people from the whole world come every year to Wies in the Allgäu; that is over two and a half thousand a day. It is almost impossible to find yourself alone here.

For which reason, I started out very early in the morning, and lo and behold, it was very quiet inside for almost twenty minutes.

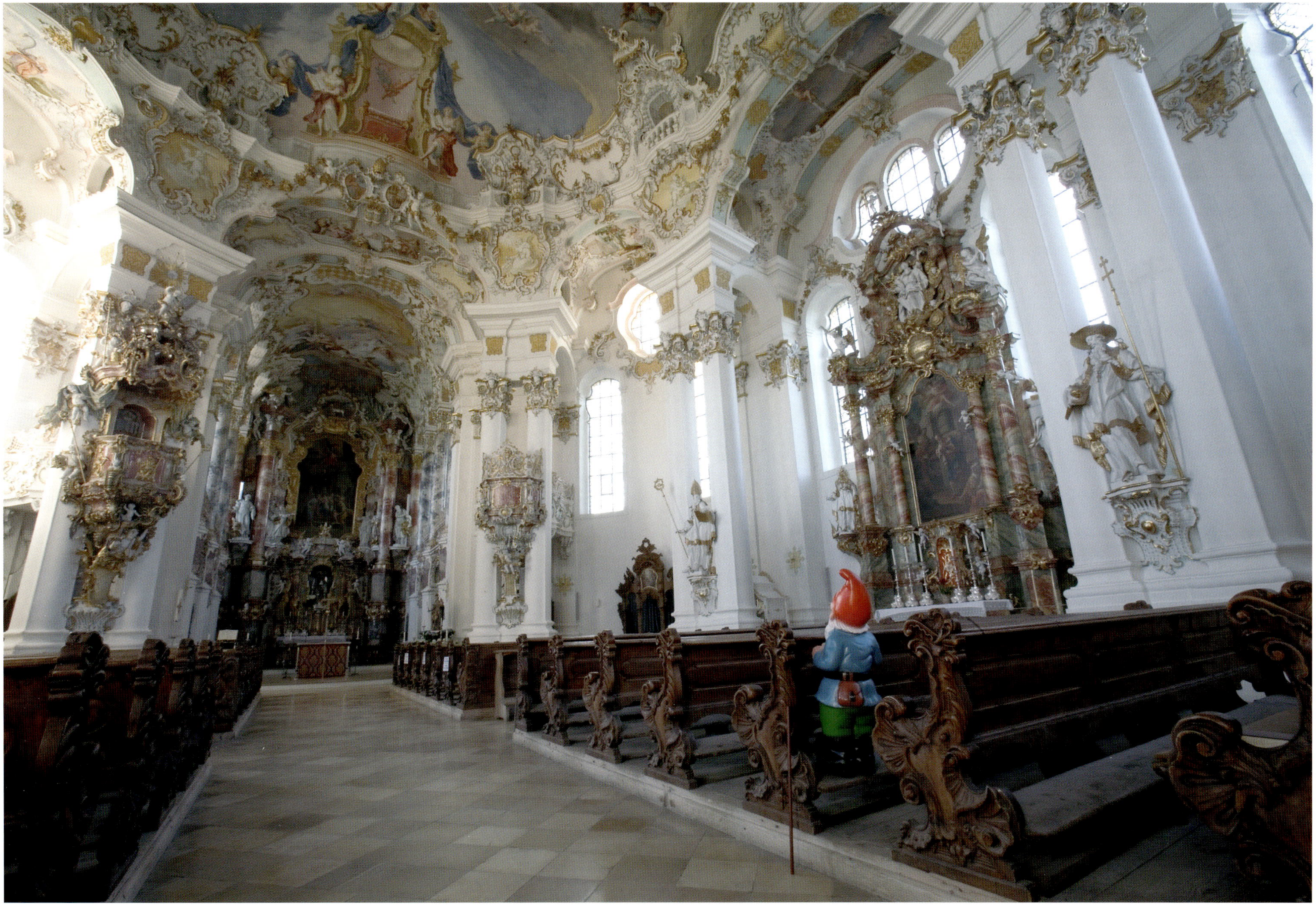

WATZMANN, KÖNIGSSEE

Vor langer, langer Zeit herrschte im Berchtesgadener Land einmal ein grausamer König, Watzmann mit Namen. Der hatte eine grausame Frau und sieben grausame Kinder. Sie alle verbrachten ihr Leben damit, Menschen und Tiere zu quälen, und hatten ihre Freude daran. Das ging so jahraus, jahrein, und niemand konnte ihnen Einhalt gebieten in ihrem herzlosen Tun.

Eines Tages aber hat es König Watzmann dann doch zu arg getrieben. Da zerstampfte er mit den Hufen seines Pferdes ein altes Mütterchen, das mit seinem Enkelkind auf dem Schoß vor dem Haus auf einer Bank saß. Doch damit nicht genug, er hetzte auch noch seine Hunde auf die Mutter und den Vater des Kindes, die zu Hilfe eilen wollten, und ließ sie zerfleischen. Da reckte das sterbende Mütterchen in seinem letzten Atemzug die blutige Hand zum Himmel und verfluchte den grausamen König mit seiner ganzen grausamen Sippe: Zu Stein sollten sie werden alle miteinander!

Und das Mütterchen wurde erhört. Der König, seine Frau und die sieben Kinder sind in mächtige schroffe Felsen verwandelt worden, da vorne im Südwesten kann man sie sehen, dort liegt die schreckliche Familie nun seit uralten Zeiten, 2713 Meter hoch reckt sich der König. Ihr aller Blut aber hat sich am Fuß der Berge in zwei Seen gesammelt: dem Obersee und dem Königssee, die sind heute leider unter dichten Nebelschwaden verborgen.

Da liegt er nun also kalt und unbeweglich, der Watzmann, seine Grausamkeit aber, die hat er nicht verloren, und er lässt die Menschen nicht in Ruhe. Er lockt sie ständig in seine berüchtigte Ostwand und quält sie wie in alten Zeiten, wenn sie hinaufsteigen. Bald hundert hat er schon in den Tod stürzen lassen.

WATZMANN, KÖNIGSSEE

A long, long time ago in the county of Berchtesgaden, there reigned a cruel king by the name of Watzmann. He had a cruel wife and seven cruel children. They spent all their life tormenting man and mouse and took great pleasure in doing so. This went on year in, year out, and no one was able to put a stop to their heartless deeds.

One day, however, King Watzmann went too far. With the hooves of his horse he trampled a little granny who was sitting on a bench in front of a house with a grandchild on her lap. As if that weren't enough, he set his dogs on the child's mother and father, who rushed to help, and had them torn to pieces. With her dying breath the old granny raised her bloodied hand to heaven and cursed the cruel king and his whole cruel brood: they should all be turned to stone.

And the little woman was heard. The king, his wife and seven children have been turned into mighty, steep cliffs. You can see them to the southwest. There, the whole terrible family has stood since ancient times. The king towers 2713 metres high. At the foot of the mountain, all their blood has collected into two lakes: the Obersee and the Königssee. But today, they are unfortunately hidden under patches of fog.

There it looms, cold and immovable, the Watzmann; his cruelty, however, has not worn off at all. He just won't leave people in peace. He lures them constantly to his infamous east wall and, when they climb it, torments them as in days of old. Almost one hundred of them have plummeted from here to their death.

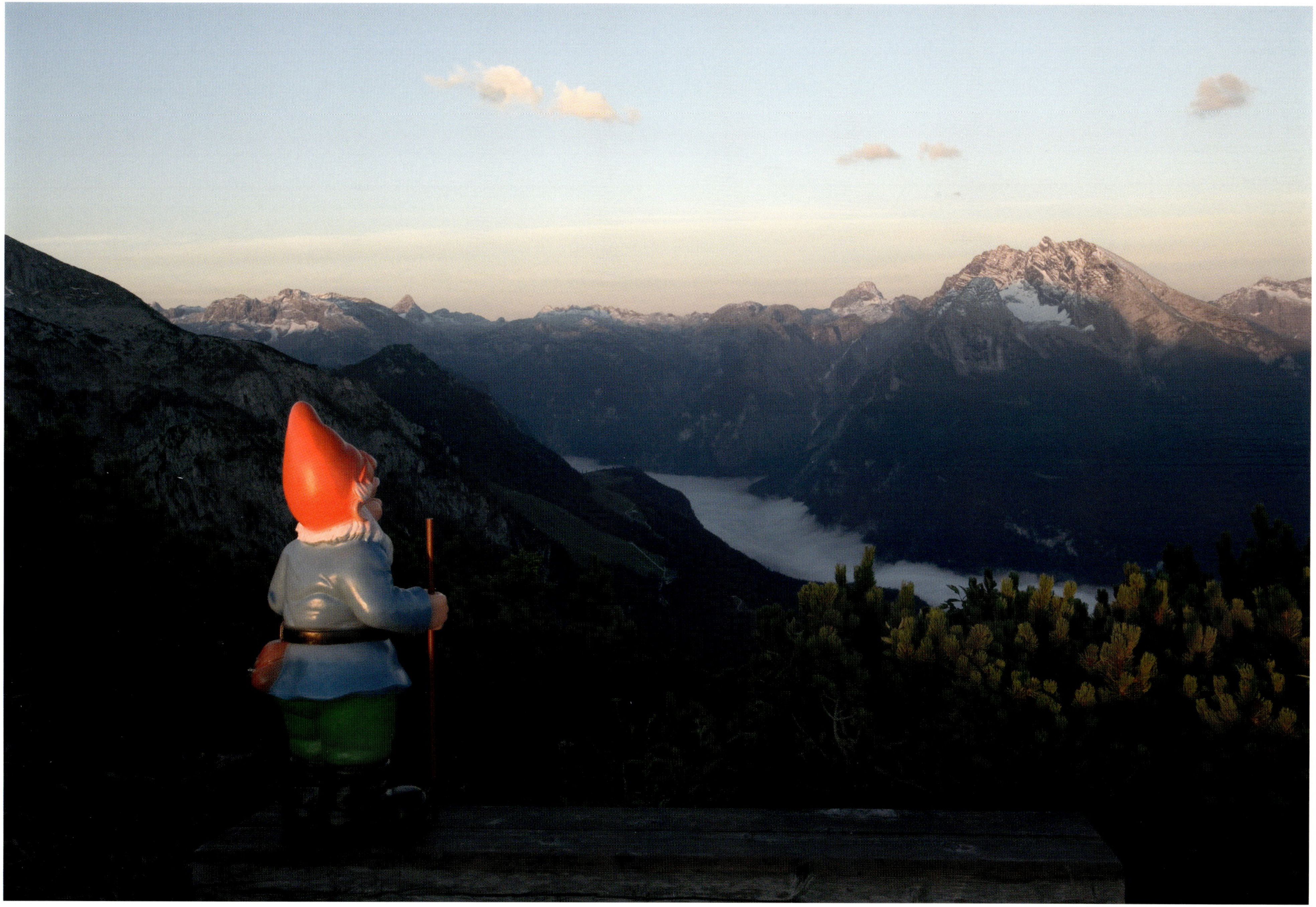

BOOTSHAUS, KÖNIGSSEE

Darin werden mir wohl die meisten zustimmen, die irgendwann einmal hier waren: Von den vielen schönen Seen in Bayern ist der Königssee am Fuß der berühmten Watzmann-Ostwand der allerschönste.

Er ist zwar bloß sechs Kilometer lang und misst an der breitesten Stelle grade mal 1200 Meter, aber er bietet Platz für eine Flotte, wie es sie auf der ganzen Welt kein zweites Mal gibt: 18 wunderschöne schlanke Holzboote fahren die Besucher den See hinauf und hinunter, und wenn die einmal alle zusammen unterwegs sind, herrscht hier ein ordentliches Gedränge.

Mit höchstens zwölf Kilometern in der Stunde geht's aber sehr gemächlich zu. Und fast völlig geräuschlos und vollkommen abgasfrei. Von Beginn der Schifffahrt auf dem Königssee sind nämlich alle Boote mit einem Elektroantrieb ausgestattet.

1909 ist ein solches Boot zum ersten Mal über den See gefahren. Das älteste der heutigen Flotte stammt aus dem Jahr 1920. Jeweils zwei Boote teilen sich ein eigenes Bootshaus, die stehen nebeneinander am Seeufer in Schönau, und alle Boote werden auf der eigenen Werft gewartet und, wenn nötig, überholt und instand gesetzt.

Vom Kapitän hab' ich gehört, dass ihn der Königssee an einen norwegischen Fjord erinnert. Das hat mich neugierig gemacht. Vielleicht komme ich dort ja auch noch mal hin, ich glaube, da würde es mir gefallen.

BOATHOUSE, KÖNIGSSEE

Probably most of the people who have ever been here would share the opinion, namely, that of all the many beautiful lakes in Bavaria, Lake Königssee – which lies below the famous East Face (the Watzmann-Ostwand) – is the most beautiful.

It is certainly not big being only six kilometres long and at its widest pointmeasuring just 1200 metres across, but it offers room enough for a fleet of boats such as cannot be found anywhere else in the world: 18 beautiful, slender wooden boats ferry visitors up and down the lake, and when they are all out-and-about at the same time, it makes for quite a turnout.

A maximum twelve kilometres an hour sets a very leisurely pace, all the while almost soundless and completely without exhaust fumes. From the very beginning, boats on the Königssee have been equipped with electric motors.

In 1909, the first such boat set out across the lake. The oldest one in today's fleet was built in 1920. Two boats share one boathouse; they stand side by side at the lakeshore in Schönau, and all the boats are serviced at their own shipyard and, when necessary, overhauled and repaired there.

The captain told me that the lake reminded him of a Norwegian fjord. This has made me curious. Perhaps I will one day get around to going there, as it sounds like my kind of place.

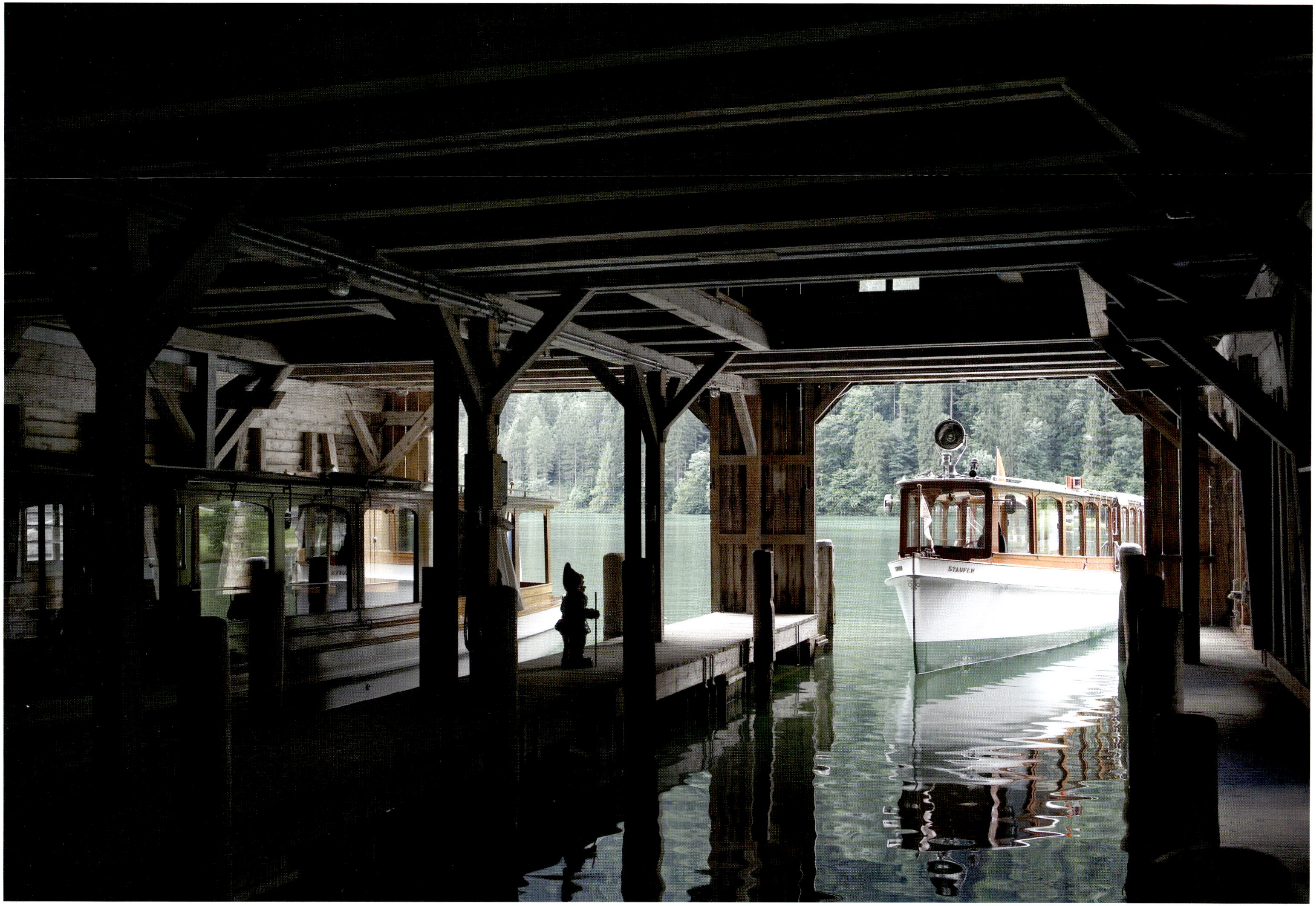

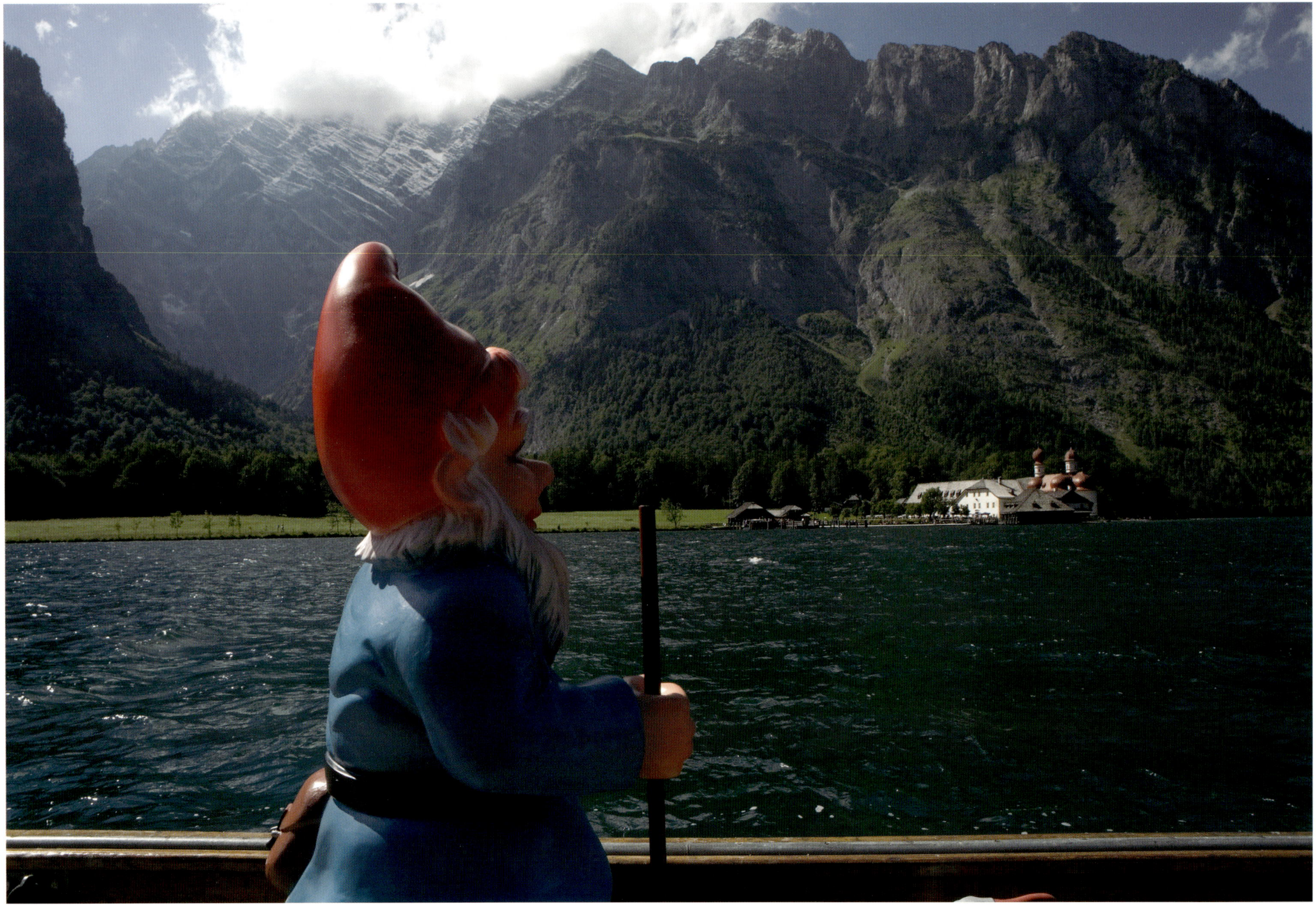

ST. BARTHOLOMÄ, KÖNIGSSEE

Sankt Bartholomäus ist der Schutzheilige der Sennerinnen und der Almbauern, aber wer weiß das heutzutage noch? Damit der Heilige gut untergebracht ist und seine Aufgabe erfüllen kann, haben ihm die Bauern schon im 12. Jahrhundert auf der Hirschau, das ist ein Schwemmkegel des Eisbachs am Westufer des Königssees, eine Kapelle gebaut. Ende des 17. Jahrhunderts war sie in so schlechtem Zustand, dass sie weitgehend neu errichtet werden musste. Inzwischen war noch ein Jagdschloss dazu gekommen, in dem sich zuerst die Pröbste und Chorherren von Berchtesgaden und später die Wittelsbacher erholt haben. Heute erholen sich hier, unterhalb der Watzmann-Ostwand, Touristen, denn aus dem Jagdschloss ist ein Restaurant geworden.

Am bequemsten kommt man mit dem Schiff dorthin. Wer's aber lieber unbequem hat, der kann auch ein paar Stunden zu Fuß gehen; das ist allerdings sehr beschwerlich. Aber St. Bartholomä ist ja schließlich eine Wallfahrtskapelle.

ST. BARTHOLOMEW, KÖNIGSSEE

Saint Bartholomew is the patron saint of Alpine herdswomen and farmers, but who still knows this today? In order to provide the saint with good accommodation so he can fulfil his duties, the farmers built him a chapel as long ago as the 12th century, located on the Hirschau, which is an alluvial cone formed by the Eisbach river on the west bank of Lake Königssee. At the end of the 17th century, the chapel was in such a bad state of repairs that it had to be extensively rebuilt. In the meantime, a hunting lodge was added, where first the provosts and canons from Berchtesgaden and later the Wittelsbach family relaxed. Today, below the East Face (Watzmann-Ostwand), it is tourists who do likewise, for the hunting lodge has become a restaurant.

The easiest way to get here is by boat; but if you prefer the hard way, you can reach it after a long and arduous hike. Remember, St. Bartholomew is, after all, a pilgrimage chapel.

NEUES SCHLOSS HERRENCHIEMSEE

Das ehrgeizigste Bauprojekt des Bayernkönigs Ludwig II. war das Schloss Herrenchiemsee. Dafür hat er sich das größte Vorbild genommen, das man damals finden konnte: Versailles. Aber Bayern war nicht Frankreich, und sein französischer Namensvetter Ludwig XIV. hatte im 17. Jahrhundert noch ganz andere Möglichkeiten als ein bayrischer »Märchenkönig« 200 Jahre später. Ludwig, von Gottes Gnaden König von Bayern, ist schließlich das Geld ausgegangen. 1885 musste er die Arbeiten am Schloss einstellen. Ein Jahr später ist er im Starnberger See ertrunken. Die Spiegelgalerie ist immerhin fertig geworden, und sie sieht fast so aus wie das Vorbild in Versailles. Ganz in der Nähe des Schlosses, im ehemaligen »Chorherrenstift«, hat im August 1948 übrigens der Verfassungskonvent getagt, um das Grundgesetz für die zukünftige Bundesrepublik auszuarbeiten.

HERRENCHIEMSEE NEW PALACE

The most ambitious project that King Ludwig II of Bavaria undertook was that of building the castle Herrenchiemsee. He took as his model the greatest one available at the time: Versailles. But Bavaria was not France, and his French namesake, Ludwig XIV (Louis XIV) had quite a few more possibilities on hand in the 17th century than a Bavarian »fairytale« king 200 years later. Ludwig, by the grace of God King of Bavaria, simply ran out of money and in 1885 he had to stop work on it. One year later, he drowned in Lake Starnberg. The Gallery of Mirrors was, however, completed, and it looks almost exactly like its namesake in Versailles. Very close to the new palace, namely in the former »Chorherrenstift«, a monastery, the Constitutional Convention took place in August 1948 to work out the »Grundgesetz« (Basic Law) for the future Federal Republic.

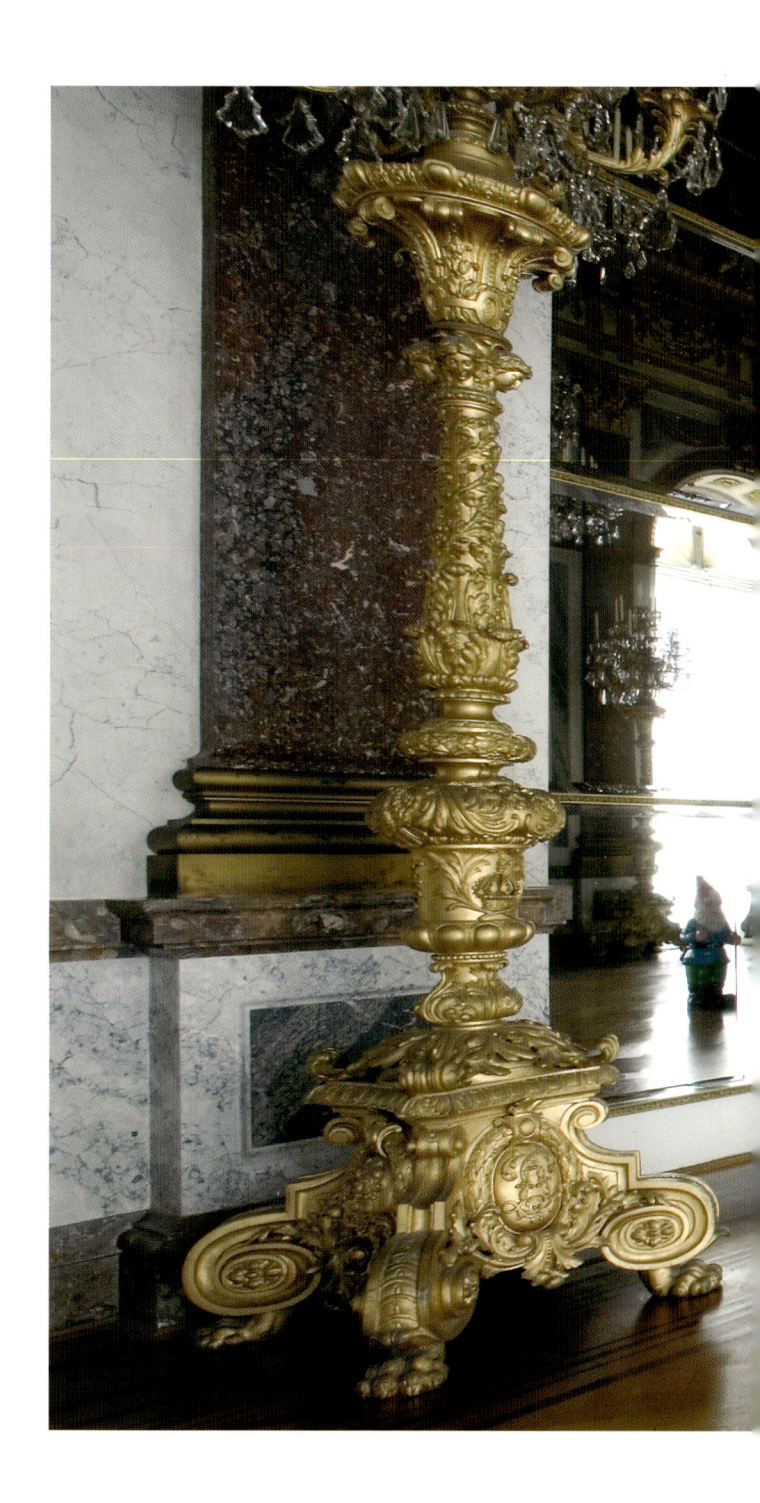

69

MÜNCHEN

München ist die Hauptstadt von Bayern, dem größten deutschen Bundesland; Bayern ist siebenundzwanzigeinhalb Mal so groß wie das Saarland. Bayern gehört zwar auch zur Bundesrepublik, aber eigentlich nicht so richtig, jedenfalls nicht so wie die anderen Bundesländer: Die Bayern haben 1949 als einzige das Grundgesetz nicht unterzeichnet. Sie leben nämlich in einem »Freistaat« und legen besonders großen Wert auf ihre Eigenständigkeit.

Vom Aussichtshügel im Münchener Olympiapark hat man einen wunderschönen Blick nach Süden über die Frauenkirche und den Rathausturm auf das Alpenpanorama zwischen Kufstein und Garmisch-Partenkirchen. Manche sagen ja, München sei die nördlichste Stadt Italiens – hauptsächlich wegen der Architektur und der Kunst. Von hier aus ist es nach Mailand, Verona oder Venedig jedenfalls näher als nach Berlin oder Hamburg, man muss nur über die Alpen rüber.

In der Münchener Innenstadt gibt es keine Hochhäuser. Kein Gebäude darf dort höher sein als die Türme der Frauenkirche, knapp 100 Meter, und deshalb ist der Blick auf die Berge auch nicht verstellt. Vor allem bei Föhn, das ist ein Fallwind am Nordrand der Alpen, ist die Sicht besonders gut. Dann hat man den Eindruck, das ganze Gebirge käme noch ein paar Kilometer näher an die Stadt herangerückt.

Die Baumeister der Münchener Frauenkirche müssen übrigens sehr weitsichtige Männer gewesen sein. Der »Dom zu unserer Lieben Frau« ist am Ende des 15. Jahrhunderts fertig geworden, da hatte die Stadt grade mal 13.000 Einwohner. Selbst wenn die sich alle auf einmal in der Kirche versammelt hätten, wäre sie noch längst nicht voll gewesen, da passen nämlich noch 7000 mehr rein.

MUNICH

Munich is the capital city of Bavaria, Germany's largest state; Bavaria is twenty-seven-and-a-half times as big as the Saarland. Bavaria is, in fact, also part of the Federal Republic, but actually not properly so, at least not like the other federal states. The Bavarians were the only ones not to sign the Basic Law in 1949. That is to say, they live in a »free state« and very much cherish their independence.

From the lookout hill in Munich's Olympic Park you get a wonderful view to the south – past the Frauenkirche and Rathaus tower – to the panorama of the Alps between Kufstein and Garmisch-Partenkirchen. Many say that Munich is Italy's most northern city, chiefly because of its architecture and art. From here, in any case, Milan, Verona and Venice are closer than Berlin or Hamburg. You need only cross the Alps.

There are no high buildings in Munich's inner city. No building there is allowed to exceed the height of the Frauenkirche towers, just short of 100 metres, which is the reason our view of the Alps is unhindered. Especially when the »Föhn« is blowing, a wind on the northern rim of the Alps, the view is vividly clear. You get the impression that the whole mountain chain has moved several kilometres closer to the city.

The builders of Munich's Frauenkirche must have been very far sighted and optimistic. When this »Cathedral to Our Dear Lady«, was completed at the end of the 15th century, the city had just about 13,000 inhabitants. Even if all of them had assembled in the church at once, it would not have been nearly full; there would have still been room for 7000 more.

71

72

OLYMPIAPARK, MÜNCHEN

Wenn man heute durch den Olympiapark in München geht, möchte man ja kaum glauben, dass diese Anlage schon in den 60er Jahren des letzten Jahrhunderts entworfen, geplant und gebaut worden ist. Als am 26. August 1972 die XX. Olympischen Sommerspiele eröffnet wurden, war die ganze Welt begeistert von dieser leichten, beschwingten, transparenten Zeltlandschaft der Stuttgarter Architekten Günter Behnisch & Partner.

Nur der Bund der Steuerzahler hat genörgelt und das Zeltdach als »verschwenderischste Inspiration der Welt« bezeichnet. Dabei sind die Kosten dafür mit dem Verkauf der Zehn-Mark-Münzen gedeckt worden. In nur 11 Monaten sind für das Tragwerk insgesamt 436 Kilometer Drahtseile gespannt und an 12 bis zu 80 Meter hohen Pylonen befestigt worden. 25.000 Bauarbeiter aus 24 Nationen haben in mehr als 6 Millionen Arbeitsstunden die gesamte Anlage in der Rekordzeit von knapp 3 Jahren fertig gestellt.

Der Olympiapark ist nicht nur eine Ansammlung von Sportplätzen und Sporthallen, sondern eine richtige Parklandschaft mit Hügeln und Tälern und einem See in der Mitte, und in jedem Jahr kommen 5 Millionen Menschen aus München und aus aller Welt hierher, um ihre Freizeit zu verbringen.

OLYMPIC PARK, MUNICH

Walking through the Olympic Park in Munich today, you would hardly believe that these grounds were designed, planned and built as long ago as the 1960s. When the XXth Summer Olympic Games were opened on August 26, 1972, the whole world was enthused by the light-hearted, airy and transparent tent landscape of the Stuttgart architects Günter Behnisch & Partner.

Only the Taxpayers' Federation whined that the tent roof was the »most profligate inspiration in the world«. And this although the costs were covered by the sale of specially minted ten Deutschmark coins. In only eleven months a total of 436 kilometres of wire rope for the supporting structure was spanned and attached to twelve pylons up to 80 metres in height. 25,000 building workers from 24 nations completed the work on the entire complex in over 6 million working hours in the record time of less than three years.

The Olympic Park is not only a collection of sports fields and halls, but a regular park landscape with hills and valleys and a lake in the middle. And every year, 5 million people from Munich and the whole world come here for their recreational pleasure.

SIEGESTOR, MÜNCHEN

Ludwig I. ist 1825 zum bayrischen König gekrönt worden und hat 1848 zugunsten seines Sohnes Maximilian II. abgedankt. Ludwig war ein großer Verehrer der antiken Kultur und Architektur. Das kann man vor allem an der Walhalla bei Regensburg ablesen, aber auch am Münchener Königsplatz und am Siegestor. Dass die bayrische Hauptstadt heute so aussieht, wie sie aussieht, verdankt sie zum großen Teil König Ludwig I.

Er wurde 1786 in Straßburg geboren und ist 1868 in Nizza gestorben. Er war ein sehr moderner Herrscher und ein weltoffener obendrein. Er hat zum Beispiel dafür gesorgt, dass 1835 zwischen Nürnberg und Fürth die erste deutsche Eisenbahn in Betrieb ging. Das Frachtgut bei der Jungfernfahrt war übrigens ein Fass Bier.

Wo die Münchener Maxvorstadt aufhört, fängt Schwabing an, und genau dort steht das Siegestor. Ludwig I. hat es 1843 in Auftrag gegeben – »dem bayrischen Heere zum Ruhme« –, es ist aber erst 1852 fertig geworden. Für das Siegestor hat er sich den Konstantinsbogen in Rom zum Vorbild genommen.

Obendrauf steht eine mächtige Bavaria mit einer Löwen-Quadriga. Der Löwe ist das bayrische Wappentier, er kommt in dieser Gegend aber sonst nicht vor, allenfalls in Bronze, in Stein, in Porzellan oder in zoologischen Gärten.

SIEGESTOR, MUNICH

Ludwig I of Bavaria was crowned king in 1825 and in 1848 abdicated in favour of his son, Maximilian II. Ludwig was a great admirer of ancient culture and architecture. This you can see, above all, at the Walhalla near Regensburg, but also at Munich's Königsplatz and the Siegestor (Triumphal Arch). It is King Ludwig II that we mostly have to thank for the way the Bavarian capital looks today.

He was born 1786 in Strasbourg and died 1868 in Nice. He was a very modern ruler and, to top it all, open-minded. For instance, he saw to it that in 1835 the first German railway went into operation between Nuremberg and Fürth. The cargo it carried on its maiden voyage was, by the way, a barrel of beer.

Where the Munich Maxvorstadt ends, Schwabing begins, and that is exactly where the Siegestor stands. Ludwig I commissioned it in 1843 – »to the glory of the Bavarian army« – but it wasn't completed till 1852. The Triumphal Arch was modelled after the Constantine Arch in Rome.

On the top stands a mighty Bavaria riding a quadriga drawn by lions. The lion is on the Bavarian coat of arms, not that he otherwise frequents this region, except in bronze, in stone, in porcelain or in the zoo.

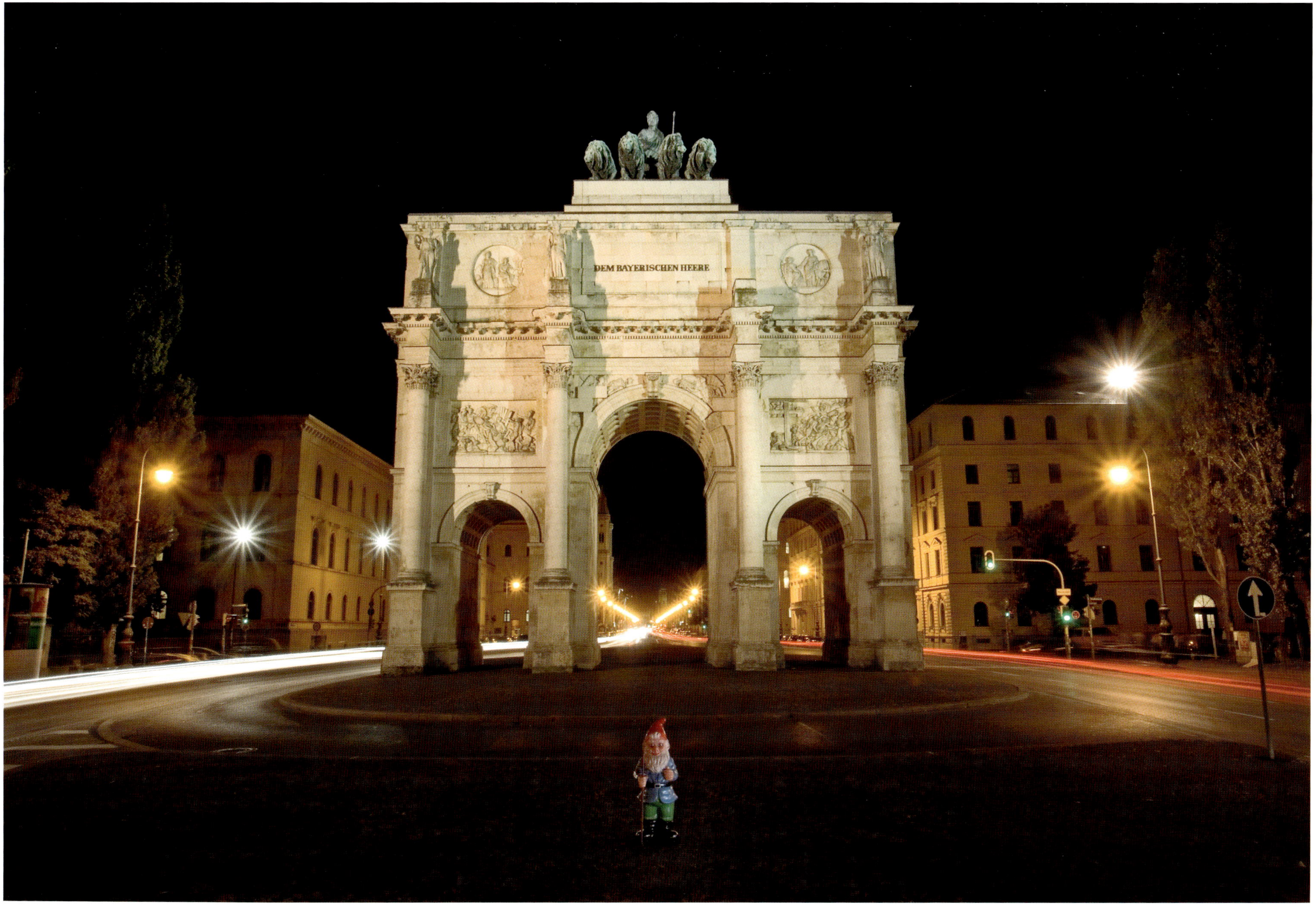
DEM BAYERISCHEN HEERE

ALTE PINAKOTHEK, MÜNCHEN

Kurz nach seiner Krönung zum bayrischen König hat Ludwig I. beschlossen, seinen Untertanen einen großen Teil der Kunstwerke zugänglich zu machen, die seine Vorfahren im Laufe der Zeit zusammengetragen und in ihren Schlössern verteilt hatten – über 700 Gemälde aus dem 14. bis 18. Jahrhundert. Und weil es kein geeignetes Gebäude dafür gab, hat er seinen Baumeister Leo von Klenze beauftragt – denselben übrigens, der die Walhalla bei Regensburg gebaut hat –, eines zu entwerfen: So ist die Pinakothek am Königsplatz in München entstanden.

Als sie 1836 nach zehn Jahren Bauzeit eröffnet wurde, war sie die größte Gemäldegalerie der Welt. Die Münchener konnten zuerst aber nichts Rechtes damit anfangen, und obwohl der Eintritt frei war, haben sie lieber auf der Wiese davor Picknick gemacht. (Zur »Alten« ist die Pinakothek erst geworden, als 1975 bis 1981 direkt gegenüber die zweite, die »Neue« gebaut wurde.)

Seit der Eröffnung ist die Sammlung immer weiter vervollständigt worden. Das 4,6 mal 6 Meter große »Jüngste Gericht« in der so genannten Düsseldorfer Galerie gehörte von Anfang an dazu. Rubens hatte es für den Hochaltar der Jesuitenkirche in Neuburg an der Donau gemalt, aber die vielen nackten Körper waren nicht im Sinne der Geistlichkeit, und damit die Gläubigen nicht auf unpassende Gedanken kamen, haben sie die heiklen Stellen mit Tüchern verhängt.

Wenn man wirklich alles sehen will, was Rubens auf 27 Quadratmetern gemalt hat, sollte man sich ruhig ein Weilchen Zeit nehmen. Und für die anderen 1800 Gemälde würde ich glatt meinen Jahresurlaub nehmen, wenn ich nur wüsste, wo ich ihn beantragen sollte.

OLD PINAKOTHEK, MUNICH

Shortly after his coronation King Ludwig I of Bavaria decided to make accessible to his subjects a large part of the artworks that his family had collected over the years and had scattered among different castles – over 700 paintings from the 14th to the 18th centuries. And because there was no suitable building on hand to accommodate them, he commissioned his architect, Leo von Klenze – the same man, by the way, who built the Walhalla near Regensburg – to design one. That is how the Pinakothek at Königsplatz in Munich came about.

When it was opened in 1836 after ten years of construction, it was the biggest painting gallery in the world. The people of Munich didn't know quite what to make of it, and although entrance was free, they preferred picnicking on the lawn outside. (The Pinakothek was not called the »Old« till – from 1975 to 1981 – the »New« one was built directly across from it.)

Since its opening, the collection has been continually enlarged. But the 4.6 by 6 metre »Last Judgement« in the so-called Düsseldorf Gallery has been there from the beginning. Rubens painted it for the high altar of the Jesuit church in Neuburg on the Danube, but the many naked bodies were not exactly in keeping with the ideas of the clergy. So, to protect the faithful from improper thoughts, the critical parts were concealed under bits of cloth.

If you really want to see all 27 square metres of what Rubens painted, then simply allow yourself to take the time. And as for all the other 1800 paintings, I would honest to goodness sacrifice my annual holiday, if I only knew where I was supposed to apply for it.

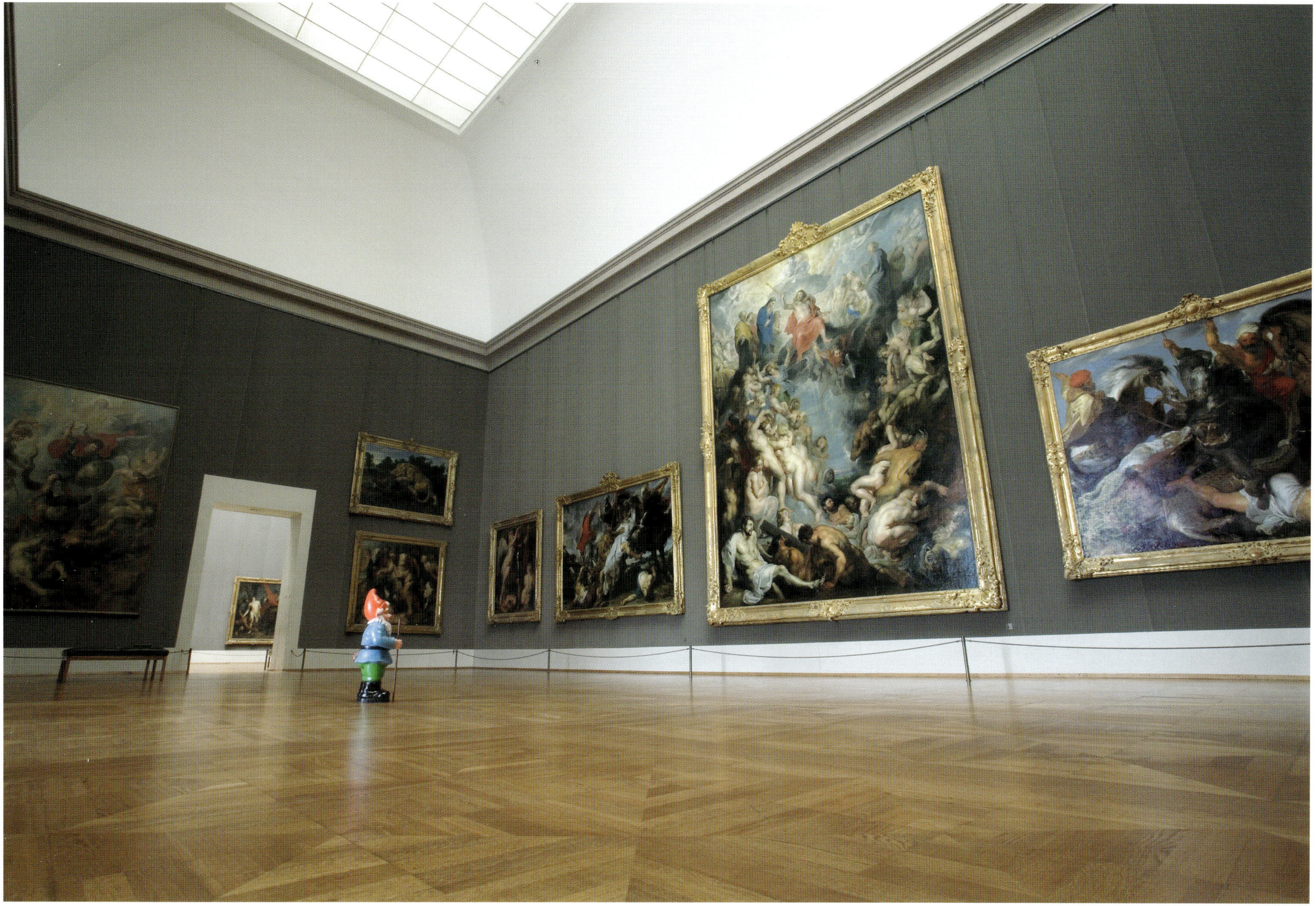

MÜLLER'SCHES VOLKSBAD, MÜNCHEN

Bis um die Mitte des 19. Jahrhunderts war es in Europa mit der Hygiene noch nicht weit her. Aber dann hat jemand herausgefunden, dass jeder Mensch schon dadurch eine Menge für seine Gesundheit – und auch für die von andern – tun kann, dass er sich ab und zu mal die Hände ordentlich mit Seife wäscht. Das hat damals hauptsächlich die Ärzte überrascht, und die wollten es zuerst gar nicht glauben.

Aber schließlich haben sie sich doch überzeugen lassen, und mit der Hygiene wurde es bald sehr viel besser, nicht nur bei den Ärzten. Zu den Folgen gehört unter anderem auch die Einrichtung von öffentlichen Badeanstalten, die hier und da Volksbäder hießen.

Etwa zur selben Zeit wie die Idee der Volksgesundheit ist übrigens auch die Idee der Volksbildung entstanden. Inzwischen gibt es Dutzende von Zusammensetzungen mit »Volk«: von der Volksschule und der Volksmusik über den Volkswagen, das Volkseigentum und die Volksrepublik bis zum Volkstrauertag – aber jetzt bin ich abgeschweift, zurück nach München:

Das größte, schönste und zur Bauzeit modernste und teuerste war das Müller'sche Volksbad in München. Die Baukosten lagen bei 1,8 Millionen Goldmark, damals eine riesige Summe.

Entstanden ist es zwischen 1897 und 1901. Eigentlich war das ja die Zeit des Jugendstils, aber der Bauherr und Stifter, der Münchener Ingenieur Karl Müller, war anscheinend ein großer Liebhaber des Barock, und so ist es zu dieser interessanten Stilmischung gekommen. Inzwischen ist es aufwändig saniert worden und zählt jetzt wieder zu den schönsten Hallenbädern in Europa.

MÜLLER'SCHES VOLKSBAD, MUNICH

Up to the mid-19th century, hygiene was not at all a very pressing matter. But then someone discovered that a person can do a lot for his health – and also for the health of others – if he from time to time washes his hands thoroughly with soap. At the time this doctors more than anyone, and they at first surprised didn't want to believe it.

But, in the end, they allowed themselves to be convinced and, with hygiene on board, things got very much better, not only for doctors. One of the results was the installation of indoor public swimming pools, which here and there were called »folk baths«.

Around the same time as the idea of people's health was bandied about, by the way, the idea of people's education also began to emerge. In the meantime, there have been dozens of combinations in German with the word »Volk«: from the folk school (community college) and folk music, via Volkswagen, folk (communal) property, the Folk (People's) Republic of East Germany, up to Folk Mourning Day (national remembrance day) – but now I'm digressing. Let's return to Munich:

The largest, loveliest and, at the time of its construction, the most modern and most expensive was the Müller'sche Volksbad in Munich. The building costs came to 1.8 million Goldmark, which was then an enormous sum.

It was built from 1897 to 1901. This was, in fact, the era of Jugendstil or Art Deco, but the owner and sponsor, the Munich engineer Karl Müller, was apparently a great fan of the Baroque. So this interesting mixture of style became the fascinating result. In the meantime, it has been lavishly refurbished and is again one of the most beautiful indoor pools in Europe.

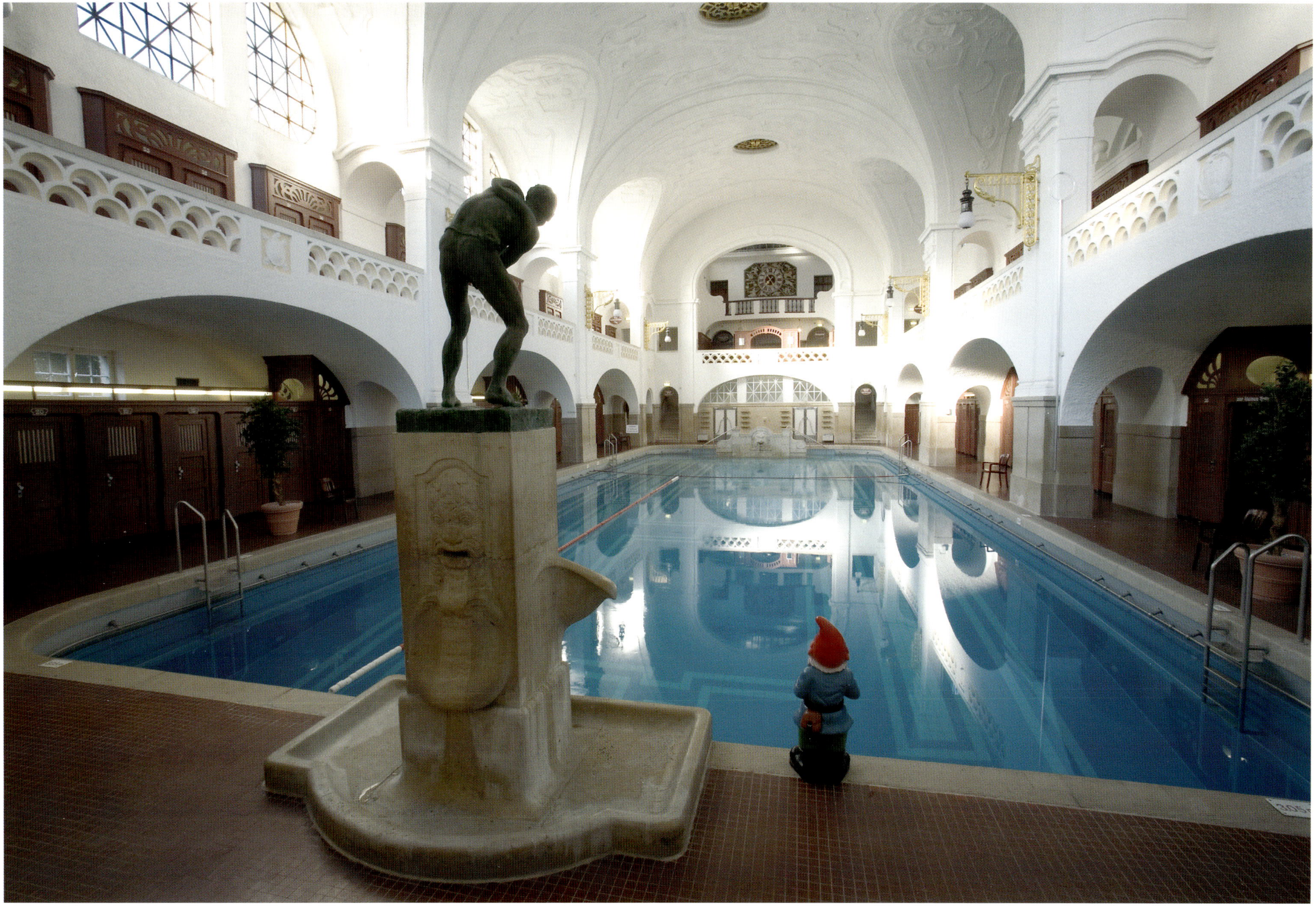

HALLERTAU

Der Georgitag 1516 ist für das Bier in Deutschland das wichtigste Datum. An diesem 23. April hat der bayrische Herzog Wilhelm IV. zusammen mit seinem jüngeren Bruder Ludwig X. das »Reinheitsgebot« erlassen. Das ist zwar nicht die älteste, aber sicher die bekannteste Lebensmittelverordnung der Welt, und sie besagt eigentlich nichts anderes, als dass Bier nur aus den Bestandteilen Hopfen, Malz, Wasser und Hefe gebraut werden darf. Daran hat sich im Grunde bis heute nichts geändert. (Was es mit der Hefe eigentlich auf sich hat, das wusste man vor 500 Jahren noch nicht genau.)

Bier ist zusammen mit dem Wein das älteste Getränk der Welt; schon die Ägypter und die Mesopotamier haben Bier gebraut. Und: Sie haben dabei auch schon Hopfen verwendet. Der macht das Bier haltbar und herb, das ist ganz wichtig für den Geschmack. Nicht nur deswegen hat das Bier der alten Germanen, der süßliche Met, mit dem Bier von heute kaum etwas gemeinsam.

Der Hopfen – er gehört zu den Hanfgewächsen – ist eine Kletterpflanze. Sie windet sich im Uhrzeigersinn an Leitdrähten bis in 7 Meter Höhe und wächst am Tag manchmal 30 Zentimeter. Die Hopfendolden müssen nach der Ernte sofort getrocknet werden, damit sie nicht verderben.

Die Anbaufläche für Hopfen beträgt weltweit 59.000 Hektar, knapp ein Drittel davon liegt in Deutschland und das meiste in der Hallertau, dem größten zusammenhängenden Hopfenanbaugebiet der Welt: 17.800 Hektar. Kein Wunder, dass die Hallertauer ihrem Hopfen in Wolznach ein eigenes, wunderschönes Museum gebaut haben, wo man alles erfahren kann, was es über den Hopfen zu wissen gibt.

HALLERTAU

Georgi Day, 1516, is the most significant date in the German calendar for beer. On the April 23, of that year, Duke Wilhelm IV of Bavaria, together with his younger brother Ludwig X, proclaimed the »Reinheitsgebot« or purity law. Although this is not the oldest, it is surely the best known food regulation in the world, and it says nothing other than that beer may only consist of the ingredients hops, malt, water and yeast.
And, up to today, nothing has basically changed. (The role yeast played in all this was rather a mystery five hundred years ago.)

Beer, together with wine, is the oldest beverage in the world; beer had already been brewed by the Egyptians and the Mesopotamians. And: they used hops to do it, an ingredient that helps preserve beer, gives it its tartness, and is in general an essential taste factor. This is not the only reason the beer drunk by the old Germanic tribes, their legendary honeyed mead, has hardly anything in common with today's brew.

Hop – a species of hemp – is a climbing plant. It winds clockwise along wires strung up to a height of 7 metres and can grow as much as 30 centimetres a day. Once picked, the flower clusters must be dried immediately so that they don't spoil.

The worldwide area of cultivation for hops is 59,000 hectares, just short of a third of which lie in Germany and most of it in Hallertau, the world's largest continious area of cultivation for hops: 17,800 hectares. No wonder that the people of Hallertau have built the hop plant a wonderful museum of its own in Wolznach, where you can find out everything there is to know about hops.

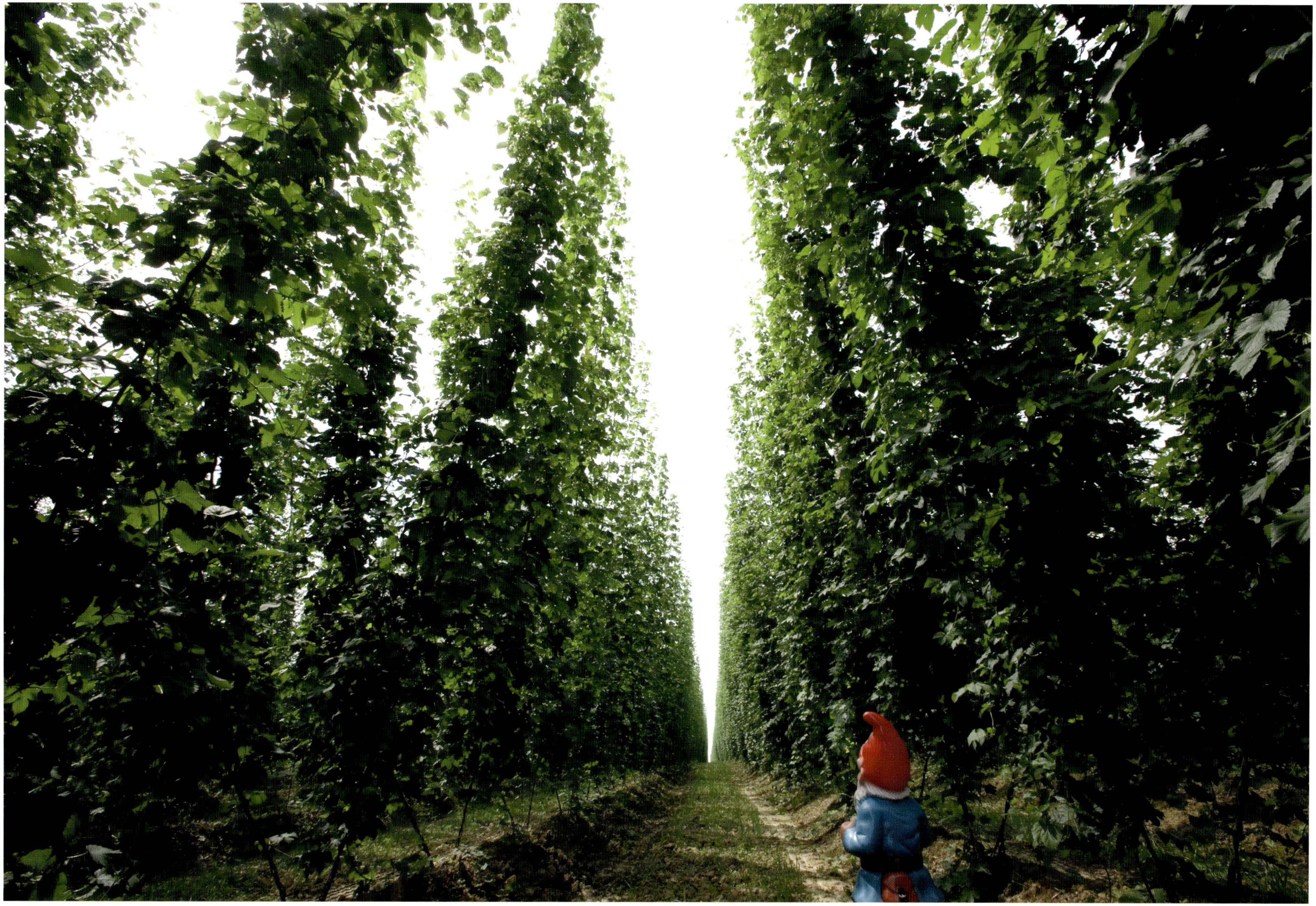

ORTSSPITZE, PASSAU

Wie ist das eigentlich, wenn sich zwei Flüsse treffen und zusammenfließen? Welcher mündet da in welchen? Gut, meistens ist die Sache klar, aber nehmen wir mal die Donau bei Passau im Südosten von Bayern. Die kommt hier an der »Ortsspitze« von links, kurz vorher fließt noch die kleine Ilz hinein, und von rechts kommt der Inn. Der ist hier ungefähr 40 Meter breit und bringt 10 Prozent mehr Wasser mit als die Donau. Trotzdem ist an dieser Stelle Schluss für ihn, und beide fließen zusammen als Donau weiter. Und warum? Ganz einfach: Die Donau ist seit ihrer Quelle im Osten des Schwarzwalds schon 648 Kilometer unterwegs, der Inn von seinem Quellgebiet im Schweizer Engadin aber erst 517. Das sind 131 Kilometer zu wenig.

Obwohl – eine richtige Quelle hat die Donau eigentlich gar nicht. Am Anfang besteht sie aus zwei Flüsschen, der Breg und der etwas kleineren Brigach, die fließen hinter Donaueschingen zusammen und nennen sich erst von da ab Donau. Manche meinen aber auch, dass die Donau eigentlich schon an der Bregquelle beginnt, dann kämen sogar noch mal 49 Kilometer dazu.

Von Passau aus fließt die Donau durch Österreich, das kann man da hinten am Horizont schon sehen, durch Ungarn und sieben weitere Länder bzw. dran vorbei, an Moldawien zum Beispiel nur über eine Strecke von 570 Metern.

Nach ungefähr 2850 Kilometern verschwindet die Donau schließlich in Rumänien über ein riesiges Delta im Schwarzen Meer. In Europa gibt es übrigens nur noch einen längeren Fluss, und das ist die Wolga.

ORTSSPITZE, PASSAU

What goes on when two rivers meet and merge? Which one flows into which? All right, most of the time it's clear, but let's take the Danube at Passau in southeast Bavaria. It arrives here at the town's »tip« where, shortly before, the little Ilz has flowed into it from the left and from the right, the Inn. The latter is about forty metres broader than the Danube at this point and transports ten percent more water. Yet despite this, the Inn ends here and both flow on together only as the Danube. Why? Quite simple: the Danube, from its source in the eastern Black Forest, has been underway for 648 kilometres, whereas the Inn, from its source in the Swiss Engadine, for only 517 kilometres. That's 131 kilometres too few.

Actually – the Danube does not really have a proper source at all. It begins as two little rivers, the Breg and the somewhat smaller Brigach, which flow together at Donaueschingen and, it is only from here that they become the Danube. Some people believe, however, that the Danube actually begins at the source of the Breg, which would add another 49 kilometres on to it.

From Passau, the Danube flows through Austria – which you can see here on the horizon – through Hungary and seven other countries or past them, for instance Moldavia for a mere 570-metre stretch.

After around 2850 kilometres, the Danube crosses a huge delta in Rumania and disappears into the Black Sea. Incidentally, there is only one river that is longer in Europe, and that is the Volga.

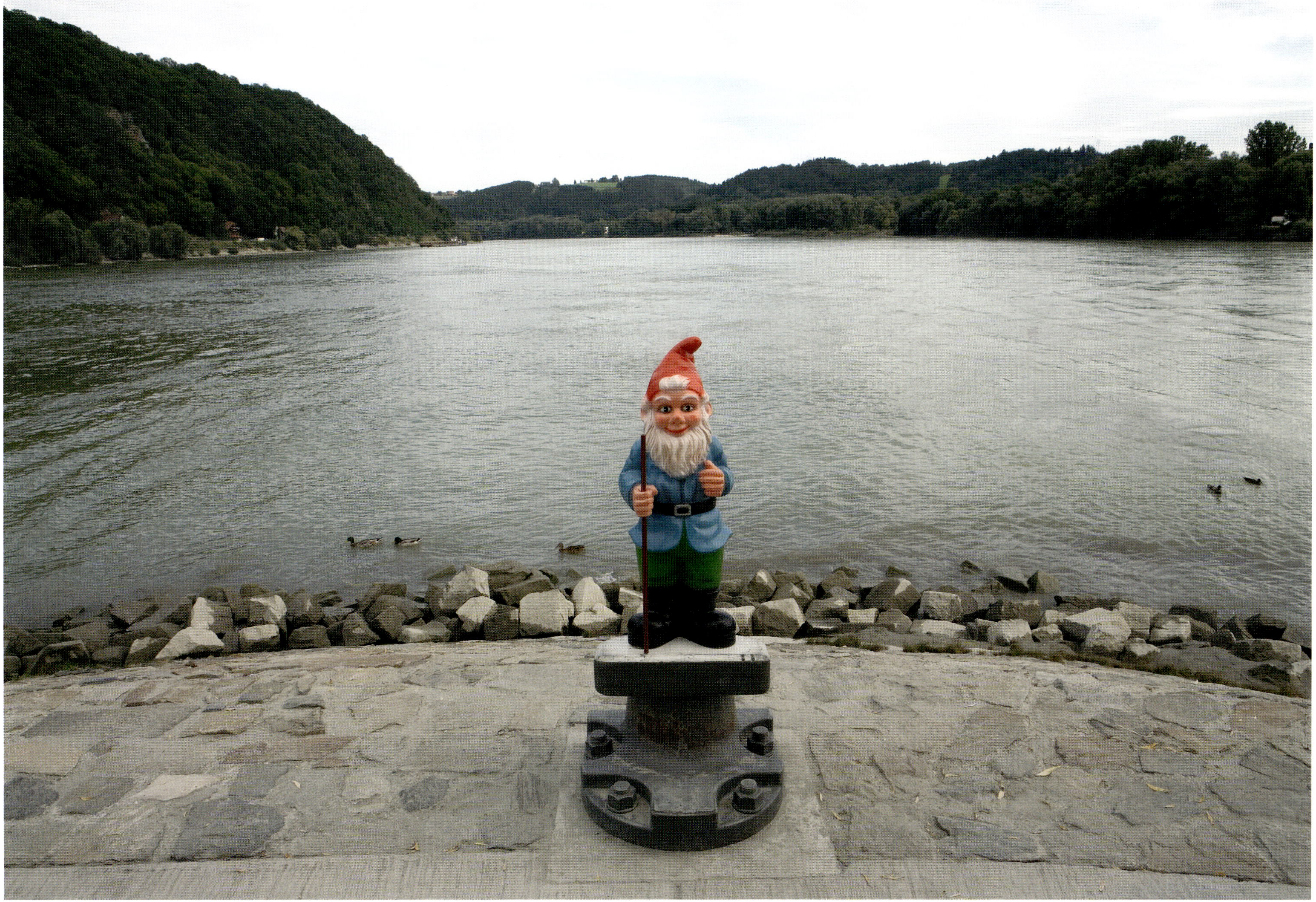

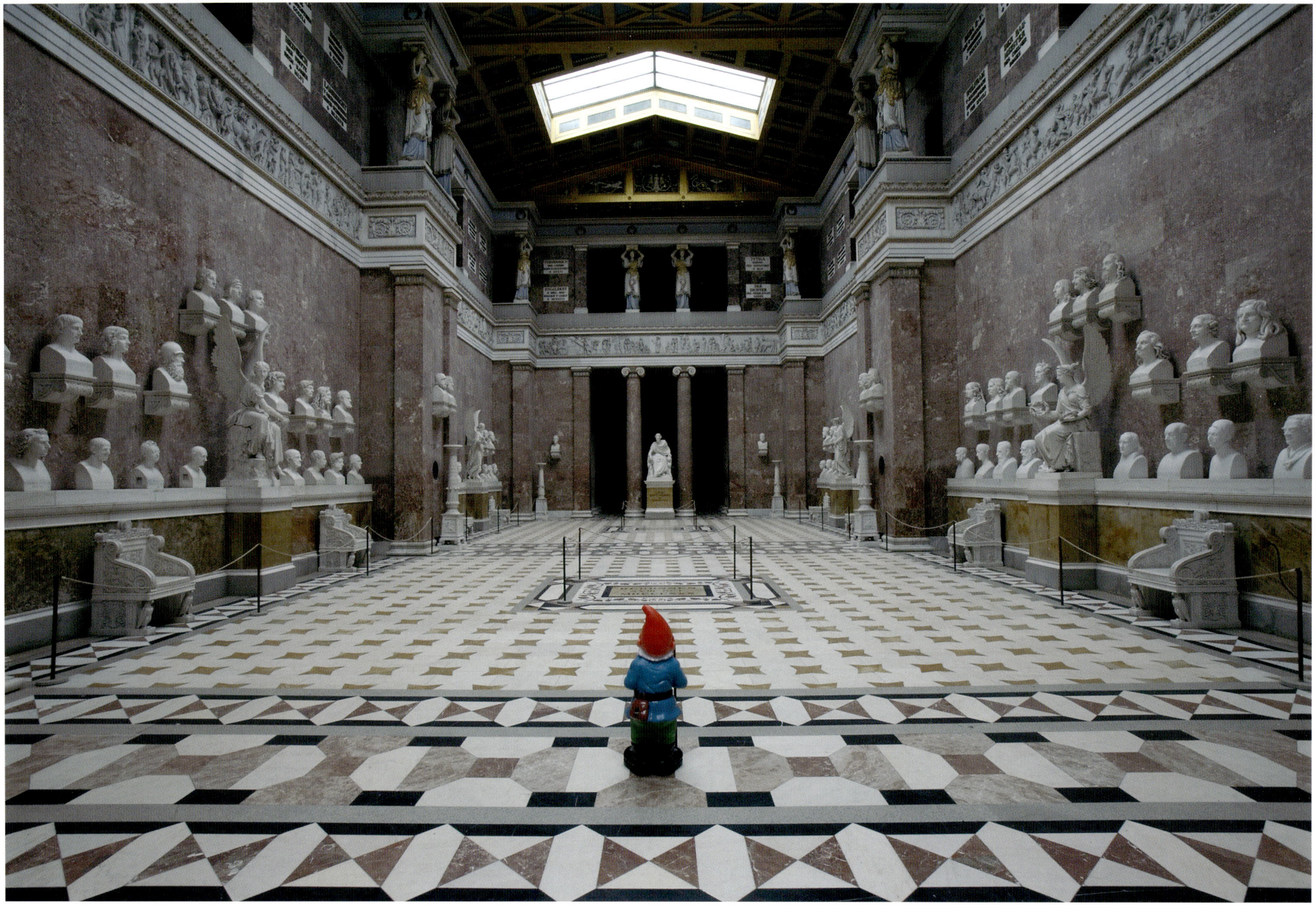

WALHALLA, DONAUSTAUF

Ein griechischer Tempel mitten in Bayern, hoch über der Donau östlich von Regensburg? Und im Fries Szenen aus der Schlacht im Teutoburger Wald? Der kann ja wohl keine zweitausend Jahre alt sein.

Das ist er auch nicht, und griechisch sieht er bloß aus. Das Vorbild für die »Walhalla« steht zwar auf der Akropolis, aber der Tempel bei Donaustauf ist genauso deutsch und ungefähr genauso alt wie die Hofkirche in München, der Königsplatz, die Glyptothek und die alte Pinakothek. Das stammt alles vom selben Architekten: Leo von Klenze, dem Lieblingsbaumeister des bayrischen Königs Ludwig I.

»Walhalla« ist ein germanisches Wort und heißt »Totenhalle«. Sie ist von 1830 bis 1842 gebaut worden, als die Deutschen dachten, sie brauchten auch einen besonderen Ort, an dem sie ihre großen Landsleute und Vorbilder aus der Geschichte verehren können. Im 19. Jahrhundert hatte man andere Vorstellungen als heute, und so kommt es, dass jetzt viele von denen, die hier versammelt sind, kaum noch einer kennt.

Bei der Einweihung 1842 waren es insgesamt 160. Bis 2005 sind 31 dazugekommen. 127 Marmorplastiken und 64 Gedenktafeln sind jetzt zu bestaunen, von Alarich über Blücher, Katharina die Große, Einstein und Konrad Adenauer bis zu Sophie Scholl.

Hier reinzukommen ist nicht ganz leicht. Wer in die »Walhalla« einziehen will, muss erstens mindestens 20 Jahre tot sein, und zweitens braucht er die Zustimmung vom bayrischen Ministerrat.

WALHALLA, DONAUSTAUF

A Greek temple in the middle of Bavaria, high above the Danube to the east of Regensburg? And on the frieze, scenes from the battle of Teutoburger Wald? There's no way this can be two thousand years old.

Which it isn't, in fact. And it only looks Greek. Though the model for the »Walhalla« is, of course, the Acropolis, it is just as German and just about as old as the Hofkirche, the Königsplatz, the Glyptothek and the Old Pinakothek, in Munich. And all of which were built by the same man: Leo von Klenze, the favourite architect of King Ludwig I of Bavaria.

»Walhalla« is a Germanic word and means »hall of the dead«. It was built from 1830 to 1842 at a time when the Germans thought they needed a special place where they could honour their great fellow countrymen and historical predecessors. In the 19th century, they had different ideas than we do, and so it is that many of those assembled here are almost unknown to us today.

At the inauguration in 1842, there were a total of 160 items; 31 have since been added. 127 marble statues and 64 commemorative plaques can now be marvelled at, from Alarich via Blücher, Catherine the Great, Einstein and Konrad Adenauer, all the way to Sophie Scholl.

To get a place in here is not very easy. Anyone wanting to take up residence in the »Walhalla« has, first of all, to have been dead for at least twenty years, and secondly he/she must have the Bavarian Council of Ministers' seal of approval.

MARKGRÄFLICHES OPERNHAUS, BAYREUTH

Die meisten Menschen glauben ja, Musik in Bayreuth besteht nur aus Richard Wagners Opern. Das stimmt aber nicht ganz. Mitten in der Stadt steht ein barockes Opernhaus, das ist gut 120 Jahre älter und vor allem viel schöner als das Festspielhaus auf dem »Grünen Hügel«. Ein schöneres soll es in ganz Europa nicht geben. Es ist zwischen 1746 und 1750 im Auftrag des Markgrafen Friedrich und seiner Frau, der Markgräfin Wilhelmine, der Lieblingsschwester Friedrichs des Großen, gebaut worden und bis heute fast unverändert erhalten geblieben. Für die besonders prachtvolle Innenausstattung waren die italienischen Theaterbaumeister Giuseppe und Carlo Galli Bibiena zuständig.

Als Richard Wagner auf der Suche war nach einem geeigneten Ort für seine Festspiele, hat er 1871 auch die markgräfliche Oper inspiziert. Das Bühnenhaus mit seiner raffinierten Maschinerie, damals das größte in Deutschland, war jedoch für seine Ansprüche und Vorstellungen zu klein. Aber in Bayreuth gefiel es ihm, und so hat er ein Jahr später den Grundstein für sein eigenes Festspielhaus gelegt. Das ist 1876 mit dem »Rheingold« eröffnet worden. Seitdem pilgern jedes Jahr Opernfreunde aus aller Welt nach Franken.

Für einen permanenten Spielbetrieb ist das markgräfliche Opernhaus heute nicht mehr geeignet. Es wird hauptsächlich während der Fränkischen Festwochen für barocke Opernaufführungen genutzt und ab und zu auch als Filmkulisse.

MARGRAVE'S OPERA HOUSE, BAYREUTH

Most people believe that music in Bayreuth consists only of Richard Wagner's operas. But that's not quite true. In the middle of the town there stands a Baroque opera house that is a good 120 years older and, above all, much more beautiful than the Festival Opera House on the »green hill«. In fact, there is supposedly none lovelier in all of Europe. It was built between 1746 and 1750 on the order of Margrave Friedrich and his wife, Wilhelmine – Friedrich the Great's favourite sister – and has remained almost unchanged till today. The Italian theatre architects Giuseppe and Carlo Galli Bibiena designed its especially magnificent interior.

When Richard Wagner was looking for a suitable place for his festival in 1871, it was the Margrave's Opera House that inspired him, though its stage area with its ingenious machinery – at the time the largest in Germany – was too small to satisfy Wagner's requirements. But he had taken a fancy to Bayreuth, and so a year later, he had the cornerstone for his own festival house laid here. It opened in 1876 with »The Rhinegold«. And ever since, opera lovers from the whole world have made their annual pilgrimage to Franconia.

The Margrave's Opera House is today no longer suitable for a full season of performances. It is mainly in use during the Franconian Festival of Baroque Opera, and at times also as a cinematic backdrop.

87

RESIDENZ, WÜRZBURG

Die Würzburger Residenz ist »das einheitlichste und außergewöhnlichste aller Barockschlösser, einzigartig durch ihre Originalität, ihr ehrgeiziges Bauprogramm und die internationale Zusammensetzung des Baubüros«, sie ist »eine Synthese des europäischen Barock« und außerdem »einer der strahlendsten Fürstenhöfe Europas«.

So hat die Unesco 1981 die Aufnahme der Bischöflichen Residenz in ihre Liste des Kulturerbes der Menschheit begründet, als drittes Baudenkmal in Deutschland nach dem Aachener und dem Speyerer Dom.

Balthasar Neumann war erst 33 Jahre alt, als ihm der Fürstbischof Johann Philipp Franz von Schönborn 1720 den Auftrag zum Bau der Residenz gab. Als sie 24 Jahre später im Rohbau fertig gestellt war, gehörte Neumann zu den berühmtesten und einflussreichsten Baumeistern des 18. Jahrhunderts.

Wenn eine Anlage von solcher Größe gebaut wird, wirken viele unterschiedliche Fachleute mit unterschiedlichen Vorstellungen und Fähigkeiten mit, und das geht oft zu Lasten der Einheitlichkeit. Eine der großen Leistungen von Balthasar Neumann liegt auch darin, dass er alle unterschiedlichen Entwürfe zu einer vollkommenen Einheit gebracht hat.

Der Innenausbau und die Ausstattung zogen sich anschließend noch über 30 Jahre hin. Zu den besonderen Sehenswürdigkeiten zählt das stützenfrei überwölbte Treppenhaus, für das der italienische Maler Giambattista Tiepolo das größte Deckenfresko der Welt geschaffen hat. Es hat die Bombardierung im Zweiten Weltkrieg fast unversehrt überstanden.

Der Blick aus dem Fenster zeigt den gotischen Würzburger Dom mit seinen vier Türmen westlich der Residenz.

RESIDENCE, WÜRZBURG

The Würzburg Residence is »the most homogenous and most extraordinary of all Baroque palaces, unique by virtue of its originality, its ambitious building programme and the international character of its workshop«; it is »a synthesis of the European Baroque« and, in addition, »one of the most brilliant courts of Europe.«

This is how Unesco described and justified its 1981 listing of the episcopal residence as a cultural heritage site, Germany's third architectural monument after the cathedrals in Aachen and Speyer.

Balthasar Neumann was only 33 years old when in 1720, the Prince Bishop Johann Philipp Franz von Schönborn commissioned him to build the residence. By the time it was structurally complete 24 years later, Neumann had become the most celebrated and most influential architect of the 18th century.

When a complex of such size is built, many different types of artisans with different ideas and capabilities are involved, often at the expense of homogeneity. One of Balthasar Neumann's great achievements, among other things, is that he brought all the various designs into perfect unison.

The interior design and furnishings then dragged on a good 30 years more. Among the special attractions is the vaulted stairwell support-free, for which the Italian painter Giambattista Tiepolo created the world's largest ceiling fresco. It miraculously survived the bombardment during World War II almost intact.

The view from the window shows the Gothic Würzburg Cathedral with its four towers, located to the west of the residence.

89

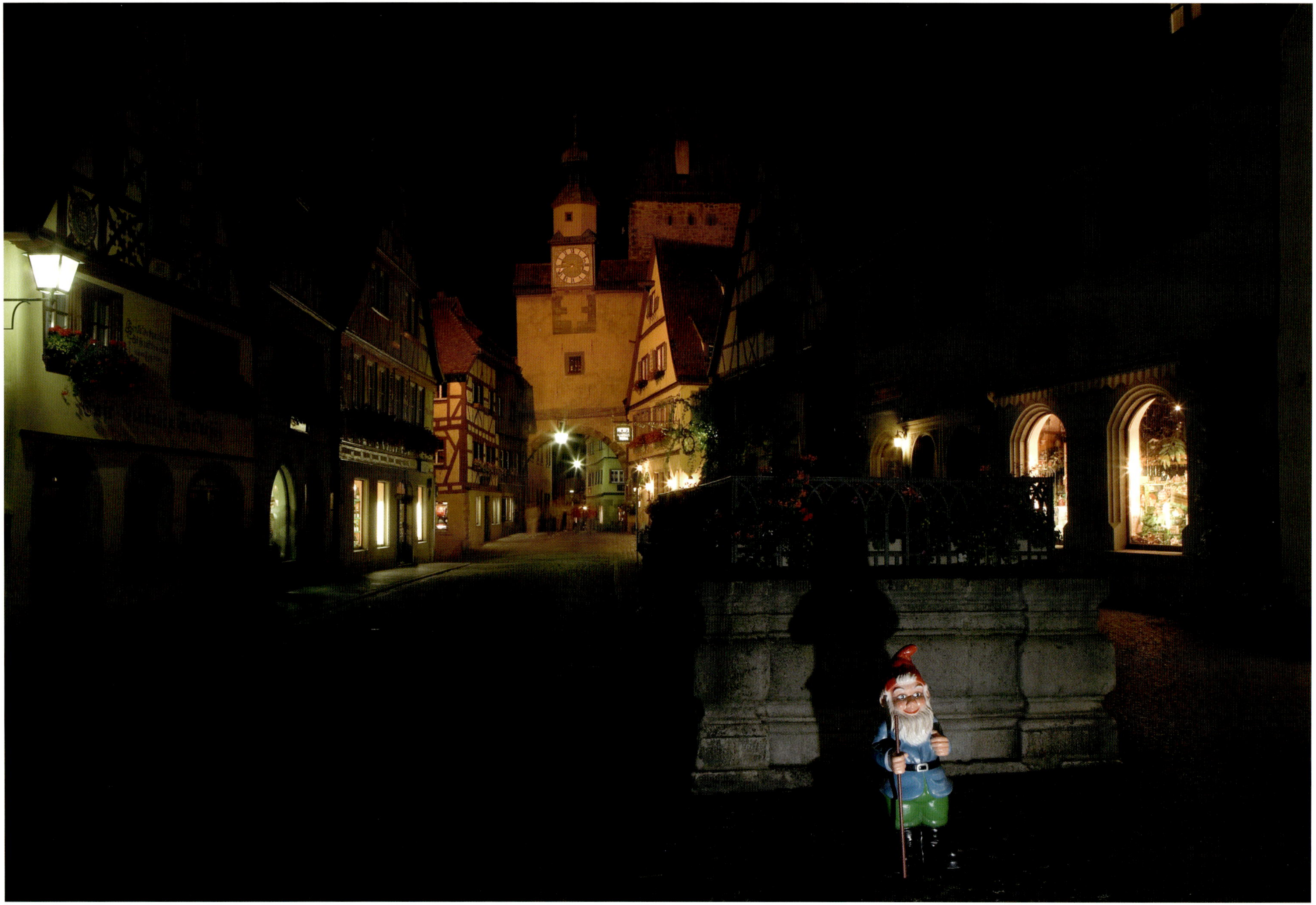

ROTHENBURG OB DER TAUBER

Wenn man mit dem Auto von Ulm Richtung Norden fährt, erscheint ungefähr nach einer Stunde am westlichen Horizont eine Stadtsilhouette wie aus dem Märchen. Nein, nicht Disneyland, sondern das Original: Rothenburg ob der Tauber.

Wer durch die Straßen und Gässchen geht, bekommt einen wunderbaren Eindruck davon, wie die Menschen vor drei-, vier- oder fünfhundert Jahren in Deutschland gelebt haben. Nach dem Zweiten Weltkrieg allerdings war die Stadt zu einem großen Teil zerstört. Das kann man sich heute gar nicht mehr vorstellen, denn die Rothenburger haben sie komplett wieder aufgebaut – genau so, wie sie vorher war.

Jedes Jahr kommen über zwei Millionen Besucher aus der ganzen Welt zum Staunen nach Rothenburg – ein ganz schöner Ansturm für eine Stadt mit elfeinhalbtausend Einwohnern. Viele sehen sich im Sommer das Festspiel »Der Meistertrunk« an, das auf eine Begebenheit aus dem 17. Jahrhundert zurückgeht: 1631, mitten im Dreißigjährigen Krieg, wird das protestantische Rothenburg von dem katholischen General Tilly mit 60.000 Mann belagert. Tilly stürmt die Stadt und verurteilt den Bürgermeister und den gesamten Stadtrat zum Tode. Da greift sich der Bürgermeister Georg Nusch einen Krug mit 13 Schoppen Wein – das sind dreiviertel Liter! – und trinkt ihn in einem Zug aus. Das hat den blutrünstigen Feldherrn so beeindruckt, dass er die Rothenburger anschließend in Ruhe ließ.

Ein Rat noch zum Schluss: Wer nach Rothenburg kommt, sollte wenigstens bis zum Abend bleiben, dann wird es noch märchenhafter – etwa so wie hier auf dem Bild mit Blick auf das Rödertor an der östlichen Stadtmauer.

ROTHENBURG OB DER TAUBER

After about an hour's drive north of Ulm, a town silhouette looms up on the horizon like a picture out of a fairytale. No, not Disneyland but the real thing: Rothenburg ob der Tauber.

When you walk through the streets and alleyways, you get a wonderful impression of how people lived in Germany three, four or five hundred years ago. However, the city was largely destroyed during World War II, a fact you can hardly imagine today, for the people of Rothenburg have completely rebuilt it – just like it was before.

Every year, over two million visitors come to Rothenburg from all over the world to marvel at it – quite an invasion for a town with eleven-and-a-half thousand inhabitants. Many come to see the festival play »Der Meistertrunk«, which goes back to an event from the 17th century: In 1631, in the midst of the Thirty Years War, Protestant Rothenburg was besieged by the Catholic General Tilly and his 60,000 men. Tilly stormed the city and sentenced the mayor and all the men on the city council to death. Suddenly, Mayor Georg Nusch grabbed a pitcher filled with the contents of 13 large glasses of wine – which is three and a quarter litres – and drank it down in one go. This so impressed the bloodthirsty general that he subsequently left Rothenburg in peace.

A final word of advice: anyone coming to Rothenburg should at least stay until evening when it then becomes even more fairytale-like – as you can see here is the photograph with its view of the Röder Gate at the eastern city wall.

NEUES PALAIS, POTSDAM

Als Friedrich II. 1763 siegreich aus dem Siebenjährigen Krieg gegen Österreich nach Hause kam, haben ihn alle nur noch den Großen genannt. Dagegen hatte er nichts einzuwenden, und sofort nach dem Krieg hat er im Park von Sanssouci mit dem Bau des Neuen Palais begonnen. Auf der einen Seite brauchte er jetzt nämlich dringend ein repräsentatives Gebäude, um seine Gäste oder Kollegen standesgemäß unterzubringen. Auf der andern Seite wollte er damit aller Welt aber auch zeigen, dass der preußische Staatshaushalt trotz des teuren Krieges noch längst nicht erschöpft war. Der Bau des 220 Meter langen Schlosses dauerte fast genauso lange wie der voraufgegangene Feldzug.

Damit den Besuchern des Königs aber auch unmissverständlich klar wurde, bei wem sie zu Gast waren, hat Friedrich im großen Marmorsaal neben den acht Kurfürsten von Brandenburg auch Statuen von Cäsar, Karl dem Großen, Kaiser Konstantin und Rudolf von Habsburg aufstellen lassen.

Trotzdem hat er das Palais nicht sehr gemocht, es war ihm mit seinen mehr als 200 Räumen wohl zu groß und zu ungemütlich. Sehr viel lieber hat er sich in seinem »Weinberghäuschen« aufgehalten, dem kleinen feinen Schloss Sanssouci. Das hatte er sich noch vor dem Krieg nach seinen eigenen Skizzen bauen lassen.

Nach dem Tod Friedrichs des Großen wusste keiner so richtig, wofür man den Riesenbau eigentlich verwenden sollte. Erst der letzte deutsche Kaiser hat das Schloss wieder als Wohnung genutzt. Bis zu seiner Abdankung im November 1918 hat Wilhelm II. hauptsächlich im Neuen Palais residiert. Und als moderner Kaiser, der er war, hat er eine Dampfheizung und elektrisches Licht installieren lassen.

NEW PALACE, POTSDAM

When Friedrich II of Prussia returned home victorious in 1763 at the end of the Seven Years' War against Austria, no one addressed him by any other title than the Great, to which he certainly had no objection. And immediately after the war, he began to build the New Palace in the park of »Sanssouci«. On the one hand, he now urgently needed a representative building to accommodate his guests and colleagues in a suitable manner. On the other, he wanted to show the world that Prussia's national budget was a long way from exhausted, despite the expense of the war. The construction of the 220-metre-long palace lasted almost as long as the preceding military campaign.

Moreover, so that it was unmistakably clear to the king's visitors what kind of man their host was, Friedrich had statues erected in the large marble hall: Caesar, Charlemagne, the Emperor Constantine and Rudolf of Hapsburg, alongside the eight prince-electors of Brandenburg.

And yet, he didn't very much like the palace with its over 200 rooms; it was simply too big and too uninviting. He much preferred staying at his »Weinberghäuschen« (vineyard cottage), that is the small but fine Sanssouci Palace. He had had it built before the war according to his own design.

After Friedrich the Great's death, no one quite knew what to do with such a white elephant of a building. Not till the last German emperor moved in was the castle ever again used as a residence. Up to the time of his abdication in November 1918, Wilhelm II lived the major part of the time in the New Palace. And like the modern emperor he was, he had steam heating and electric light installed.

93

SPARGELFELDER, BEELITZ

Gemüse kommt im deutschen Liedgut praktisch nicht vor. Nicht die Mohrrübe, nicht der Wirsing, nicht die Bohne, auch den Porree will niemand besingen und noch nicht einmal den Blumen- oder den Rosenkohl. Es gibt aber mindestens eine Ausnahme: den Spargel. Wenn nämlich die Comedian Harmonists in ihrem Lied »Veronika, der Lenz ist da« den Frühling begrüßen, heißt es an einer entscheidenden Stelle: »… die ganze Welt ist wie verhext, Veronika, der Spargel wächst!« Und zwar bis zu einem Zentimeter in der Stunde.

Der Spargel ist also ein typisches Frühlingsgemüse, und man sagt, er hat ganz besondere Eigenschaften. Manche meinen sogar, er ist das Gemüse überhaupt. In Deutschland gibt es ein paar Gegenden, wo er besonders gut gedeiht: in Schwetzingen zum Beispiel, in Walbeck oder in Beelitz, südwestlich von Berlin. Spargelliebhabern läuft bei diesen Namen das Wasser im Mund zusammen, nicht nur im Frühling, dann aber vor allem. Was der Spargel für die Gegend um Beelitz bedeutet, kann man daran sehen, dass er in Schlunkendorf ein eigenes Museum bekommen hat.

Die Spargelzeit dauert ungefähr von Mitte April bis spätestens Ende Juni. Der beste Spargel wird gestochen, bevor er aus der Erde ans Tageslicht kommt. Ganz weiß und fest muss er sein, 22 Zentimeter lang und höchstens 26 Millimeter dick, er darf keine blauen Spitzen haben, das macht ihn bitter, und er muss quietschen, wenn man die Stangen aneinander reibt. Am besten schmeckt er, wenn er morgens gestochen, mittags gekauft und abends zubereitet wird.

Inzwischen wird Spargel ja auch an Weihnachten und zu jeder anderen Jahreszeit angeboten, aber darüber kann unsereiner allenfalls die Nase rümpfen und geduldig abwarten, bis der nächste Lenz kommt.

ASPARAGUS FIELDS, BEELITZ

Vegetables go practically unmentioned in German songs. The carrot, the cabbage, the bean and the leek: no one wants to sing about them, nor about the cauliflower or brussel sprout. But there is at least one exception: the asparagus. When the Comedian Harmonists greet the spring in their song »Veronika, der Lenz ist da« (Veronica, spring has come), at a crucial point they continue: »… the world is under a spell, Veronica, the asparagus is rising!« And rise it does, at a rate of up to one centimetre an hour.

Asparagus is a typical spring vegetable, and it's said to have very special qualities. Some even consider it *the* vegetable per se. In Germany there are a few regions where it thrives especially well: in Schwetzingen, for example, in Walbeck or in Beelitz, southwest of Berlin. Asparagus devotees begin to drool on hearing the name Beelitz and not only (but above all) in spring. What the asparagus means to the region around Beelitz can be seen from the fact that in Schlunkendorf it has been given its very own museum.

The asparagus season lasts from mid-April to the end of June at the latest. The best asparagus is cut before it ever emerges from the soil and sees daylight. It must be entirely white and very firm, 22 centimetres long and 26 millimetres thick at the most; blue tips must be avoided, for they make it bitter. And it must squeak when the stalks are rubbed together. It tastes best when it's cut in the morning, bought at midday and cooked in the evening.

In the meantime, asparagus can also be had at Christmas and every other season, but our sort can only turn up our noses at such an idea and wait patiently for the next spring to come.

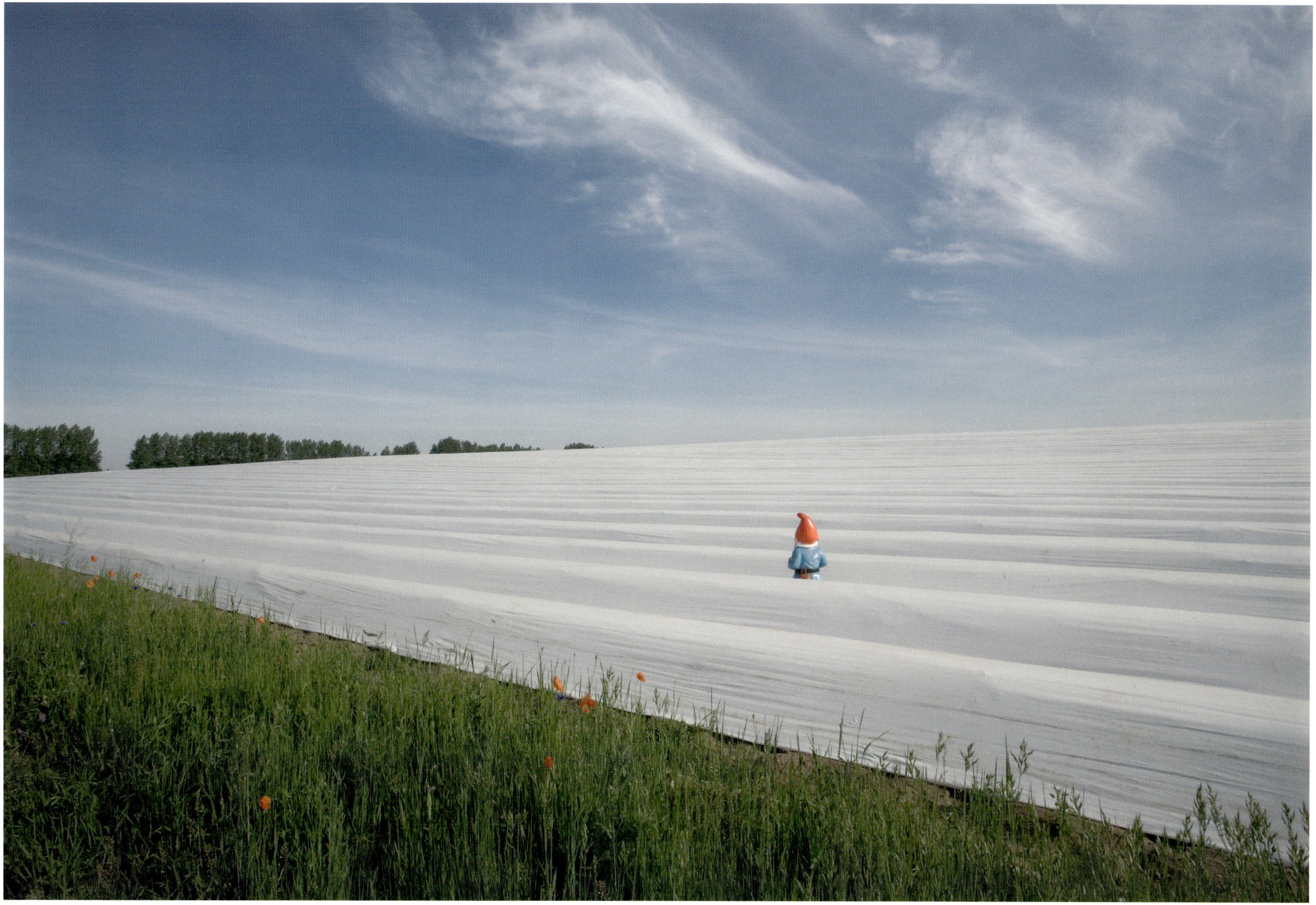

SPREEWALD

Die berühmten Spreewälder Gurken kenne ich ja schon lange, und dass es im Spreewald unzählige Kanäle gibt – die heißen hier Fließe –, das wusste ich auch. Aber dass es hier so schön ist, vor allem im Frühling und im Sommer, hab' ich mir nicht vorstellen können. Fast tausend Kilometer von diesen Fließen gibt's insgesamt, und überall sieht man solche flachen Kähne herumfahren, die sind hier das Hauptverkehrsmittel.

Die Spree entspringt in der Nähe von Bautzen und verzweigt sich bei Cottbus über fast 500 Quadratkilometer in ein so genanntes Binnendelta. Anschließend wird sie wieder ein ganz normaler Fluss, fließt im Südosten von Berlin in den Großen Müggelsee und dann weiter durch die ganze Stadt und mündet im Westen bei Spandau in die Havel.

18.000 Tier- und Pflanzenarten gibt es im Spreewald, und damit sie alle erhalten bleiben, hat die Unesco das ganze Gebiet zum geschützten Biosphären-Reservat erklärt.

Drei Tierarten sind allerdings schon lange verschwunden: 1650 ist der letzte Bär erlegt worden, 1746 der letzte Elch, und 1844 ging's dem letzten Wolf an den Pelz.

SPREEWALD

The famous Spreewald cucumbers are something I've known about for a long time, as I also knew that in the Spreewald forest there are countless canals – that are here called »Fliesse«. But the fact that it's so beautiful here, above all in spring and summer, I couldn't have imagined. There are almost one thousand kilometres of these canals in all, and flat-bottomed punts, which are the main means of transportation, are everywhere in evidence.

The source of the Spree River begins at Bautzen and branches out near Cottbus to a so-called inland delta of almost 500 square kilometres. It subsequently turns into a quite normal river again, flows to the southeast of Berlin into the lake, Grosser Müggelsee, and from there on through the entire city to flow into the Havel in the west near Spandau.

18,000 species of fauna and flora can be found in the Spreewald, which is why Unesco declared the whole area a protected biosphere reserve.

There are, however, three animal species that already vanished long ago: in 1650, the last bear was shot and killed, in 1746, the last elk and in 1844, the last wolf was hunted down.

97

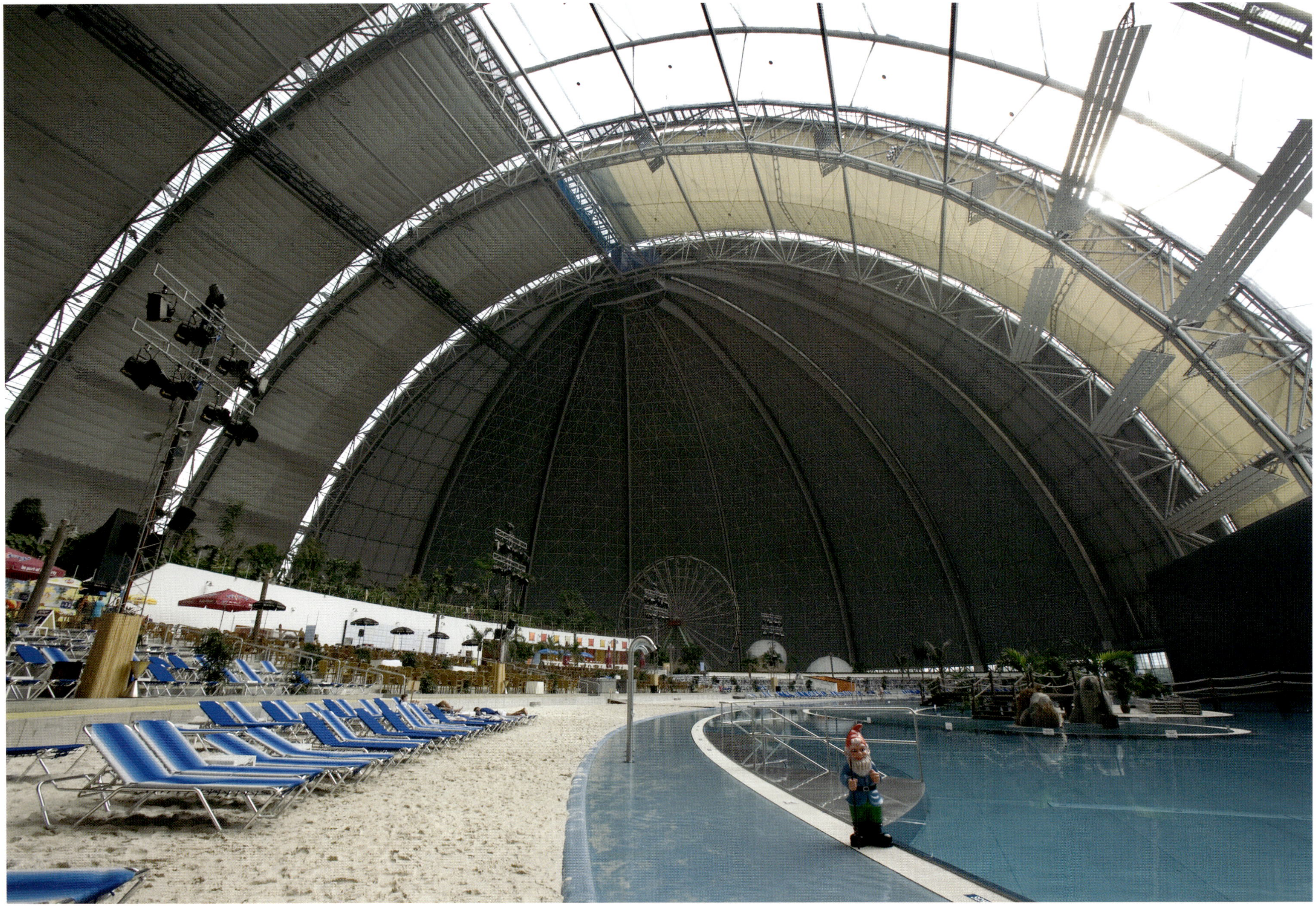

TROPICAL ISLANDS, KRAUSNICK

Kennt ihr den Unterschied zwischen einem Flugzeug und einem Luftschiff? – Ein Flugzeug fliegt, ein Luftschiff fährt. Das ist seit den Zeiten der Brüder Montgolfier schon so. Und weil ein Luftschiff fährt, kann es zwischendurch auch mal Halt machen. Ein Flugzeug kann das nicht, jedenfalls nicht mitten in der Luft, es bewegt sich nach ganz anderen physikalischen Gesetzen.

Und was hat das mit »Tropical Islands« zu tun? Ganz einfach: Hier in Brand, sechzig Kilometer südlich von Berlin, sollten eigentlich Luftschiffe vom Stapel laufen, riesige »Cargo-Lifter«, die große Lasten überall dorthin transportieren können, wo es zum Beispiel keine richtigen Straßen und keine Landebahnen gibt. Und zum Bau von solchen 260 Meter langen Kolossen ist hier die größte freitragende Halle der Welt errichtet worden: 360 Meter lang, 260 Meter breit und 107 Meter hoch. Aber dann ist dem Unternehmen leider das Geld ausgegangen.

Was sollte jetzt aus der nutzlosen Werfthalle werden? Es hat nicht viel gefehlt, und man hätte sie wieder abgerissen. Aber dann haben Unternehmer aus Malaysia davon gehört, haben die Halle gekauft und das Innere im Handumdrehen in einen wetterfesten, tropischen Freizeitpark verwandelt.

Jetzt gibt es dank dem malaysischen Unternehmergeist mitten in Brandenburg 66.000 Quadratmeter Tropenlandschaft, mit Sandstrand, balinesischem Langhaus, Lagune, Beachvolleyball, Disco und Showveranstaltungen – 24 Stunden am Tag, 365 Tage im Jahr.

TROPICAL ISLANDS, KRAUSNICK

Do you know the difference between a plane and an airship? A plane flies, an airship glides. That has been the case since the time of the Montgolfier brothers. And because an airship glides, it can stop and hover from time to time. A plane can't do this, at least not in the air; its propulsion follows quite different laws of physics.

And what does all this have to do with »Tropical Islands«? It's quite simple: here in Brand, sixty kilometres south of Berlin, the idea was to turn out airships, giant »cargo-lifters« that could transport huge loads to places where there are no real roads and no airstrips. For the construction of such 260-metre-long colossuses, the greatest self-supporting hangar in the world was built: 360 metres long, 260 metres wide and 107 metres high. But then, unfortunately, the money ran out.

What was supposed to become of this useless white elephant of a hangar? It didn't need much and it would have been torn down. But then an entrepreneur from Malaysia heard of it, bought the hall and transformed its interior, in no time at all, into a weatherproof, tropical leisure centre.

So now, thanks to Malaysian entrepreneurship, we have – in the middle of Brandenburg – a 66,000-square-metre tropical landscape with sandy beach, Balinese longhouse, lagoon, beach volleyball, a disco and show performances – 24 hours a day, 365 days a year.

ERLEBNISPARK LUFTFAHRT & TECHNIK, FINOWFURT

Tu 134, Mi 8T, MiG 15UTI, Jak-28R, Ka 26, Il 14P, MiG 23S, Z-37 A, AN 2, FW 190, TU 134 – Namen aus längst vergangenen Zeiten, Typenbezeichnungen für sowjetische Flugzeuge und Hubschrauber, die jahrzehntelang auf dem Flugplatz Finowfurt nordöstlich von Berlin stationiert waren.

Angefangen hat es in Finowfurt in den 20er Jahren, als man mit Flugzeugen noch auf größeren Äckern und Wiesen starten und landen konnte. Erst 1937 ist ein richtiger Militärflugplatz draus geworden, den die deutsche Luftwaffe bis kurz vor Kriegsende genutzt hat.

Am 15. Mai 1945, eine Woche nach der Kapitulation des Deutschen Reiches, sind hier zum ersten Mal sowjetische Flugzeuge gelandet. Die Sowjets sind dann 48 Jahre geblieben, und im September 1993 ist die letzte Einheit Richtung Weißrussland wieder abgezogen. Da war auch in Finowfurt der Kalte Krieg zu Ende.

Anschließend haben sich Flugzeugbegeisterte, Techniker und ehrenamtliche Luftfahrthistoriker darangemacht, auf dem Platz ein Museum einzurichten, haben ausrangierte militärische und zivile Flugzeugtypen und Hubschrauber zusammengetragen und restauriert. Die kann sich heute jeder aus der Nähe betrachten.

AVIATION & TECHNOLOGY THEME PARK, FINOWFURT

Tu 134, Mi 8T, MiG 15UTI, Jak-28R, Ka 26, Il 14P, MiG 23S, Z-37 A, AN 2, FW 190, TU 134 – names from bygone times, type designations for Soviet airplanes and helicopters that have been stationed at the Finowfurt Airfield, northeast of Berlin for decades.

It all began in Finowfurt in the 1920s, when you could still start and land airplanes on large fields and meadows. Not till 1937 did this become a proper military airfield which the German Luftwaffe used until shortly before the end of the war.

On May 15, 1945, a week after the German capitulation, Soviet airplanes landed for the first time. They then stayed on for 48 years, and in September 1993, the last unit withdrew in the direction of Belarus. This meant that the Cold War had finally come to an end in Finowfurt, too.

Since then, airplane enthusiasts, technicians and volunteer aviation historians got to work to install a museum on the site and assembled and restored scrapped military and civilian airplanes and helicopters. Interested members of the public can now view them close up.

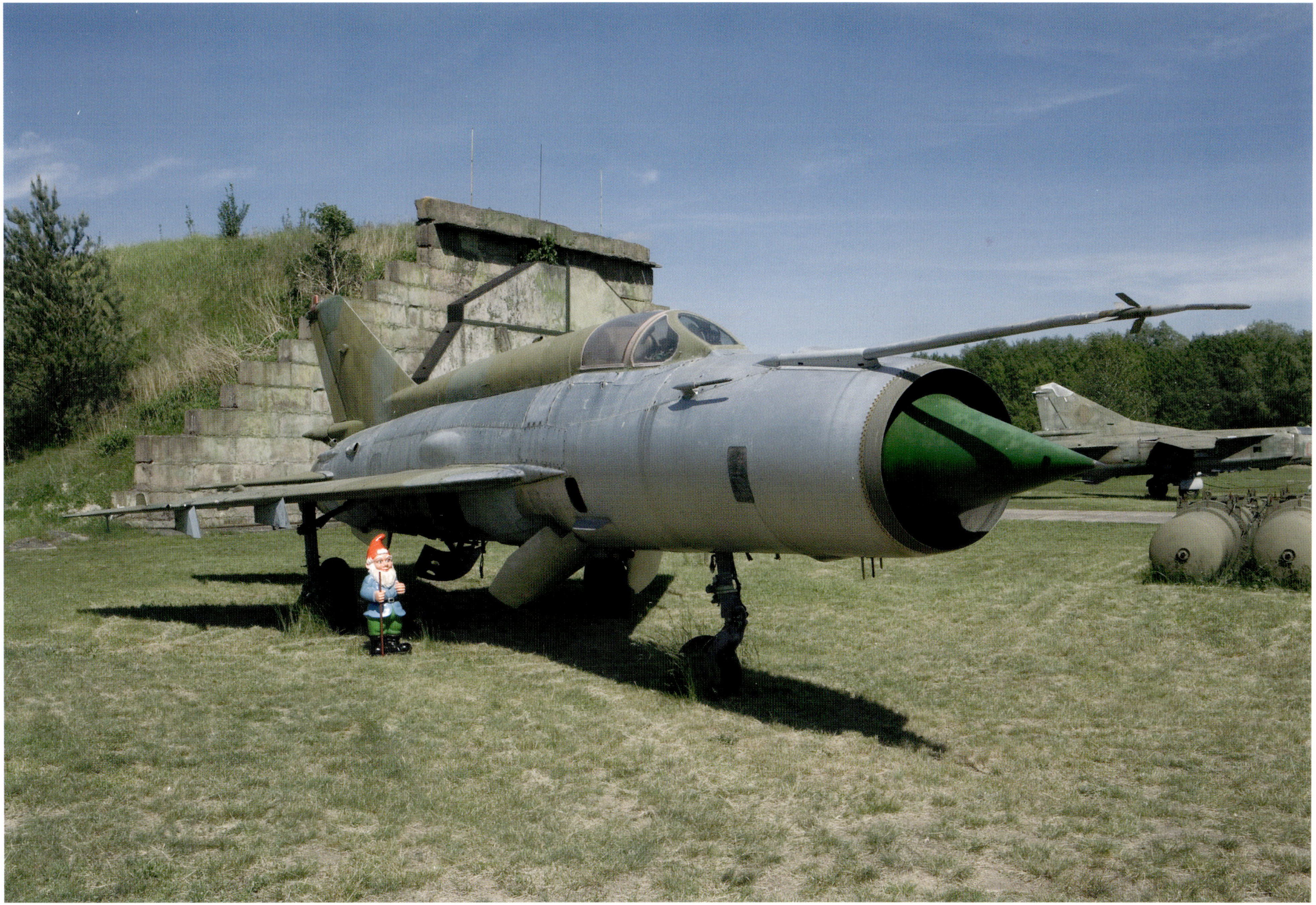

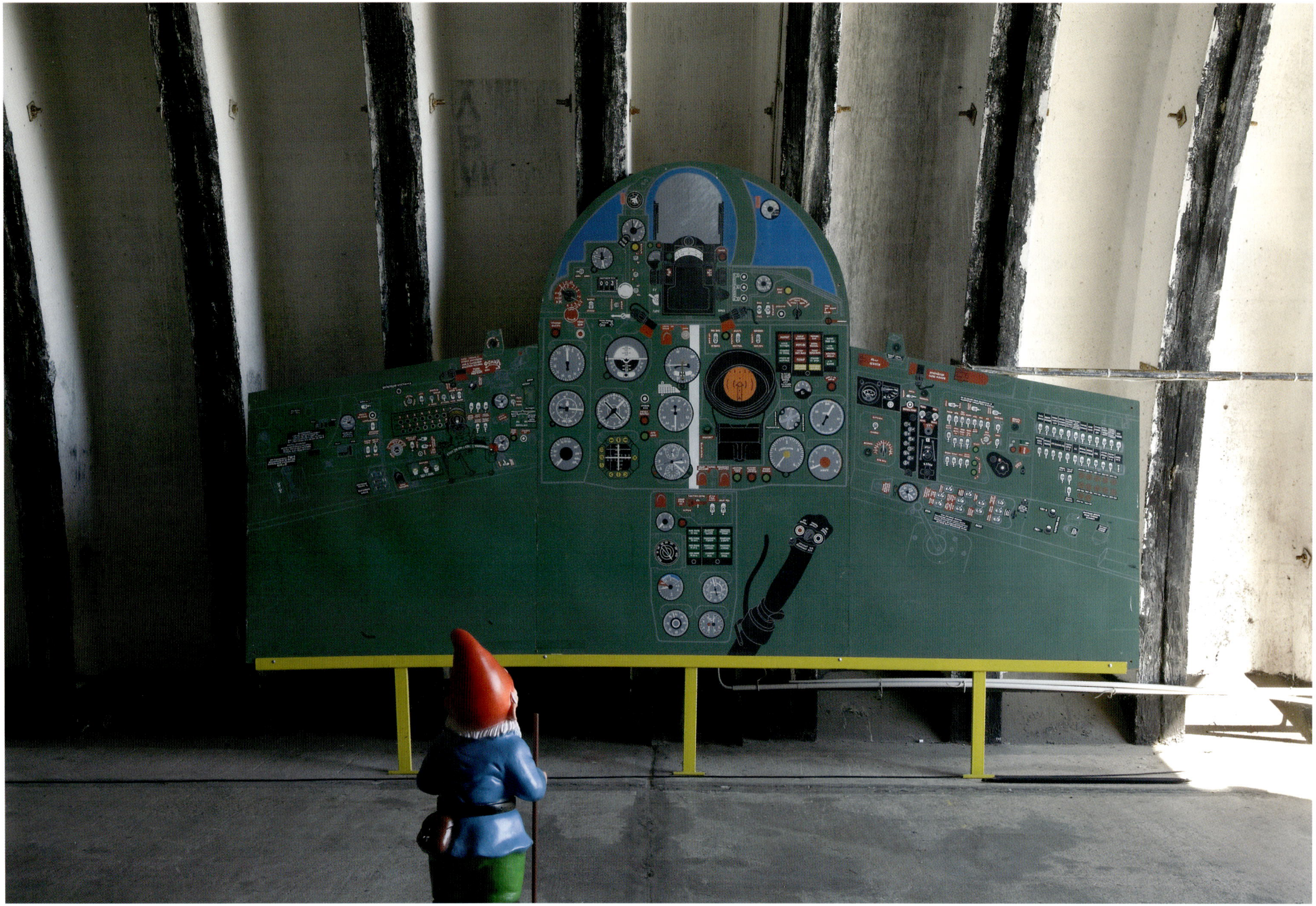

ERLEBNISPARK LUFTFAHRT & TECHNIK, FINOWFURT

Und so hat die Rote Armee für den Kalten Krieg trainiert: Vor dieser Schautafel in einem der Bunker haben sowjetische Fluglehrer angehende Piloten mit den Instrumenten im Cockpit eines Kampfflugzeugs vertraut gemacht.

Fliegen scheint ja gar nicht so kompliziert zu sein, wie ich immer dachte. Wenn ich jünger wäre, würde ich es vielleicht auch versuchen.

AVIATION & TECHNOLOGY THEME PARK, FINOWFURT

And this is the way that the Red Army trained for the Cold War; in a bunker in front of this mock-up, Soviet aviation instructors familiarized trainee pilots with the instruments in the cockpit of a fighter plane.

Flying doesn't seem to be at all as complicated as I always thought. If I were younger, I would perhaps try it myself.

SCHIFFSHEBEWERK, NIEDERFINOW

Wer hätte gedacht, dass schon Kaiser Karl der Große die Idee hatte, einen Kanal vom Main zur Donau zu bauen? Im 9. Jahrhundert hatten seine Fachleute allerdings noch nicht genügend Erfahrung mit dem Kanalbau, und deswegen ist das Projekt erst über 1100 Jahre später zu Ende gebracht geworden.

Wenn man mit Schiffen von einem Fluss-System in ein anderes kommen will, zum Beispiel vom Main in die Donau oder von der Havel in die Oder, muss man die Wasserscheide zwischen den beiden überwinden, das heißt, man muss die Schiffe über einen Berg bringen.

Die Bauarbeiten für den ersten Kanal, der die Havel nördlich von Berlin mit der Oder verbinden sollte, begannen im Jahr 1605. Er war über 38 Kilometer lang und hatte elf Schleusen, ist aber im Dreißigjährigen Krieg zerstört worden. Dann hat, rund 100 Jahre später, Friedrich der Große wieder einen Kanal gebaut, der war 43 Kilometer lang, musste 38 Meter Höhenunterschied überwinden und hatte zunächst zehn, später dann 17 Schleusen.

Anfang des 20. Jahrhunderts konnte der 150 Jahre alte Kanal den Schiffsverkehr aber nicht mehr bewältigen, also wurde ein neuer gebaut. Der hatte nur noch fünf Schleusen, vier davon bildeten in Niederfinow eine »Schleusentreppe« mit jeweils neun Metern Hub. Aber bald stauten sich auch hier wieder die Schiffe.

Jetzt musste etwas ganz Neues her. 1934 wurde das Schiffshebewerk Niederfinow eröffnet und als ein Weltwunder der Technik bestaunt. Es hebt bis heute 80 Meter lange und 9,5 Meter breite Schiffe mit 1,7 Metern Tiefgang in fünf Minuten 36 Meter hoch. Bei der letzten großen Überholung gab es kaum etwas zu beanstanden. Aber dieser Schiffsaufzug reicht inzwischen auch schon nicht mehr aus. Direkt nebenan wird ein neuer gebaut, der soll 2012 fertig sein.

THE SHIP LIFT, NIEDERFINOW

Who would have thought that Charlemagne had already had the idea of building a canal from the Main to the Danube? In the 9th century, however, his experts did not have enough experience in canal construction, which is why the project was not realized until over 1100 years later.

If you want to go by ship from one river system to another – for instance from the Main to the Danube or from the Havel to the Oder – you have to overcome the watershed between the two, which means, you must get the ship to mount a hill.

The first attempt to connect the Havel north of Berlin with the Oder by way of a canal began in the year 1605. It was over 38 km long and had eleven locks, all destroyed during the Thirty Years War. Then, about 100 years later, Friedrich the Great had another built. It was 43 kilometres long, had to overcome 38 metres difference in height and had at first ten, later seventeen, locks.

At the beginning of the 20th century, however, the 150-year-old canal could no longer handle the shipping traffic, so a new one was built. This had only five locks, four of which made up a »stairway of locks« in Niederfinow, each with a lift of 9 metres. But once again, ship traffic soon became congested.

Now something quite new was needed. In 1934, the ship lift at Niederfinow opened and was marvelled at worldwide as a technological wonder. Today it still lifts ships that are 80 metres long and 9.5 metres wide with a 1.7 metres draught, and it lifts them 36 metres in five minutes. At its last major inspection, there was almost nothing wrong. Nevertheless, in the meantime this ship lift is again barely sufficient to handle the traffic. A new one is being built, right next to it, to be finished in 2012.

105

»BREMER STADTMUSIKANTEN«, BREMEN

Der Hahn auf der Katze auf dem Hund auf dem Esel – die vier sind ein ziemlich seltsames Quartett aus einem Märchen der Brüder Grimm. Als »Bremer Stadtmusikanten« haben sie es zu Ruhm und Ehre gebracht, obwohl sie nie in Bremen waren.

Und das kam so: Sie haben sich zusammengetan, weil sie nicht geschlachtet werden oder sonstwie ihr Leben lassen wollten – das stand nämlich jedem von ihnen bevor. Darum sind sie unter dem Wahlspruch »Etwas Besseres als den Tod findest du überall« nach Bremen aufgebrochen und wollten sich dort als Stadtmusikanten bewerben; angekommen sind sie hier aber nicht. Sie haben nämlich unterwegs an einem Haus in der Umgebung Halt gemacht, haben die Bewohner, eine Räuberbande, daraus vertrieben, haben Bremen Bremen sein lassen und sich im Räuberhaus niedergelassen, denn »… den vier Bremer Musikanten gefiel's aber so wohl darin, dass sie nicht wieder hinauswollten.« Als Musikanten sind sie jedenfalls nicht weiter in Erscheinung getreten; für das Bremer Musikleben ist das aber vielleicht gar kein so großer Verlust.

Auf der anderen Seite: Wenn man ihnen schon ein Denkmal baut, wo sollte es denn sonst stehen wenn nicht mitten in Bremen neben dem Rathaus?

»BREMEN TOWN MUSICIANS«, BREMEN

The cock on the cat on the dog on the donkey – the four are quite an oddball quartet from a Brother Grimm fairytale. As the »Bremen Town Musicians« they achieved honour and fame, although they were never in Bremen.

And it came about this way. They had got together in the first place, because they didn't want to be slaughtered or done away with, which was what each of them was faced with. For which reason they set off for Bremen under the motto: »Something better than death can be found anywhere.« Once in Bremen, they wanted to be taken on as town musicians, but they never did arrive. While on the road, they came across a house on the outskirts where they wanted to stay the night, but then chased away the gang of thieves who lived there, left Bremen to look out for itself and settled down in their new-found home: »… the four Bremen town musicians felt so content there that they never wanted to leave.« In any case, they never again appeared on the scene as musicians, which was perhaps not such a big loss for Bremen's musical life.

On the other hand: if a memorial is built to commemorate them, where better should it stand than smack in the middle of Bremen, next to the town hall?

107

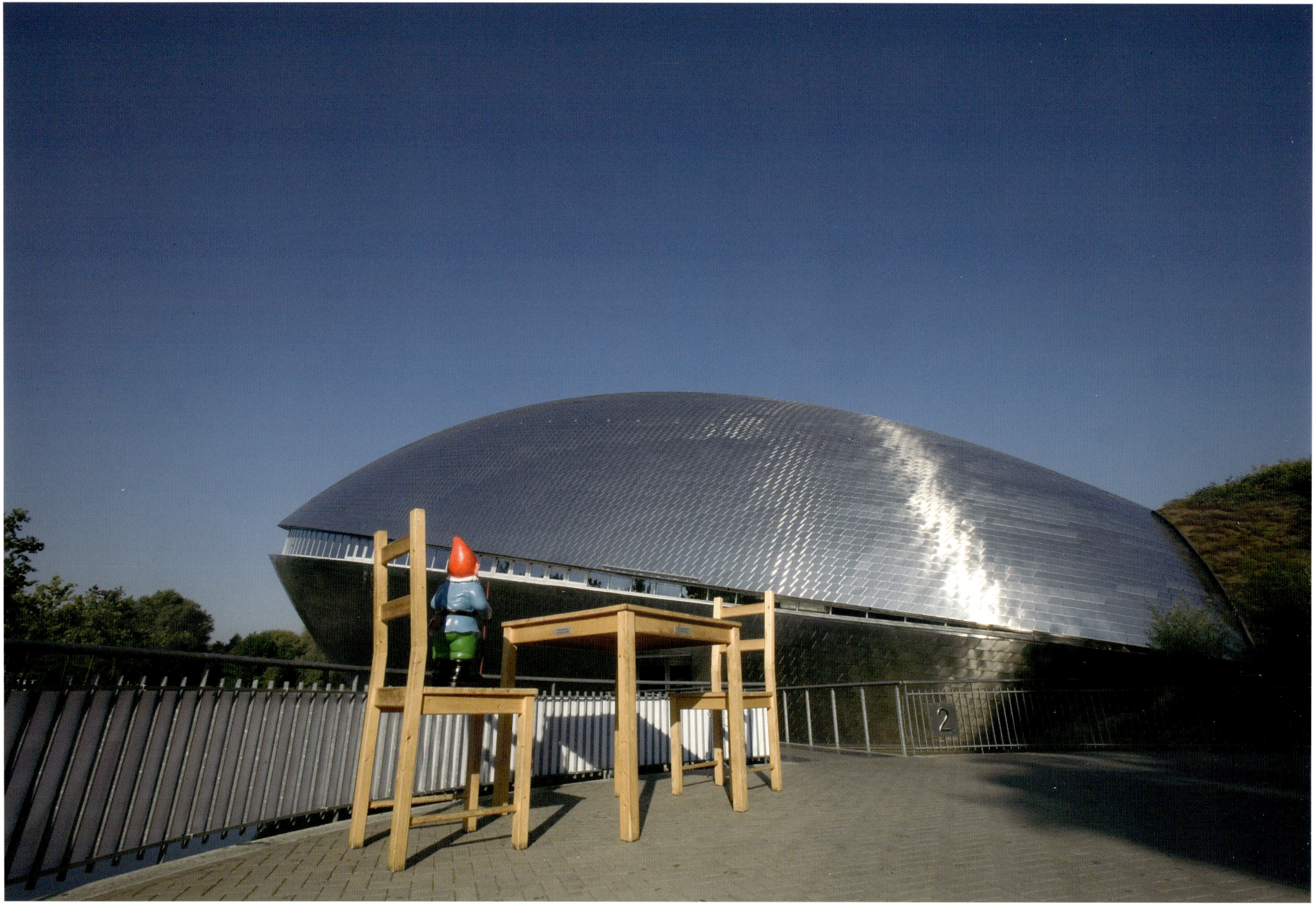
2

UNIVERSUM-SCIENCE-CENTER, BREMEN

Die Ansichten über dieses glänzende, raumschiffartige Gebilde mit seinen 44.000 Schindeln aus Edelstahl gehen auseinander. Manche sind überzeugt, es handelt sich um einen Wal, für andere sieht es mehr nach einer Muschel aus. Das Universum-Science-Center in Bremen ist 70 Meter lang, 22 Meter breit und 27 Meter hoch – die Maße sprechen also eher für einen Wal.

Im Bauch dieses Wales – oder, damit auch die andern zu ihrem Recht kommen: im Innern der Muschel – wird an 250 Stationen unter den Oberbegriffen Mensch, Erde, Universum erklärt und gezeigt, wie Wissenschaft und Forschung funktionieren, wozu sie gut sind, was sie herausfinden und was sie mit den Menschen und ihrem Alltag zu tun haben. Das Museum, und das ist hier das Besondere, ist aber nicht nur zum Gucken und Staunen da, sondern auch zum Anfassen, Probieren und Experimentieren.

Als das Science-Center im Jahr 2000 fertig war, haben die Verantwortlichen und die Betreiber auf 300.000 Besucher im Jahr gehofft, aber es sind sehr schnell über 500.000 geworden. Es scheint also was dran zu sein an der Wissenschaft – die Menschen scheinen wissen zu wollen, was es damit auf sich hat, es kommt eben nur drauf an, wie man sie präsentiert.

UNIVERSUM SCIENCE CENTRE, BREMEN

Opinions are divided on what this shiny, spaceship-like construction is with its 44,000 high-grade steel shingles. Some are convinced it is a whale, others think it looks more like a seashell. The Universum Science Center in Bremen is 70 metres long, 22 metres wide and 27 metres high – so, given its dimensions, it is more likely to be a whale.

In the belly of this whale – or (to give the others their say) inside this shell – 250 stations, under the headings man, earth and universe, explain and show how science and research function, what they're good for, what they find out, and what they have to do with human beings and their everyday lives. The museum – and that is what is special here – is not just to look and marvel at, but to be touched, tested and experimented with.

When the Science Center was finished in the year 2000, those responsible and the operators hoped for 300,000 visitors a year, but these quickly turned into over 500,000. There seems to be something about science that makes people want to know what's behind it; it's all a question of how it's presented.

HAMBURG

»Schmuddelwetter«, so nennt man das in Hamburg, wenn der Himmel mal wieder so aussieht wie hier auf dem Bild. Und er sieht oft so aus. Gleich fängt's an zu regnen. Das stört die Hamburger aber nicht besonders, und wenn ich Hamburger wäre, würde es mich wahrscheinlich auch nicht stören.

Hamburg ist das Tor zur Welt. Das sagen nicht nur die Hamburger, das kann man auch schon mal in Köln oder in Stuttgart hören. Das heißt aber doch genau genommen, die Welt fängt erst hinter Hamburg an. Und jetzt frage ich mich: Was liegt denn eigentlich davor? Die Welt kann es ja schon mal nicht sein.

Hinter mir ganz links am Bildrand ist übrigens das Hamburger Wahrzeichen zu sehen, der »Michel«, das ist der Turm der Michaeliskirche, und rechts ein kleiner Teil vom Hafen.

HAMBURG

»Schmuddelwetter« or drab weather is what one says in Hamburg when the weather once again looks like it does on the photo. And it often looks like this. That doesn't upset the Hamburg people so much, and if I was one of them, it probably wouldn't upset me either.

Hamburg is the gateway to the world. Not only those from Hamburg say this; you can hear it occasionally said in Cologne or Stuttgart, too. Taken precisely, it means the world first begins on the other side of Hamburg. Which makes me wonder: what is it that lies on this side? In any case, it can't be the world.

Behind me to the far left, incidentally, you can see Hamburg's trademark, the tower of the Michaelis Church, and to the right, a small part of the harbour.

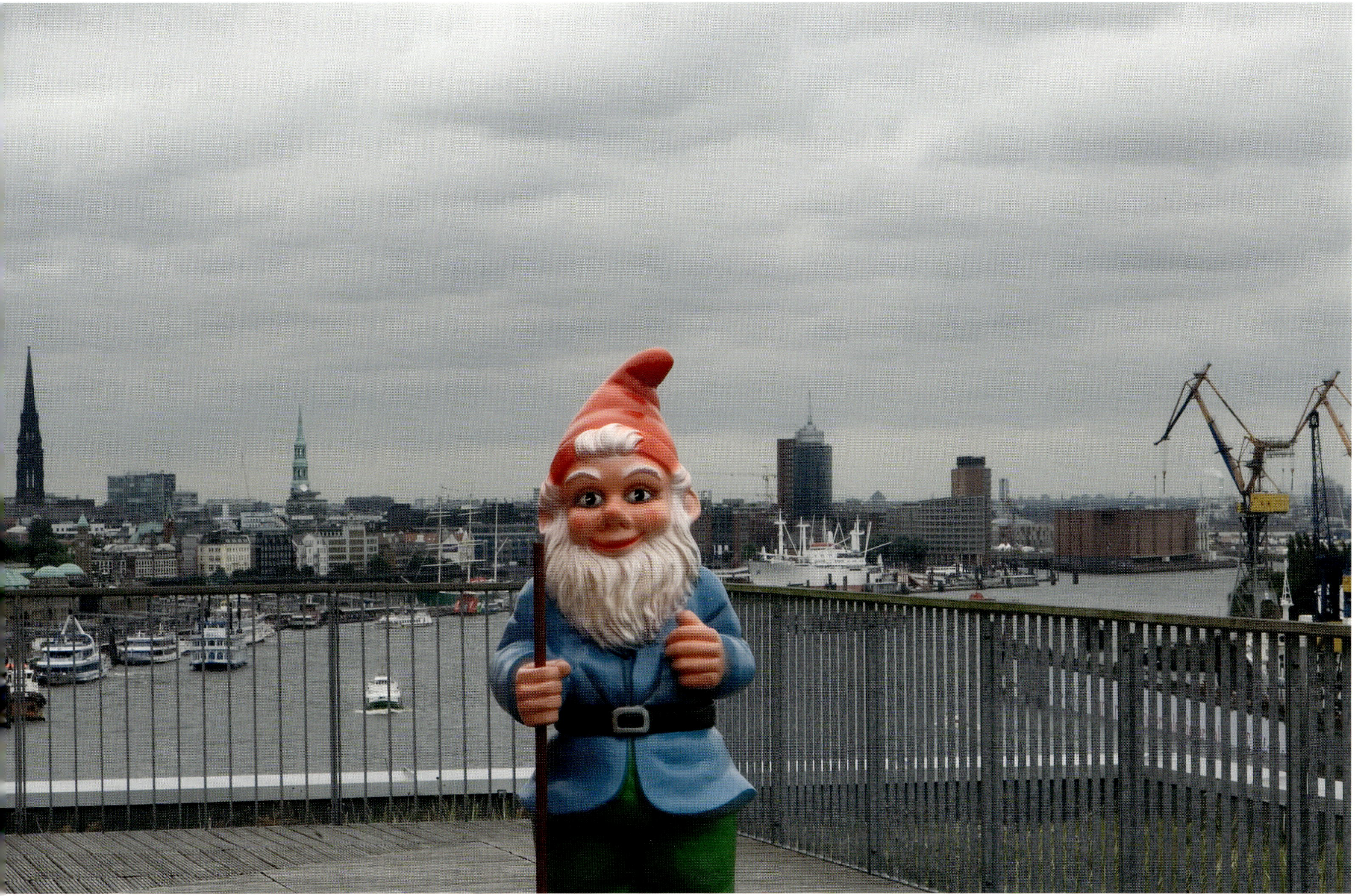

Wandrahmsfleet-
Brücke

SPEICHERSTADT, HAMBURG

Hamburg ist seit dem Mittelalter eine Hafenstadt und war als Mitglied der »Hanse« lange Zeit ein Handelsplatz mit eigenen Zollgrenzen. Die Waren aus Übersee konnten über die vielen Kanäle, die heißen hier Fleete, bequem in die verschiedenen Lagerhäuser gebracht werden. Das ist einer der Gründe für die vielen Brücken in der Stadt. Hamburg hat nämlich mehr Brücken als irgendeine andere Stadt auf der Welt, weit mehr als Venedig und Amsterdam zusammen, nämlich genau 2479, und vielleicht sind es sogar noch ein paar mehr.

Nach der Gründung des Deutschen Reiches musste auch Hamburg auf Druck des Kanzlers Bismarck 1881 sein altes Zollprivileg als Hansestadt aufgeben, allerdings unter der Bedingung, dass sich die Hamburger auf ihrem Stadtgebiet eine Freihandelszone einrichten konnten, ein Gebiet also, wo Waren weiterhin zollfrei umgeschlagen werden konnten.

So ist der Plan für die Speicherstadt entstanden. Baubeginn war 1883. Da war der Kölner Dom grade seit drei Jahren fertig, und die Gotik war überall groß in Mode. Deswegen ist auch der größte zusammenhängende Lagerhauskomplex der Welt im neugotischen Stil gebaut worden, mit Backsteinfassaden über Stahlskeletten und mit moderner Technik im Innern. Jeder Block hat eine Wasser- und eine Straßenseite.

Die gesamte Speicherstadt steht auf 3,5 Millionen Eichenpfählen, die ungefähr zwölf Meter tief in den Untergrund getrieben werden mussten, so ähnlich wie in Venedig 900 Jahre zuvor. Dort sind es allerdings noch ein paar Millionen mehr.

WAREHOUSE CITY, HAMBURG

Hamburg has been a seaport since the Middle Ages and, as a member of the Hanseatic League, has long been a trading centre with its own customs' barriers. Goods from overseas could easily be shipped in to the various warehouses via the many canals which here are called »Fleete«. This is the reason for the many bridges in the city. Hamburg, namely, has more bridges than any other city in the world, far more than Venice and Amsterdam put together, 2479 in all, and maybe even a few more than that.

In 1881, after the German Reich was founded, Hamburg – under pressure from Chancellor Bismarck – had to suspend its old customs privilege as a Hanseatic city, however only under condition that the city could set up its own free trade area on its territory, that is, an area where goods could be handled free of customs.

That's how the plan for this warehouse city came about. Construction was started in 1883. In that year the Cologne Cathedral in its new completed state was three years old, and Gothic was very fashionable. This is the reason that the world's largest connected warehouse complex was built in Neo-Gothic style, with brick facades over a steel skeleton construction and an interior equipped with modern technology. Each block of warehouses faces the water on one side and the street on the other.

The entire warehouse city stands on 3.5 million oak palisades, which had to be driven underground about twelve metres, similar to Venice built almost 900 years before, but which naturally boasts a couple million more.

»ZUR RITZE«, HAMBURG

Zur Zeit der großen Segelschiffe gab es fast in allen Hafenstädten der Welt Manufakturen, die Taue oder Seile hergestellt haben. Um die langen Seile richtig zu verdrillen, brauchte man viel Platz, und die Gebäude, die Seilereien, in denen das gemacht wurde, waren normalerweise ein paar hundert Meter lang. Einer von diesen Orten, wo Seile hergestellt wurden, war die Hamburger Reeperbahn. »Reep« heißt nämlich nichts anderes als Seil, und eine Strickleiter zum Beispiel heißt in der Seemannssprache heute noch »Fallreep«.

In allen Hafenstädten auf der Welt gibt es Viertel, in denen sich die Matrosen amüsieren, wenn sie nach der langen Zeit auf See an Land gehen. In Hamburg heißt dieses Viertel Sankt Pauli, und da genau mittendrin liegt die 930 Meter lange weltbekannte Reeperbahn. Seile werden dort allerdings schon lange nicht mehr gemacht, und zum Amüsieren kommen nicht nur Matrosen her. Anfang der 60er Jahre des vorigen Jahrhunderts sind zum Beispiel die Beatles in einigen Lokalen von Sankt Pauli aufgetreten. Und anschließend haben sie Karriere gemacht.

Eine der berühmtesten Kneipen an der Reeperbahn ist die »Ritze«. Der Wirt Hanne Kleine war Anfang der 80er Jahre Box-Landesmeister im Mittelgewicht und hat damals im Keller unter seinem Lokal einen Boxclub eingerichtet. Das hat sich schnell herumgesprochen, und in den Jahren danach hat fast jeder, der Boxhandschuhe anziehen konnte, irgendwann mal hier im oder am Ring gestanden, hat Sparringsrunden absolviert oder gegen den Sandsack gehauen.

»ZUR RITZE«, HAMBURG

In almost every seaport, at the time of the big sailboats, there were workshops that manufactured cable or rope. To twist the long ropes properly, you needed a lot of room, and the buildings in which this was done were normally several hundred metres long. One of the places where cable was produced was Hamburg's Reeperbahn. »Reep« means nothing other than rope and »Reeperbahn« rope lane, while in sailor language today a rope ladder is still called a »Fallreep«.

In every seaport in the world, there are districts where sailors go on shore leave to have fun after a long time at sea. In Hamburg, this district is called Sankt Pauli, and smack in its midst lies the 930 metres long, world (in)famous Reeperbahn. Ropes, however, haven't been made here in a long time, and it is certainly not only sailors who come here for entertainment. At the beginning of the 1960s, for instance, the Beatles played gigs in several St. Pauli bars. And afterwards went on to fame.

One of the most famous bars on the Reeperbahn is the »Ritze«. The owner, Hanne Kleine, was the state's middleweight boxing champion in the early 1980s and had a boxing club installed in the basement under his bar. Word of this spread quickly, and in the following years almost anybody able to pull on boxing gloves stood here in or at the ring to do some sparring or a round with the punching bag.

PRINCE RODNEY
WATTS
BRUNO
SCOTT LE DOUX
MARK KAYLOR
RAY GILBODY
RIVAL BOUT II
BOXEN
Georg Steinherr
VELENSEK
HERNANDEZ
PROFI-BOXEN
FRITZ WIENE PRASENT
BERUFS-BOXEN
EUROPAMEISTERSCHAFT
STERLING
TIGER
EVERLAST
BOXEN
GRUGAHALLE ESSEN
HANSEHALLE
EVERLAST

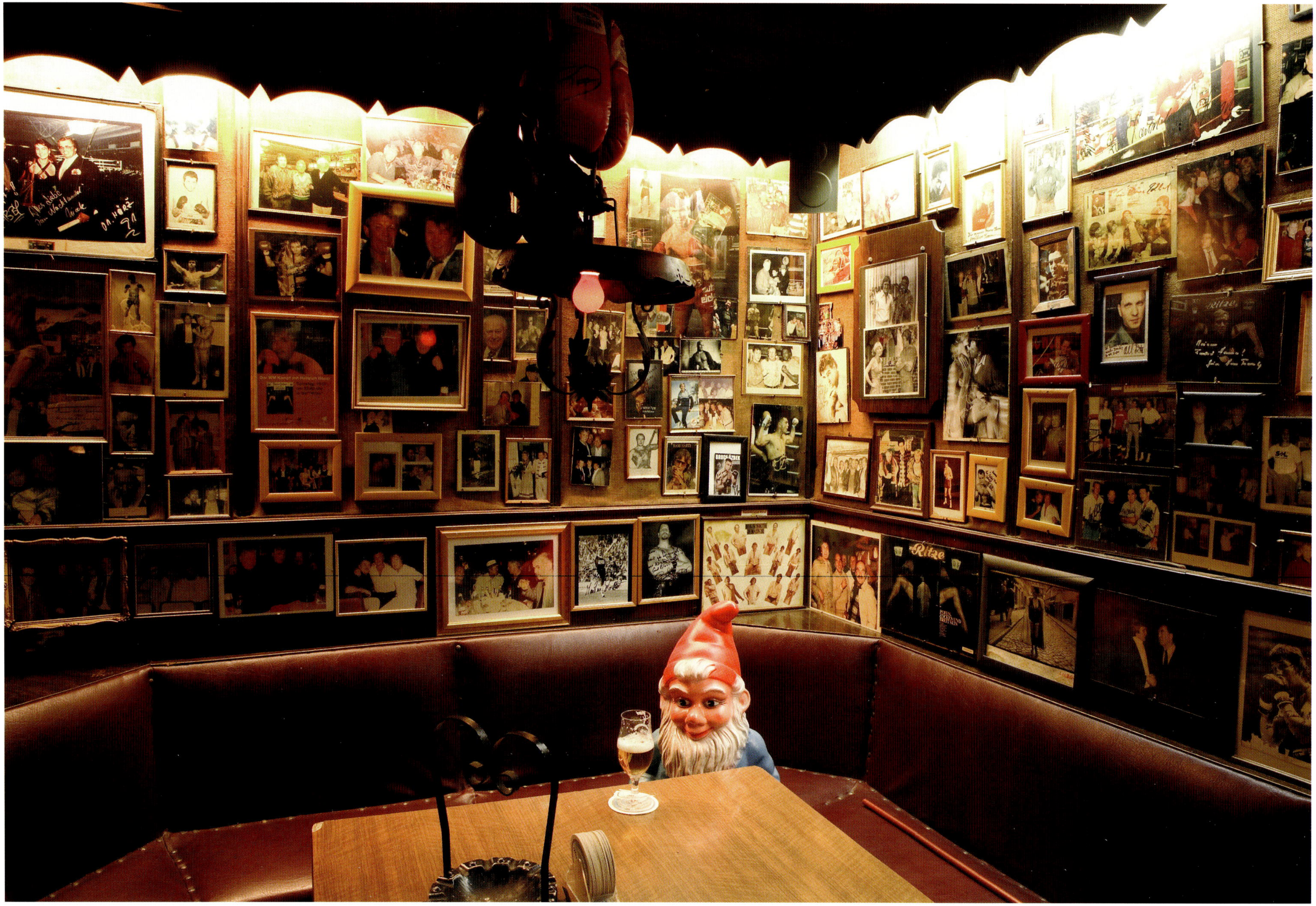
Ritze

»ZUR RITZE«, HAMBURG

Beer was now urgently needed. Boxing is strenuous and makes you thirsty, even when watching it. Perhaps that's the real reason Hanne has set up a boxing club in the cellar. After all, he's not been a boxer for a long time, rather, his main profession has been that of a barkeeper.

All around the walls you can see them: the boxers, trainers and promoters who have played a role these past decades in or at the ring. And everybody who was anybody in the sport have been down in this cellar at one time or other: Max Schmeling, Bubi Scholz, Norbert Grupe, Henry Maske, Axel Schulz, Dariusz Michalszewski. And with them many other stars, big names and small.

DEUTSCHES WOHNZIMMER, HAMBURG

Wie sieht das durchschnittliche deutsche Wohnzimmer aus? Ganz einfach: so wie auf dem Bild nebenan. Das meinen jedenfalls die Fachleute von der Hamburger Werbeagentur Jung von Matt, und sie haben lange und aufwändige Untersuchungen angestellt, um das herauszubekommen. So oder so ähnlich richten sich nach ihren Erkenntnissen die meisten Menschen in Deutschland ihre Wohnzimmer ein: mit Schrankwand, Sitzgruppe, Auslegware, Sideboard, Couchtisch, Fernseher und plus/minus 30 Büchern. In Bremen, Detmold, Berlin, Köln, Niedermohr oder Tübingen, in Kassel, Haßloch, Leipzig, Bamberg, Greifswald oder Buxtehude.

Aber ihr ahnt es vielleicht schon: Das hier ist nicht einfach nur ein Wohnzimmer – nein: Es ist in Wirklichkeit ein Konferenzraum, den die Hamburger Reklamespezialisten eingerichtet haben, damit sie immer daran denken, in welcher Umgebung ein großer Teil von dem verwendet und verbraucht wird, wofür sie Werbung machen.

Außen hängt ein Türschild, auf dem steht: Deutschlands häufigstes Wohnzimmer. Hier wohnen Sabine, Thomas und Sohn Alexander. Sabine (39) und Thomas (42) sind beide berufstätig. Sabine halbtags, weil Alexander (12) noch zur Schule geht. Thomas fährt einen VW-Passat und sieht gerne fern. Am liebsten Formel 1 und Fußball. Die Lieblingsfreizeitbeschäftigung von Sabine ist Telefonieren. Ansonsten kocht sie gerne. Da sich Sabine gerade mit einer Freundin trifft und Thomas noch arbeitet, steht ihr Wohnzimmer für Konferenzen zur Verfügung. Hereinspaziert!

GERMAN LIVING ROOM, HAMBURG

What does the average German living room look like? Quite simple: just like on this picture. At least, that's what the experts at the Hamburg advertising agency Jung von Matt believe, and they went to a lot of trouble and undertook exhaustive studies to find this out. According to them, most people in Germany furnish their living room in this, or a similar, way: with a large wall unit, sofa suite, carpeting, sideboard, coffee table, TV and around thirty books. In Bremen, Detmold, Berlin, Cologne, Niedermohr or Tübingen, in Kassel, Hassloch, Leipzig, Bamberg, Greifswald or Buxtehude.

But you probably already see which way the wind's blowing: this is not simply just a living room – oh no. It is in actual fact a conference room that the Hamburg advertising specialists have furnished so that they have, ever present, the type of surroundings in which a major part of the things they advertise are being put to use.

Outside hangs a sign which states: Germany's most frequent type of living room. Here live Sabine, Thomas and son Alexander. Sabine (39) and Thomas (42) both work, Sabine part-time because Alexander (12) still goes to school. Thomas drives a VW Passat and likes to watch television, preferably Formula 1 or soccer. Sabine's favourite pastime is talking on the phone. Apart from that she likes to cook. Since Sabine is just meeting up with a friend and Thomas is still at work, their living room is available for conferences. Step right in!

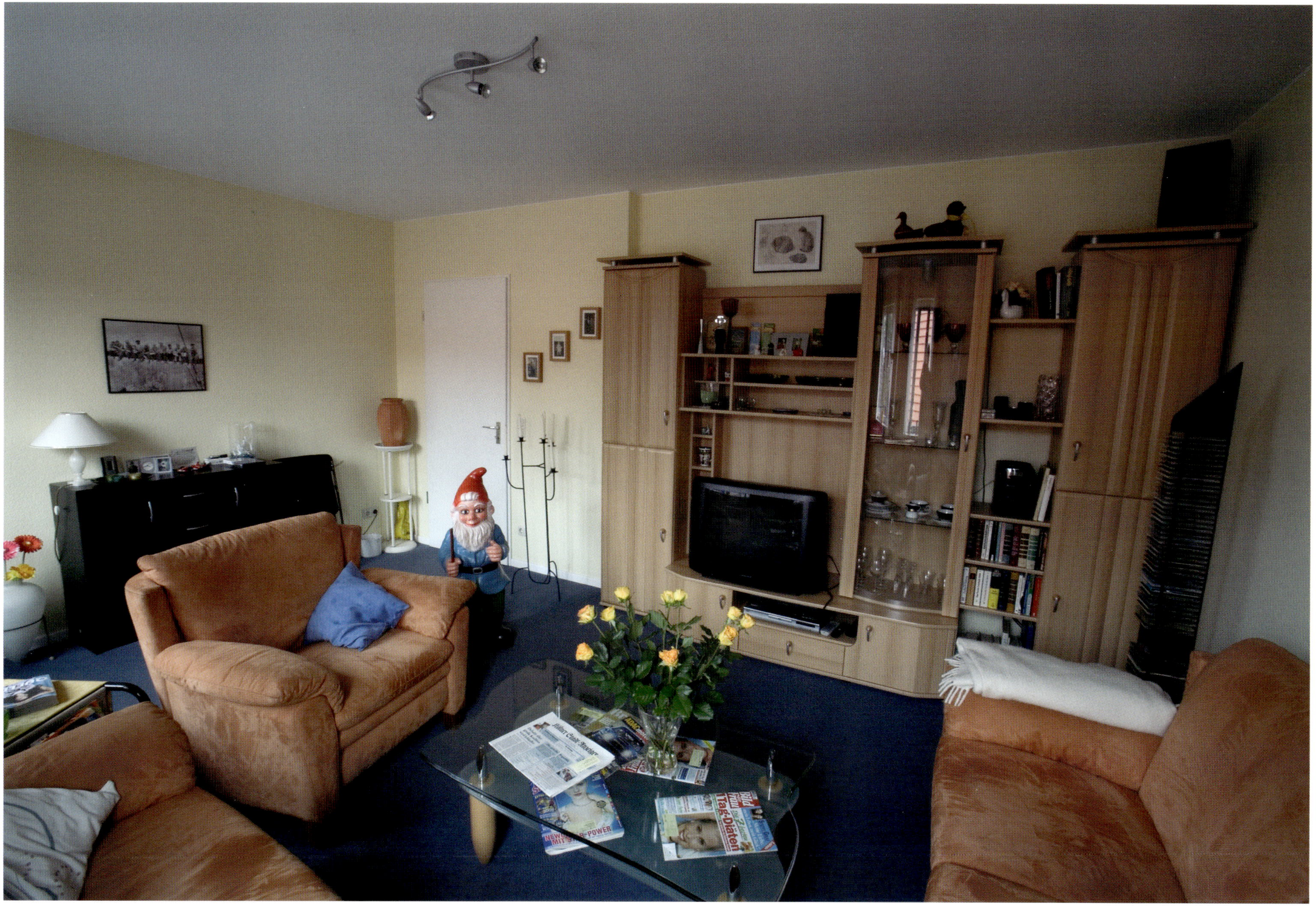

FULDA-UFER, KASSEL

1982 hat sich der amerikanische Künstler Claes Oldenburg vorgestellt, dass das Wahrzeichen von Kassel, der Herkules auf der Wilhelmshöhe, eine riesige Spitzhacke von dort oben in die Stadt hinunterwirft. Und tatsächlich: Seitdem steckt diese Hacke sechs Kilometer vom Herkules entfernt in der Wiese am Ufer der Fulda, zwölf Meter hoch und fünf Tonnen schwer. Das war im Jahr der siebten »documenta«.

Diese berühmte Ausstellung für moderne Kunst ist 1955 von dem Kasseler Maler und Kunstprofessor Arnold Bode zusammen mit kunstliebenden Bürgern der Stadt gegründet worden und hat Kassel in der ganzen Welt bekannt gemacht. Eigentlich war sie damals nur als Rahmenprogramm für die Bundesgartenschau gedacht, aber sie war so erfolgreich, dass man sie vier Jahre später noch einmal veranstaltet hat. Da war sie noch erfolgreicher, und deswegen haben die Kasseler beschlossen, sie regelmäßig stattfinden zu lassen, zuerst alle vier, ab 1967 alle fünf Jahre, und seitdem ist alle Welt immer wieder auf die nächste »documenta« gespannt.

Der Halbgott Herkules übrigens soll die Olympischen Spiele im antiken Griechenland gegründet haben (dort hieß er Herakles); sie wurden seit 776 v. Chr. alle vier Jahre ausgerichtet. Soweit ich weiß, war der Spitzhackenweitwurf aber schon damals keine olympische Disziplin.

FULDA-UFER, KASSEL

In 1982, the American artist, Claes Oldenburg, imagined that Kassel's trademark, the Hercules statue on the Wilhelm's Height, had thrown a giant pickaxe down into the city from there. And indeed: ever since then, this pickaxe juts out of the grass on the banks of the Fulda, six kilometres from Hercules, the pickaxe itself twelve metres high and weighing five tons. That was the year of the 7th »documenta«.

This famous exhibition for modern art was founded in 1955 by the Kassel artist and art professor, Arnold Bode, together with the city's art-loving citizens, and made Kassel into a worldwide name. At the time, it was only viewed as a fringe event to the Bundesgartenschau (Germany's national garden show), but it was so successful that four years later it was repeated. This was even more successful and the reason why Kassel decided to hold one regularly, at first every four years and, since 1967, every five years. And now the whole world is forever expectantly awaiting the next »documenta«.

Incidentally, the demigod Hercules is the one who supposedly initiated the ancient Olympic Games in Greece (there he was called Heracles). They have taken place every four years since 776 B.C. As far as I know, pickaxe-throwing was not an Olympic discipline, even at that time.

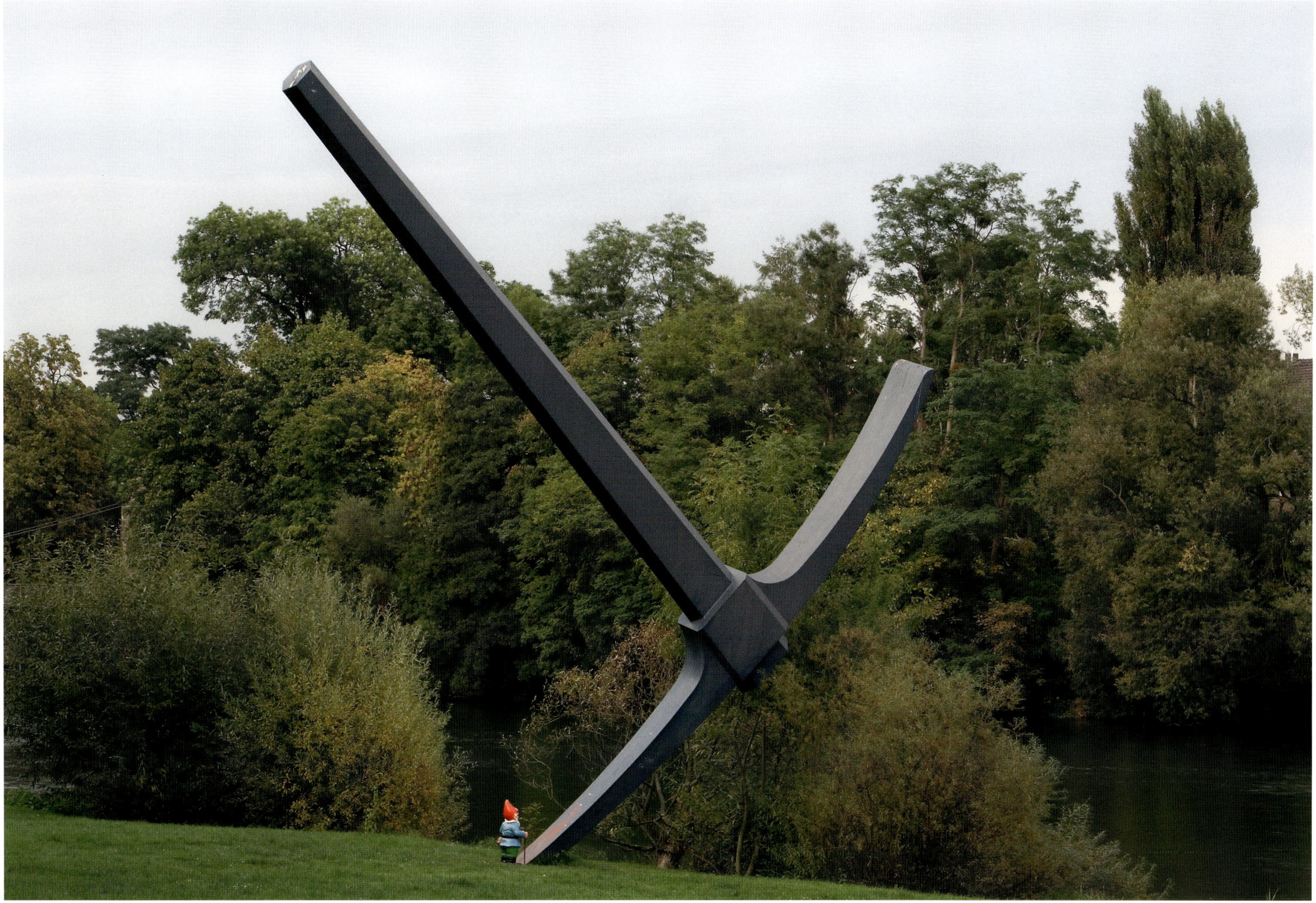

FRANKFURT AM MAIN

Die romanischen und gotischen Kathedralen waren über tausend Jahre die größten und höchsten Gebäude in Europa und auf der Welt. Dann kam zur Pariser Weltausstellung 1889 der Eiffelturm, 300 Meter hoch und 6000 Tonnen schwer, der stellte für lange Zeit alles in den Schatten. Aber ein richtiges Gebäude ist dieser zwecklose Gittermast ja wirklich nicht. Er ist sehr hoch, sieht ganz elegant aus, man kann raufsteigen und runtergucken, aber das ist eigentlich schon alles. Es gibt da zwar ein Restaurant, aber keine Wohnung, und Eiffels Büro oben in der Spitze wird schon lange nicht mehr genutzt. Der Ingenieur wollte mit seinem Turm ja auch bloß zeigen, was er machen kann, wenn man ihn nur lässt.

In den anderen Städten in Europa blieb erst mal alles beim Alten, da gab es keine Eiffeltürme. Auch in Frankfurt war der spätgotische Kaiserdom mit seinen 95 Metern bis 1960 das höchste Gebäude der Stadt – bis zum Bau des 120 Meter hohen Henninger-Turms.

1957 war per Gesetz die Deutsche Bundesbank nach Frankfurt gekommen, die Börse entwickelte sich nach und nach zur wichtigsten in Deutschland, und die Stadt war auf dem Weg zu einem weltweit bedeutenden Finanzplatz.

Banken brauchen aber vor allem Büros. Der Boden in den Innenstädten wurde immer knapper und teurer. Die Luft darüber gab's dagegen umsonst. Also hat man in die Höhe gebaut, in Frankfurt wie überall auf der Welt. Zuerst bescheiden, dann immer höher, und schließlich wurden Rekorde angepeilt oder gebrochen. Die 300 Meter hohe Zentrale der Commerzbank ist derzeit das höchste Gebäude in Europa.

Mit seinen annähernd 20 Hochhäusern sieht Frankfurt heute amerikanischer aus als alle anderen deutschen Großstädte.

FRANKFURT AM MAIN

For over a thousand years the Romanesque and Gothic cathedrals were the biggest and highest buildings in Europe and the world. Then, at the 1889 Paris World's Fair, the Eiffel Tower was presented. At 300 metres high and weighing 6000 tons, it overshadowed everything else for a long time. But this no-purpose, latticed tower is not a real, honest-to-God building. It is very high, looks elegant, you can go up it and look down from it, but there it ends. It does have a restaurant, but no living quarters, and Eiffel's office at the very top has not been in use for a very long time. With his tower, the engineer had only wanted to show what he could do if one would only let him.

In the other cities in Europe, everything at first remained as it was; there were no Eiffel Towers. Also in Frankfurt, the 95-metre-high late-Gothic Kaiserdom Cathedral was the tallest edifice in the city – until the construction of the 120-metre-high Henninger Tower in 1960.

In 1957, the Deutsche Bundesbank, per decree, set up headquarters in Frankfurt; the stock exchange evolved little by little into the most important one in Germany, and the city was on its way to becoming a significant worldwide financial centre.

What banks need, above all, is office space. Building plots in city centres became ever scarcer and more expensive. The air above them, on the other hand, cost nothing. So upwards things went, in Frankfurt as everywhere else in the world. At first modestly, then ever higher, and finally sights were set on breaking records. The 300-metre-high headquarters of the Commerz Bank is, at present, Europe's highest building.

With its high-rise buildings numbering close to 20, Frankfurt – among Germany's big cities – today looks more American than any other German city.

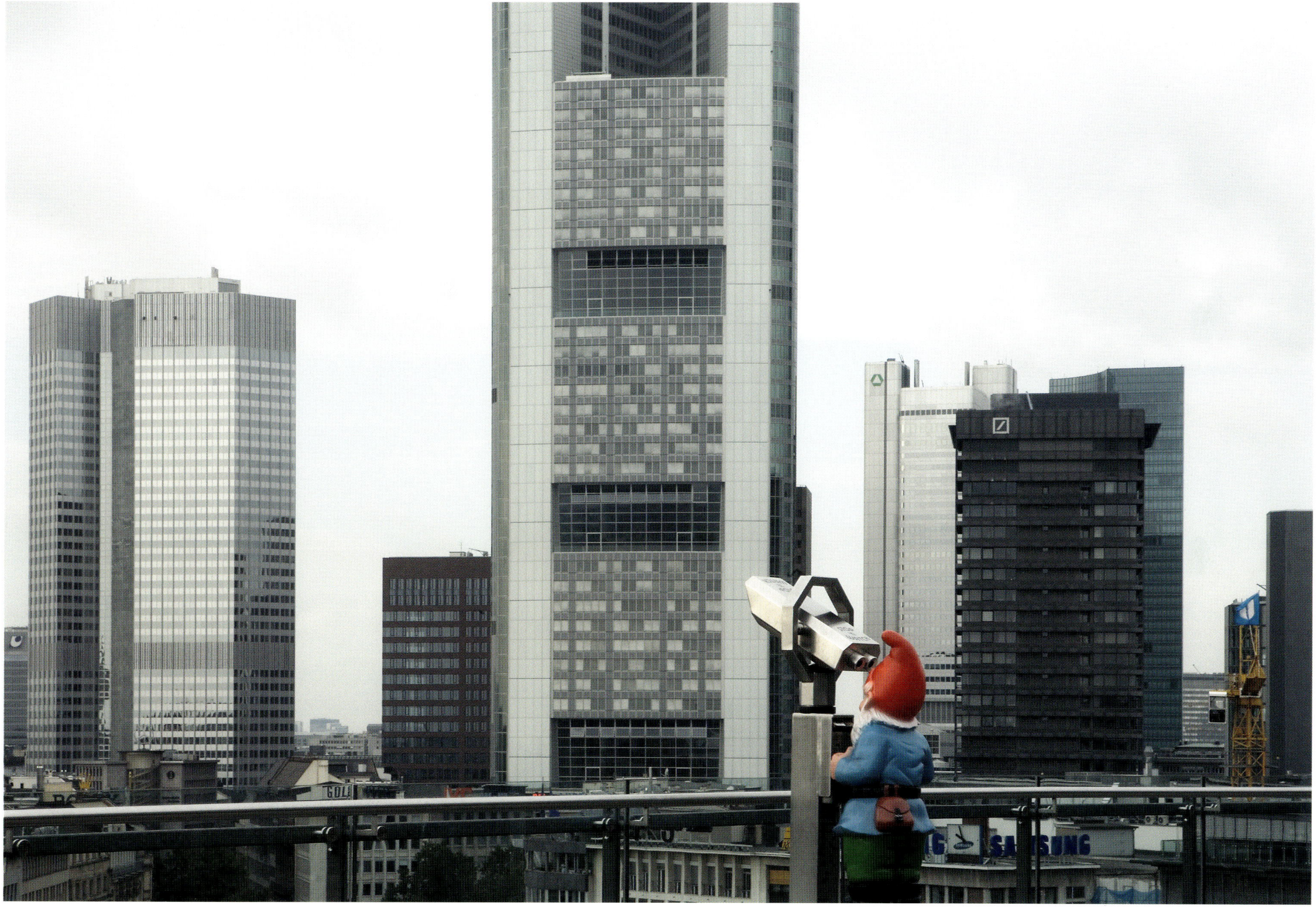

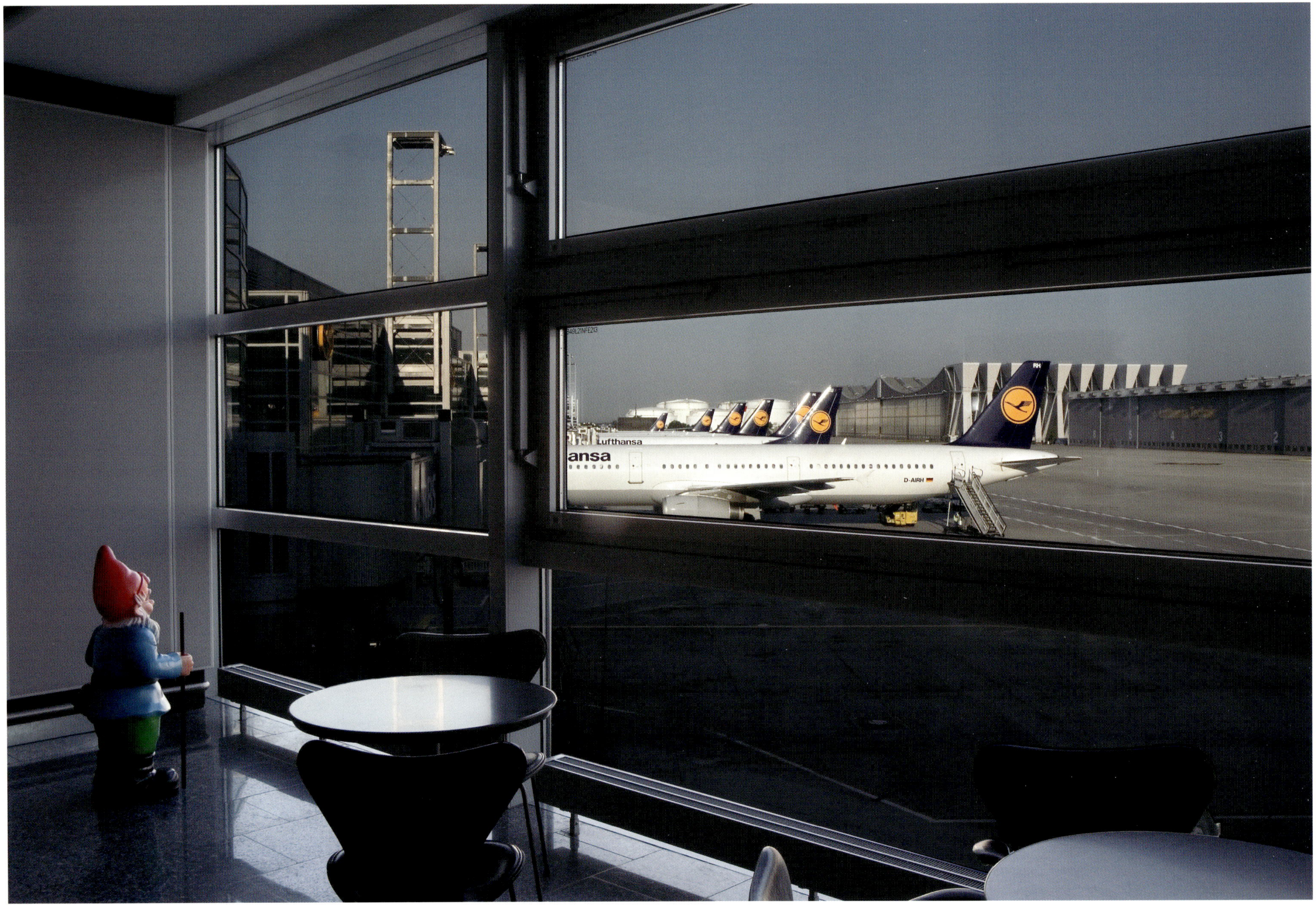
Lufthansa
ansa
D-AIRH

**LUFTHANSA-TERMINAL,
FLUGHAFEN FRANKFURT/MAIN**

Schwer zu sagen, mit wem es eigentlich angefangen hat, das Fliegen: mit Daidalos auf Kreta, mit Leonardo da Vinci, dem Schneider von Ulm, den Brüdern Montgolfier, mit Otto Lilienthal oder doch erst mit Wilbur und Orville Wright?

Die Brüder Montgolfier sind nach dem Prinzip »leichter als Luft« aufgestiegen, aber Otto Lilienthal war gut 100 Jahre später der erste, der mit dem Prinzip »schwerer als Luft« erfolgreich war. Für ihn und seine Flugapparate war der Storch das große Vorbild. 1896 ist er bei einem seiner Flugversuche tödlich verunglückt. In den Jahren danach ging es rasant aufwärts mit der Fliegerei: immer schneller, immer höher, immer weiter.

Im Vergleich mit dem Storch gilt der Kranich als der elegantere Vogel, und deshalb hat ihn die Lufthansa wohl auch zu ihrem Firmenzeichen gemacht (zumal der Storch ja auch andere Aufgaben hat). Die erste Version des stilisierten Kranichs stammt von 1918. Leicht verändert wurde er 1926 beim Zusammenschluss des Deutschen Aero Lloyd mit dem Junkers Luftverkehr zur »Deutsche Luft Hansa Aktiengesellschaft« das Wappentier der ersten Luftfahrtgesellschaft der Welt. Am 6. April hat sie mit 162 Flugzeugen den Liniendienst aufgenommen und nannte sich ab 1936 »Lufthansa«. 1939 reichte ihr interkontinentales Streckennetz schon bis nach Thailand und Chile. Nach dem Zweiten Weltkrieg ist die Gesellschaft aufgelöst worden. Nach der Neugründung 1955 hat sie sich schnell wieder zu einer der erfolgreichsten Fluggesellschaften der Welt entwickelt.

Heute gehen im Jahr weltweit 1,7 Milliarden Passagiere mit dem Flugzeug auf Reisen, hier auf dem Frankfurter Flughafen, dem zweitgrößten in Europa, fliegen jährlich allein über 50 Millionen ab oder kommen an.

**LUFTHANSA TERMINAL,
FRANKFURT/MAIN AIRPORT**

It's hard to say who started it all, this business of flying: Daedalus on Crete, Leonardo da Vinci, the tailor from Ulm, the Montgolfier Brothers, Otto Lilienthal, or was it really Wilbur and Orville Wright?

The Montgolfier Brothers gave their balloons lift on the principle of »lighter than air«, but Otto Lilienthal, a good 100 years later, was the first to have proven success with the principle of »heavier than air«. It was the stork that was the model for him and his flying apparatus. He even discovered what the curvature of the wings had to do with it all. He crashed fatally in 1896, during one of his attempts to fly. In the following years, the flying business really took off: always faster, always higher, always farther.

In comparison with the stork, the crane is considered the more elegant bird, for which reason Lufthansa chose it for its company logo (particularly as the stork has other duties). The first version of the stylised crane goes back to 1918. It was changed slightly in 1926 when Deutscher Aero Lloyd merged with Junkers Luftverkehr to become »Deutsche Luft Hansa AG«, and the crane became the ›coat of arms‹ for the first airline company in the world. On April 6, it began regular flights with 162 planes and from 1936 on called itself »Lufthansa«. As early as 1939, its intercontinental routes extended as far as Thailand and Chile. Post-World War II, the company was dissolved. After its re-establishment in 1955, it quickly developed into one of the most successful airline companies in the world.

Today, 1.7 billion passengers from all over the world travel by aeroplane each year. At Frankfurt Airport alone, the second largest in Europe, over 50 million passengers depart or arrive every year.

**KEMPINSKI GRAND HOTEL,
HEILIGENDAMM**

Franz Friedrich I., Großherzog von Mecklenburg, soll der erste gewesen sein, der 1793 in der Gegend von Heiligendamm seinen Sommerurlaub verbracht hat. Es muss ihm dort sehr gut gefallen haben, denn in den folgenden Jahren hat er alles dafür getan, dass der kleine Ort westlich von Rostock und Warnemünde zum ersten und zum elegantesten Seebad von Deutschland ausgebaut wurde.

Aber erst 1870 war die klassizistische Anlage aus Bade- und Logierhäusern komplett fertig. Bis in die 30er Jahre des vergangenen Jahrhunderts war Heiligendamm ein beliebtes Urlaubsziel für den Hochadel aus ganz Europa. Dann war für über 60 Jahre damit Schluss.

Erst nach der deutschen Wiedervereinigung konnte Heiligendamm wieder an die alten Zeiten anknüpfen. Mit Hilfe von zahlungskräftigen Investoren ist hier in sorgfältiger Restaurierungsarbeit ein Fünf-Sterne-Hotel entstanden, eine Anlage aus sechs einzelnen klassizistischen Gebäuden, die 2004 zum schönsten Hotel der Welt gewählt worden ist: das Kempinski Grand Hotel Heiligendamm. Wäre ich in der Jury gewesen, hätte ich auch dafür gestimmt.

**KEMPINSKI GRAND HOTEL,
HEILIGENDAMM**

Franz Friedrich I, Grand Duke of Mecklenburg, was supposed to have been the first who spent his summer holiday in the region of Heiligendamm in the year 1793. He must have liked it here very much, for in the following years he did everything to have the little town west of Rostock and Warnemünde fashioned into the most elegant seaside resort in Germany.

But not till 1870 was the classicist complex of spa and living accommodations complete. Up until the 1930s, Heiligendamm was a popular holiday spot for the upper nobility from all over Europe. This came to an abrupt end, which lasted for over sixty years.

Not till German reunification could Heiligendamm again link up with its past. With the help of wealthy investors and after careful restoration, a five-star hotel has emerged, a complex of six individual classicist buildings that, in 2004, was voted the most beautiful hotel in the world: the Kempinski Grand Hotel. If I had been on the jury, I would have voted for it, too.

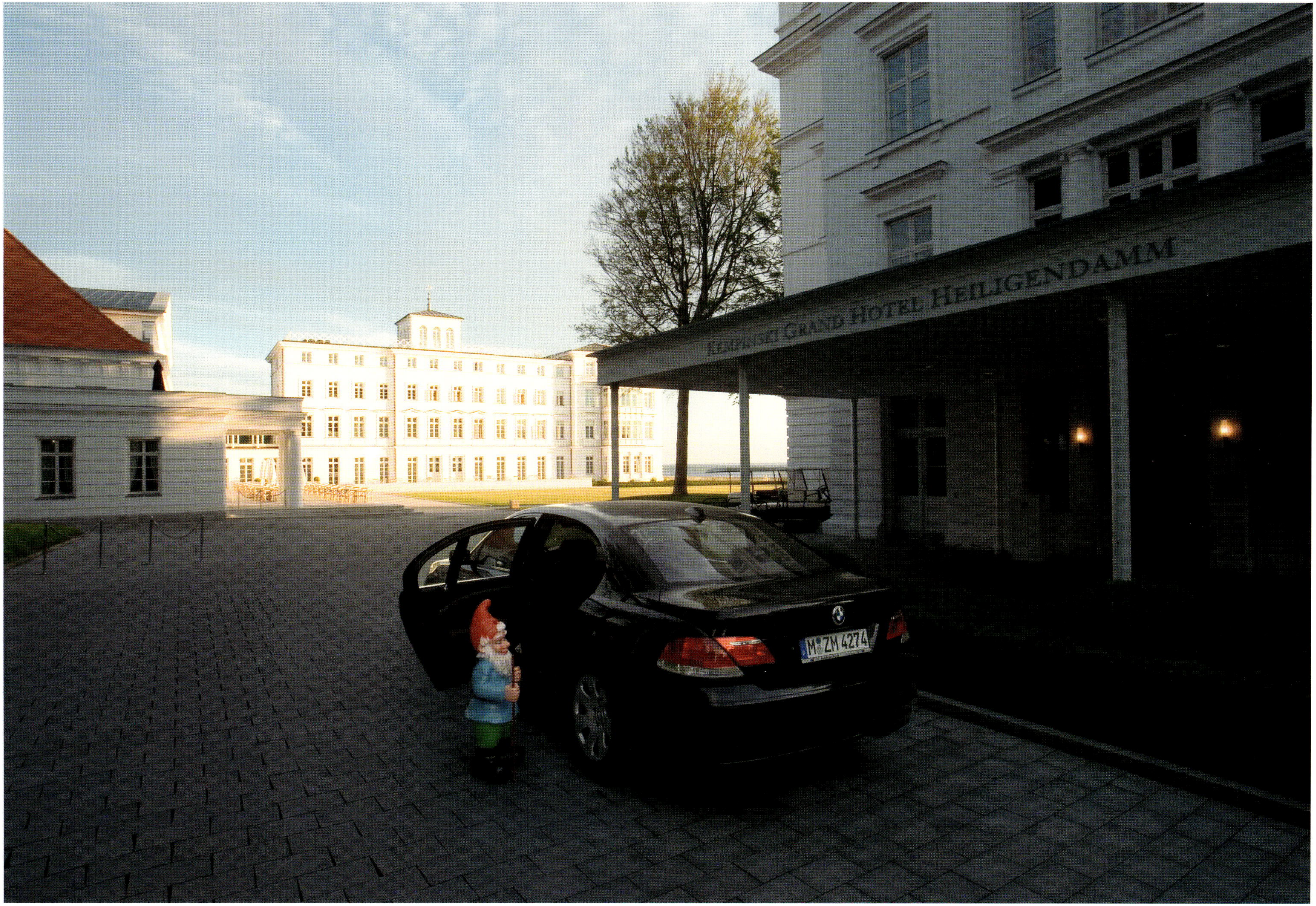
KEMPINSKI GRAND HOTEL HEILIGENDAMM
M ZM 4274

SEEBRÜCKE SELLIN, RÜGEN

Habt ihr gewusst, warum am 19. Oktober 1913 in Leipzig die »Deutsche Lebensrettungs-Gesellschaft« gegründet wurde? Der unmittelbare Anlass dafür war ein bedauerliches Unglück an der Ostküste von Rügen im Jahr zuvor. Beim Anlegemanöver des Dampfers »Kronprinz Wilhelm« an der Seebrücke von Binz war ein Querbalken gebrochen, und dadurch sind 14 Menschen ums Leben gekommen.

Rügen ist die größte deutsche Insel (926 qkm), und bis zum Bau des Rügendamms 1936 konnte man sie lediglich übers Wasser erreichen. Es gab nur kurze Bootsstege, da konnten große Schiffe aber nicht anlegen, und die Urlauber mussten mit ihrem Gepäck in kleinere Boote umsteigen, die sie an Land brachten. Also baute man 1902 in Binz einen Anleger ins Meer, eine 560 Meter lange Seebrücke zum bequemen Ein- und Aussteigen. Auf dieser Brücke konnte man auch spazieren gehen, dafür musste man aber Brückengeld bezahlen. Im strengen Winter 1942/43 haben große Eisschollen die Brücke zerstört.

Der Seebrücke in Sellin war es ein Jahr zuvor schon genauso ergangen; sie war nur vier Jahre nach der in Binz gebaut worden. Der Brückenkopf blieb zunächst stehen, musste aber schließlich 1978 abgerissen werden.

Inzwischen sind beide Brücken wieder aufgebaut, allerdings etwas kürzer als früher. Die neue Brücke in Sellin ist nur noch 395 Meter lang, aber die Gebäude sehen fast wieder so aus wie vor 100 Jahren.

Natürlich ist es hier auch tagsüber sehr schön, aber am schönsten ist es in der Dämmerung, wenn auf der Seebrücke die Lichter angehen.

SELLIN PIER, RÜGEN

Do you know why the German Lifesaving Association was founded on October 19, 1913, in Leipzig? The immediate occasion was an unfortunate accident on the east coast of Rügen the year before. The steamship »Kronprinz Wilhelm«, during docking manoeuvres, broke a crossbeam of the Binz pier, which resulted in the death of 14 persons.

Rügen is the largest German island (926 sq. km.) and until, in 1936, the Rügen Dike was built, could only be reached by water. Its short landing stages did not reach far enough out for large ships to get close enough to the shore, and holiday-makers and their luggage had to be transferred to smaller boats that then took them ashore. Therefore in 1902, a landing stage was built in Binz, a 560 metre long pier that allowed easy boarding. You could also take walks along the pier, but you had to pay a fee to do so. Unfortunately, during the very severe winter of 1942/43, large ice floes destroyed the pier.

Exactly one year before, the pier at Sellin had suffered a similar fate; it was built only four years after the one in Binz. The bridgehead was at first left standing, but eventually had to be torn down in 1978.

In the meantime, both piers have been rebuilt, although a bit shorter than before. Sellin's new pier is only 395 metres long, but the buildings on it look almost the same as they did 100 years ago.

It is naturally very beautiful here during the day, but it is the loveliest at dusk when the lights on the pier are switched on.

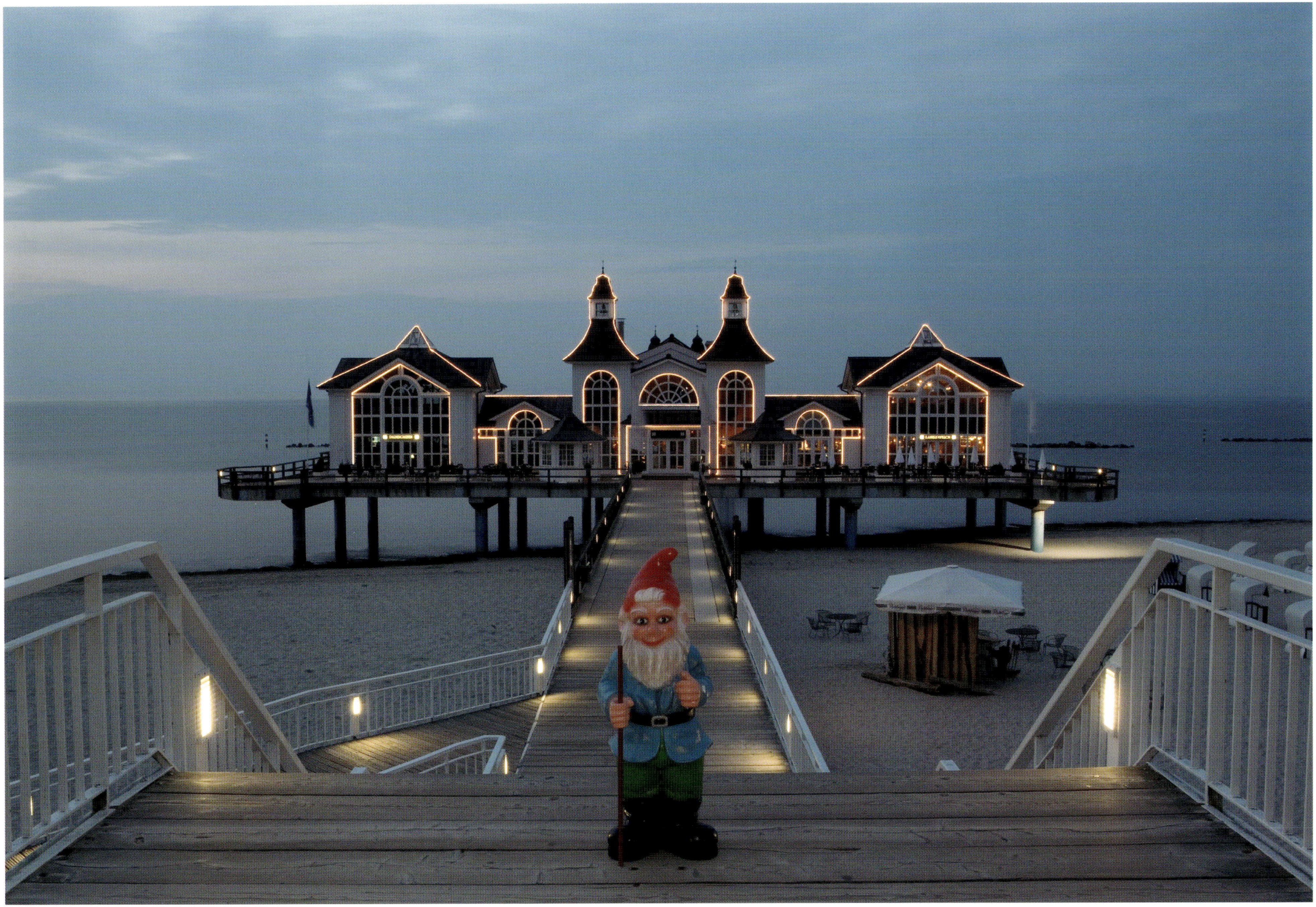

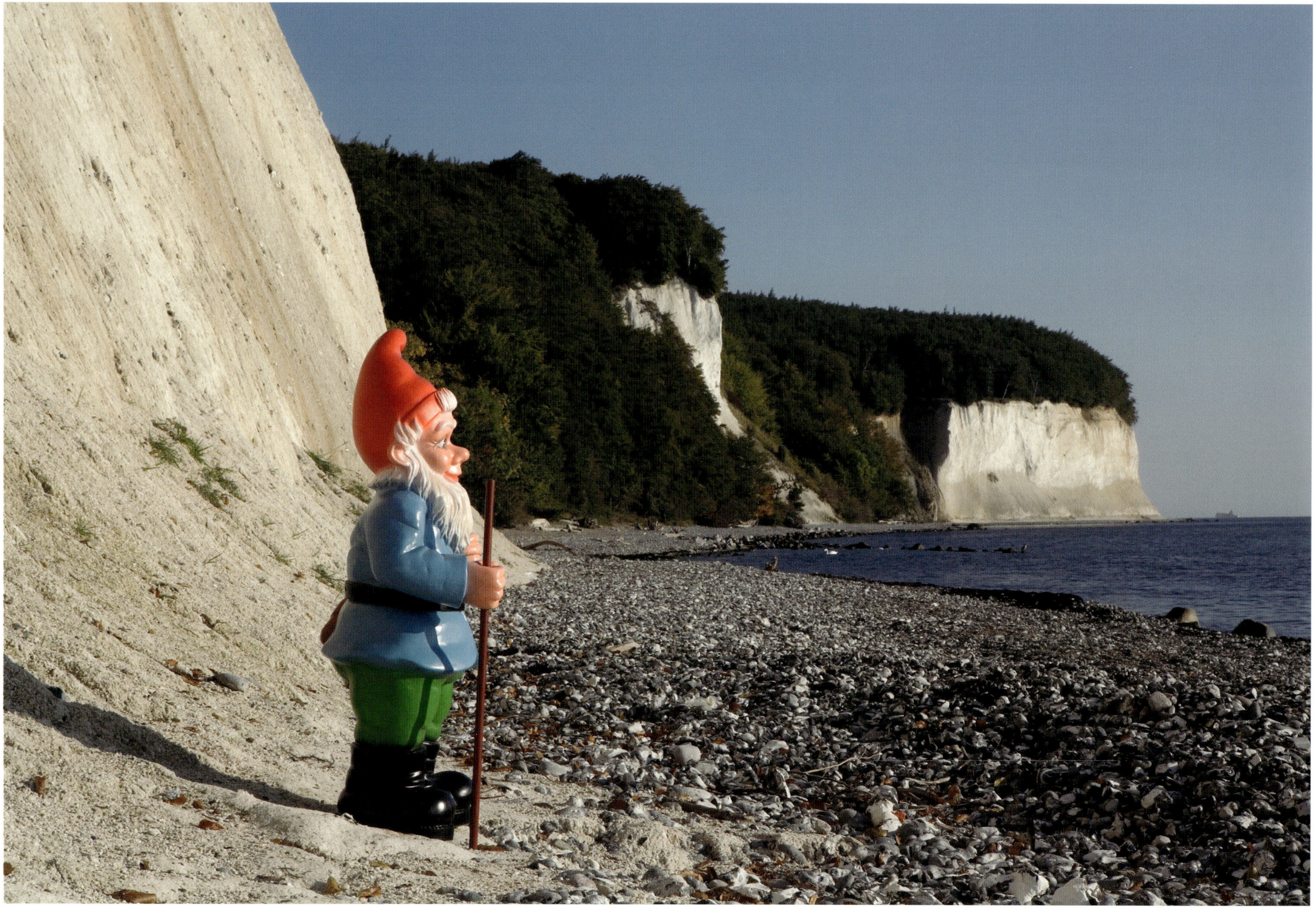

KREIDEFELSEN, RÜGEN

Wer weiß, ob die leuchtenden Kreidefelsen von Rügen heute genau so berühmt wären, wenn Caspar David Friedrich sie am Beginn des 19. Jahrhunderts nicht gemalt hätte. Und schwer zu sagen, was berühmter ist: die Felsen oder das Gemälde.

Die Kreidefelsen sind bis zu 120 Meter hoch und fallen an vielen Stellen fast senkrecht ab, aber eben weil sie so steil sind, sind sie auch sehr gefährdet: Am 24. Februar 2005 sind zum Beispiel die »Wissower Klinken« ins Meer gerutscht. Das Meer ist da ganz unromantisch, und irgendwann gibt's von den Kreidefelsen vielleicht nichts anderes mehr als Bilder. Aber ein paar tausend Jahre werden sie wohl noch halten.

CHALK CLIFFS, RÜGEN

Who knows if Rügen's brilliant chalk cliffs would be as famous today if Caspar David Friedrich hadn't painted them at the beginning of the 19th century. And it's hard to say which is more famous, the cliffs or their painting.

The chalk cliffs are up to 120 metres high and at many places drop almost straight down. And because they are so steep, they themselves are very much in danger: on February 24, 2005, for instance, the two peaks of the »Wissower Klinken« slithered into the sea. The sea there is thoroughly unromantic, and perhaps sometime or other there will be nothing left of the chalk cliffs but their pictures. But they should hold out for another couple of thousand of years.

LEUCHTTURM DORNBUSCH, HIDDENSEE

Hiddensee erinnert in der Form ein wenig an ein Seepferdchen, das nach Osten schaut: eine schmale, lang gestreckte Insel westlich vor Rügen, knapp 17 Kilometer von Norden nach Süden und an der schmalsten Stelle keine 250 Meter breit.

Wer endlich mal Ruhe haben will von der Großstadt und den Autos und dem Lärm, für den ist Hiddensee genau der richtige Ort. Hier gibt es keine Autos für den privaten Gebrauch, und die wenigen Fahrzeuge für öffentliche Aufgaben haben Elektroantrieb. Dazu gehört auch ein kleiner Linienbus, der bringt hauptsächlich Schüler zur Schule und wieder nach Hause. Wer sich auf Hiddensee umschauen will, geht am besten zu Fuß, er kann aber auch eine Kutschfahrt machen oder sich ein Fahrrad mieten, davon gibt es ungefähr tausend.

Besonders bekannt gemacht hat die Insel der deutsche Dichter und Dramatiker Gerhart Hauptmann. Er ist schon als junger Mann zum ersten Mal hier gewesen und über Jahrzehnte immer wieder zurückgekommen. 1930 hat er sich schließlich das Haus »Seedorn« in dem nördlich gelegenen Ort Kloster gekauft, um dort die Sommermonate zu verbringen. Gerhart Hauptmann ist 1946 gestorben und ist auf Hiddensee beigesetzt worden, sein Haus ist heute ein Museum.

Das Wahrzeichen von Hiddensee ist der Leuchtturm auf dem Dornbusch an der Nordspitze. Er stammt aus dem Jahr 1888, hat die Kennung »2,4 Sekunden hell, 7,6 Sekunden dunkel«, und sein Licht in 90 Metern Höhe ist 24,9 Seemeilen weit zu sehen.

DORNBUSCH LIGHTHOUSE, HIDDENSEE

Hiddensee is shaped somewhat like a seahorse facing eastwards: a narrow, elongated island that lies to the west of Rügen, almost 17 kilometres long and, at it narrowest, barely 250 metres wide.

Anyone who wants a brake from the big city with its cars and noise will find Hiddensee the perfect spot. Here, no private cars are allowed, and the few vehicles needed for public purposes run on electricity. One of these is a small bus that chiefly transports children to school and home again. If you want to have a look around Hiddensee, it's best to do so on foot. You can also take a carriage ride or rent a bicycle, of which there are about a thousand.

The person who made the island especially well known was the German poet and dramatist, Gerhart Hauptmann. He came here for the first time as a young man and for decades returned again and again. In 1930, he bought »Seedorn«, a house in Kloster in the north of the island, as a summer home. Gerhart Hauptmann died in 1946 and was buried on Hiddensee; his house is today a museum.

Hiddensee's landmark is the lighthouse on the Dornbusch Heights at the island's northernmost point. It was built in 1888; its identifying code is »2.4 seconds light, 7.6 seconds dark«, and its beacon, at a height of 90 metres, is visible 24.9 nautical miles away.

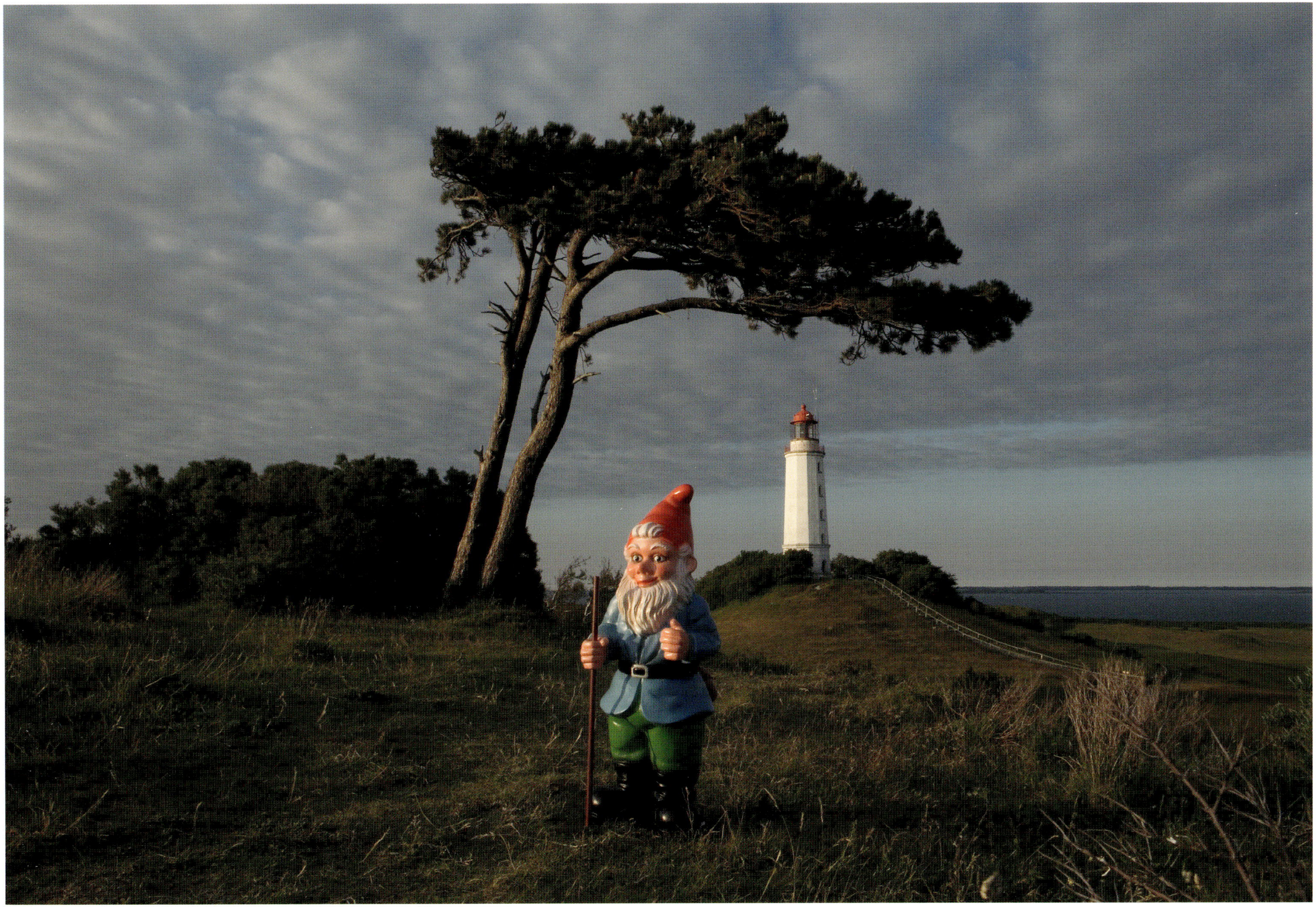

»AUTOSTADT«, WOLFSBURG

Die meisten Städte in Europa sind mindestens ein paar hundert Jahre alt, viele sind tausend, einige sogar zweitausend Jahre alt oder noch älter. Ganz neue Städte sind selten. In Deutschland sind im 19. und 20. Jahrhundert nur sieben gegründet worden: Bremerhaven (1827), Ludwigshafen (1843), Leverkusen (1862) und Wilhelmshaven (1869) sowie Wolfsburg (1938), Salzgitter (1942) und Eisenhüttenstadt (1950). Anlass für diese Gründungen war entweder der Bau von Häfen oder von Industrieanlagen.

Wolfsburg liegt 75 Kilometer östlich von Hannover. Hier sollte vor dem Zweiten Weltkrieg eigentlich der »Volkswagen« gebaut werden. Den hatte Ferdinand Porsche extra für das neue Werk konstruiert. Als »VW Käfer« ist er aber erst nach dem Krieg in Serie gegangen. Er ist zunächst nur für den Export hergestellt worden, hat anschließend das deutsche »Wirtschaftswunder« in Fahrt gebracht und war 30 Jahre später das meistgebaute Auto aller Zeiten. VW ist heute einer der größten Autokonzerne der Welt und beschäftigt mehr als 300.000 Menschen.

Die »Autostadt« in Wolfsburg wurde am 1. Juni 2000 eröffnet, zeitgleich mit der EXPO in Hannover. Sie ist eine Mischung aus Freizeitpark, Kundencenter und Auslieferungslager, wo im Jahr etwa 120.000 Autokäufer ihre Fahrzeuge persönlich abholen. In den beiden 20 Stockwerke hohen verglasten Rundtürmen warten jeweils 800 Autos auf ihre Käufer und werden automatisch für jeden einzeln herausgeholt.

Das Kraftwerk ist die Energiezentrale der Fabrik. Es steht gegenüber dem Fünf-Sterne-Hotel »Ritz-Carlton«. Das beleuchtete Rechteck hier im Vordergrund gehört zu den Attraktionen des Hotels: ein schwimmendes Schwimmbad, 8 mal 40 Meter und mit 28 Grad Wassertemperatur das ganze Jahr über geöffnet.

»CAR CITY«, WOLFSBURG

Most of the cities in Europe are at least a few hundred years old; many are 1000, several even 2000 years old or older. Completely new towns are rare. In Germany, only seven were founded in the 19th and 20th centuries: Bremerhaven (1827), Ludwigshafen (1843), Leverkusen (1862) and Wilhelmshaven (1869), as well as Wolfsburg (1938), Salzgitter (1942) and Eisenhüttenstadt (1950). The motive for their foundation was either the construction of a port or of an industrial plant.

Wolfsburg lies 75 kilometres east of Hanover. Here it was that the actual »Volkswagen« was to be built before the war. Ferdinand Porsche had specifically designed it for the new factory. But, as the »VW Beetle«, it did not go into serial production until after the war. It was at first produced only for export, but subsequently sparked the German »economic miracle« and, thirty years later, was the most-produced car of all time. Today, VW is one of the globe's largest automobile companies and employs over 300,000 people.

The »Autostadt« or »car city« in Wolfsburg was opened on June 1, 2000, at the same time as the EXPO in Hanover. It is a mixture of leisure park, customer centre and supply depot, where around 120,000 car buyers per year come to pick up their cars personally. In the two round glass towers, both 20 storeys high, 800 cars await their new owners and are automatically retrieved one by one for each customer.

The power station is the factory's energy centre. Across from it stands the five-star Ritz Carlton Hotel. The illuminated square here in the foreground is one of the hotel's attractions: a floating swimming pool, 8 by 40 metres and with a water temperature of 28°C, it is open all year round.

135

HERRENHÄUSER ALLEE, HANNOVER

Was hat der britische Prinz Charles aus dem Hause Windsor mit dem Welfen-Prinzen Ernst August von Hannover gemeinsam? Die Vorfahren. Und was unterscheidet die Verwandten voneinander? Nur Charles kann noch König werden. Die Welfen gehören zu den ältesten Adelsgeschlechtern in Europa, sie haben in Burgund, Kärnten, Sachsen, Spoleto, Bayern, Braunschweig und Hannover regiert. 1714 ist schließlich Großbritannien an die Hannoversche Linie gefallen, und die Welfen haben bis zum Jahr 1901 insgesamt fünf Könige und eine Königin gestellt, zuletzt Queen Victoria (1837-1901); von dieser Linie stammen übrigens die Windsors ab. Die fast zwei Kilometer lange Herrenhäuser Allee ist 1726 als Verbindung zwischen der Stadt Hannover und dem Welfen-Schloss angelegt worden: vier Reihen Lindenbäume und dazwischen ein Weg für Kutschen, einer für Reiter und einer für Fußgänger.

HERRENHÄUSER ALLEE, HANOVER

What do the British Prince Charles of the House of Windsor and the Guelph Prince Ernst August of Hanover have in common? Their ancestors. And the difference between them? The fact that only Charles can become king. The Guelphs belong to the oldest aristocratic dynasties in Europe, with lines reigning in Burgundy, Kärnten, Saxony, Spoleto, Bavaria, Brunswick and Hanover. Finally, in 1714, Great Britain fell to the Hanover line, and Guelphs then sat on the British throne until 1901, with five kings and finally Queen Victoria from 1837 to 1901. The Windsors are, by the way, descendents of this line. In 1726, the Herrenhäuser Allee, almost 2 kilometres long, was built as a link between the city of Hanover and the Guelph castle: four rows of linden trees and, between them, one path for carriages, one for horses and one for pedestrians.

137

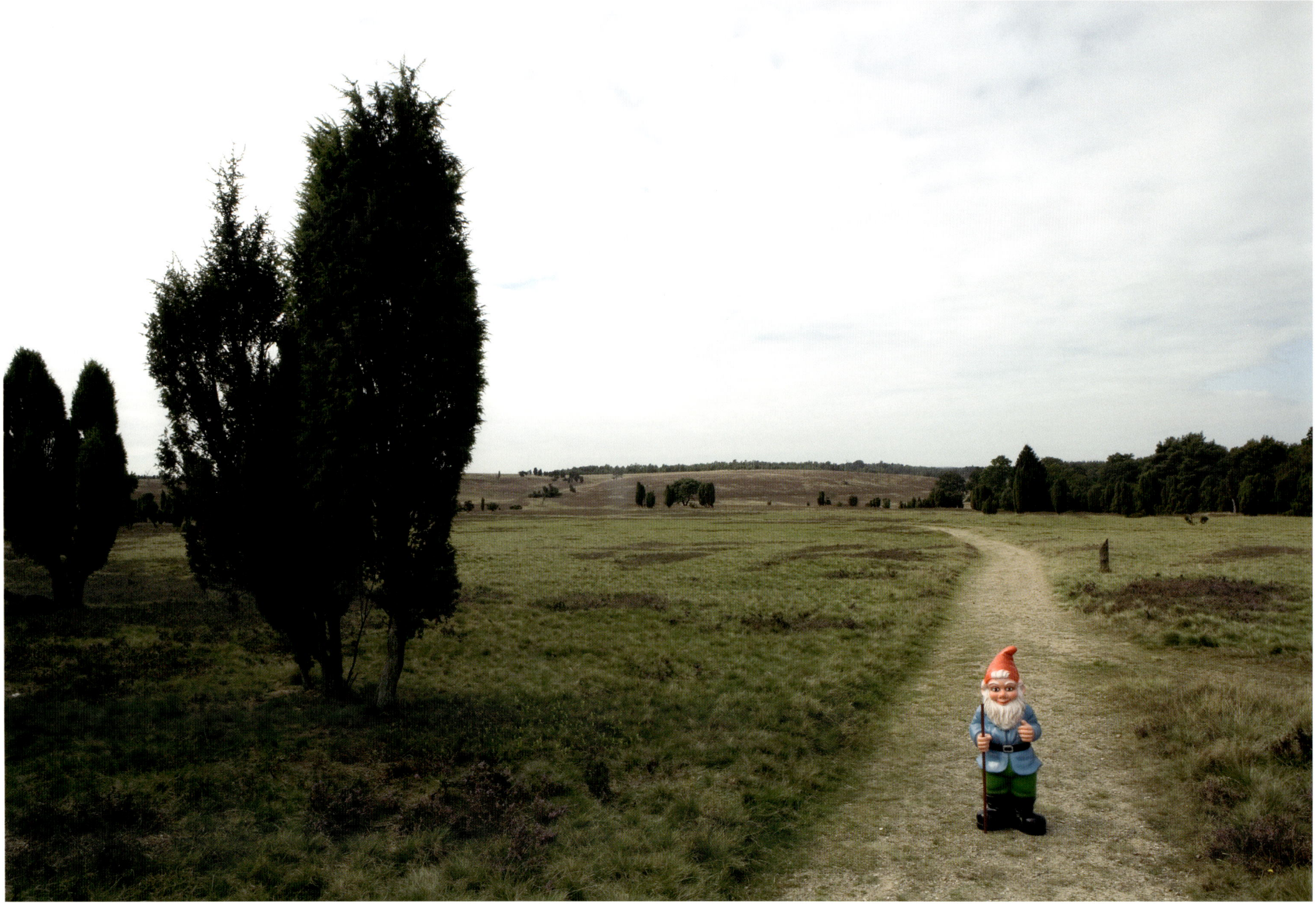

LÜNEBURGER HEIDE

Wer gerne wandert, der wird sich in der Lüneburger Heide ganz besonders wohl fühlen – ein Paradies. Der beliebteste von den vielen Wanderwegen hier ist der »Pastor-Bode-Weg«. Er führt von Egestorf nach Wilsede – oder umgekehrt –, und er heißt so, weil der »Heidepastor« Wilhelm Bode vor über 100 Jahren hier am liebsten spazieren gegangen ist.

Diesem Pfarrer haben wir es hauptsächlich zu verdanken, dass das Naturschutzgebiet Lüneburger Heide mit der Landschaft drum herum heute eines der schönsten in Deutschland ist.

Vor ein paar Millionen Jahren allerdings war die ganze Heide von der Nordsee bedeckt (die hieß damals natürlich noch nicht so). Irgendwann hat sich das Meer zurückgezogen, aber sein Salz hat es hier gelassen. Über 1000 Jahre haben die Menschen dieses Salz aus der Erde geholt, und es hat Städten wie Lüneburg, Celle oder Gifhorn jahrhundertelang Wohlstand gebracht.

Was kaum noch einer weiß: Keine 50 Kilometer südlich von hier, in Wietze, ist 1859 Erdöl gefunden worden, und zwar früher als irgendwo sonst auf der Welt; erst ein paar Monate später haben die Amerikaner in Pennsylvania ihre erste Quelle entdeckt. 1908 kamen 80 Prozent der deutschen Ölproduktion aus dieser Gegend, aber in den 60er Jahren war damit Schluss.

Öl gibt's hier also schon lange nicht mehr, nur noch ein Ölmuseum, dafür aber Schafe, die heißen hier »Heidschnucken«, Wacholder, Pferde, Bienen, Hühnengräber, Birken, Torf und natürlich – Heidekraut. Und wenn das blüht, im August und September, ist die Heide am allerschönsten. Wer ein paar Tage Zeit hat, der sollte dann mal zum Wandern hierher kommen. In diesem Jahr war die Heideblüte früher als sonst, und deshalb war ich leider ein, zwei Wochen zu spät hier.

LÜNEBURG HEATH

Anyone who enjoys long walks will feel right at home in the Lüneburg Heath – a veritable paradise. The favourite among the many hiking trails is probably the »Pastor-Bode-Weg«. It runs from Egestorf to Wilsede – or vice versa – and was named after the »heath pastor« Wilhelm Bode, who, over 100 years ago particularly loved to walk here.

It is this pastor we mostly have to thank for the fact that the nature reserve of the Lüneburg Heath and its surrounding countryside is today one of the loveliest in all of Germany.

Several million years ago, however, the North Sea (before it even had such a name) covered the entire heath. At some time or other, the sea withdrew but left its salt behind. For over 1000 years man has extracted salt from its soil, which for centuries brought prosperity to cities such as Lüneburg, Celle and Gifhorn.

What almost no one remembers: less than 50 kilometres south of here, oil was found in Wietze in 1859, and this earlier than anywhere else in the world. Not till a couple of months later did the Americans in Pennsylvania discover their first well. In 1908, 80 percent of Germany's oil was produced in this region, but it all came to an end in the 1960s.

There has been no oil here for a long time, only an oil museum. Instead there are sheep (known there as »Heidschnucken« or moorland sheep), junipers, horses, bees, dolmens, birches, peat and – naturally – heather. And when it is in bloom – in August and September – the moorland is at its most beautiful. Anyone with a few days free should make it a point to come here for long strolls. This year, the heather bloomed earlier than usual, so that I was unfortunately here one or two weeks too late.

TEUFELSMOOR

Wenn den Menschen irgendwas nicht so ganz geheuer ist, schieben sie es gern dem Teufel in die Schuhe. Es gibt den Teufelsdreck, das Teufelsei, die Teufelsinsel, die Teufelskralle oder den Seeteufel, es gibt Teufelskerle, Teufelsmessen, Teufelskreise, Teufelsschluchten und noch viele andere verteufelte Sachen. Und es gibt das Teufelsmoor.

Mit dem Teufel hatte dieses Moor ursprünglich allerdings wirklich nichts zu tun, es hieß früher »Dovelsmoor«, und damit war einfach eine »taube«, unfruchtbare Landschaft gemeint, wo es keine Bäume, keine Sträucher und keine Tiere gab und wo man auch nichts anbauen konnte: keine Kartoffeln, kein Gemüse, kein Getreide. Das ist in den letzten 250 Jahren aber anders geworden, das Moor wurde entwässert, besiedelt und bebaut. Weil's hier jedoch wie in jedem Moor tatsächlich immer wieder mal ein bisschen unheimlich wird, hatte es seinen Namen bald ein für alle Mal weg.

Das Teufelsmoor erstreckt sich nordöstlich von Bremen über eine Fläche von rund 500 Quadratkilometern. Am Südrand liegt das Dorf Worpswede. Es ist am Ende des 19. Jahrhunderts bekannt geworden, als sich viele Maler und Schriftsteller hier niedergelassen haben: Otto und Paula Modersohn, Heinrich Vogeler, Fritz Overbeck, Rainer Maria Rilke und Manfred Hausmann. Bis heute ist Worpswede der schönste Ausgangspunkt für die Erkundung des Teufelsmoors.

DEVIL'S MOOR

When something appears somewhat awesome, we tend to pin the blame on the devil. There is devil's dirt, devil's spawn, Devil's Island, devil's darning needle or dragonfly, devilfish (monkfish); there are daredevils, devil worship, devil's advocate, devil's gorges and many other devilish items. And there is Teufelsmoor (Devil's Moor).

However, this moor originally had nothing at all to do with the devil; it used to be called »Dovelsmoor«, which simply meant »empty« or infertile land, where no tree, bush or animal could thrive and where you could not get anything to grow: neither potatoes, vegetables nor grain. But this has changed over the past 250 years; the moor has been drained, settled and built on. But because here, as on every moor, it really does get rather eerie at times, the name simply stuck, once and for all.

Devil's Moor stretches northeast of Bremen, across an area of approximately 500 square kilometres. On its southern border lies the village of Worpswede, which became famous at the end of the 19th century when many painters and writers settled here: Otto and Paula Modersohn, Heinrich Vogeler, Franz Overbeck, Rainer Maria Rilke and Manfred Hausmann. And still today, Worpswede is the loveliest starting point for exploring Devil's Moor.

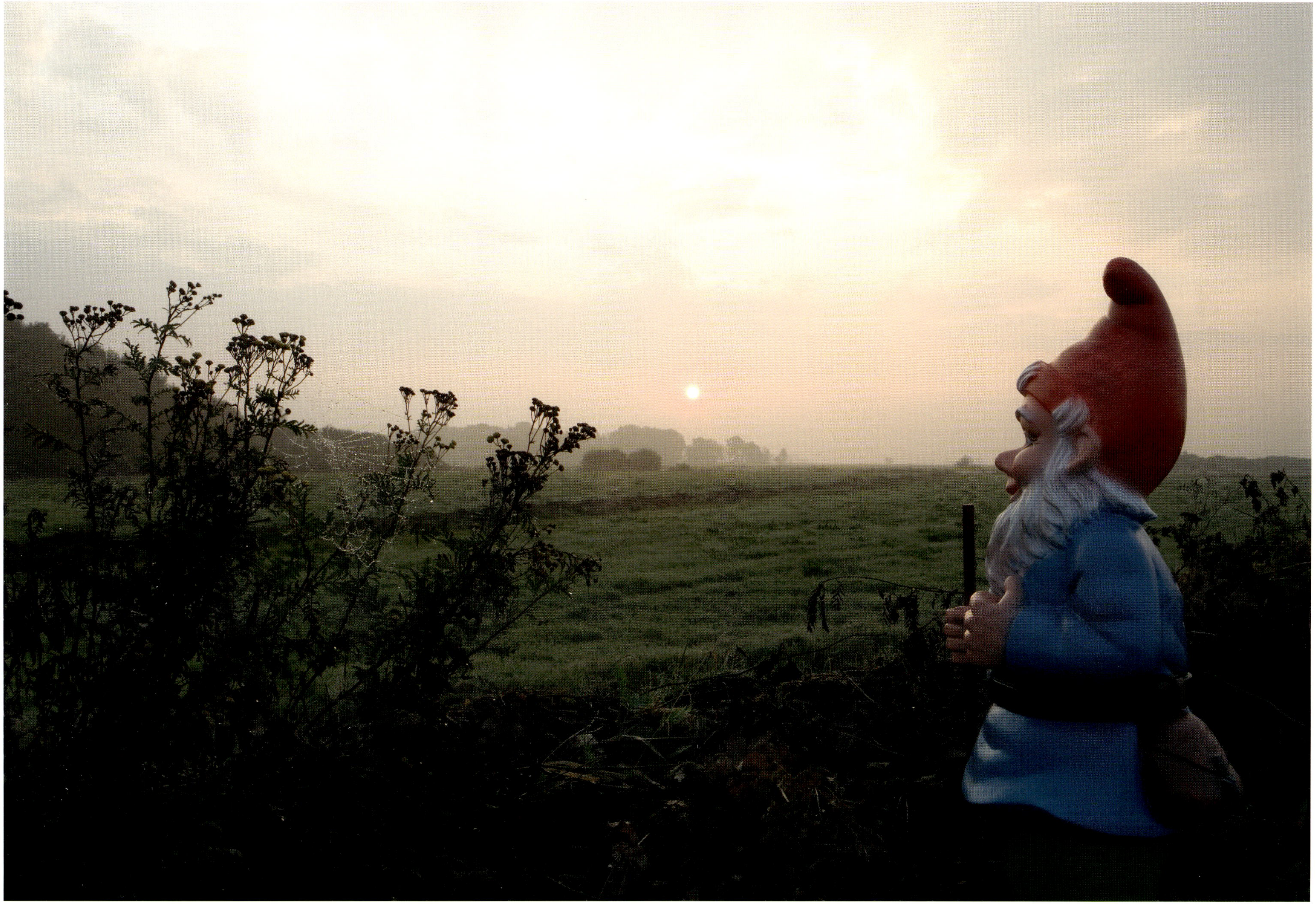

KLAPPBRÜCKE, WESTRHAUDERFEHN

In Ostfriesland – das ist der nordwestliche Teil von Niedersachsen – gehen die Uhren anders. Das kann man schon daran erkennen, dass die Ostfriesen zehnmal mehr Tee trinken als die übrigen Deutschen. In der Stadt Norden haben sie für ihr Nationalgetränk sogar ein Museum eingerichtet. Und sie treiben sonderbare Sportarten wie Boßeln, Klootschießen oder Pultstockspringen. Sie sprechen auch ein bisschen anders und können sich mit einem Holländer vermutlich leichter verständigen als mit einem Rheinländer, von Bayern oder Sachsen gar nicht erst zu reden.

Ostfriesland ist auch flacher als die südlichen Gegenden von Deutschland, der Wind weht meistens ungebremst vom Meer herein. Da kann es einen kaum überraschen, dass der größte deutsche Hersteller von Windkraftanlagen seinen Sitz in Aurich hat.

Westrhauderfehn liegt im Westen von Ostfriesland, nicht weit von Papenburg. Fehn (auch Veen, Fenn oder Venn) ist das niederdeutsche Wort für Moor. Die Ostfriesen haben schon vor Jahrhunderten angefangen, das Moor zu entwässern und Torf abzubauen. Dazu mussten sie Kanäle ziehen, durch die das Wasser abfließen konnte und auf denen sie den Torf abtransportierten. Wegen der vielen Kanäle mussten sie auch viele Brücken bauen. Aber nicht aufwändig, sondern einfach und niedrig. Wenn ein Schiff kommt, werden sie hochgeklappt. Solche Brücken kennt man ja auch aus Holland, die Grenze ist keine halbe Stunde von hier entfernt.

Von den vielen bedeutenden Persönlichkeiten, die die ostfriesische Lebensart in die Welt getragen haben, will ich nur eine nennen: Minnie Schönberg aus Dornum. Sie fuhr 1875 mit ihren Eltern nach New York, heiratete den Elsässer Simon Marrix und bekam fünf Söhne: Milton, Herbert, Leonard, Adolph Arthur und Julius Henry, besser bekannt als die Marx-Brothers.

BASCULE BRIDGE, WESTRHAUDERFEHN

In East Friesland – which is the northwest part of Lower Saxony – clocks tick to a different rhythm. You can easily recognize this by the fact that the East Frisians drink ten times more tea than all other Germans. In the town of Norden, they have even set up a museum for their national beverage. And they go in for peculiar sports such as Booßeln, Klootschießen (both ball-throwing games), or Pultstockspringen (pole vaulting over water). They also speak a different dialect and can presumably communicate more easily with a Dutchman than with someone from the Rhine or Bavaria, not to mention from Saxony.

East Friesland is also flatter than the southern regions of Germany; the wind blows in from the sea unhindered. It should thus hardly be surprising that Germany's biggest manufacturer of wind power plants has its headquarters in Aurich.

Westrhauderfehn lies in the west of East Friesland, not far from Papenburg. Fehn (also Veen, Fenn or Venn) is the Low German word for marsh or fen. Centuries ago, the East Frisians had already begun to drain the marshes and harvest the peat. To do so, they had to create canals through which the water could flow off and by which they could transport the peat. Many canals mean many bridges. Not anything lavish, but simple and low-built. When a ship passes, they are swung up. Such bridges are also familiar to us from Holland, and the border with Holland is less than half an hour away.

Of the many important personalities who have carried the East Frisian way of life out into the world, I will only mention one: Minnie Schönberg from Dornum. In 1875 she sailed to New York with her parents, married Simon Marrix from Alsace and bore him five sons: Milton, Herbert, Leonard, Adolph Arthur and Julius Henry, better known as the Marx-Brothers.

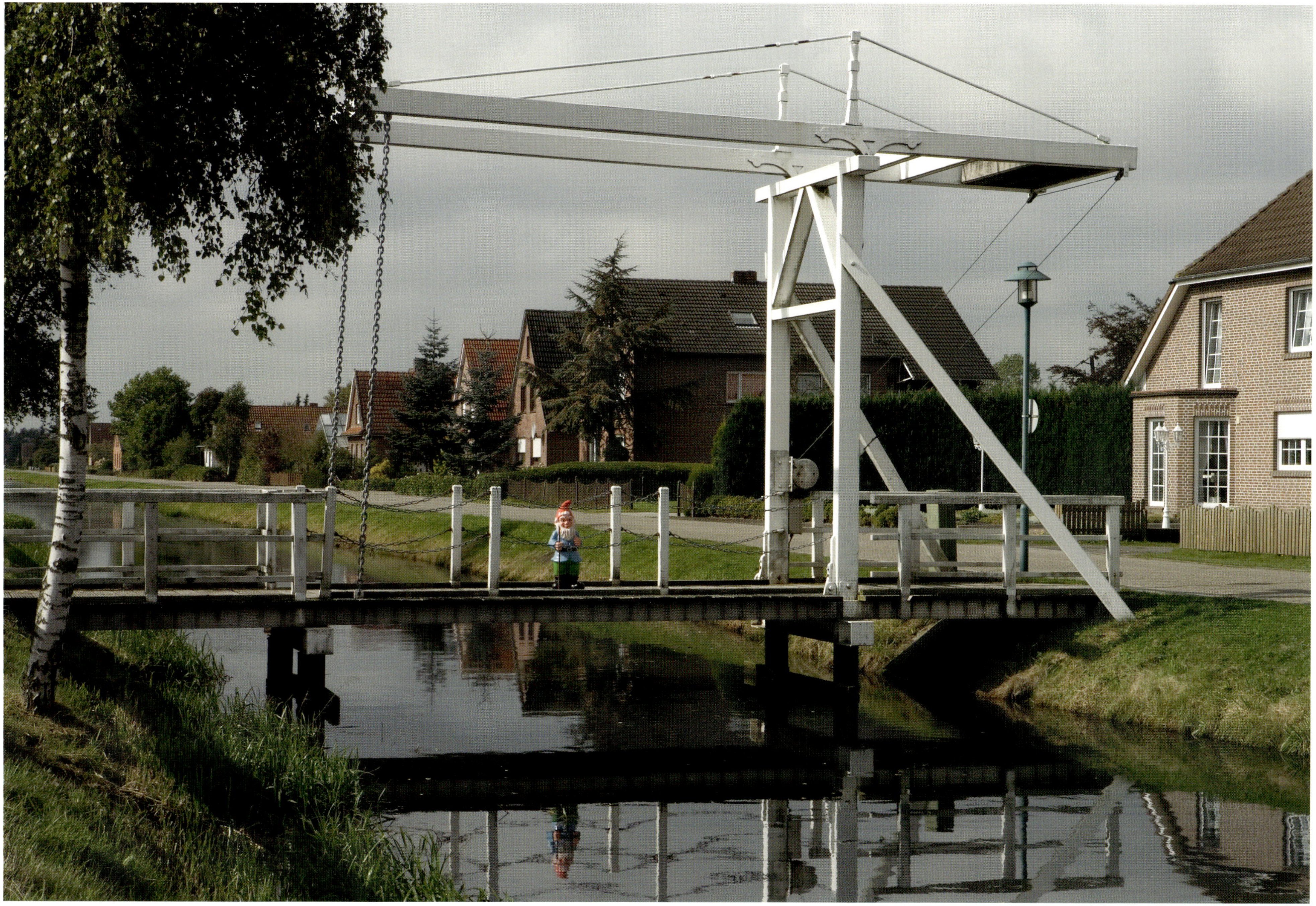

MEYER-WERFT, PAPENBURG

Könnt ihr euch vorstellen, wie man ein 300 Meter langes Schiff baut? 40 Meter breit und 60 Meter hoch? – Ich nicht. Und ich war immerhin auf der Meyer-Werft in Papenburg und hab's mit eigenen Augen gesehen. Hier läuft seit vielen Jahren eine Fähre nach der anderen, ein Kreuzfahrtschiff nach dem anderen vom Stapel; bis zu 180.000 Registertonnen können die groß werden. (Ich hab' extra noch mal ins Lexikon geschaut: Eine Registertonne – heute sagt man Raumzahl – hat 100 Kubikfuß, das sind genau 2,8316847 Kubikmeter.)

Das Ungewöhnliche ist: Die Werft liegt nicht an der Küste, so wie fast alle anderen großen Werften auf der Welt, sondern weit im Landesinnern, und die fertigen Schiffe müssen erst einmal 36 Kilometer über die ausgebaggerte Ems gezogen werden, bevor sie endlich ihre eigenen Maschinen anwerfen können.

Als das anfing mit der Meyer-Werft, im Jahr 1795, da waren die Schiffe vielleicht 20, 30 oder 40 Meter lang, sie hießen Ewer, Kuff, Schoner, Prahme, Schnau oder Tjalk, und zum Vorwärtskommen brauchten sie noch keine Maschinen und keine Schiffsschrauben, sondern Wind.

Weil man mit einer Werft aber nicht so leicht umziehen kann wie mit einer Schlosserei oder einer Schreinerei, sind die Meyers eben in Papenburg geblieben, und ihre Werft ist immer weiter gewachsen. In den beiden großen Hallen könnte man ganz bequem acht Fußballspiele gleichzeitig austragen.

MEYER SHIPYARD, PAPENBURG

Can you imagine how a 300-meter-long ship is built? Forty metres wide and sixty metres high? – I can't. And, after all, I was actually at the Meyer Shipyard in Papenburg and saw it with my own eyes. For many years now, one ferry after another, one cruise ship after another has been launched from here: up to 180,000 register tons. (I specifically looked it up in the encyclopaedia: a register ton – today we call it a unit of volume – is 100 cubic feet, which are exactly 2.8316847 cubic metres.)

What is really unusual: the shipyard is not even located on the coast, unlike nearly all other large shipyards in the world, but far inland, and the ships, when completed, have to be pulled 36 kilometres along the dredged out Ems River before they can finally switch on their engines and move under their own power.

When the Meyer Shipyard started up in the year 1795, the ships were perhaps 20, 30, 40 metres long; they were named Ewer, Kuff, Schoner, Prahme, Schnau or Tjalk, and to move forward they needed neither engines nor ship's screws, but wind.

Because you can't move a shipyard as easily as a locksmith's or a carpenter's workshop, the Meyers just stayed put in Papenburg, while the yard got bigger and bigger. In the two giant hangars, you could quite easily put on eight soccer games simultaneously.

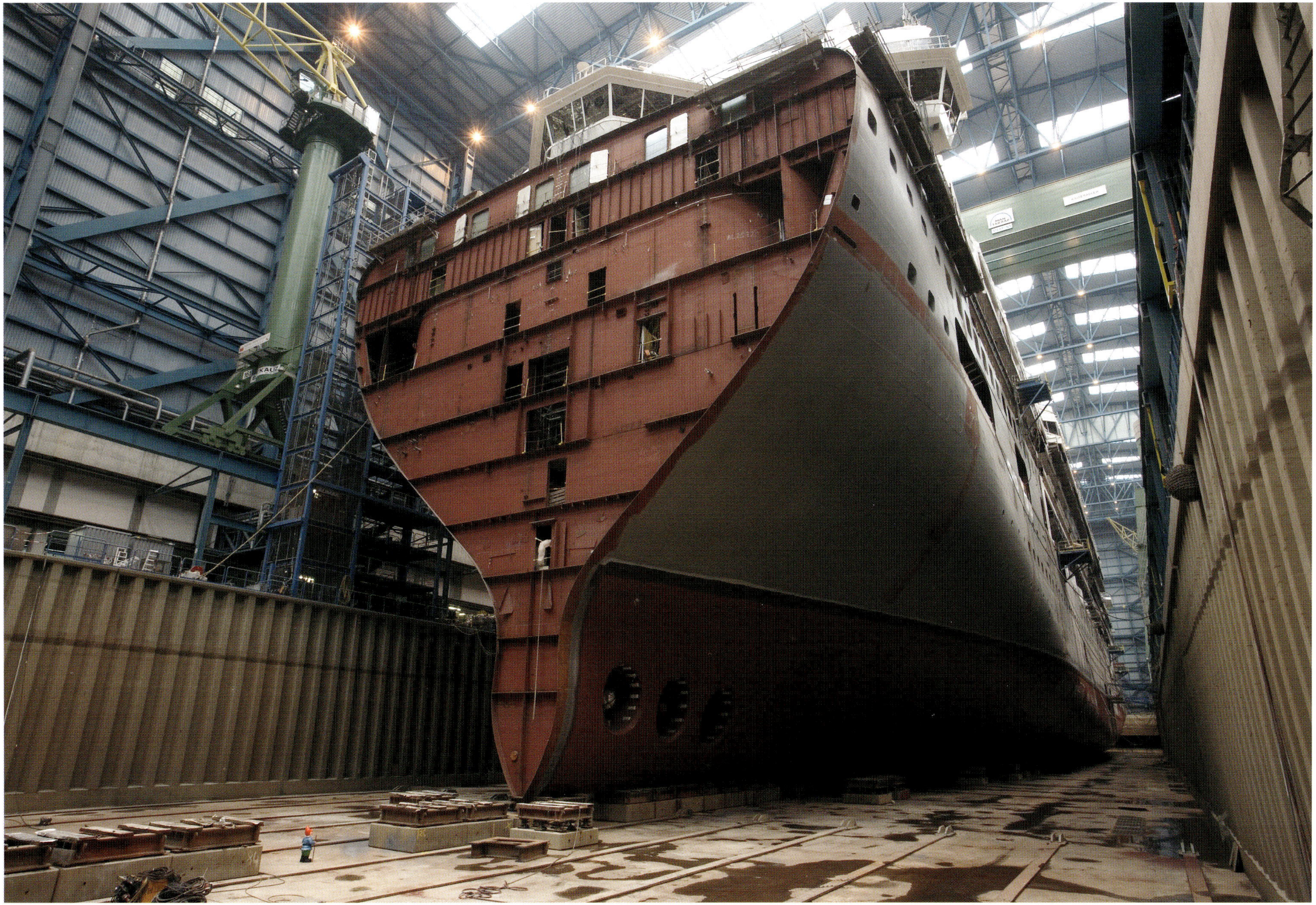

EMSLANDSCHAFT, DITZUM

Früher dachten die Menschen ja, die Erde wäre eine Scheibe. Dann hat ihnen vor ein paar hundert Jahren jemand bewiesen, dass sie in Wirklichkeit eine Kugel ist. Der kam aber ganz bestimmt nicht aus Ditzum, Hatzum, Critzum, Midlum, Jemgum oder Bingum, aus der Gegend also, wo die Ems in den Dollart fließt und anschließend um Borkum, Juist und Norderney herum in die Nordsee.

Hier, wo ich grade stehe und nach Westen schaue – keine 50 Kilometer geradeaus liegt übrigens Groningen –, hier käme kein Mensch auf die Idee mit der Kugel. Hier kann man sich auch heute noch wie vor tausend Jahren gut vorstellen, dass es so flach weiter geht und immer weiter, bis man eines Tages an den Rand der Erde kommt. Und wenn man dort nicht aufpasst, fällt man runter. Auch heute noch.

THE EMS COUNTRYSIDE, DITZUM

People used to think that the earth was flat. Then a couple of hundred years ago, someone proved to them that it was actually round. But this person quite certainly did not come from Ditzum, Hatzum, Critzum, Midlum, Jemgum or Bingum, that is, from the region where the Ems River flows into the Dollart and from there around Borkum, Juist and Nordeney and into the North Sea.

Here, just where I'm standing and looking westwards – where, incidentally, less than 50 kilometres in this direction Groningen lies – no one would ever get the idea that the earth is a sphere. Here you can still easily imagine, today, just as people did a thousand years ago, that it is a flat disc and goes on and on until, one day, you come to the edge of the earth. And if you don't take care, you can fall off. Even today.

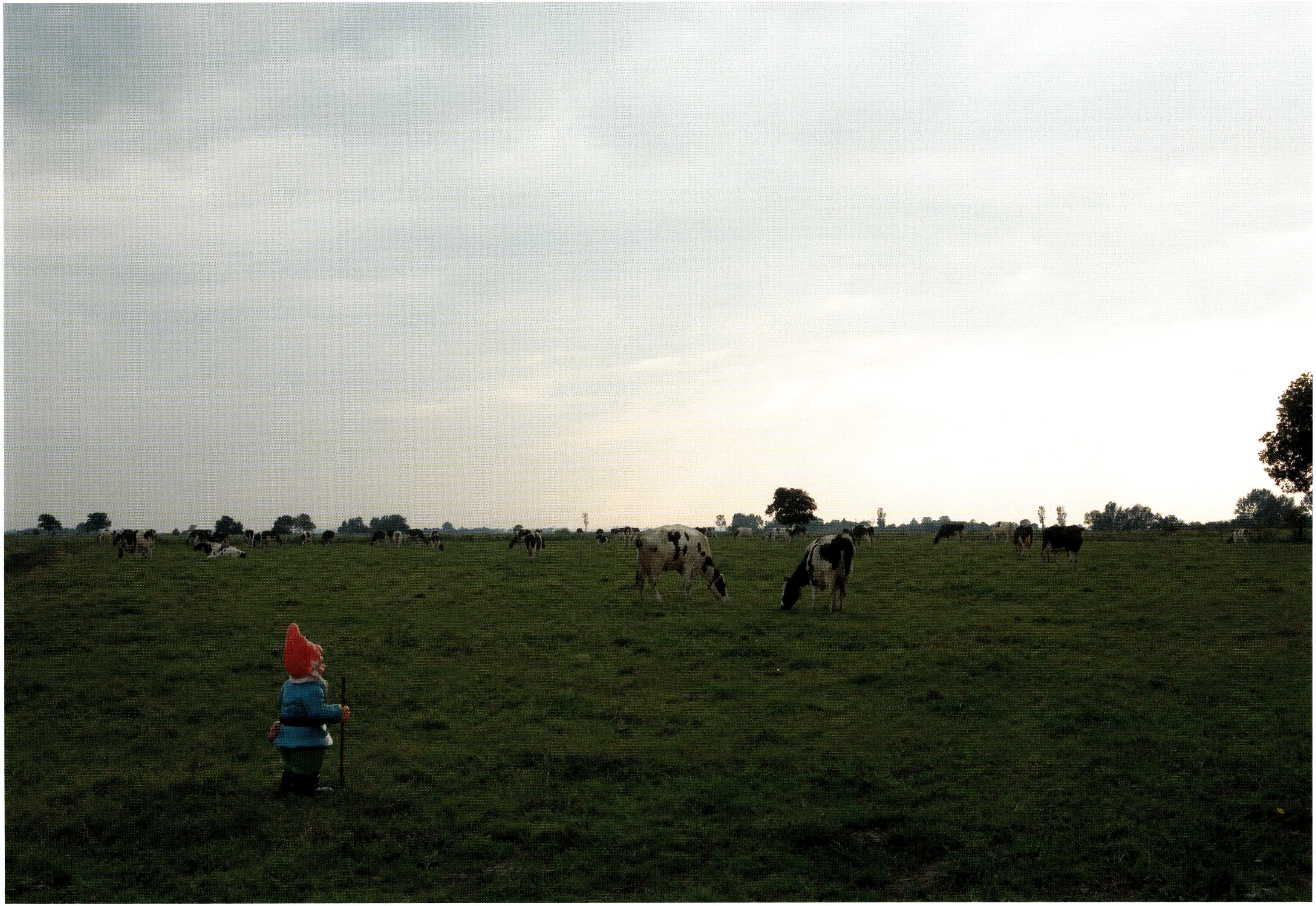

ZWILLINGSMÜHLEN, GREETSIEL

Auch wenn ich auf dem Bild vielleicht nicht sehr betrübt aussehe – in Greetsiel hatten die Menschen an diesem Tag Grund zur Trauer. Warum, das könnt ihr hinter mir an den beiden Windmühlen – Typ »Zweistöckiger Galeriehollander« – erkennen: Die Flügel stehen in der »Trauerschere«, 30 Grad rechts vom Turm. Am Tag zuvor ist nämlich Lükko Schoof gestorben, der alte Müllermeister, der hier jahrzehntelang gearbeitet hat. Das habe ich aber erst später erfahren.

Mit den Windmühlenflügeln werden auch noch andere Signale gegeben. Die Flügel stehen senkrecht: kurze Arbeitspause; die Flügel stehen im Winkel von 45 Grad: lange Arbeitspause; die Flügel stehen 30 Grad links vom Turm: »Freudenschere«, dann feiert jemand Hochzeit, oder ein Kind ist geboren worden.

In Lükko Schoofs roter Mühle wird bis heute mit Windkraft oder, wenn der Wind mal ausbleibt, mit Motorkraft Getreide zu Schrot oder Mehl gemahlen. Das kann man dort auch kaufen, pfundweise oder zu Brot und anderen gesunden Sachen verbacken; nur mit dem Kornmahlen allein lässt sich eine solche Mühle heute nicht mehr unterhalten.

Die andere Mühle ist 1972 bei einem Sturm so schwer beschädigt worden, dass sie nicht mehr genutzt werden konnte. Der »Verein zur Erhaltung der Greetsieler Zwillingsmühlen« hat sie gekauft und instand gesetzt und betreibt im Erdgeschoss eine Teestube und obendrüber eine Galerie.

THE TWIN MILLS, GREETSIEL

Even if on this picture I don't look especially sad, the people of Greetsiel had reason enough to mourn on this day. Why? You can see why from the two windmills behind me – of the type »two-storey Dutch gallery«. Their blades are fixed at a »mourning scissors« position, 30 degrees to the right of the tower. You see, Lükko Schoof, the old master miller who worked here for decades, had died the day before. But I didn't find that out till later.

The blades of the windmill are also used to send other signals: vertical blades mean a short workbreak; blades at a 45-degree angle: long workbreak; blades at 30 degrees to the left of the tower: a »happy-scissors« position that is reserved for a wedding celebration or the birth of a child.

Lükko Schoof's red mill today still grinds grain to coarse meal or flour by wind power or, when the wind fails, by motor power. You can buy these products here by the pound or ready-baked as bread and other healthy things. But such a mill cannot be maintained today only by grinding grains.

The other mill was so badly damaged in a storm in 1972 that it could no longer be used. The »Society for Maintaining the Greetsiel Twin Mills« bought and restored it, and today a tearoom is located on the ground floor, with an art gallery above it.

149

PRINZIPALMARKT, MÜNSTER

Die Münsteraner fahren dreimal mehr Fahrrad als die Einwohner in anderen Städten von ähnlicher Größe. Hier sind die Fahrradwege besser organisiert und ausgebaut als irgendwo sonst, es gibt sogar eine »Fahrrad-Autobahn« (komisches Wort), und man sieht immer wieder Städte- und Verkehrsplaner aus aller Welt, die sich mitten in Westfalen ansehen, wie man so was am besten macht.

Ihr seht mich hier auf dem Prinzipalmarkt in Münster, hinter mir die gotische Rathausfassade, rechts von mir die Lambertikirche. An ihrem Turm sind 1536 die grausam hingerichteten Anführer der Wiedertäufer, Knipperdolling, Bockelsohn und Krechting, zur Abschreckung in einem Eisenkäfig aufgehängt worden; dieser Käfig hängt immer noch dort oben.

Das Rathaus von Münster ist ein Ort mit besonderer Bedeutung für die europäische Geschichte. Um den Dreißigjährigen Krieg zu beenden, haben sich die beteiligten Parteien Frankreich und Schweden mit ihren Verbündeten und dem deutschen Kaiser vier Jahre lang in Münster und in Osnabrück versammelt. Dabei haben sie einen Vertrag ausgehandelt, mit dem das völlig verwüstete Europa neu geordnet werden sollte. Am 24. Oktober 1648 ist im später so genannten Friedenssaal direkt hinter mir der »Westfälische Friede« geschlossen worden.

Im Zweiten Weltkrieg haben Bomben das Rathaus vollkommen zerstört. Das wollten die Bürger von Münster aber nicht so einfach hinnehmen und haben 1950 mit dem Wiederaufbau begonnen. Knapp die Hälfte des Geldes dafür, 770.000 Mark, haben sie mit der »Rathauslotterie« selbst aufgebracht. Am 30. Oktober 1958, 310 Jahre nach der Verkündigung des »Westfälischen Friedens«, stand das Rathaus von Münster wieder genauso prächtig da wie im 17. Jahrhundert.

PRINZIPALMARKT, MÜNSTER

The people of Münster ride bicycles three times as much as the inhabitants of other cities of similar size. Here, the bicycle paths are better organized and designed than in other places, and there is even a »Bicycle Autobahn« (a funny term), and you can often see city and traffic planners from around the world who have come right to the heart of Westphalia to observe how best to learn from its example.

I am standing here at the Prinzipal marketplace in Münster, behind me the façade of the Gothic Rathaus, to my left the Lamberti Church. From its tower in 1536, the brutally executed leaders of the Anabaptists (Knipperdolling, Bockelsohn and Krechting) were hoisted up in iron cages to awe and deter the populace. The cages still hang there.

The Münster Rathaus or Town Hall has a special meaning in European history. With the intention of ending the Thirty Years War, the participating parties – France and Sweden with their allies, and the German emperor – assembled for four years in Münster and in Osnabrück. They worked out a treaty that was to create a new order for a thoroughly devastated Europe. On October 24, 1648, in the Peace Room (later so named), which is directly behind me, the »Treaty of Westphalia« was signed.

During World War II, bombs thoroughly destroyed the Town Hall. But Münster's citizens didn't want to leave it at that and began, in 1950, to rebuild it. They raised just short of half the sum needed themselves, DM 770,000, via the Rathaus Lottery. On October 30, 1958 – 310 years after the »Peace of Westphalia« was announced – their town hall looked just as magnificent as it did in the 17th century.

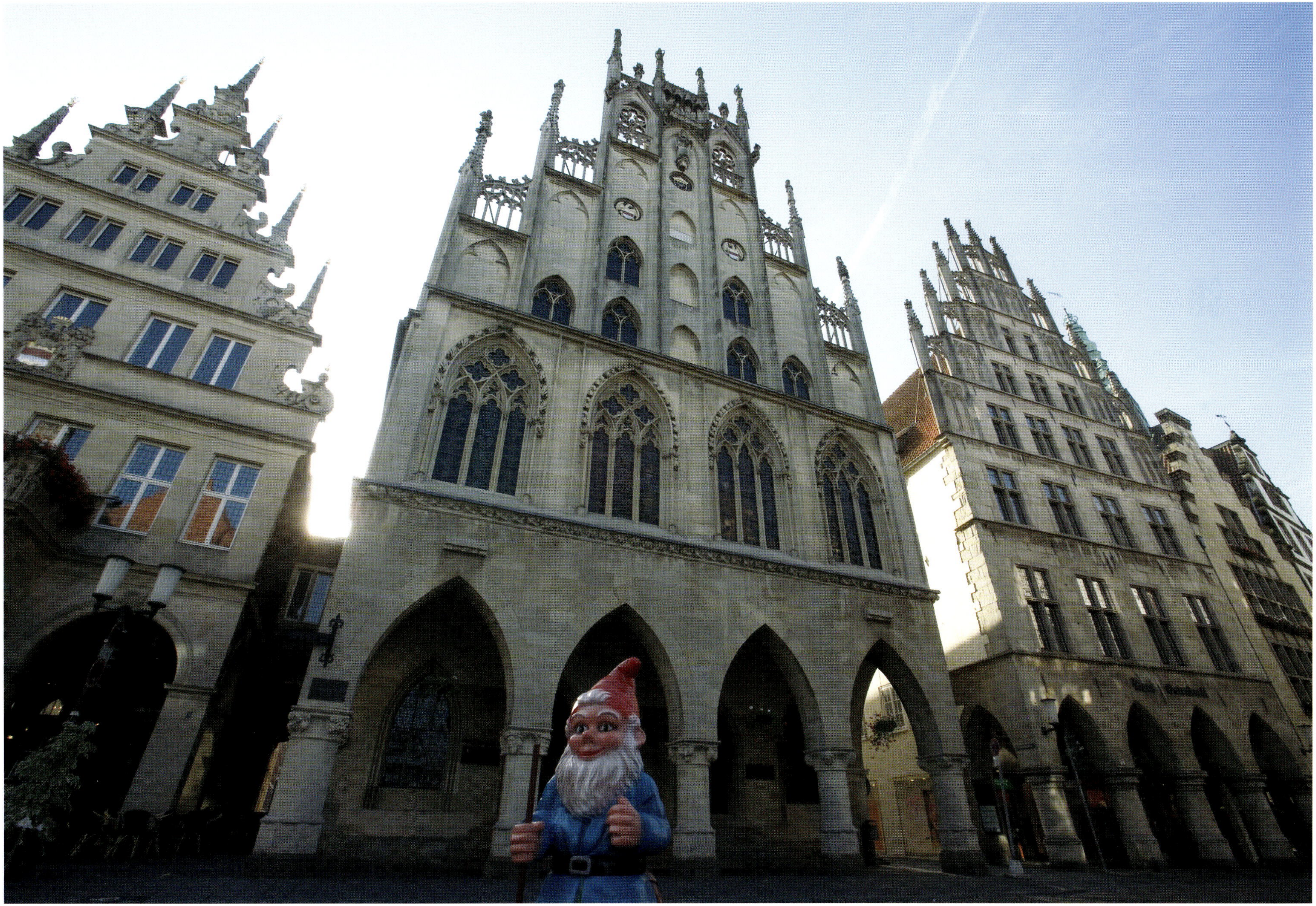

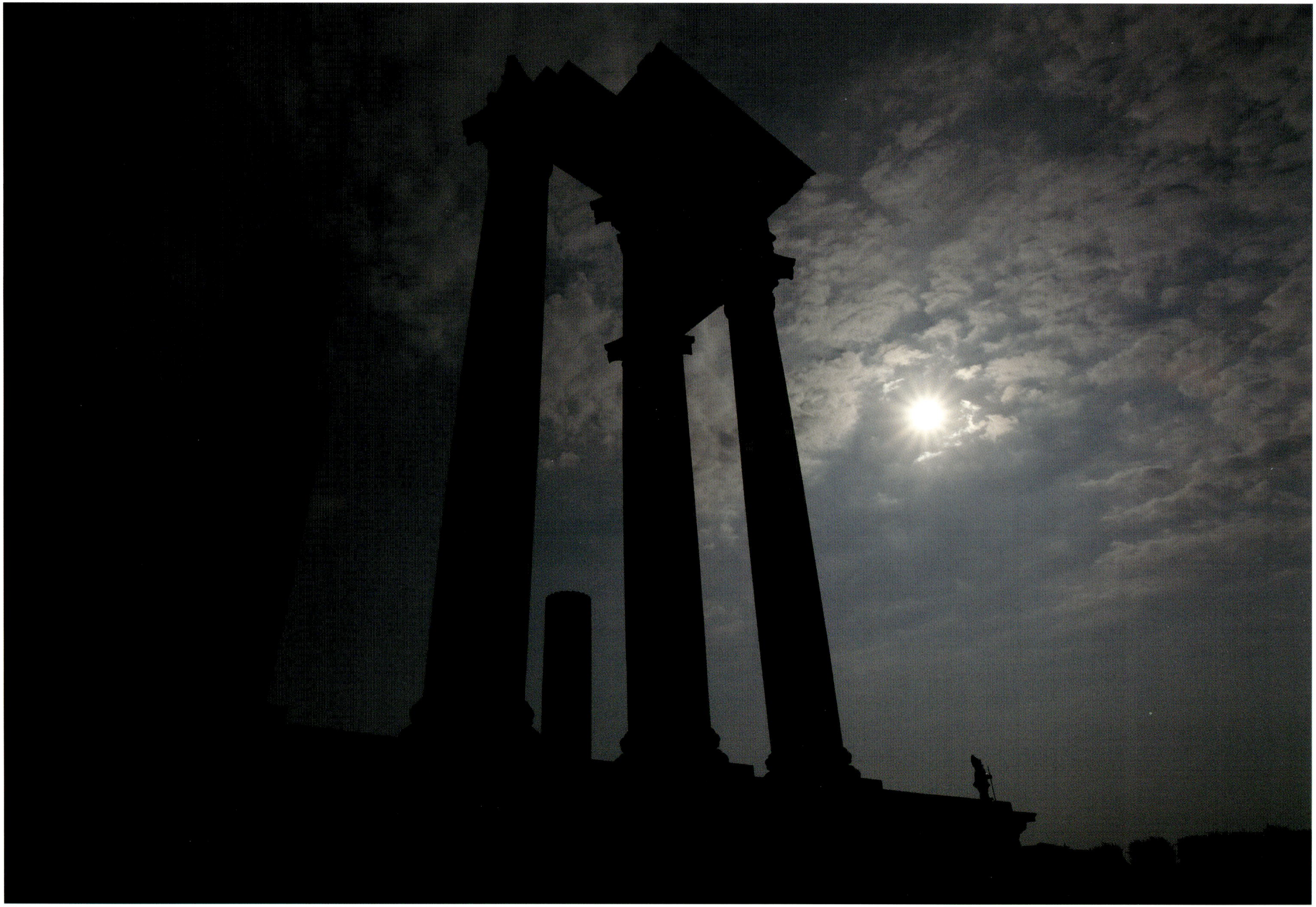

ARCHÄOLOGISCHER PARK, XANTEN

Überall wo die Römer vor 2000 Jahren hinkamen, und sie kamen ja fast überall hin, haben sie neben ihren Legionen auch ihre Kultur mitgebracht, ihre Ingenieure und Stadtplaner, ihre Architekten, ihre Götter und ihren Komfort. Im 2. Jahrhundert n. Chr. hatte das Römische Reich unter Kaiser Trajan seine größte Ausdehnung: von Ägypten bis nach Britannien und von Spanien bis nach Mesopotamien.

Damals gab es ungefähr 150 Städte, die sich »Colonia« nennen durften. Das war eine Auszeichnung, denn sie besagte, dass die jeweilige Stadt eine Stellvertreterin der Hauptstadt war. Wer hier lebte, war Bürger Roms.

Köln war zum Beispiel so eine Stadt und auch Xanten. Das hieß damals Colonia Ulpia Traiana und war so etwas wie die Metropole der Provinz Niedergermanien. Nach dem Untergang des Römischen Reiches ist auch Ulpia Traiana bald verfallen. Ganz in der Nähe ist im 8. Jahrhundert eine Kirche mit einem Stift gebaut worden, »Ad sanctos«, zu den Heiligen. Daraus wurde zuerst Xanctum, dann Xantum und schließlich Xanten.

Von der Colonia Ulpia Traiana war im 20. Jahrhundert nichts mehr zu sehen – bis auf die Fundamente eines Amphitheaters vor einem südlich gelegenen Militärlager. Alles andere war im Laufe der Jahrhunderte abgetragen und zum Bau von Xanten, seit 1263 vor allem des Xantener Doms verwendet worden. Über den Fundamenten der Römerstadt lag schließlich eine dicke Erdschicht. Ein Glücksfall für die Archäologen: Nach jahrzehntelangen Grabungen ist 1977 der Archäologische Park Xanten eröffnet worden.

Bei den Bauwerken, die heute dort zu sehen sind, handelt es sich nicht um echte Ruinen, sondern um moderne Rekonstruktionen auf den alten römischen Fundamenten.

ARCHAEOLOGICAL PARK, XANTEN

Wherever the Romans went 2000 years ago – and they went almost everywhere – they not only brought their legions, but also their culture, their engineers, their fortress builders and city planners, their architects, their gods and their taste for comfort. In the 2nd century A.D., the Roman Empire under Emperor Trajan underwent its greatest expansion: from Egypt to Brittany, from Spain to Mesopotamia.

At that time, there were around 150 cities that were allowed to call themselves »Colonia«. This was an honour, for it meant that the so-named towns stood in for the capital. Whoever lived in them was a citizen of Rome.

Cologne, for instance, was just such a city, and so was Xanten. It was then called Colonia Ulpia Traiana and was something like the metropolis of the province of Lower Germania. After the fall of the Roman Empire, Ulpia Traiana also soon declined. In the eighth century quite close by, a church with a monastery was built and called »Ad sanctos«, or to the saints. The name then became Xanctum, then Xantum and finally Xanten.

In the 20th century, nothing more could be seen of the Colonia Ulpia Traiana – except for the foundations of an amphitheatre in front of a military camp that lay to the south. Everything else had, over the centuries, been carted off to build Xanten, and particularly, from 1263 onwards, the Xanten cathedral. A thick layer of soil slowly covered the foundations of the Roman city, preserving it. This was a stroke of luck for archaeologists: after decades of digging, the Archaeological Park Xanten was opened in 1977.

As for the constructions that can be seen there today, they are not genuine ruins, but rather modern reconstructions upon the old Roman foundations.

ZOO, KREFELD

Es hat eine ganze Weile gedauert, bis ich gemerkt habe, was das Besondere ist am Krefelder Zoo. Er ist vor allen Dingen ein zoologischer *Garten* oder, noch besser: ein zoologischer *Park*. Und ich hatte bei meinem Besuch den Eindruck, als würde der Besitzer auch irgendwo hier wohnen.

Und so ist es früher tatsächlich einmal gewesen. Der Zoo ist nämlich in der Mitte des 19. Jahrhunderts in einem Park um ein kleines privates Schloss herum entstanden, das Grotenburg-Schlösschen, das sich der Krefelder Seidenfabrikant Moritz de Greiff 1846 als Sommersitz gebaut hat. (Krefeld ist seit Jahrhunderten das Zentrum der Samt- und Seidenweberei in Deutschland.) Das Schlösschen gibt es immer noch, und wenn man Glück hat, stehen ein paar Dutzend Flamingos davor.

Seit 1877 konnten auch die Krefelder Bürger den Zoo besuchen, bis 1914, dann wurde er geschlossen. 24 Jahre später ist er als städtischer Zoo wieder eröffnet worden, ein Tier*park* ist er aber zum Glück immer noch.

ZOO, KREFELD

It took awhile before I noticed what was so special about the zoo in Krefeld. It is, above all things, a zoological *garden* or, better still, a zoological *park*. And during my visit I got the impression that the owner was also living somewhere around here.

And that is, in fact, the way it once was. The zoo came about in the mid-19th century, namely within a park surrounding a small private castle, the Grotenburg Schlösschen, which the Krefeld silk manufacturer, Moritz de Greiff, built in 1846 as a summer residence. (Krefeld has, for centuries, been the centre for velvet and silk weaving in Germany.) The mini-castle still exists and, if you're lucky, you'll see a few dozen flamingos standing around in front of it.

From 1877, the Krefeld citizens were able to visit the zoo, up until 1914, when it was closed. 24 years later it was re-opened as the city zoo, but is still, happily, a zoological *park*.

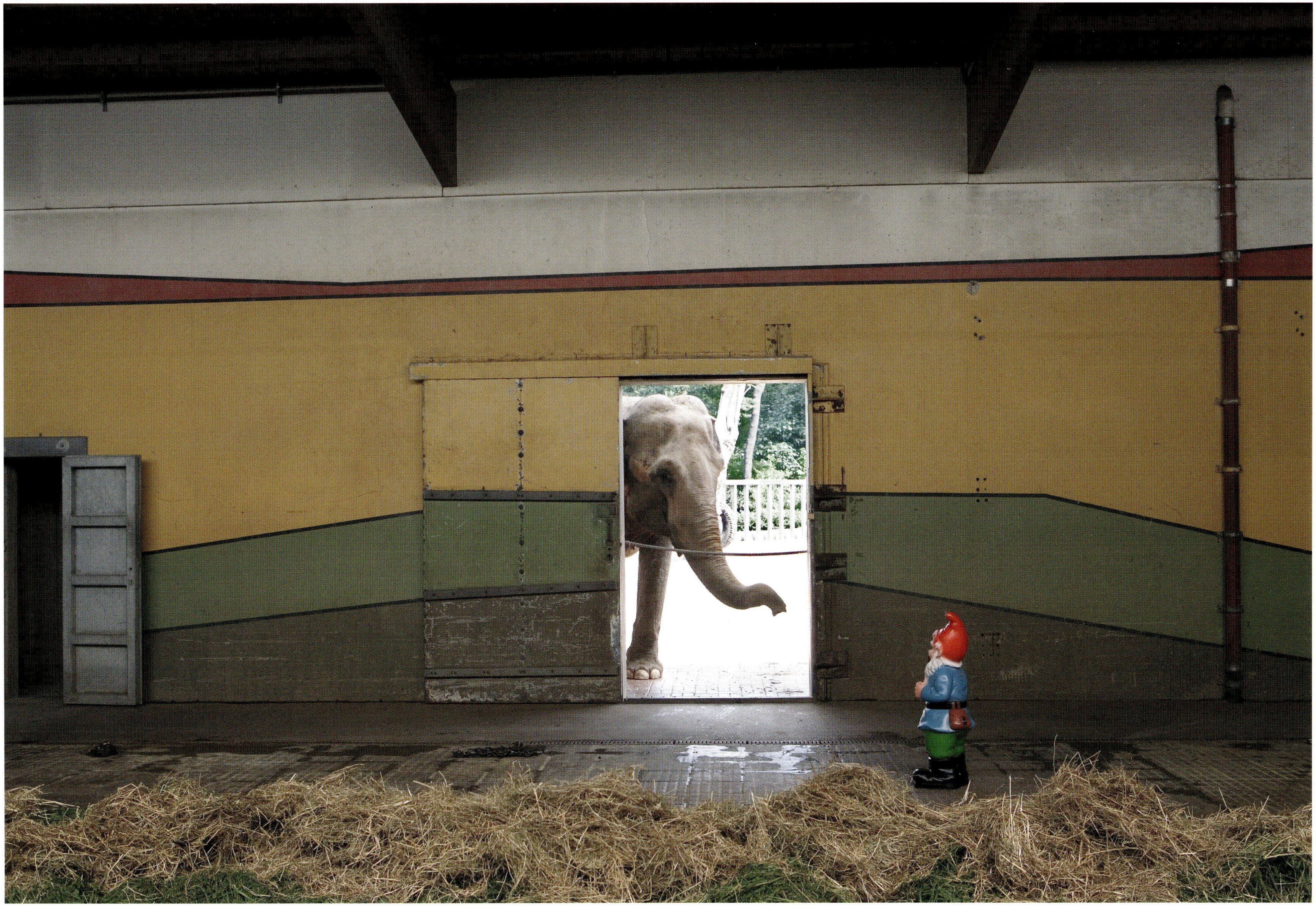

BRAUNKOHLETAGEBAU, GARZWEILER

Um das abzutransportieren, was der Schaufelradbagger »288« in 24 Stunden abräumt, bräuchte man 16.000 Fünfzehn-Tonnen-Laster oder 2400 Eisenbahnwaggons: 240.000 Tonnen Kohle. Als der »288« 1978 in Betrieb ging, war er der größte Bagger der Welt, und das ist er heute immer noch: 240 Meter lang, 96 Meter hoch, 12.840 Tonnen schwer (so viel wie 13.000 Kleinwagen), 0,6 km/h Höchstgeschwindigkeit, 100 Meter Wendekreis und 5 Mann Besatzung.

Auf dem Rad sitzen 18 Schaufeln – oder Eimer, wie sie hier sagen –, und in jede passen gut sechseinhalb Kubikmeter Kohle oder Abraum. Abraum ist das, was der Bagger erst mal wegschaffen muss, um überhaupt an die Kohle heranzukommen: Löß, Sand, Kies usw. Die Braunkohle liegt im Abbaugebiet Garzweiler in drei 10 bis 15 Meter dicken Schichten – den Flözen – 40 bis 160 Meter tief in der Erde. Aus der Kohle, die der »288« und die anderen Bagger in Garzweiler fördern – durchschnittlich 40 Millionen Tonnen im Jahr –, wird in den Kraftwerken in der Nähe Strom gemacht.

Der Unterschied zwischen Braun- und Steinkohle ist der: Die Braunkohle ist jünger und deshalb weniger hart, sie hat einen geringeren Brennwert, sie enthält mehr Wasser und liegt verhältnismäßig dicht unter der Erdoberfläche. Deshalb kann man sie im Tagebau fördern, man muss also keine Schächte und Stollen bohren wie bei der Steinkohle im Ruhrgebiet. Allerdings sind die Löcher, die dafür gegraben werden müssen, 40 bis 50 Quadratkilometer groß, so wie hier im Tagebau zwischen Aachen, Köln, Düsseldorf und Mönchengladbach.

Ich bin ja nun wirklich nicht groß mit meinen 97 Zentimetern, aber ich sage euch eins: Vor diesem Bagger kämt ihr euch alle genauso winzig vor wie ich.

BROWN COAL OPENCAST MINING, GARZWEILER

In order to transport what the bucket wheel excavator »288« clears away in 24 hours, you would need 16,000 fifteen-ton lorries or 2,400 rail freight wagons for the 240,000 tons of coal. When the »288« went into operation in 1978, it was the biggest excavator in the world and it is still so today: it is 240 metres long, 96 metres high, and, at 12,840 tons, it weighs as much as 13,000 small cars; its top speed is 0.6 km per hour with a 100-metre turning circle and a crew of 5.

The wheel is spiked with 18 shovels – or buckets as they say – and each one of them holds a good six-and-a-half cubic metres of coal or overburden. Overburden is what the excavator first has to dig through in order to reach the coal: loess, sand, gravel, etc. The brown coal lies in the Garzweiler mine field in three 10-to-15-metre thick layers – or seams – 40 to 160 metres deep in the earth. All the coal that the »288« and the other excavators in Garzweiler produce – an average of 40 millions tons a year – is transformed into electric current in local power stations.

The difference between brown coal and hard coal is this: brown coal is younger and therefore softer; it has a lower calorific value, contains more water and lies relatively close to the earth's surface. Which is why it can be opencast (or strip) mined. No vertical shafts or tunnels need be drilled, as is necessary for mining hard coal in the Ruhr. However, the holes that need to be dug have a dimension of 40-50 square kilometres, as is the case here in the opencast mine between Aachen, Cologne, Düsseldorf and Mönchengladbach.

Now, with my 97 centimetres I'm really what you'd call short, but I'll tell you this: next to this excavator, all of you would feel just as tiny as I do.

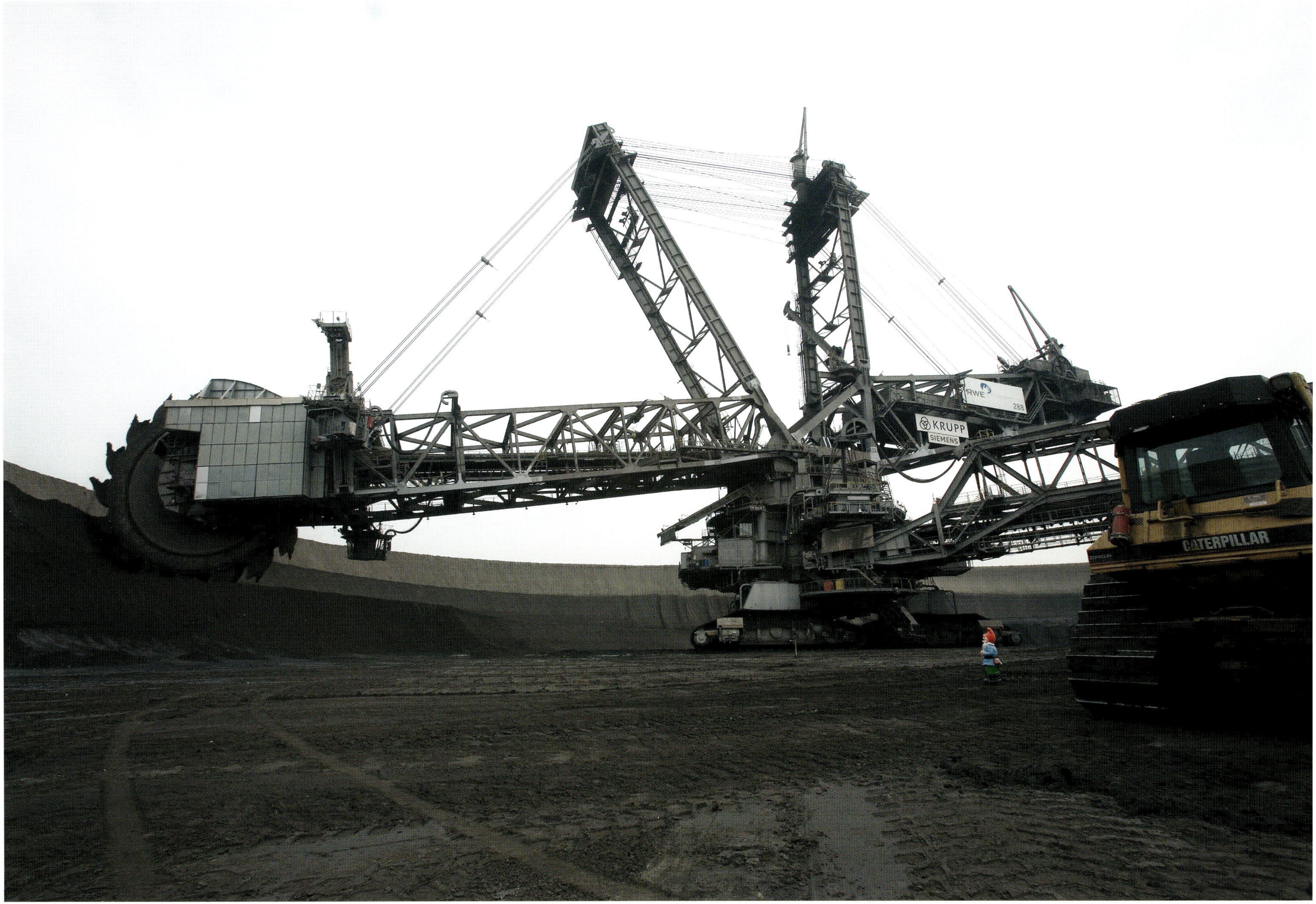
RWE
288
KRUPP
SIEMENS
CATERPILLAR

ZECHE »ZOLLVEREIN«, ESSEN

Vor allem wegen der Körpergröße ist unsereiner ja ganz gut für den Bergbau geeignet; die Stollen sind manchmal sehr niedrig, und die Menschen haben's da oft schwerer als wir. Bergmann ist bei uns ein ganz alter, hoch angesehener Beruf. Die sieben Zwerge zum Beispiel in der Geschichte von Schneewittchen – wisst ihr noch? –, die waren Bergleute und haben unter Tage nach Erz und Gold gegraben. Aber damals war der Bergbau noch reine Handarbeit.

Auf der Zeche »Zollverein« in Essen, viele hundert Jahre später, sind im Bergbau riesige Maschinen eingesetzt worden. Der Schacht XII unter dem Förderturm ist über 1000 Meter tief. In den besten Zeiten haben hier mehr als 5000 Bergleute 13.000 Tonnen Kohle am Tag von da unten raufgeholt.

Seit Dezember 2001 gehört auch die Zeche »Zollverein« zum Weltkulturerbe der Unesco. Kohlenzeche und Kultur, werdet ihr vielleicht fragen, was hat das denn miteinander zu tun? Nun, für eine Zeche braucht man Gebäude, und die kann man so oder so bauen. Die Zeche »Zollverein«, so wie sie heute dasteht, ist von 1927 bis 1932 gebaut worden – da war das Bergwerk selbst schon gut 80 Jahre alt –, und sie ist die erste Zechenanlage, bei der die gesamte Architektur aus einem Guss ist. Die Architekten Fritz Schupp und Martin Kremmer haben sie zusammen mit den Werksingenieuren geplant und nach den modernsten Prinzipien der Architektur gestaltet, wie sie damals zum Beispiel am Bauhaus in Weimar und Dessau entwickelt worden sind.

1986 ist die Zeche stillgelegt und bald darauf unter Denkmalschutz gestellt worden, danach konnte sie niemand mehr abreißen. Um ein Haar wäre das der riesigen Kokerei passiert, nur ein paar hundert Meter von hier, aber die ist heute auch ein Industriedenkmal.

»ZOLLVEREIN« MINE, ESSEN

Above all because of size, our sort is quite suited for work in a mine; the galleries are sometimes so low, and people often have more difficulty than we do. For us, minework is an old and highly regarded profession. The seven dwarfs, for example, in the fairytale of Snow White – if you remember – were mineworkers and worked underground to dig for gold and ore. But in that day and age, mining was exclusively done by hand.

At the »Zollverein« mine in Essen, many hundreds of years later, giant machines were in use for digging. Shaft XII under the winding tower is over 1000 metres deep. In its glory days, more than 5000 miners hauled up 13,000 tons of coal a day from down there.

Since December 2001, the »Zollverein« mine is also on Unesco's worlds cultural heritage list. Coal mine and culture? You will probably ask what the one has to do with the other? Well a mine needs buildings, and these can be designed either this way or that. The »Zollverein mine«, as it stands today, was built from 1927 to 1932 – when the mine itself was already 80 years old – and it is the first mine complex in which the architecture was all of one piece. The architects Fritz Schupp and Martin Kremmer planned it together with the mining engineers and designed it according to the most modern architectural principles as they were then being developed at the Bauhaus in Weimar and Dessau.

In 1986, the mine was shut down and soon afterwards became a listed building so that no one could then tear it down. That very nearly happened to the giant coking plant only a couple of hundred metres from here, but it too is, in the meantime, listed as an industrial monument.

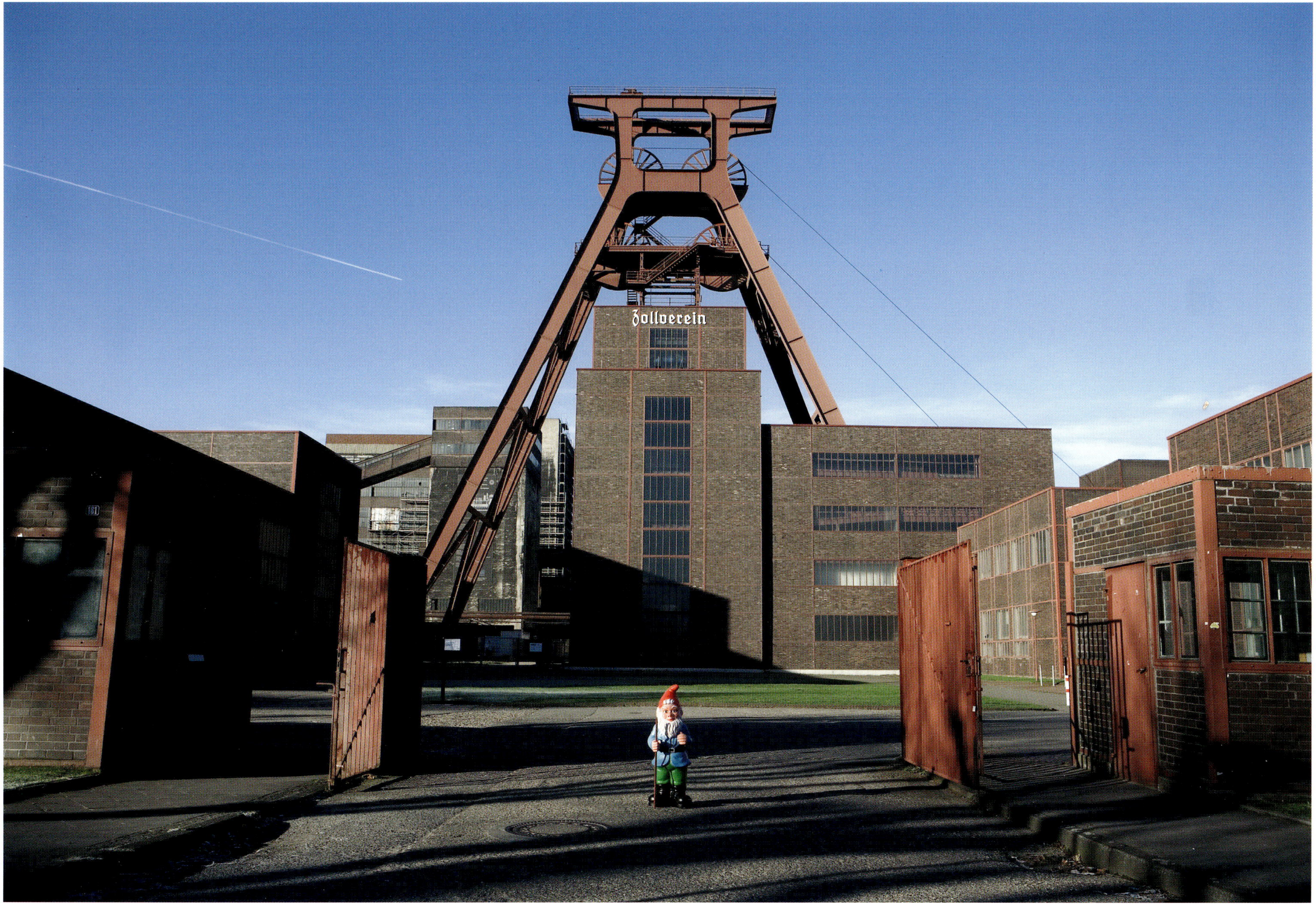
Zollverein

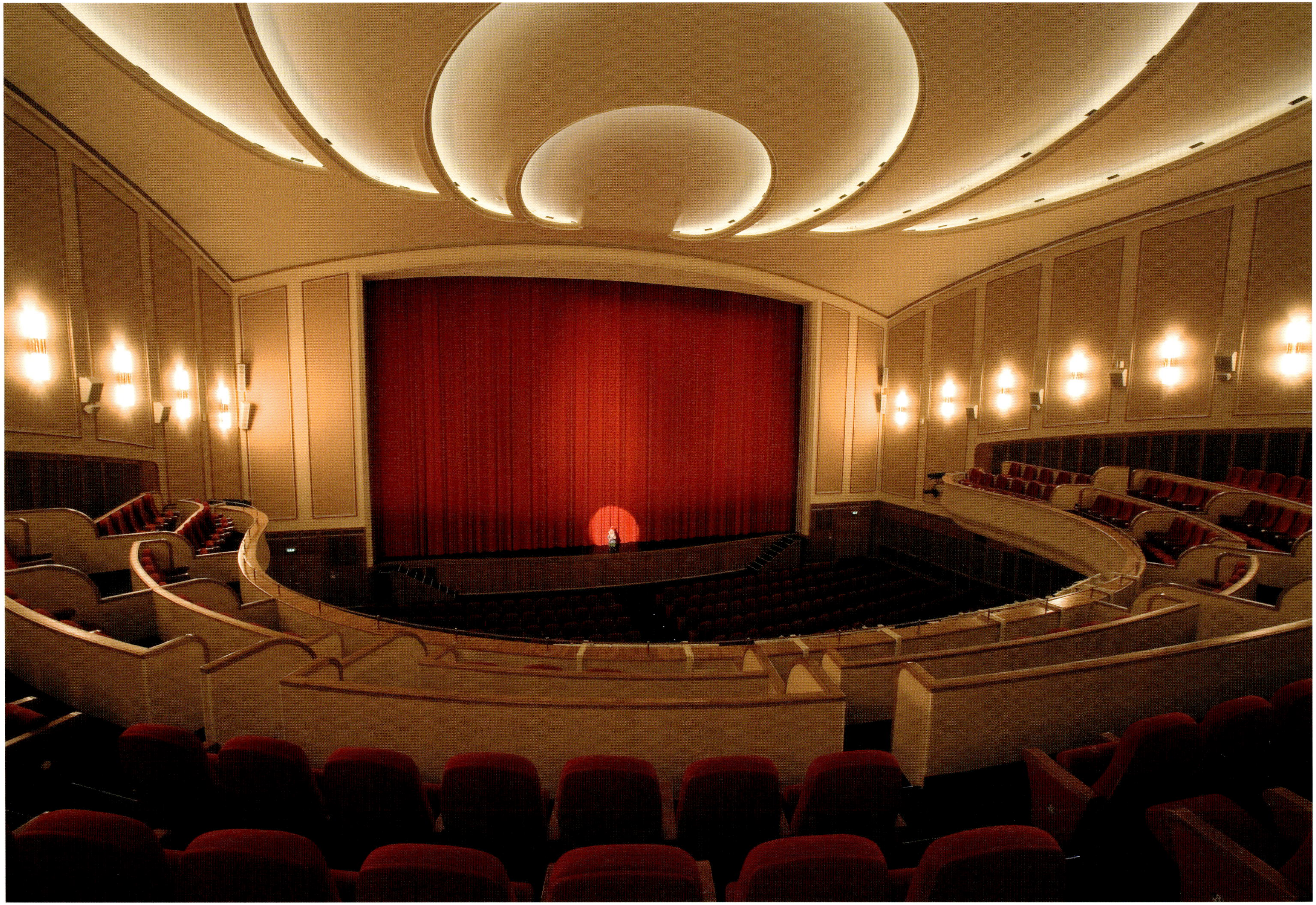

»LICHTBURG«, ESSEN

Früher hießen die Kinos Lichtspielhäuser, Lichtspieltheater oder sogar Lichtspielpaläste und hatten so wunderbare Namen wie Urania, Universum, Astra oder Luna. Heute heißen sie Multiplex, Cinemaxx oder so ähnlich und bestehen aus einem Dutzend gestapelter Vorführsäle. Ob das Kino dadurch schlechter geworden ist, kann ich nicht sagen, davon verstehe ich zu wenig, aber anders geworden ist es ganz bestimmt. Und wenn jemand wissen will, wo der Unterschied liegt, dann sollte er sich einmal auf den Weg nach Essen machen und sich dort in der »Lichtburg« einen Film anschauen.

Als die »Lichtburg« 1928 eröffnet wurde, gab es in Essen immerhin schon 24 Lichtspielhäuser, darunter, nur ein paar hundert Meter entfernt, die »Schauburg« der UFA mit 2000 Plätzen. So viele hatte die »Lichtburg« natürlich auch. Zur Eröffnung spielte das hauseigene Orchester und danach die größte Wurlitzer-Orgel in Europa. Und die Projektion war hochmodern: Die Filme wurden »ohne Pausen nach den Aktschlüssen« projiziert.

Nach 1928 ist die »Lichtburg« noch zweimal eröffnet worden: 1950 nach der Zerstörung im Krieg und im Frühjahr 2003 nach einer gründlichen Renovierung. Nach wie vor ist die »Lichtburg« ein Film-»Theater«, das heißt, hier gibt es auch andere Sachen zu sehen und zu hören als Filme: Musik, Theater, Kabarett.

Nun bin ich ja kein typischer Kinogänger. Aber wenn ich mir mal wieder einen Film ansehen sollte, dann nur in der »Lichtburg«. Und anschließend würde ich mir vielleicht in der Filmbar einen Kräuterlikör genehmigen. Hier haben sie seit den späten 20er Jahren alle gesessen, die großen Leinwandheldinnen und -helden: von Zarah Leander und Luis Trenker über Louis Armstrong, William Holden, Marika Rökk, Gary Cooper und Jean Marais bis zu Pierce Brosnan.

»LICHTBURG«, ESSEN

Cinemas used to be called picture-theatres in German or even picture-palaces and used to have wonderful names like Urania, Universum, Astra or Luna. Today, they are called Multiplex, Cinemaxx or the like and are made up of a dozen projection rooms piled one onto the other. Whether the cinema has been downgraded as a result, I don't know enough about it to say, but in any case it has certainly changed. And if someone wants to know where the difference lies, he should make his way to Essen and the »Lichtburg« to watch a film.

When the »Lichtburg« was opened in 1928, there were already 24 movie houses among which, only a few hundred metres away, was the UFA's »Schauburg« that seated 2000. Of course, the »Lichtburg« also provided as many seats. At its opening, the house's own orchestra played, followed by a performance of the largest Wurlitzer organ in Europe. And its projection system was cutting edge for the time: films were projected »without breaks between the scenes«.

After 1928, the »Lichtburg« was opened twice again. In 1950, after its destruction in the war and once more in the spring of 2003 after a thorough renovation. As it was from the beginning, the »Lichtburg« is a movie »theatre«, that is, there are other things to see and hear than films: namely, music, plays and cabaret.

Now I'm not what you call a typical moviegoer. But when I do want to see a film, then only in Essen at the »Lichtburg«. And afterwards, I would perhaps allow myself an aperitif at the film bar. Ever since the 1920s, here is where all those screen greats have sat around: from Zarah Leander and Luis Trenker via Louis Armstrong, William Holden, Marika Rökk, Gary Cooper and Jean Marais, all the way to Pierce Brosnan.

RHEINWIESEN, DÜSSELDORF

»Satzung für die Benutzung der Oberkasseler Rheinwiesen der Landeshauptstadt Düsseldorf vom 2. Dezember 1975, § 2, Zweck: Die Rheinwiesen dienen der Düsseldorfer Bevölkerung ausschließlich zur Erholung.« Jetzt bin ich allerdings kein Düsseldorfer und kann nur hoffen, dass ich hier nichts falsch gemacht habe. (Als Fußballtorwart tauge ich jedenfalls schon mal nichts.)

Ich bin ja auch nur hier herübergekommen, weil man von den Rheinwiesen in Oberkassel den schönsten Blick auf das neue Viertel am alten Hafen mit diesen seltsamen Häusern hat. »Wie Bauklötze, die vom Himmel gefallen sind« sehen die Gebäude aus, die der berühmte amerikanische Architekt Frank Gehry am Neuen Zollhof gebaut hat; so hat er sie selber mal beschrieben.

Und Recht hat er. Mir sind sie auf den ersten Blick auch ein bisschen unaufgeräumt vorgekommen, so schief und verschachtelt, wie er sie da ans Ufer gestellt hat. Aber innen stehen die Tische, Stühle und Schränke alle waagerecht, und die Menschen leben und arbeiten dort genauso wie anderswo. Seit 1999 sind die Häuser jedenfalls eine der größten Attraktionen in der Stadt, und je länger ich sie mir angesehen habe, desto besser haben sie mir gefallen.

Fernsehtürme könnte man so aber wahrscheinlich nicht bauen. Der in Düsseldorf stammt aus dem Jahr 1982, er ist nach dem Stuttgarter Modell von 1954 gebaut, 240 Meter hoch, mit einer Aussichtsplattform in 170 Metern Höhe und einem Drehrestaurant in der Etage darüber. Von dort oben kann man bei guter Sicht fast 70 Kilometer weit sehen.

RHINE MEADOWLAND, DÜSSELDORF

»Statute for the use of the Oberkassel Rhine meadowland of the state capital Düsseldorf from December 2, 1975, para. 2. Objective: the Rhine meadowland is to serve the people of Düsseldorf exclusively for recreation.« Now I am not a citizen of Düsseldorf and can only hope I didn't do anything wrong by being here. (In any case, I am completely worthless as a football goalie.)

I only came over here because from the Rhine meadowland in Oberkassel you get the best view of the new quarter at the old harbour with its strange architecture. »Like building blocks fallen from the sky« is the way the American architect Frank Gehry once described what he'd built at the Neuer Zollhof.

And he's right there. At first glance, they seemed to me a bit disorderly, so crooked and higgledy-piggledy in the way he set them up on the riverbank. But inside, the tables, chairs and shelves are all horizontally aligned, and people live and work here just as they do anywhere else. Since 1999, these buildings have been one of the chief attractions in the city, and the longer I look at them, the better I like them.

But television towers could probably not be built in this way. Düsseldorf's tower is from 1982 and was modelled on Stuttgart's 1954 TV tower. It is 240 metres high, with a viewing platform at 170 metres and a revolving restaurant on the floor above. From there, clear weather permitting, you can see to a distance of almost 70 kilometres.

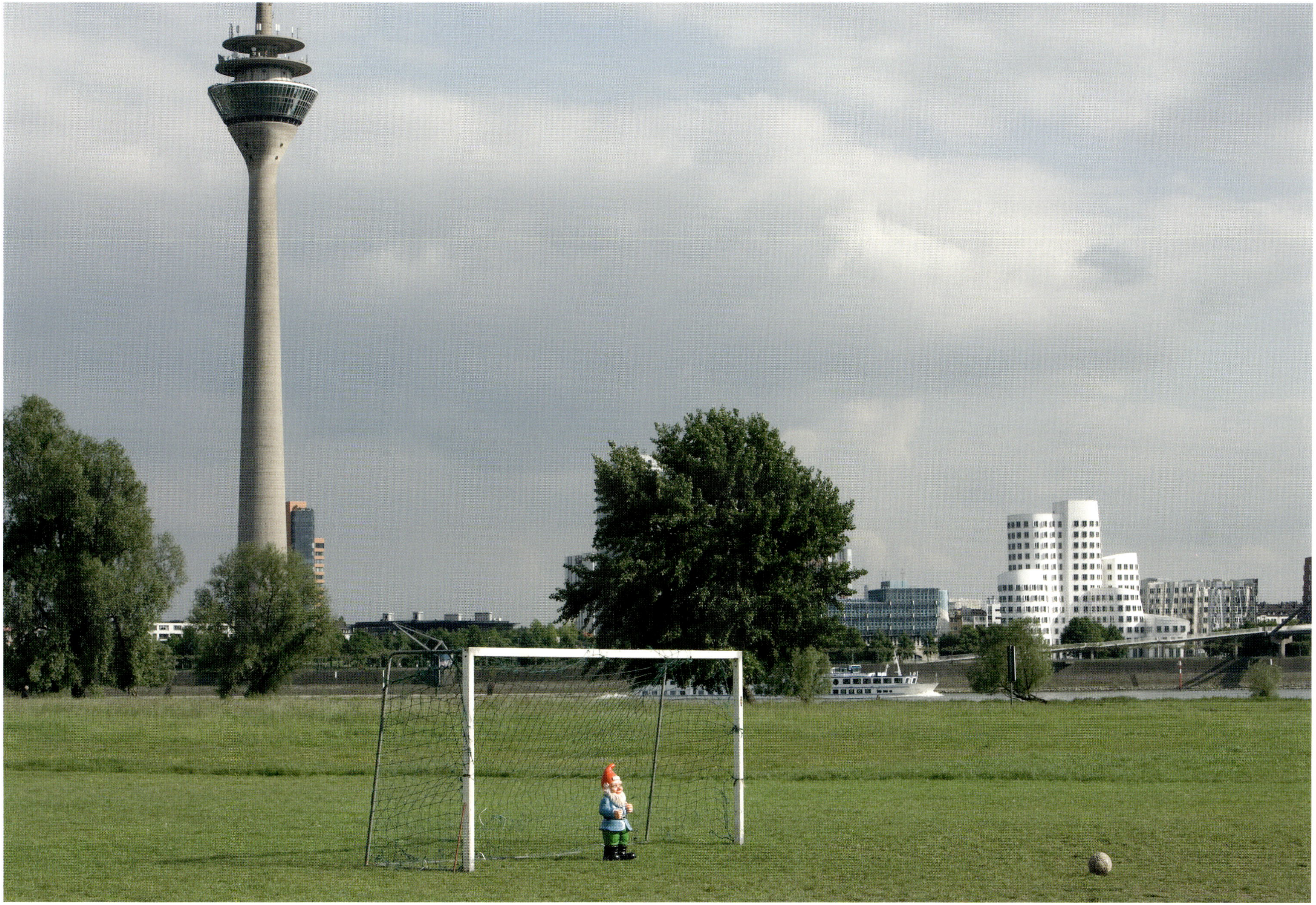

MODE-MESSE CPD, DÜSSELDORF

Was meine Kleidung angeht, bin ich ja sehr genügsam, die Modeschöpfer, die Schneider und die Textilindustrie können an mir nicht viel verdienen. Ich nähe mir fast alles selbst, meistens im Winter, wenn es im Garten nichts zu tun gibt; meine Schuhe, meine Hose, meine Jacke, mein Gürtel und meine Mütze haben schon immer so ausgesehen wie heute.

Aber ich wollte doch mal herausfinden, warum die Menschen im Frühling und im Herbst immer so aus dem Häuschen geraten, wenn das Neueste aus den großen und kleinen Modeateliers vorgestellt wird. Und deshalb habe ich mich bei der Modemesse CPD in Düsseldorf angemeldet. Wenn man wissen will, was die Menschen im nächsten Jahr drunter und drüber anziehen – auf dieser Messe kann man's erfahren. Ungefähr 1500 Firmen aus aller Welt zeigen hier, was sie sich dazu im letzten halben Jahr haben einfallen lassen.

Die CPD – das heißt »Collections Premieren Düsseldorf« – wird seit 1982 von der IGEDO veranstaltet. Die IGEDO ist 1949 zu dem Zweck gegründet worden, Modemessen zu veranstalten. Die fünf Buchstaben sind die Abkürzung für »Interessengemeinschaft Damenoberbekleidung«, und sie waren bald in aller Welt bekannt. Seit 2002 wird in Düsseldorf aber auch Mode für Männer gezeigt.

Vor zwei Stunden sind hier junge Frauen mit Kleidern hin- und hergelaufen, wie ich sie noch nie gesehen habe – die Kleider meine ich. Wo ich hier stehe, das heißt in der Modesprache »Catwalk«; das muss irgendwas mit Katzen zu tun haben, aber ich hab' hier bisher noch keine gesehen oder gehört.

FASHION FAIR CPD, DÜSSELDORF

As to my clothing, I am easy to satisfy; fashion designers, tailors and the textile industry can't earn much from me. I sew almost everything myself, mostly in the winter when there's nothing doing in the garden. My shoes, my trousers, my jacket, my belt and my cap have always looked just the way they do today.

But I wanted to see why the people in spring and autumn go so overboard when the very newest from the big and small fashion studios is presented. Which is why I announced my coming to the Fashion Fair CPD in Düsseldorf. If you want to know what people will be wearing next year on top and underneath, you can find out at this fair. Around 1500 companies from around the world show here what they have come up with over the past half year.

The CPD – which stands for »Collections Premieren Düsseldorf« – has been put on since 1982 by the IGEDO. IGEDO itself was founded in 1949 with the aim of organizing fashion shows. Its five letters stand for the »Women's Outer Garments Interest Group« in German, and it soon became known worldwide. In the meantime, since 2002, men's fashions are also being shown in Düsseldorf.

About two hours ago, strutting back and forth here were young women in fashionable dress like I never saw before – the clothing I mean. I am now standing on what is called the »catwalk«, which must have something to do with cats. But I have not seen or heard a single one.

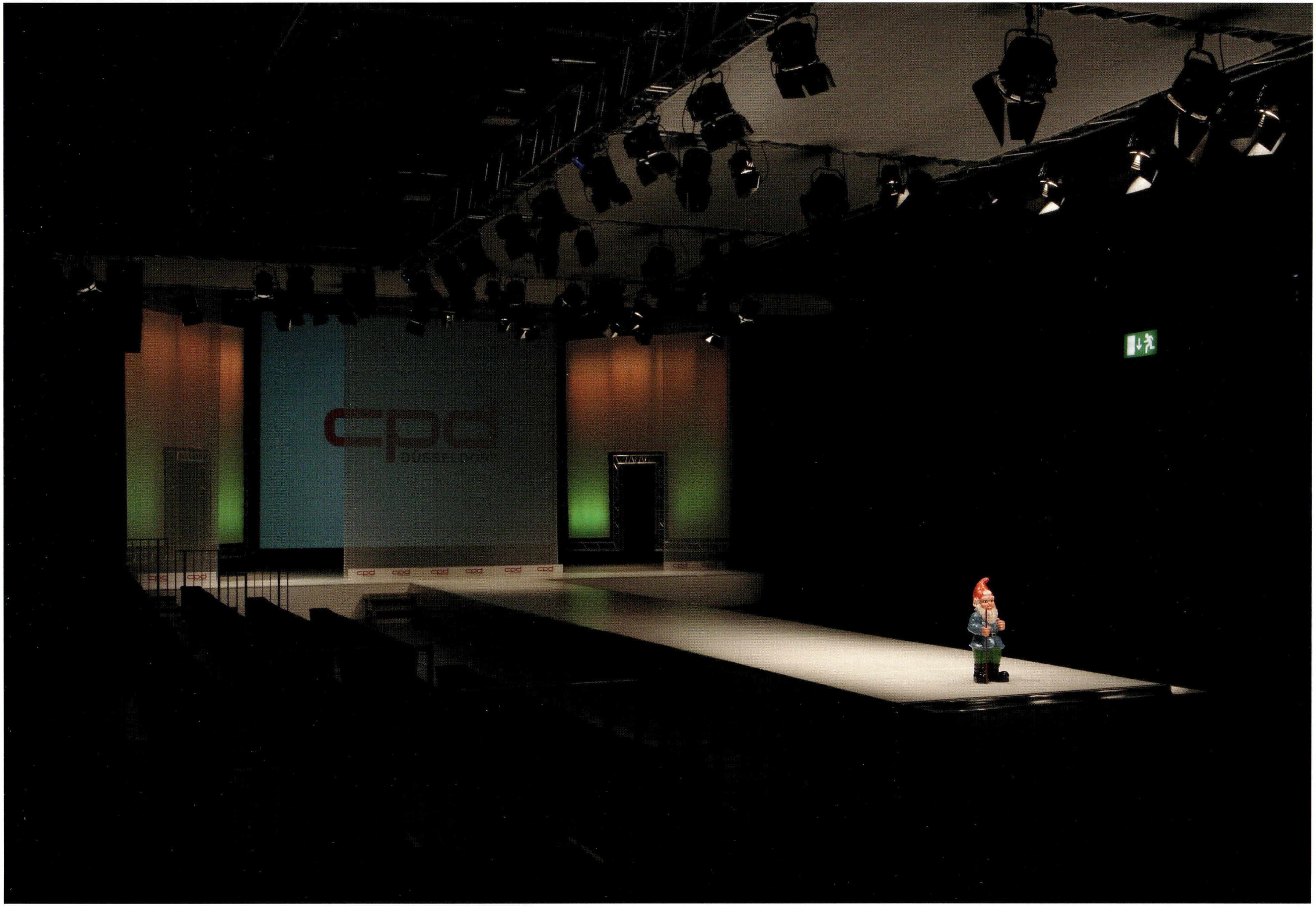
cpd

LENNEP, BERGISCHES LAND

Wenn das Bergische Land seinen Namen von den Bergen hätte, die es hier ja reichlich gibt, müsste es nach den Vorschriften der Grammatik korrekterweise Bergiges Land heißen. So heißt es aber nicht. Es hat seinen Namen vielmehr von den Grafen und Herzögen von Berg, die hier über viele Jahrhunderte das Sagen hatten. Die allerdings haben sich anscheinend tatsächlich nach irgendeinem Berg benannt: Ein früher Vorfahre namens Adolf hat sich im Jahr 1068 den Namen »vom Berge« zugelegt bzw., weil das vornehmer klang, »de monte«.

Das Bergische Land gehört zum rechtsrheinischen Schiefergebirge. Schiefer ist ein dunkelgraues Sedimentgestein, das sich leicht bearbeiten und in dünne Platten spalten lässt. Damit kann man sehr schön Dächer decken und Wände verkleiden.

Lennep ist ein Stadtteil von Remscheid, südlich von Wuppertal, und liegt mitten im rechtsrheinischen Schiefergebirge. Und deswegen sind hier sehr viele alte Fachwerkhäuser mit Schiefer verkleidet.

Vielleicht erinnert sich der eine oder der andere noch an seine ersten Schreibversuche, mit Griffeln auf quietschenden Schiefertafeln. So eine Tafel hängt heute noch an meinem Küchenschrank, da schreib' ich immer drauf, was ich einkaufen muss.

LENNEP, BERGISCHES LAND

If Bergisches Land had taken its name from the hills, of which there are many here, it would, according to German grammar, need to be correctly called Bergiges Land, or hilly land. But it is not. It got its name from the counts and dukes of Berg, who for many centuries called the shots here. They, however, were in fact apparently named after some mountain or other: an early ancestor by the name of Adolf took the name »vom Berge« in the year 1068, or actually he took »de monte«, because it sounded more distinguished.

Bergisches Land is part of the slate mountains on the right side of the Rhine. Slate is a dark grey sedimentary rock that can be easily worked and split into thin layers, which are very handy for roofing and wall panelling.

Lennep is a district of Remscheid, south of Wuppertal, and lies in the midst of the slate mountains on the right bank of the Rhine. Hence this is the reason why so many of the old half-timbered houses here are covered in slate.

Perhaps one or two of you remember your first attempts at writing, which could have been with a slate pencil on a squeaky slate. Just such a blackboard hangs on my kitchen cupboard. I use it to jot down my shopping list.

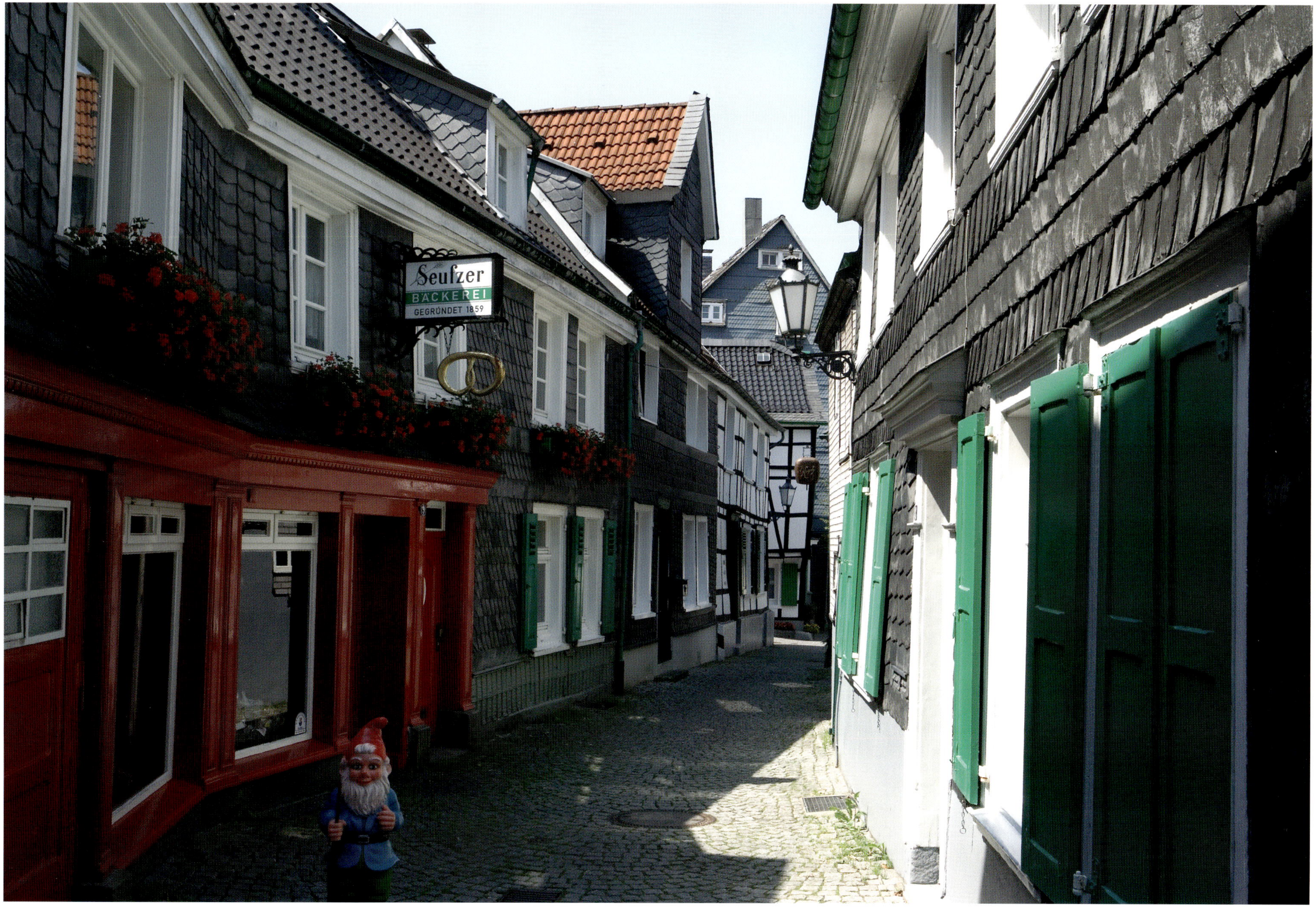
Seufzer
BÄCKEREI
GEGRÜNDET 1859

SCHWEBEBAHN, WUPPERTAL

Der berühmteste Fahrgast der weltbekannten Wuppertaler Schwebebahn ist ein junger Elefant namens Tuffi. Sein Zirkus hatte ihn am 21. Juli 1950 mit der Bahn auf eine Reklamefahrt geschickt, das hat ihm wohl keinen richtigen Spaß gemacht, vielleicht hatte er auch bloß Höhenangst, jedenfalls ist er während der Fahrt ausgestiegen und in die Wupper gesprungen. Zum Glück ist ihm dabei nichts weiter passiert, und abends stand er wieder in der Manege.

Als die Schwebebahn nach drei Jahren Bauzeit 1901 eingeweiht wurde, war sie eine Weltsensation und hat Wuppertal, die Stadt mit den meisten öffentlichen Treppen in Deutschland, auf einen Schlag berühmt gemacht.

Die Bahn hängt an 486 Stützen und Brücken und befördert seit mehr als 100 Jahren ihre Fahrgäste – heute sind es im Jahr ungefähr 23 Millionen – hauptsächlich über dem Flussbett der Wupper, vorbei an 20 Haltestellen, über die 13,3 Kilometer lange Strecke von Elberfeld nach Barmen und wieder zurück; dafür braucht sie jeweils ungefähr 35 Minuten.

Rein verkehrstechnisch gilt die Schwebebahn als Straßenbahn »besonderer Bauart«, und so sieht sie ja auch aus, und so hört sie sich auch an, nur dass die Schienen nicht drunter liegen, sondern drüber. Sie kennt keine Staus, keine Kreuzungen und keine roten Ampeln und deshalb auch keine Verspätungen. Sie ist das zuverlässigste und sicherste Verkehrsmittel der Welt. Außer Tuffi ist niemand hinausgefallen. Und selbst das Unglück vom 12. April 1999, als durch eine Unachtsamkeit bei Modernisierungsarbeiten 5 Fahrgäste starben und 47 verletzt wurden, ändert wenig an dieser Bilanz.

SUSPENSION RAILWAY, WUPPERTAL

The most famous passenger to ride on the world-renowned Wuppertal suspension railway was a young elephant called Tuffi. His circus sent him out in one of the suspension cars on July 21, 1950, as an advertising gag, but to him it didn't seem funny. Perhaps he was just afraid of heights. In any case, during the ride he clambered out and jumped into the Wupper River. Fortunately nothing happened to him and in the evening he was back with the circus.

When the suspension railway was inaugurated in 1901 after a 3-year period of construction, it was a global sensation and made Wuppertal – the city with the most outdoor flights of stairs in Germany – famous in a single blow.

The railway hangs from 486 supports and bridges and has carried its passengers for over 100 years – today approximately 23 million of them every year – mainly across the river bed of the Wupper, past 20 stops, along the 13.3 kilometre stretch from Elberfeld to Barmen and back, which takes around 35 minutes in each direction.

Viewed from a technological-transport aspect, the suspension train is, in truth, a special type of tram; that's what it looks like and what it sounds like, only that the tracks are not underneath but on top. It is bothered neither by traffic jams, junctions or red lights, and is therefore never late. It is the most reliable and the safest means of transportation in the world. No one has ever fallen out, except for Tuffi. And even the accident on April 12, 1999 – when, because of carelessness during modernization work, 5 passengers died and 47 were injured – changes this net balance very little.

169

DOM, KÖLN

Der Kölner Dom ist die einzige gotische Kathedrale, die mit Hilfe von Dampfmaschinen gebaut wurde. Und das kam so:

Nach der Grundsteinlegung 1248 haben die Kölner genauso fleißig daran gearbeitet wie andere Baumeister an ihren Kathedralen, aber weil dieser Dom länger, breiter und höher werden sollte als alle anderen, hat's dann doch länger gedauert als geplant. Die Begeisterung nahm allmählich ab, nach der Reformation kamen kaum noch Pilger in die Stadt, das Geld wurde knapp, und nach dreihundert Jahren war schließlich auch der gotische Stil aus der Mode; in Europa war mittlerweile Renaissance.

1560 stellte das Domkapitel die Bauarbeiten ein, und nicht der Dom, sondern der riesige hölzerne Baukran auf dem Turmstumpf war von da an das Kölner Wahrzeichen. Die halbfertige Kirche stand fast dreihundert Jahre als größte Bauruine des Abendlandes am Rheinufer, und kein Mensch hat mehr damit gerechnet, dass der Dom jemals fertig werden würde.

Aber im 19. Jahrhundert kam die Gotik wieder in Mode. Auf Anregung des Preußen-Königs Friedrich Wilhelm IV. gründeten Kölner Bürger 1841 den Zentralen Dombau-Verein und legten 1842 den Grundstein für den Weiterbau. 1880, also keine 40 Jahre später, sah der Dom mit Hilfe von modernster Technik endlich so aus, wie ihn sich der Erzbischof Konrad von Hochstaden und sein Baumeister Gerhard 732 Jahre vorher gedacht hatten.

Er ist 146 Meter lang, 86 Meter breit und 157 Meter hoch, er wiegt 300.000 Tonnen, und wenn man ihn heute noch einmal bauen wollte, dann müsste man gut 10 Milliarden Euro aufbringen.

COLOGNE CATHEDRAL

Cologne's Cathedral of St. Peter and Mary is the only Gothic cathedral that has been built with the help of steam engines. And it happened like this:

After the foundation stone was laid in 1248, Cologne's artisans worked just as diligently at erecting it as other builders did their cathedrals, but because this one was to be longer, wider and higher than all the others, it took longer than was planned. Enthusiasm gradually waned. After the Reformation, hardly any pilgrims visited the city anymore; money became scarce, and after three hundred years, the Gothic style was out of date. In the meantime it was the Renaissance that reigned in Europe.

In 1560, the cathedral chapter decided to halt all work, and from then on it was not the cathedral but the gigantic wooden crane on the stub of the tower that was Cologne's trademark. The half-finished church stood on the Rhine for almost three hundred years as the occident's largest construction site; no one thought that it would ever be completed.

But in the 19th century, Gothic came into fashion again. Encouraged by King Friedrich Wilhelm IV of Prussia, Cologne's citizens founded the Central Cathedral Building Association in 1841 and, in 1842, laid the cornerstone for further work on it. In 1880, hardly 40 years later, the cathedral, with the help of the most modern technology, finally looked the way Archbishop Konrad von Hochstaden and his master builder Gerhard had imagined it 732 years previously.

It is 146 metres long, 86 metres wide and 157 metres high; it weighs 300,000 tons and, if we wanted to build it again today, would cost a good 10 billion Euro.

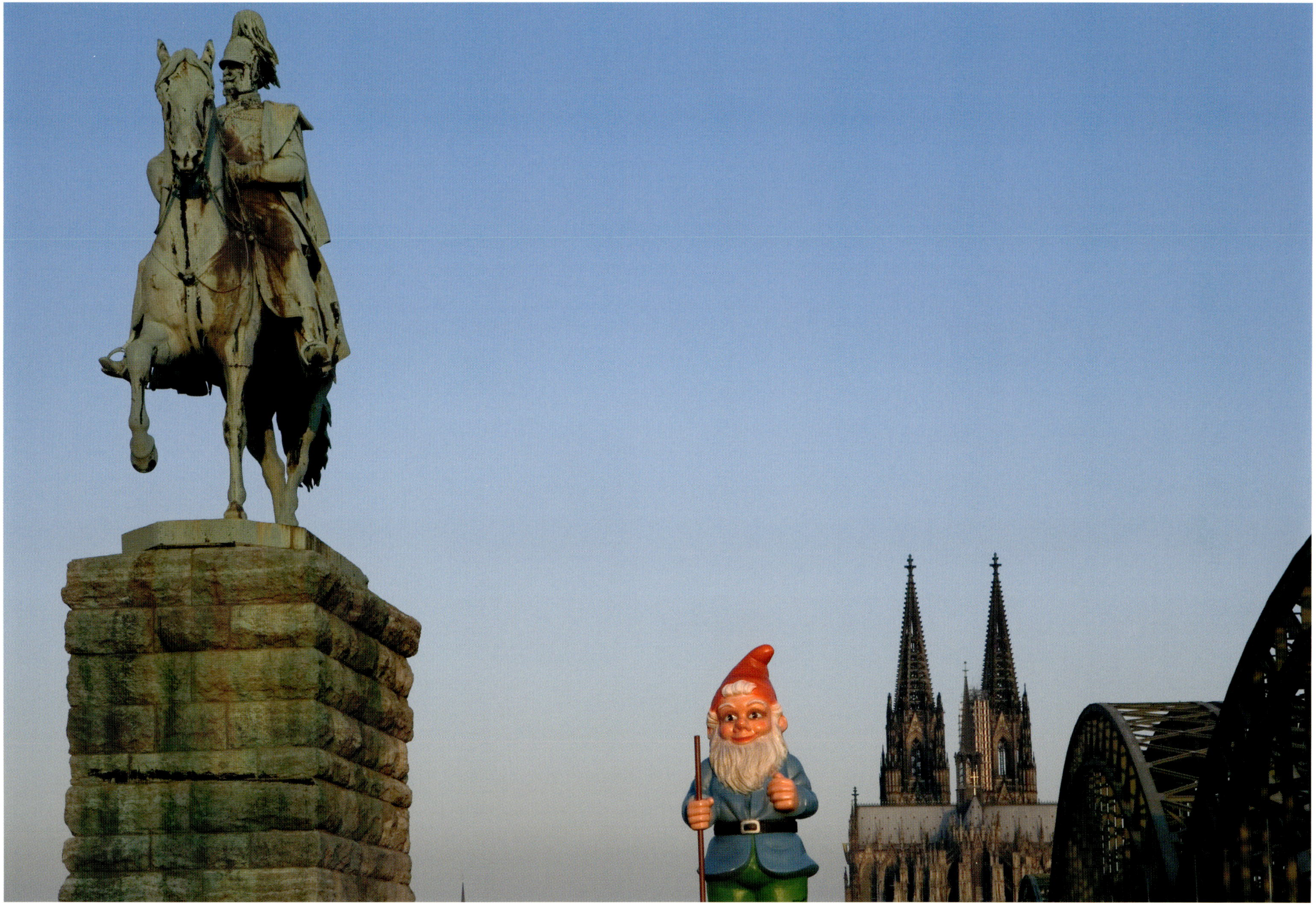

»LINDENSTRASSE«, KÖLN

Von den berühmten Straßen in Deutschland, wie zum Beispiel dem Kurfürstendamm, der Reeperbahn, der Maximilianstraße, der Königsallee oder dem Jungfernstieg, ist die Lindenstraße bei weitem die jüngste. Am 8. Dezember 2005 ist sie genau 20 Jahre alt geworden.

Die Lindenstraße ist eine Münchener Vorortstraße, aber es ist nicht die, die man auf dem Münchener Stadtplan findet. Wer zu der Lindenstraße will, von der hier die Rede ist, muss nach Köln fahren, aber hier ist es auch nicht die auf dem Stadtplan. Trotzdem wusste der Taxifahrer sofort, wie man hinkommt: *die* Lindenstraße ist eine 150 Meter lange Filmkulisse auf dem Studiogelände des Westdeutschen Rundfunks in Köln-Bocklemünd, im Nordwesten der Stadt.

Wer aber genauer wissen will, wie es dort aussieht, wer da wohnt und was hier die Woche über so alles passiert ist, der bleibt am besten zu Hause und stellt am Sonntag um 18 Uhr 50 den Fernseher an, so wie es im Durchschnitt vier bis fünf Millionen andere Zuschauer auch machen.

Die »Lindenstraße« ist eine deutsche Fernsehserie, und zwar die erste, die nicht von vornherein auf eine bestimmte Zahl von Folgen festgelegt war. Sie wird wahrscheinlich so lange laufen, wie es die Zuschauer wollen. Erfunden hat sie der Münchener Regisseur Hans W. Geißendörfer, und das Besondere daran ist unter anderm, dass in der Handlung immer wieder ganz aktuelle Ereignisse aus dem wirklichen Leben, manchmal auch solche aus den Tagen kurz vor dem Sendetermin, eine Rolle spielen. Hier kommt alles das vor, was die Menschen vor dem Fernsehapparat bewegt, aufregt oder langweilt: Liebe, Hass, Geburt und Tod, Hochzeit, Scheidung, Krankheit und jede Menge Klatsch und Tratsch.

»LINDENSTRASSE«, COLOGNE

Of all the famous streets in Germany – such as the Kurfürstendamm, the Reeperbahn, the Maximilianstrasse, Königsallee or the Jungfernstieg – Lindenstrasse is by far the youngest. On December 8, 2005, it was exactly 20 years old.

Lindenstrasse is a street on the outskirts of Munich, but it is not the one you would find on a Munich city map. Anyone who wants to go to *the* Lindenstrasse we are talking about, must go to Cologne, but here it is also not on the map. Yet despite this, the taxi driver knew exactly how to get there: *the* Lindenstrasse is a 150-metre-long stage set on the studio lot of the WDR radio station in Cologne-Bocklemünd in the northwest of the city.

Anyone who wants to find out exactly what it looks like and who lives here and what happens here during the week, stays home Sundays and switches on the TV at 6:50 pm, just as an average 4 to 5 million other viewers also do.

»Lindenstrasse« is a German TV series and, in fact, the first that was not fixed from the beginning to a set number of episodes. It will probably run as long as viewers want it to. It was an idea thought up by the Munich director Hans W. Geißendörfer, and what is special about it is, among other things, that current events from real life – sometimes even those that happened shortly before the broadcast – are repeatedly worked into the plot. Here, everything is put on show that moves, excites or bores the viewers sitting in front of the TV set: love, hate, birth and death, wedding, divorce, sickness and plenty of gossip and hearsay.

173

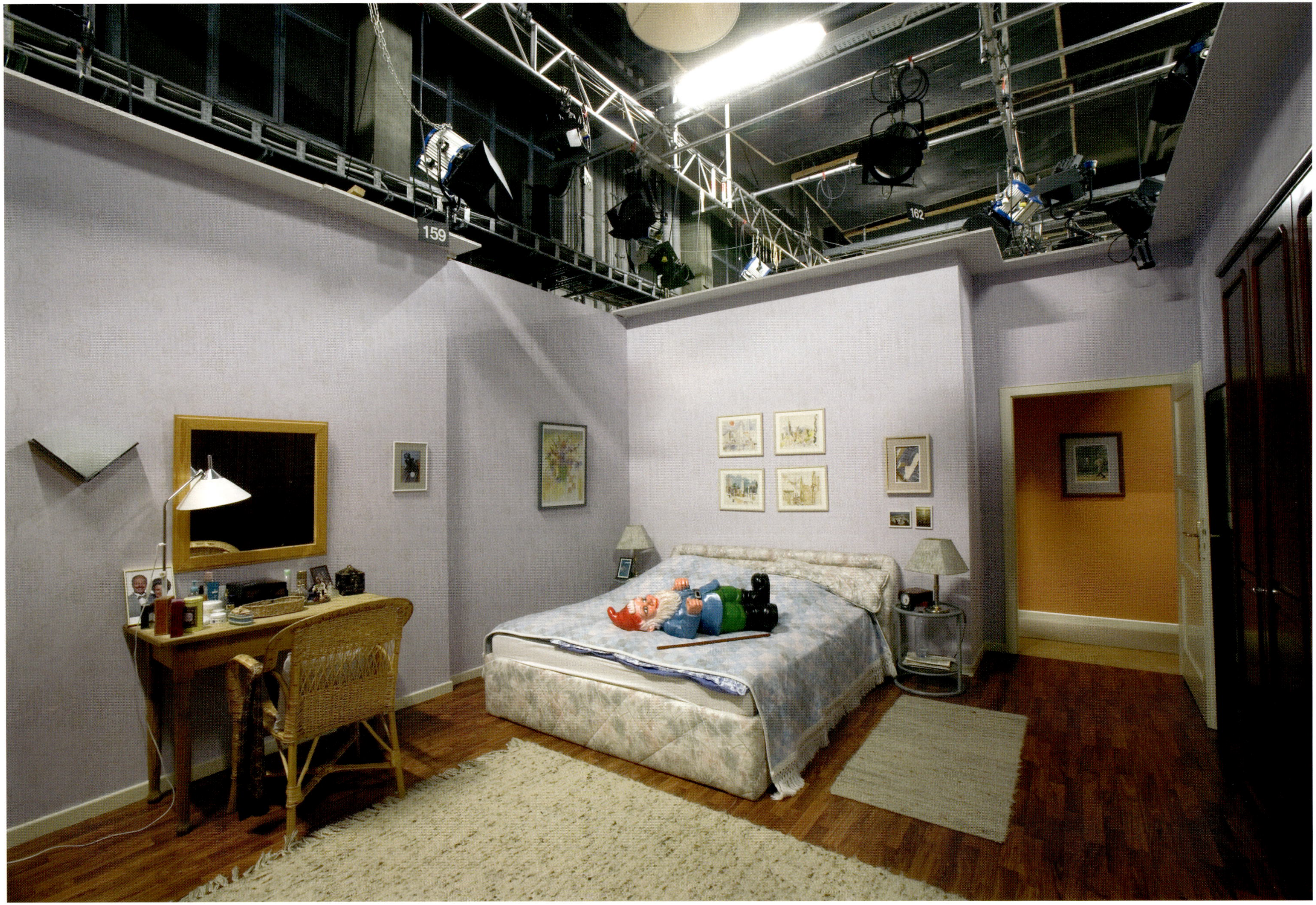
159
162

»LINDENSTRASSE«, KÖLN

Das ist das Schlafzimmer in der Wohnung von Mutter Beimer, Lindenstraße Nr. 3. Sie hat mir erlaubt, mich hier mal kurz auszuruhen. Helga Beimer – und die Schauspielerin Marie Luise Marjan, die sie spielt – ist von Anfang an dabei. Bis zum 8. Dezember 2005 hat sie in 1045 Folgen mitgemacht und hat alle Schicksalsschläge und Katastrophen überlebt. Sie hat in dieser Zeit drei Kinder großgezogen, sie hat sich scheiden lassen und hat sich schließlich selbständig gemacht. Auch den Tod ihres Sohnes Benny (Busunfall im November 1995) und die 30 anderen Todesfälle, darunter drei Morde – der schönste ist der mit der Bratpfanne –, hat sie gut weggesteckt.

Neben Frau Beimer/Marjan sind noch acht andere Personen von Anfang an dabei. Insgesamt haben in den ersten 20 Jahren 150 Schauspieler und viele Gäste – darunter sogar der aus der amerikanischen Serie »Dallas« bekannte Larry Hagman alias J. R. Ewing – mitgespielt.

Inzwischen gibt es über 220 wissenschaftliche Arbeiten über die Serie, und einmal war sie sogar schon Thema einer Habilitationsschrift. Am Anfang hatte sie es aber keineswegs leicht. Eine große Zeitung aus Frankfurt hat 1985 mit gerunzelter Stirn geschrieben: »Das sollen wir sein? Sind wir so langweilig, so säuerlich moralisch, so einfältig und lebensmüde? Und selbst wenn wir so wären: Müssen wir uns dabei auch noch zuschauen? Nein, so schlecht muss das Leben nicht spielen.« Die Zuschauer sehen das jedenfalls anders.

Falls es aber mit der Serie tatsächlich einmal zu Ende gehen sollte, hat der Erfinder Hans W. Geißendörfer schon lange »einen fantastischen Plan für die letzten zehn Folgen«.

»LINDENSTRASSE«, COLOGNE

This is the bedroom in mother Beimer's flat at Lindenstrasse 3. She said I could stretch out and take a short break here. Helga Beimer – and the actress Marie Luise Marjan who plays her role – has been here from the beginning. Up to December 8, 2005, she had taken part in 1045 episodes and survived many »slings and arrows of outrageous fortune«. During this time, she raised three children, got divorced and finally became self-employed. She even managed to cope with the death of her son Benny (bus accident in November 1995) and the 30 other cases of death, among which were three murders – the best of all being the one with the frying pan.

Along with Ms. Beimer/Marjan, eight other people have been here from the beginning. During the first 20 years, a total of 150 actors took part, plus many guests, including Larry Hagman alias J. R. Ewing from the American series »Dallas«.

In the meantime, the series has spawned 220 scholarly articles and it was once even the theme of a post-doctoral thesis. Nonetheless, it didn't have it easy at the beginning. A major Frankfurt newspaper wrote in 1985, with furrowed brow: »This is supposed to be us? Are we that boring, that grimly moralistic, that simple-minded and world-weary? And even if we are: do we have to watch ourselves being so? No, life does not have to turn out that badly.« In any event, for 20 years now the viewers have been of a different opinion.

But in case the series should at some time come to an end, its author Hans W. Geißendörfer has, long since, thought out »a fantastic plan for the last ten episodes«.

GESTÜT RÖTTGEN, KÖLN

Mindestens zwei Kölner Spezialitäten sind auf der ganzen Welt bekannt: der Dom und »4711«, das beliebte Kölnisch Wasser oder Eau de Cologne.

1918 hat Peter Mühlens, der Fabrikant, der dieses Erfrischungswasser damals herstellte, östlich von Köln ein Schloss mit einem großen Park gekauft und im Renaissance-Stil aus- und umbauen lassen, das Schloss Röttgen. Peter Mülhens war nicht nur Schloss-, sondern auch Pferdeliebhaber und hat 1924 ein Gestüt gegründet: das Gestüt Röttgen. Es ist bis heute eines der schönsten und erfolgreichsten nicht nur in Deutschland, sondern in ganz Europa.

Nach dem Zweiten Weltkrieg hat sich der britische Militärgouverneur und Hohe Kommissar Robertson in Schloss Röttgen eingerichtet, und Peter Mülhens musste samt Familie ins Gestütsmeisterhaus umziehen. Während dieser Zeit hat Konrad Adenauer hier mit Robertson darüber beraten, was aus dem zerstörten Nachkriegsdeutschland werden sollte. Im Mai 1949 wurde die Bundesrepublik gegründet, Adenauer wurde Bundeskanzler, und 1953 durfte die Familie Mülhens wieder in ihr Schloss zurück.

Im Gestüt Röttgen konnte man sich dann in aller Ruhe wieder auf die Vollblutzucht konzentrieren – und mit Erfolg: Die Pferde und Jockeys aus Röttgen haben alles gewonnen, was es im Galoppsport zu gewinnen gibt, sogar das berühmteste Rennen der Welt, den »Prix de l'Arc de Triomphe« in Paris im Jahr 1975.

Damit die empfindlichen Vollblüter hier so ungestört wie möglich trainieren und sich vermehren können, ist der ganze wunderschöne Park von einer neun Kilometer langen Mauer eingefasst. Hier wär' ich auch gerne Pferd.

RÖTTGEN STUD FARM, COLOGNE

At least two Cologne specialties are known throughout the world: the cathedral and »4711«, the popular Kölnisch Wasser or eau de cologne.

In 1918, Peter Mühlens, the manufacturer who created this refreshing eau de toilette, bought a castle to the east of Cologne, Schloss Röttgen, surrounded by a large park and rebuilt and expanded it in Renaissance style. Peter Mühlens was not only a fan of castles but of horses, and he founded a stud farm in 1924: Gestüt Röttgen. It is still today one of the most beautiful and most successful, not only in Germany, but in the whole of Europe.

After World War II, the British military governor and High Commissioner Robertson took over Schloss Röttgen, and Peter Mühlens had to move his entire family into the house of the stud farm master. During this time, Konrad Adenauer consulted with Robertson about what would become of a devastated postwar Germany. In May 1949, the Federal Republic was founded; Adenauer became chancellor and in 1953 the Mühlens family was allowed to move back into their castle.

At the stud farm one could again concentrate in peace on breeding thoroughbreds – and this with visible success: the horses and jockeys from Röttgen won everything there was to win in racing, even the most famous race of them all, the »Prix de l'Arc de Triomphe« in Paris in 1975.

So that the sensitive thoroughbreds can train and multiply with as little disturbance as possible, the entire scenic park is enclosed within a nine-kilometre-long wall. I myself wouldn't mind being a horse here at all.

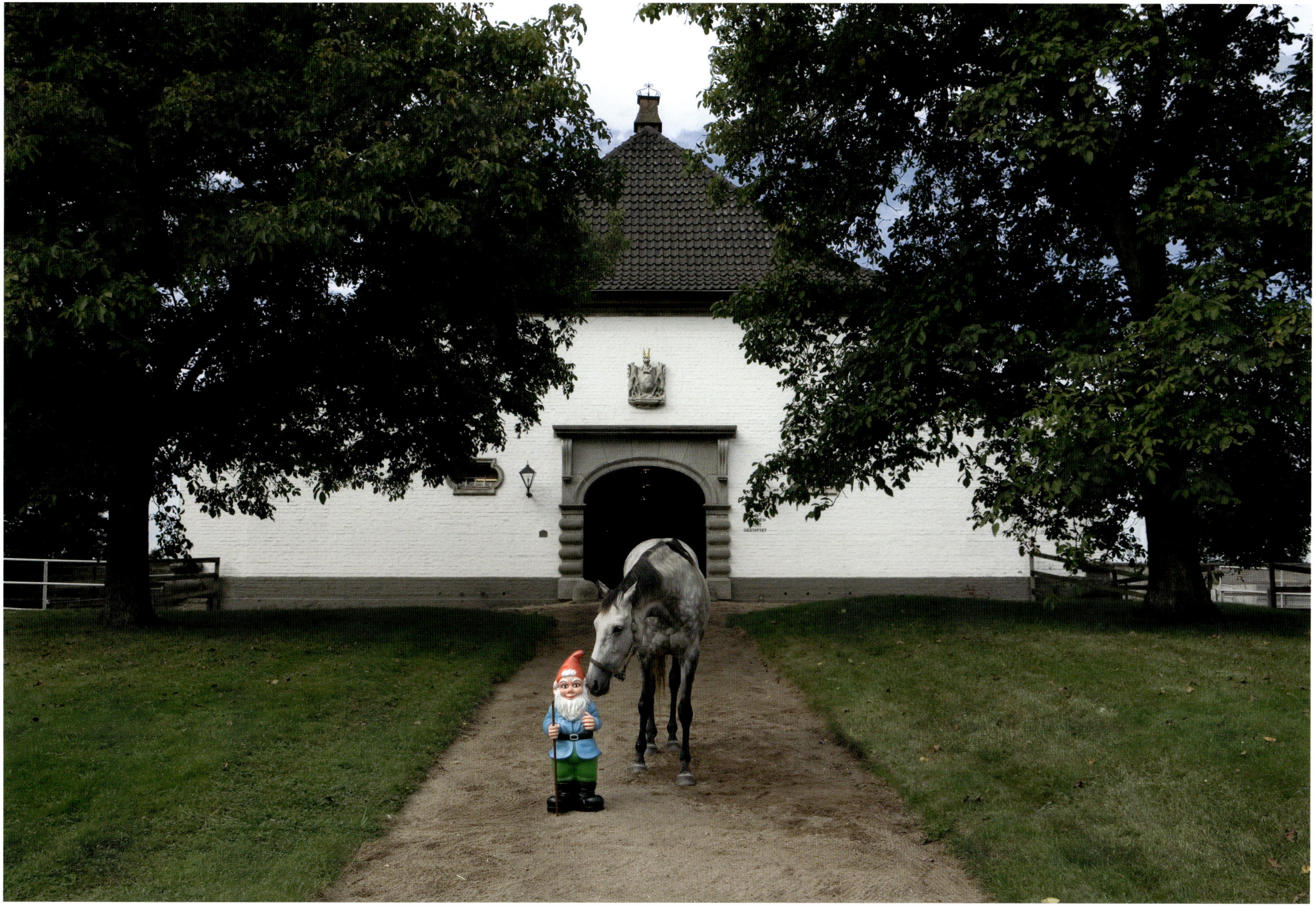

MUSEUM ALEXANDER KOENIG, BONN

Um ein Haar wäre das Haus, in dem ich hier stehe, Bundeskanzleramt geworden. Und zwar 1949. Konrad Adenauer hatte hier jedenfalls schon mal sein Büro eingerichtet.

Bonn war nach dem Zweiten Weltkrieg genauso zerstört wie die meisten deutschen Großstädte. Nur ein paar repräsentative Gebäude waren heil geblieben, und man konnte sie als vorläufige Regierungsgebäude nutzen; eins davon war das Naturkundemuseum Alexander Koenig.

Am 1. September 1948 hat hier zum ersten Mal der »Parlamentarische Rat« getagt. Der war eine provisorische Nationalversammlung und hatte hauptsächlich die Aufgabe, eine neue Verfassung auszuarbeiten. Und weil die auch nur provisorisch war, hat man sie eben nicht Verfassung genannt, sondern »Grundgesetz«. Das ist am 23. Mai 1949 verkündet worden und am nächsten Tag in Kraft getreten; es heißt übrigens heute noch so.

Konrad Adenauer ist dann der erste Bundeskanzler geworden (bis 1963), Bonn wurde Hauptstadt (bis 1990) und Regierungssitz (bis 1999). Der erste Bundespräsident, Theodor Heuss, ist 1951 schräg gegenüber in die »Villa Hammerschmidt« eingezogen, die früher ebenfalls der Familie Koenig gehörte. Der Bundeskanzler hatte sich schon nebenan im »Palais Schaumburg« eingerichtet.

Das Museum Koenig war bald wieder ein richtiges Museum, und mit über sieben Millionen Präparaten gehört es heute zu den größten Naturkundemuseen der Welt. Als der Parlamentarische Rat 1948 in der großen Halle tagte, hat man die präparierten Giraffen übrigens mit Tüchern verhüllt. Die und viele andere Tiere stehen heute noch da und werden bestaunt. Aber bei meinem Besuch waren sie alle für kurze Zeit vergessen, und die Attraktion war ich.

MUSEUM ALEXANDER KOENIG, BONN

It was only by the skin of its teeth that this house I am standing in did not become the Federal Chancellery. That was in 1949. Konrad Adenauer had even set up an office here for himself.

After World War II, Bonn was as much in ruins as most German cities. Only a few representative buildings remained whole and could be used as provisional government buildings. One of them was the Alexander Koenig Natural History Museum.

On September 1, 1948, the Parliamentary Advisory Board began a series of meetings here. It was a provisional national assembly and its main task was to work out a new constitution. And because it was only provisional, it was not called a constitution, but a »Grundgesetz« or basic law. It was officially announced on May 23, 1949, and came into effect the next day and is, still to this day, called the Basic Law.

Konrad Adenauer became the first German chancellor (until 1963); Bonn became the capital (until 1990) and the seat of government (until 1999). In 1951, the first German president, Theodor Heuss, moved across the street from the museum into the »Villa Hammerschmidt«, which used to belong to the Koenig family, too. And the chancellor set himself up next door in the »Palais Schaumburg«.

The Koenig Museum soon went back to being a proper museum, and is, with over seven million specimens, today one of the world's largest natural history museums. During the time the Parliamentary Board held its meetings in the great entrance hall, the preserved giraffes were covered in cloth. They and many other animals continue to inhabit the premises and are there to be wondered at. But during my visit, they were forgotten for a short time and I was the big attraction.

179

MONTABAUR

Im Jahr 1217 kam der Trierer Erzbischof Dietrich von Wied von einem Kreuzzug aus dem Heiligen Land zurück. Zum Erzbistum Trier gehörte auch das – damals zerstörte – Castellum Humbacense auf einem Berg im Westerwald mit dem Dorf Humbach ganz in der Nähe. Er ließ es wieder aufbauen, unter anderem um den Grafen von Nassau in Schach zu halten. Der hatte ihn nämlich zuvor zwei Jahre lang eingekerkert; so etwas war unter Grafen, Fürsten und Erzbischöfen damals überhaupt nichts Ungewöhnliches. Und weil ihn der Berg mit dem neuen Schloss an einen Hügel erinnerte, den er auf dem Kreuzzug in Galiläa gesehen hatte, nannte er die ganze Anlage »Mons Tabor«.

Wenn der Erzbischof heute von Montabaur aus ins Heilige Land ziehen wollte, könnte er ein paar hundert Meter vom Schloss entfernt in den ICE nach Frankfurt steigen, dort ins Flugzeug, und ein paar Stunden später wäre er in Jerusalem. Zur Zeit der Kreuzzüge waren die Ritterheere auf solchen Reisen meistens Jahre unterwegs und mussten ständig gegen die Heiden kämpfen. Aber Kreuzzüge sind gottseidank seit vielen hundert Jahren nicht mehr üblich, und Erzbischöfe haben heute sowieso andere Aufgaben.

MONTABAUR

In 1217, the Archbishop Dietrich von Wied of Trier returned from a crusade to the Holy Land. His diocese of Trier included the Castellum Humbacense – at the time destroyed – which was located on a hill in the Westerwald, very close to the village of Humbach. The archbishop had it, rebuilt, amongst other reasons, in order to keep the Count of Nassau at bay. It was this count who had previously held the archbishop prisoner for two years. Such goings-on were nothing unusual among counts, princes and archbishops at the time. And because the summit with the new castle reminded him of a hilltop in Galilee, the archbishop called the whole complex »Mons Tabor«.

If today the archbishop were to go off to the Holy Land, he could board the Intercity Express (ICE) to Frankfurt a couple of hundred metres from the castle, from there climb aboard an aeroplane and, in a couple of hours, be in Jerusalem. At the time of the Crusades, knights were on the road for years and constantly had to battle heathens. But thank the Lord, crusades have not been the »in« thing for several hundreds of years, and archbishops today have other tasks to attend to.

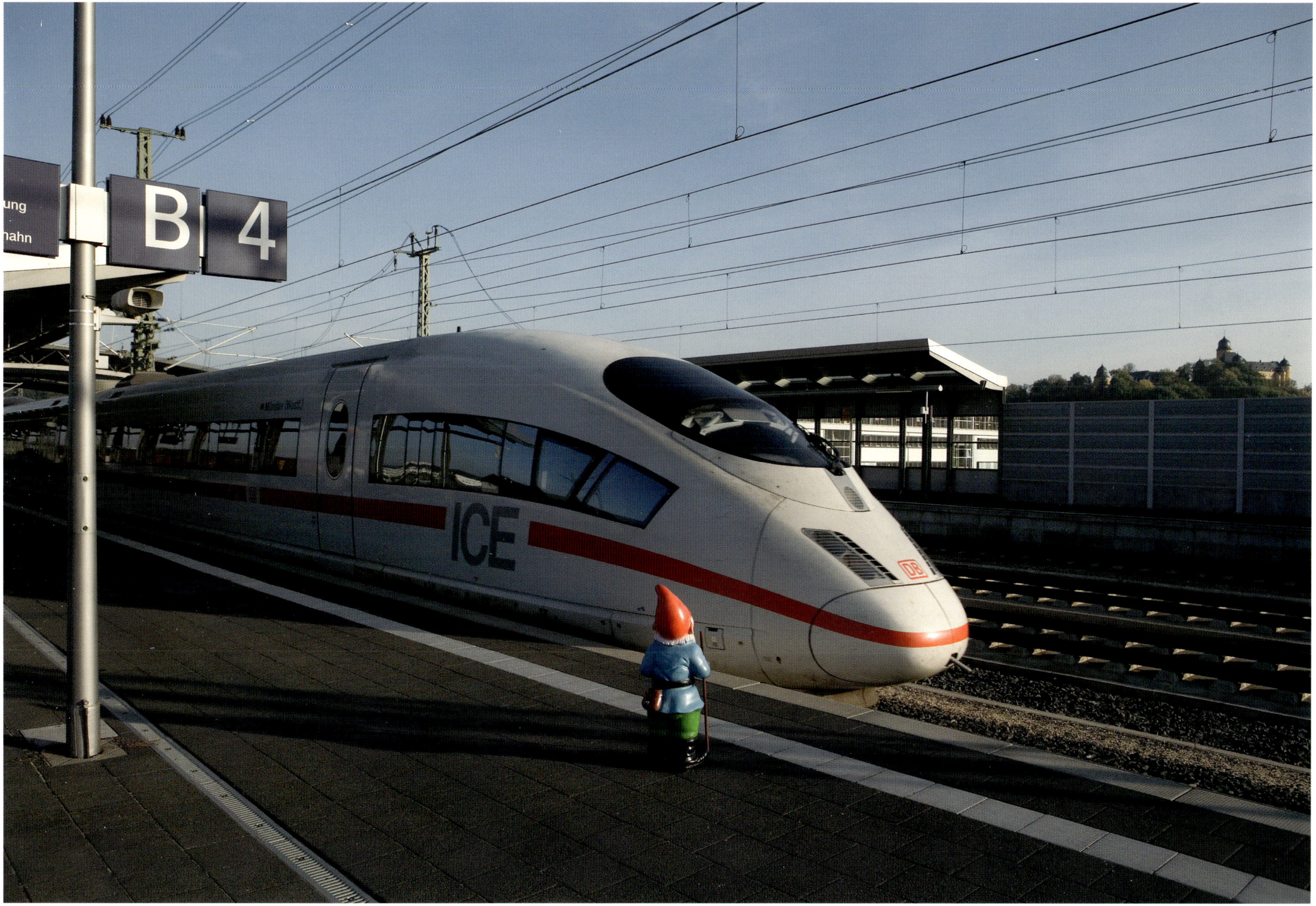
B
4
ICE
DB

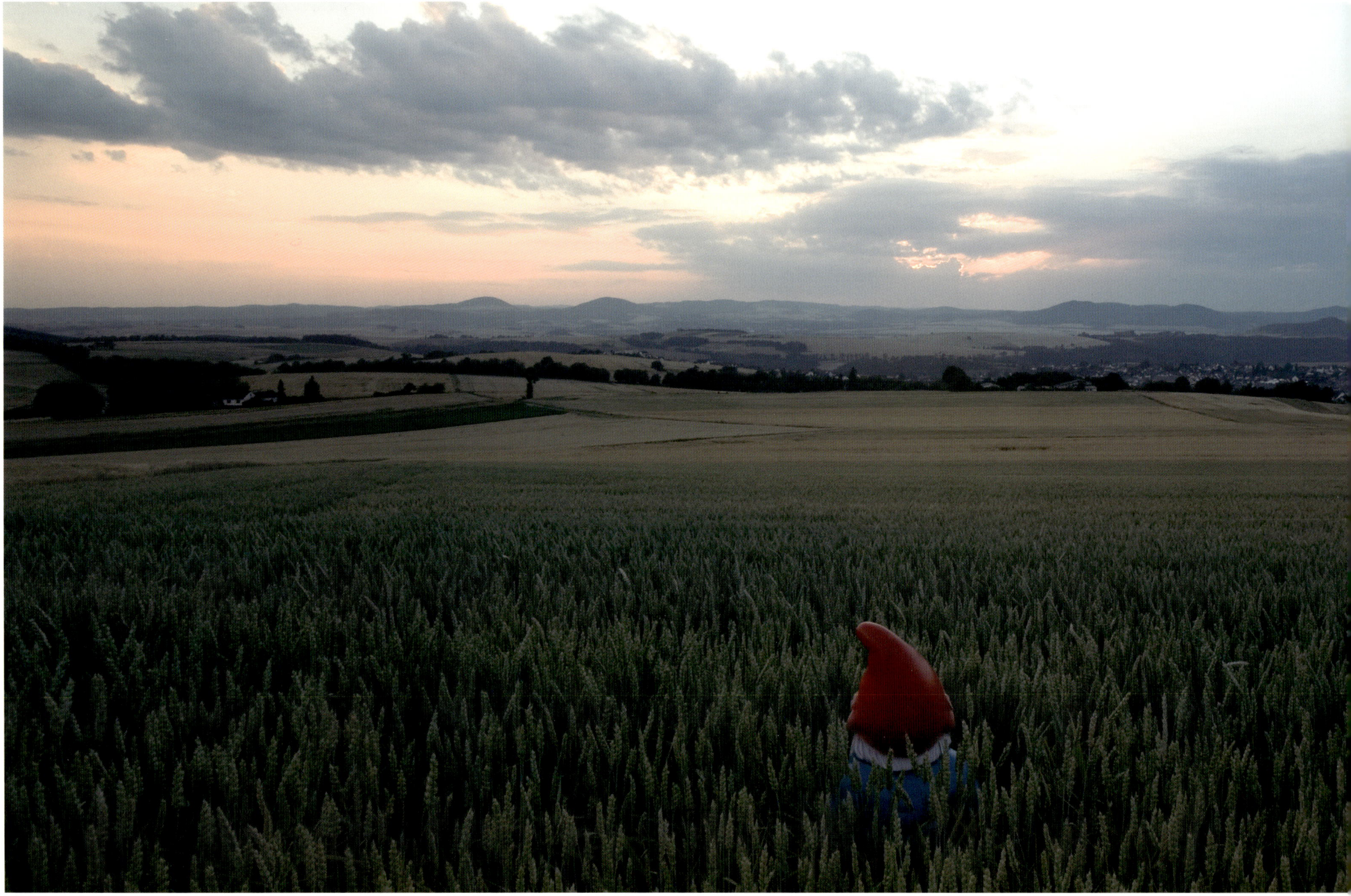

OCHTENDUNG, EIFEL

Die Eifel liegt, ähnlich wie Hawaii, über einem »HotSpot«. In 32 Kilometern Tiefe wartet 1.000 bis 1.400 Grad heißes flüssiges Gestein auf die nächste Gelegenheit zum Ausbruch. Über solchen Magmakammern hebt sich die Erdkruste unablässig, im Fall der Eifel sind das im Jahr ein bis zwei Millimeter. Im Laufe eines Menschenlebens macht das immerhin rund 15 Zentimeter aus, und aus Sicht der Geologen ist das ein ganz rasantes Tempo.

In den letzten 700.000 Jahren gab es hier etwa einhundert Vulkanausbrüche. Nach einem Vulkanausbruch ist im Durchschnitt erst mal zehn- bis zwanzigtausend Jahre Ruhe. Der letzte liegt inzwischen ungefähr 10.000 Jahre zurück. Theoretisch kann es also jeden Tag wieder losgehen, und hin und wieder bebt die Erde in dieser Gegend ja auch ein bisschen. In den letzten Tagen war hier aber alles ruhig.

OCHTENDUNG, EIFEL

The Eifel, like Hawaii, lies above a »hot spot«. At a depth of 32 kilometres, molten rock at a temperature of 1,000 to 1,400° C is just waiting for the next opportunity to erupt. It is above such magma chambers that the earth's crust constantly pushes upwards: in the case of the Eifel, one to two millimetres a year. And that does after all, come to 15 centimetres during a person's lifetime and, for geologists, that's breakneck speed.

Over the past 700,000 years, around one hundred eruptions have occurred. After an eruption, there is peace and quiet for an average of about 10,000 to 20,000 years. The last one took place approximately 10,000 years ago. This means, theoretically at least, it could all start up again any day now, and from time to time the ground in this region does tremble a bit. Over these last few days, however, everything's been cool.

NÜRBURGRING

Autorennen gibt es fast schon so lange, wie es Autos gibt. Regelrechte Rennwagen sind erst ein paar Jahrzehnte später gebaut worden. Und das gilt auch für Rennstrecken, denn für ein Rennen brauchte man früher nichts weiter als eine normale Straße. Aber es gibt zwischen klassischen und modernen Rennstrecken einen wichtigen Unterschied: Früher haben die Fahrer ihre Geschwindigkeit der Strecke angepasst, heute ist es umgekehrt.

Was das heißt, kann man am Nürburgring sehen. Die »schönste Rennstrecke der Welt« liegt mitten in der Eifel, gut 40 Kilometer südlich von Bonn. Eine wunderbare Landstraße ohne Gegenverkehr, durch Wälder und Wiesen, über Berge und Täler. Sie ist zwischen 1925 und 1927 gebaut worden, war ursprünglich 22,8 Kilometer lang, hatte 73 Kurven und Steigungen bis zu 17 Prozent. Zwischen der höchsten und der niedrigsten Stelle liegen fast 300 Meter.

Der Sieger im ersten Rennen 1927 war Rudolf Caracciola auf einem Kompressor-Mercedes SSK. Nach ihm ist diese Steilkurve benannt: das Caracciola-Karussell. Am Horizont sieht man die Ruine der Nürburg, nach der der Ring benannt ist. Sieben Jahre später bekam der erste Mercedes-Rennwagen hier den Namen »Silberpfeil«. Seit 1977 finden auf der Nordschleife keine Formel-1-Rennen mehr statt, sondern nur noch Tourenwagen- und Langstreckenrennen. Wenn kein Rennen stattfindet, kann jedermann gegen Gebühr mit dem eigenen Auto seine Fahrkünste erproben.

NÜRBURGRING

Automobile races are almost as old as cars themselves. But cars meant exclusively for racing were not built till several decades later. And the same goes for racetracks, because in that day and age, a race needed nothing more than a normal road. But between classic and modern racecourses there is an important difference. Drivers used to adjust their speed to suit the road, whereas today the reverse is true.

What that has come to mean, you can see at the Nürburgring. The »most beautiful racetrack in the world« lies at the heart of the Eifel, a good 40 kilometres south of Bonn. A wonderful country road with no oncoming traffic: through woods, over meadows and hills and across valleys. It was built between 1925 and 1927, was originally 22.8 kilometres long, had 73 curves, and gradients up to 17 percent. There is a difference of 300 metres between the highest and the lowest points.

The winner of the first race in 1927 was Rudolf Caracciola, driving a compressor Mercedes SSK. The steeply banked corner is named after him: the Caracciola Carousel. On the horizon, you can see the ruins of the Nürburg, which gave its name to the track. Seven years later, the first Mercedes racing car was baptized the »Silberpfeil« or Silver Arrow. Since 1977, Formula 1 racing no longer takes place on the northern loop, only touring car and long distance races. When no races are scheduled, anyone willing to pay the fee can try out his driving skills here, using his own car.

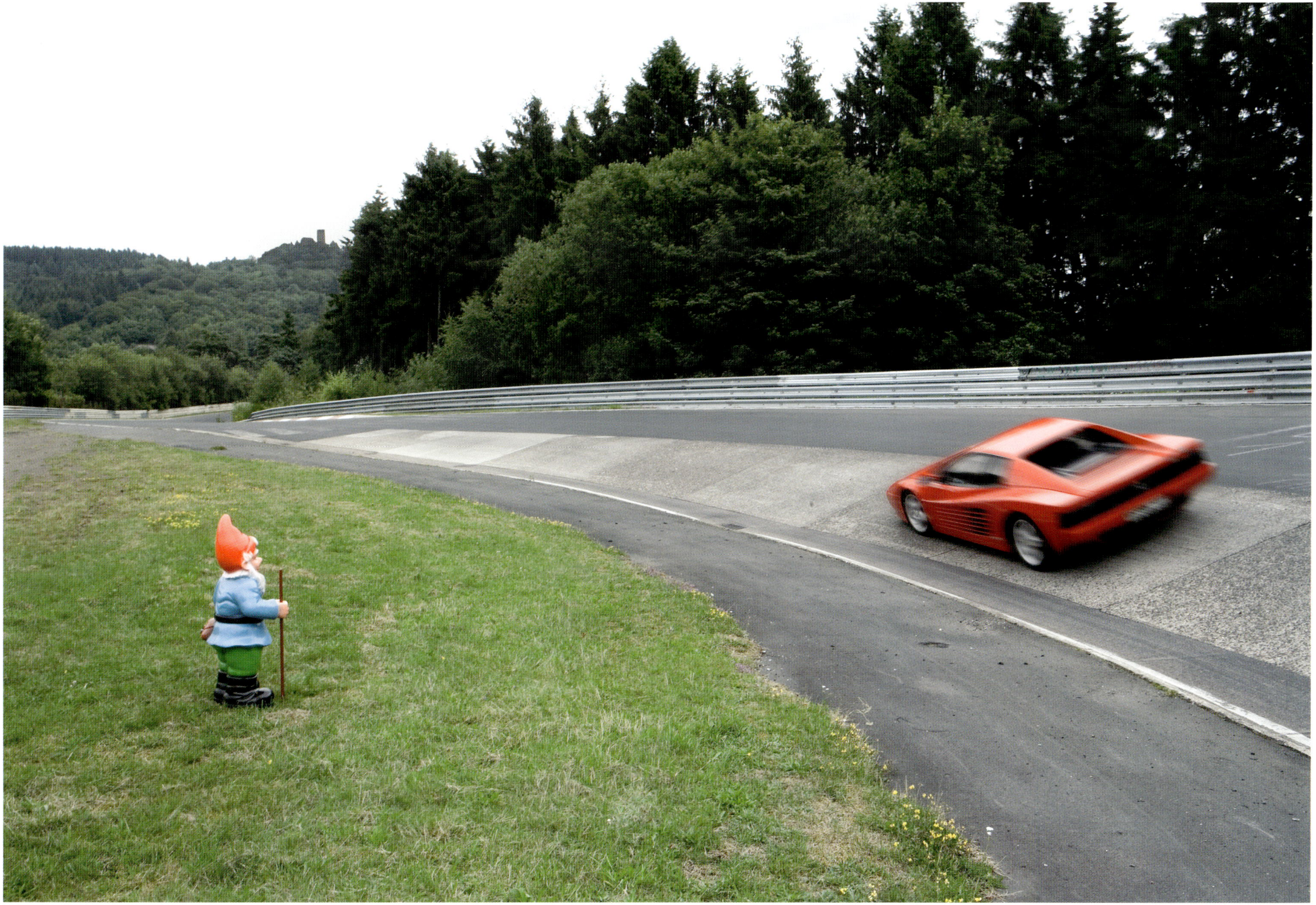

BURG ELTZ, WIERSCHEM

Über 7000 Burgen und Burgruinen gibt es in Deutschland, und es ist wirklich nicht ganz leicht zu sagen, welche die eindrucksvollste oder schönste ist. Aber ich bin sicher, dass die Burg Eltz zumindest unter die ersten drei käme. Es ist ja kein Zufall, dass sie auf der Rückseite eines alten Fünfhundert-Mark-Scheins abgebildet war. Zu den besterhaltenen Burgen gehört sie auf alle Fälle, und die Eigentümer tun alles, damit das auch so bleibt.

Die Burg ist seit 850 Jahren im Familienbesitz, aber die Burgherren wohnen hier schon lange nicht mehr. Der jetzige Eigentümer, Dr. Karl Graf von und zu Eltz-Kempenich, genannt Faust von Stromberg, lebt in Frankfurt und im Eltzer Hof zu Eltville am Rhein.

Angefangen hat alles mit Friedrich I., dem Kaiser Barbarossa. Der hat im Jahr 1157 dem Ahnherrn Rudolf eine kleine Burg an dem Flüsschen Elz geschenkt, nicht weit von der Mosel, südwestlich von Koblenz; Reste davon sind heute noch zu sehen. Der Beschenkte nannte sich von da an Rudolf von Elz; irgendwann kam noch ein »t« dazu. In den folgenden Jahrhunderten ist die Burg in mehreren Etappen ausgebaut und vergrößert worden, die Burgherren wurden immer mächtiger und einflussreicher. Sie wurden Domherren, Universitätsrektoren und sogar Kurfürsten.

Als eine der wenigen Burganlagen in Deutschland ist die Burg Eltz all die Jahrhunderte unversehrt geblieben. Selbst den Pfälzischen Erbfolgekrieg, in dem die meisten Burgen ringsum zerstört wurden (und in dem Ludwig XIV. das Heidelberger Schloss sprengen ließ), hat die Burg Eltz überstanden. Hans Anton zu Eltz-Üttingen war damals zufällig ein hoher Offizier im französischen Heer. Ihr endgültiges Aussehen hat die Burg zwischen 1845 und 1888 erhalten, als Graf Karl zu Eltz die Anlage mit großem Einsatz erweitert und restauriert hat.

BURG ELTZ, WIERSCHEM

There are over 7000 castles and fortress ruins in Germany, which makes it extremely difficult to say which is the most impressive or the most beautiful. But I am sure that Burg Eltz would at least be counted among the top three. It's not by chance that it is pictured on the reverse side of an old five hundred Mark note. In any case, it is one of the best preserved, and the owners do everything in their power to keep it that way.

For 850 years, the Burg has been family-owned, although the castellans have not lived here for a long time. The present owner, Dr. Karl Graf von und zu Eltz-Kempenich, otherwise known as Faust von Stromberg, lives in Frankfurt as well as at the Eltzer Hof in Eltville on the Rhine.

It all began with Friedrich I, Emperor Barbarossa. In 1157, he awarded the family ancestor Rudolf a small fortress on the river Elz, not far from the Moselle, southwest of Koblenz. You can still today see its remains. From then on, the recipient called himself Rudolf von Elz, and, at some time or other, a »t« was added. Over the following centuries, the castle was added on to and consolidated in stages, while the castle proprietors grew ever more powerful and more influential. They became canons of the church, university chancellors and even prince-electors.

As one of the few castle complexes in Germany, Burg Eltz has remained intact over all these centuries. It even survived the French-Palatinate War of Succession unimpaired, during which most of the neighbouring castles were destroyed and Louis XIV ordered Heidelberg Castle to be blown up. It might have helped that Hans Anton zu Eltz-Üttingen happened, at the time, to be a senior officer in the French army. The Burg took on its final look between 1845 and 1888, when Graf Karl zu Eltz made a great effort to restore and enlarge it.

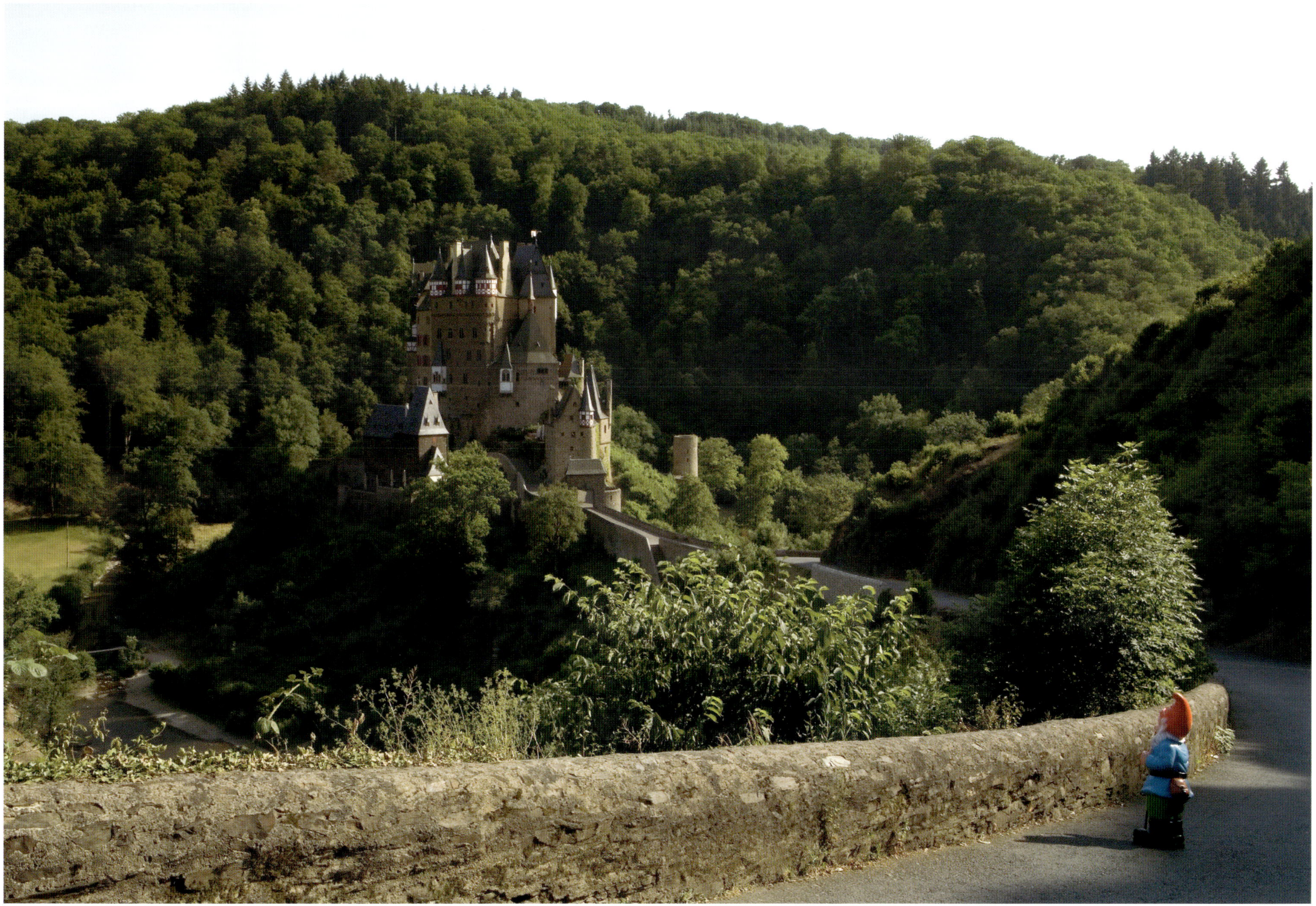

MOSELSCHLEIFE, KRÖV

Der kleine 2500-Seelen-Ort Kröv an der Mosel wäre wahrscheinlich nicht bekannter als andere Orte in der Umgebung, wenn hier nicht ein Wein angebaut würde, dessen Namen vornehmere Menschen, wenn überhaupt, allenfalls hinter vorgehaltener Hand aussprechen: den »Kröver Nacktarsch«.

Die Herkunft dieses Namens ist aber wahrscheinlich gar nicht so derb, wie er sich anhört, und es gibt dafür verschiedene Erklärungen. Die bekannteste und beliebteste ist die, bei der zwei kleinen Jungs der nackte Hintern versohlt wird, weil sie sich unerlaubterweise im Weinkeller herumgetrieben haben. Abbildungen davon findet man überall in Kröv. Für sehr viel wahrscheinlicher halte ich es aber, dass die Kröver das lateinische Wort »nectareus« im Laufe der Zeit zu »Nacktarsch« umgeschliffen haben, der Weg vom einen zum andern ist ja wirklich nicht sehr weit. »Nectareus« heißt aber einfach »aus Nektar« oder »süß wie Nektar«, was ins Weindeutsch übersetzt nichts anderes bedeutet als »lieblich«. Liebliche Weine allerdings, so hat mir ein Kellermeister gesagt, sind heute nicht mehr so sehr gefragt.

Lieblich ist und bleibt aber die Landschaft. Zwischen Bernkastel-Kues und Cochem mäandert die Mosel so sehr, dass man meinen könnte, sie möchte diese Gegend am liebsten gar nicht mehr verlassen. Mir ging's ganz ähnlich, nur kann ich nicht mäandern.

MOSELLE LOOP, KRÖV

The small village of Kröv on the Moselle River with its 2500 inhabitants would probably not be any better known than any other of its neighbours if it weren't for the fact that one of their wines has a name that respectable people, if at all, only whisper behind a raised hand: »Kröver Nacktarsch« or »Naked Arse«.

The origin of the name »Naked Arse« is, however, probably not at all as crude as it seems and has inspired a variety of explanations. The best known and the most popular is the story that two little boys had their naked buttocks spanked for playing around in the off-limits wine cellar. You will find illustrations of this scene all over Kröv. But I find it much more likely that the people of Kröv corrupted the Latin word »nectareus«, turning it into the word »Nacktarsch« over the years, for the distance between the two is really not all that great. »Nectareus« simply means »from nectar« or »sweet as nectar«, which in wine-speak simply means »sweet«. However, the winegrower told me that sweet wines today are no longer much in demand.

What is, however, definitely sweet and lovely is the countryside. Between Bernkastel-Kues and Cochem, the Moselle meanders so much that it makes you think that it would love best of all to stay in this region. Which is the way I felt too, but I'm no good at meandering.

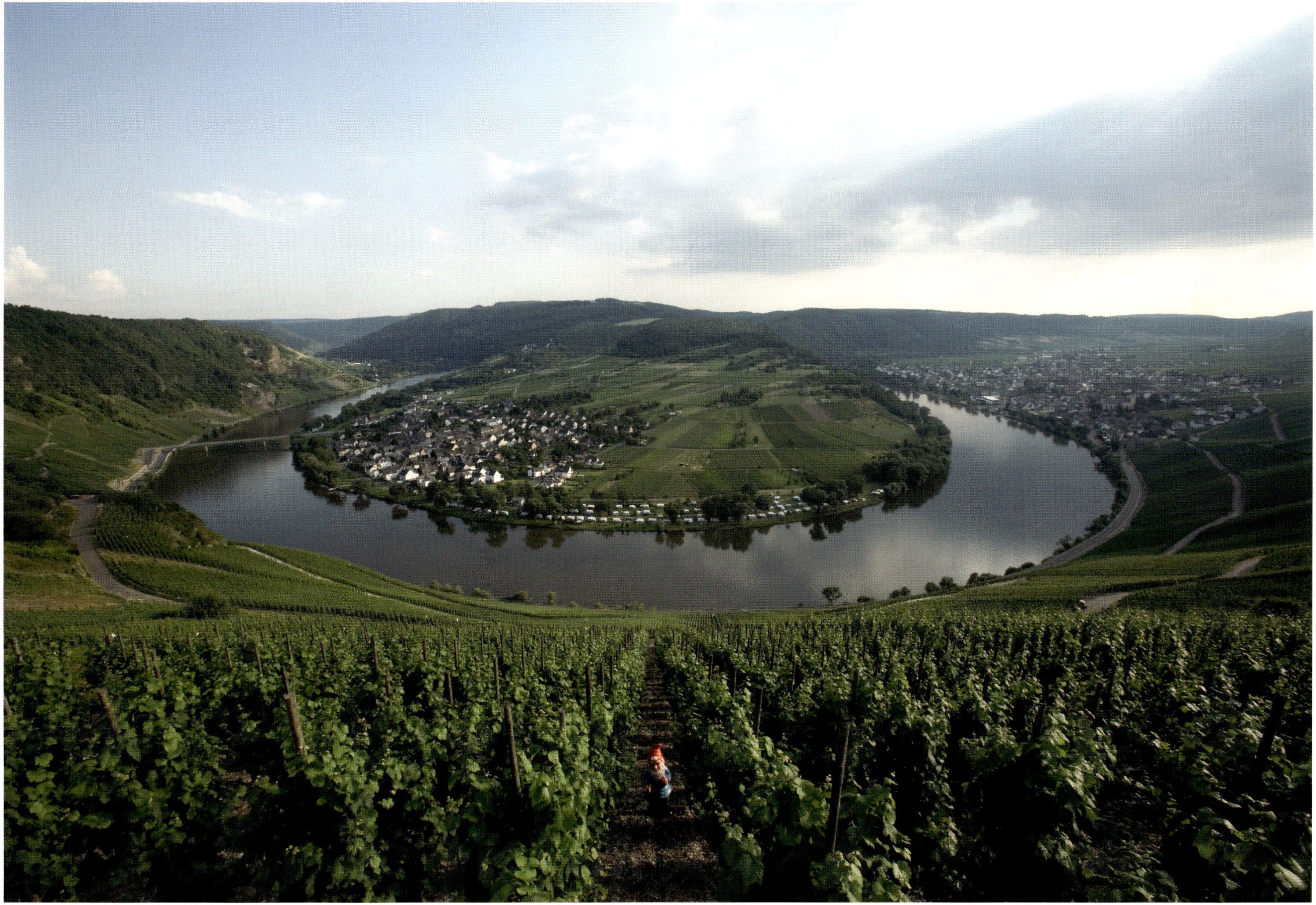

190

MÄUSETURM, BINGEN

Der Mäuseturm im Rhein bei Bingen hat mit Mäusen eigentlich nichts zu tun. Er ist ein alter Zollturm, an dem die rheinauf und rheinab fahrenden Schiffe Maut bezahlen mussten. Und aus »Maut« ist wahrscheinlich »Maus« und später »Mäuse« geworden. (Vielleicht kommt der Name aber auch von »musen«, einem alten Wort für »spähen«, denn der Mautturm war gleichzeitig ein Wachturm.) Aber dann erzählt man noch die Legende vom hartherzigen Mainzer Erzbischof Hatto aus dem 10. Jahrhundert, der im Turm bei lebendigem Leibe von Mäusen aufgefressen worden sein soll. Einen Turm gab es zu der Zeit zwar noch gar nicht, aber von sowas lassen sich Legenden ja bekanntlich nicht weiter stören.

Als der Turm – so viel ist sicher – im 14. Jahrhundert gebaut wurde, hat er ganz anders ausgesehen als heute. Nach 300 Jahren ist er zerstört worden und stand fast 200 Jahre lang als Ruine auf der Insel im Fluss. So neugotisch, wie er jetzt da steht, stammt er aus dem Jahr 1858. Um diese Zeit haben die Kölner grade ihren Dom zu Ende gebaut, und der Dombaumeister bekam vom preußischen König den Auftrag, dann auch gleich den Mäuseturm als Wach- und Zollturm wieder aufzubauen; Bingen gehörte damals nämlich zu Preußen, genauso wie Köln, Sylt, Breslau oder Königsberg.

Der Rhein fließt durch eine der ältesten Kulturlandschaften in Europa. Seit 2000 Jahren ist er einer der wichtigsten Verkehrswege zwischen dem Mittelmeerraum und Nordeuropa. Der Mäuseturm markiert den südlichen Eingang zum »Weltkulturerbe Oberes Mittelrheintal«, das sich über 65 Kilometer von hier bis nach Koblenz erstreckt – eine der schönsten Landschaften in Deutschland. Alle ein bis zwei Kilometer trifft man hier auf eine Burg, ein Schloss oder eine Festung. Und auf Weinberge: Nirgendwo sonst auf der Welt wird an so steilen Hängen Wein angebaut wie in diesem Tal.

MÄUSETURM, BINGEN

The Mouse Tower on the Rhine near Bingen has, in fact, nothing to do with mice. It is an old customs tower, where the ships that plied their way up and down the river had to pay a toll, in German »Maut«. And from the word »Maut« probably came the word »Maus« and later the plural »Mäuse«. (Perhaps, though, the name came from »musen«, an old word for »spähen/to spy«, since the tower was, at the same time, a watchtower.) But then legend specifically has it that in the 10th century, the hard-hearted archbishop of Mainz, Hatto, is supposed to have been eaten alive by mice here in the tower. No tower actually existed here at the time, but legends, as we know, don't pay attention to such things.

When the tower – this much is well established – was built in the 14th century, it looked quite different from today. It was destroyed 300 years later and stood on the island in the river as a ruin for almost 200 years. Its neo-Gothic look that it has today goes back to the year 1858. Around this time, the people of Cologne had just about finished building their cathedral, and the Prussian king commissioned the cathedral's master builder to reconstruct the Mäuseturm as a watchtower and toll tower. Bingen was, at the time, part of Prussia, as were Cologne, Sylt, Breslau and Königsberg.

The Rhine flows through one of the oldest cultural landscapes in Europe. For 2000 years, it has been among the most important traffic routes between the Mediterranean and Northern Europe. The Mäuseturm marks the southern entrance to the »World Cultural Heritage Site – the Upper Middle Rhine Valley«, that stretches 65 kilometres from here to Koblenz – one of the most beautiful areas of countryside in Germany. Every one or two kilometres, you come across a fortress, a castle or a fortification. And vineyards: nowhere else in the world is wine grown on such steep slopes as in this valley.

AMSELWEG, HASSLOCH

Habt ihr schon mal den Namen Haßloch gehört? Nein? Das ist nicht verwunderlich, den kennt wirklich kaum einer. Nach Haßloch fährt man auch nicht so wie zum Beispiel nach Rothenburg, Heidelberg oder Weimar. Das ist aber ein Fehler, denn die Deutschen haben fast alle irgendwie damit zu tun. In gewisser Weise ist Haßloch die wichtigste Stadt im Land. Sie ist nämlich vollkommen durchschnittlich und grade deshalb ganz besonders geeignet, wenn man herausfinden will, was den Menschen hierzulande gefällt und was nicht: Haßloch ist der Testmarkt der Bundesrepublik.

Es könnte wahrscheinlich auch irgendeine andere Stadt von dieser Größe sein, aber Haßloch hatte etwas, das keine andere Stadt bieten konnte: das erste Netz fürs Kabelfernsehen. Das war die Voraussetzung für ein Gerät, einen Decoder, mit dem zusätzliche Werbung ins Programm eingeblendet wird. Außerdem haben 3000 Haushalte hier besondere Chipkarten für sämtliche Einkäufe.

Vieles von dem, was irgendwann einmal in einem Supermarktregal stehen oder liegen soll, muss sich zuerst hier bewähren. Was die Haßlocher nicht kaufen oder sich nicht ansehen, kommt auch sonst nirgendwo in die Geschäfte oder auf den Fernsehschirm. Organisiert und ausgewertet wird das alles seit 1986 von der Gesellschaft für Konsumforschung in Nürnberg.

Wenn ihr wollt, könnt ihr Haßloch jetzt auch schon wieder vergessen. Aber wenn ihr das nächste Mal einkaufen geht oder den Fernseher einschaltet, fallen euch die Leute von Haßloch vielleicht wieder ein.

AMSELWEG, HASSLOCH

Have you ever heard of Hassloch? No? That's no wonder, for hardly any one has. You don't go to Hassloch as you would for instance to Rothenburg, Heidelberg or Weimar. But that's a mistake, for nearly all Germans have somehow or other a legacy here. In a certain way, Hassloch is the most important city in the country. It is thoroughly average and, for this reason, especially suitable if someone wants to find out what people in this country like or dislike: Hassloch is the testmarket for the Federal Republic.

Any other town of this size would probably serve just as well, but Hassloch has something that no other town can offer: the first cable TV network. This was the prerequisite for a device, the decoder, with which additional commercials are slotted into the television programme. In addition, 3000 households have special chip cards that register all their purchases.

Everything that at sometime or other finds, or will find, a place on a supermarket shelf must prove itself here. What the people of Hassloch don't buy or don't watch does not appear in shops or on TV anywhere else. The Society for Consumer Research in Nuremberg has organized and evaluated this since 1986.

If you so wish, you can now choose to forget Hassloch once again. But when you go shopping the next time or switch on the telly, you may very well recall the people of Hassloch.

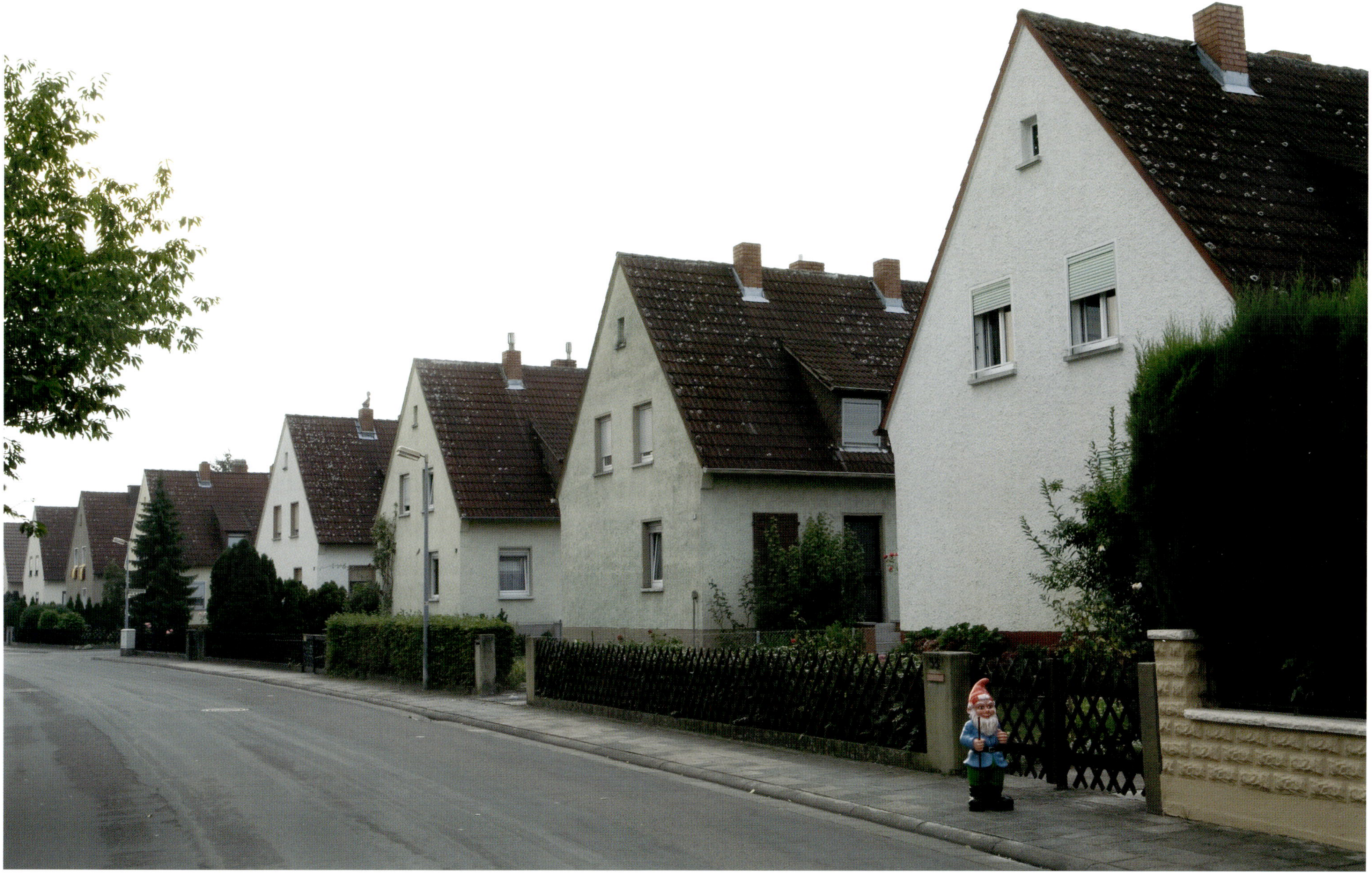

STAHLWERK, VÖLKLINGEN

Das Saarland kommt immer dann in den Nachrichten vor, wenn wieder einmal ein Größenvergleich gebraucht wird: »Eine Fläche von der Größe des Saarlands« heißt es oft, wenn man sich eine Vorstellung von irgendwas machen soll – aber wer weiß denn schon, wie groß das Saarland eigentlich ist? Es ist ziemlich genau dreimal so groß wie Berlin, nämlich exakt 2568 Quadratkilometer.

67 davon beansprucht die Stadt Völklingen im Westen an der französischen Grenze, und dort steht eines der ehemals größten und modernsten Hüttenwerke der Welt: die Völklinger Hütte. 1965 haben hier 17.000 Menschen Stahl gekocht und gewalzt. Die Hütte musste 1986, zehn Jahre nach der weltweiten Stahlkrise, stillgelegt werden. Zunächst wusste niemand, was man damit machen sollte, aber abgerissen hat man sie immerhin nicht. Zum Glück, denn so hat die Unesco 1994 die komplett erhaltene Völklinger Hütte als erstes Industriedenkmal zum »Weltkulturerbe« erklärt.

Der Vorläufer war 1873 gegründet worden und wurde 1879 schon wieder stillgelegt. 1881 hat Carl Röchling das Werk gekauft und mit seinen Brüdern Theodor und Fritz das »Völklinger Eisenwerk Gebrüder Röchling« gegründet. 1885 wurde dort der größte Hochofen der Welt angeblasen. In den Jahren danach führte Carl Röchlings Sohn Hermann wichtige Neuerungen in das Herstellungsverfahren ein und machte die Völklinger Hütte zur leistungsfähigsten Eisenhütte in Europa.

STEELWORKS, VÖLKLINGEN

The Saarland always gets into the news when there is any need for a comparison in size: »an area the size of the Saarland« is often said when you have to picture something. But who even knows how big the Saarland actually is? It is fairly precisely three times as big as Berlin, namely exactly 2568 square kilometres.

67 of those square kilometres are claimed by the city of Völklingen to the west and on the border, with France, and there stands the once biggest and most modern steelworks in the world: the Völklinger Hütte. In 1965, there were 17,000 people who smelted and rolled steel here. The works had to be shut down in 1986, ten years after the worldwide steel crisis. At first, no one knew what to do with the complex, but at least it wasn't torn down. Fortunately. For in 1994, Unesco declared the completely intact Völklinger Hütte a »world cultural heritage site«, the first industrial monument to be so.

Its predecessor was founded in 1873 and was already shut down by 1879. In 1881, Carl Röchling bought the factory and, with his brothers Theodor and Fritz, founded the »Völklinger Eisenwerk Gebrüder Röchling«. In 1885, the biggest blast furnace in the world was started up here. In the following years, Carl Röchling's son, Hermann, introduced important innovations in the methods of production and made the Völklinger Hütte into the best performing ironworks in Europe.

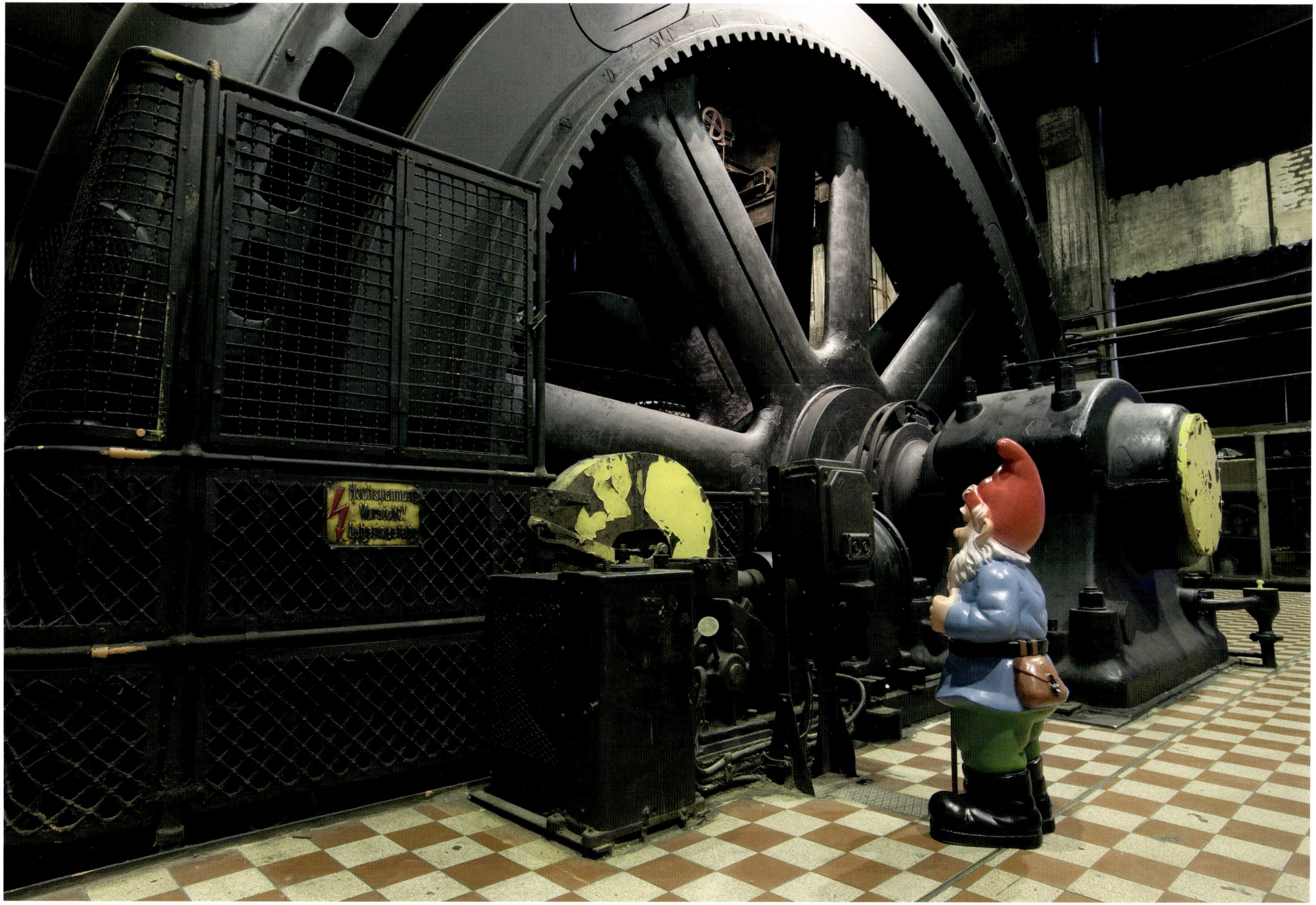
Hochspannung
Vorsicht!

UNTERMARKT, GÖRLITZ

Fast 50 Jahre lang war die Neiße eine scharf bewachte Grenze zwischen der DDR und Polen, sozialistischer Bruderstaat hin, sozialistischer Bruderstaat her. 50 Jahre lang hat diese Grenze auch ein paar Städte in zwei Teile geschnitten. Zum Beispiel Görlitz, 51° 09' N, 14° 59' O – viel weiter östlich kann man in Deutschland nicht leben. Seit 1945 ist der östliche Teil von Görlitz eine polnische Stadt: Zgorzelec.

Als der Kalte Krieg zu Ende war, sind die beiden Stadtteile rechts und links der Neiße allmählich wieder zusammengewachsen, und zwar so weit, dass sie sich schließlich gemeinsam um den Titel einer Kulturhauptstadt Europas für das Jahr 2010 beworben haben: Görlitz/Zgorzelec.

Wie durch ein Wunder ist Görlitz im Zweiten Weltkrieg nicht zerstört worden. In keiner anderen Stadt in Deutschland stehen noch so viele Häuser aus dem Mittelalter, der Renaissance und dem Barock: fast 4000 Baudenkmäler. Und deswegen kann man die Görlitzer auch gut verstehen, wenn sie ihre Stadt für die schönste in Deutschland halten.

Eines der schönsten Häuser ist die ehemalige Ratsapotheke im alten Stadtkern am Untermarkt mit dem doppelstöckigen Erker an der Ecke. Seit der Restaurierung ist hier das Ratscafé drin, und da habe ich in einem Renaissancegewölbe die berühmten Nusstörtchen gegessen. Ganz besonders hat mir das Dach mit den drei Augen gefallen, und ich bin sicher, dass die später am Abend zufallen, wenn das Haus müde wird.

Zum Schluss aber noch was ganz Verrücktes: Seit 1995 überweist ein unbekannter Gönner jedes Jahr eine Million Mark an einen Münchener Anwalt, damit in Görlitz Häuser renoviert oder restauriert werden können. Und bis heute weiß kein Mensch, von wem diese »Altstadtmillion« kommt.

UNTERMARKT, GÖRLITZ

For almost 50 years, the Neisse River was a closely watched border that divided East Germany from Poland, socialist bedfellows or no. For 50 years, this border also cut a couple of towns in two. For example Görlitz, 51° 09' N, 14° 59' E – and you can't go much further east and still live in Germany. Since 1945, the eastern part of Görlitz has been a Polish city: Zgorzelec.

When the Cold War was over, both sections of the city on the right and left of the Neisse slowly grew together again, so much so that, in tandem, they have applied for the title of European Cultural Capital 2010: Görlitz/Zgorzelec.

It's almost a miracle that Görlitz was not destroyed in World War II. In no other city in Germany are there so many buildings from the Middle Ages, the Renaissance and the Baroque still standing: almost 4000 architectural treasures. Which makes it easy to understand that the citizens of Görlitz consider their town to be Germany's most beautiful.

One of the most beautiful buildings of them all is the former Ratsapotheke or Council's Apothecary in the heart of the old town at Untermarkt, with its two-storey bay window on the corner. Since its restoration it has become a café and that is where, under its Renaissance vault, I munched on one of their famous nut tarts. What I especially like is the roof with its three eyes, which I'm sure close late at night when the house gets sleepy.

But I'll end with a really curious story: since 1995, an unknown patron has wired one million Deutschmark every year to a Munich solicitor for the renovation or restoration of houses in Görlitz. And still today, no one knows who it is who donates this »old-town million«.

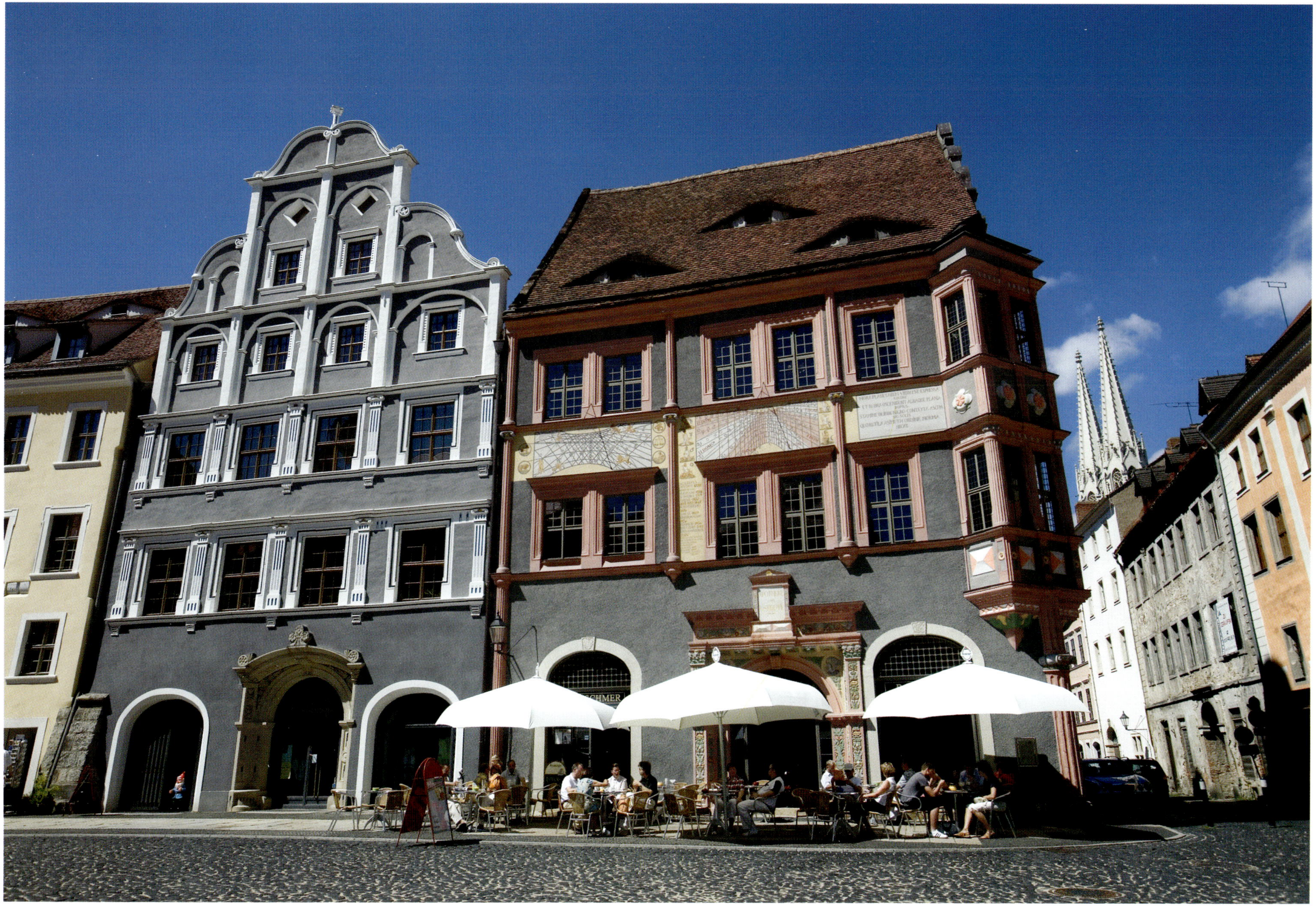

LOHMEN, SÄCHSISCHE SCHWEIZ

Habt ihr's entdeckt? Direkt über mir? Seht nur mal genauer hin. – Der Himmel hatte nämlich ein Herz für mich, als ich Ende Mai von Dresden nach Lohmen gewandert bin, dem »Tor zur Sächsischen Schweiz«.

Und wisst ihr, was »Brassica napus« ist? Nein? Wusste ich bis vor kurzem auch nicht, aber jetzt stehe ich grade mitten drin: Raps. Der macht die Landschaft im Mai und im Juni so wunderbar gelb. Und nun wollt ihr sicher auch noch wissen, was der Raps eigentlich für eine Pflanze ist. Na gut, ich werd's euch sagen:

Der Raps ist ein amphidiploider Bastard und gehört zur Familie der »Brassicaceae«, das sind Kreuzblütengewächse, zu denen auch der Senf und der Kohl gehören. (Ich stöbere halt ab und zu mal gern in meinem Lexikon. Das ist zwar nicht mehr ganz neu, aber bisher hab' ich alles gefunden, was ich suche.) Aus Raps macht man hauptsächlich Öl, zum Braten und für den Salat, vor allem aber für Schmiermittel. Rapsöl schmeckte früher ziemlich bitter und war deshalb ein »Arme-Leute-Öl«. Das ist aber inzwischen anders.

An diesem Rapsfeld habe ich ja auch nur kurz wegen der Wolke Halt gemacht, denn eigentlich bin ich nach Lohmen gekommen, um mir hier die Steinbrüche anzusehen. Der Name »Lohmen« stammt wahrscheinlich vom altslawischen »lomu«, was nichts anderes heißt als »Steinbruch«. Im Elbsandsteingebirge haben die Menschen schon vor über 1000 Jahren Steine gebrochen, um Burgen, Kirchen oder Häuser zu bauen.

Aus Lohmen kommt übrigens auch ein großer Teil der Steine, die sie in der Dresdner Frauenkirche verbaut haben, beim Neubau wie vor 250 Jahren. Und die Lohmener Dorfkirche besteht aus demselben Stein und sieht auch ein bisschen so aus wie das große Vorbild in Dresden.

LOHMEN, SAXON SWITZERLAND

Have you found it? Directly above me? Take a closer look. Someone up there had a heart for me when I set out on a hike at the end of May from Dresden to Lohmen, the gateway to Saxon Switzerland.

And do you know what »Brassica napus« is? No? Neither did I till recently, but I am now standing in the midst of it: rape. It is what turns the countryside so gloriously yellow in May and June. And now you probably also want to know what kind of plant rape is. O. K., I'll tell you:

Rape is an amphidiploid bastard and belongs to the Cruciferae family, to which mustard and cabbage also belong. (I like to browse through my dictionary now and again. It's no longer very new, but up to now it has always told me what I wanted to know.) Rapeseed is cultivated mainly for its oil, which is used for frying and for salad dressings, but above all as a lubricant. Rape oil used to taste rather bitter and was thus considered a »poor-man's oil«. But that has since been remedied.

I stopped at this field of rapeseed only for a short spell, attracted by the cloud, because I actually came to Lohmen to see the stone quarries. The name »Lohmen« probably comes from Old Slavic »lomu«, which means nothing other than »quarry«. Over 1000 years ago, stone was already being quarried in the Elbe Sandstone Mountains in order to build castles, churches or houses.

By the way, it's from Lohmen that a large number of the stones were taken to build Dresden's Frauenkirche (Church of Our Lady), today as well as 250 years ago. And Lohmen's village church is made of the very same stone and even looks a bit like its grand predecessor in Dresden.

199

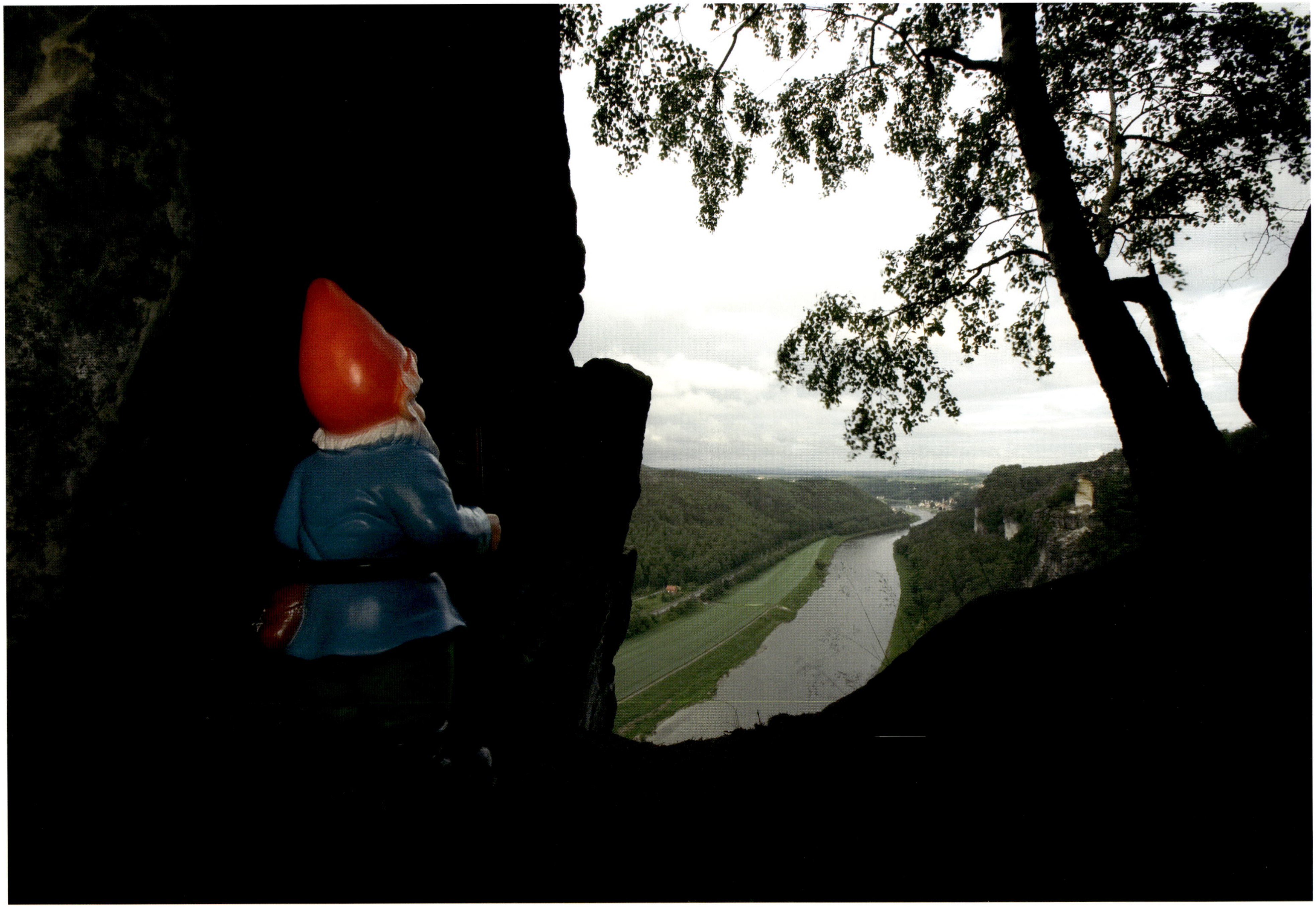

BASTEI, ELBSANDSTEINGEBIRGE

Es ist doch erstaunlich, wie viele »Schweizen« – oder wie heißt sonst die Mehrzahl von Schweiz? – wie viele Schweizen es also nördlich von Basel, Zürich und Sankt Gallen gibt; zum Beispiel die »Sächsische Schweiz« und gleich nebenan in Tschechien die »Böhmische Schweiz«. Sogar in Holstein soll es eine geben und auch in anderen flachen Landstrichen, wo alles sofort Berg heißt, was höher ist als 50 Meter.

Die »Sächsische Schweiz« hat ihren Namen allerdings direkt von zwei Original-Eidgenossen bekommen, nämlich von zwei Künstlern aus dem Schweizer Jura, die im 18. Jahrhundert zum Studieren an die Dresdner Akademie gekommen sind. Sie haben häufig Ausflüge zum Malen ins Elbsandsteingebirge gemacht, keine 30 Kilometer südöstlich von Dresden, und haben sich hier sofort wie zu Hause gefühlt. Der Große Zschirnstein ist ja auch immerhin 560 Meter hoch.

Rechts und links der Elbe gibt es mehr als 1000 Klettergipfel und 12.000 Kletterwege, über die man nach oben kommt. Aber auch für anspruchslose Fußgänger und Wanderer wie mich gibt es hier viele Strecken, auf denen man einfach gradeaus gehen kann.

Die berühmteste Felsenformation der Gegend ist die Bastei, 194 Meter über der Elbe, da stehe ich und schaue den Fluss hinunter nach Westen. Der Ort ganz da hinten am Ufer ist übrigens die Stadt Wehlen. Die Bastei war früher tatsächlich einmal Teil einer Festung, der Felsenburg Neurathen; sie hat im frühen 19. Jahrhundert dem berühmten Maler Caspar David Friedrich für sein Bild »Felsenschlucht« als Motiv gedient. Und wie es sich für eine ordentliche Schweiz gehört, gibt es hier auch ein Berghotel. Das liegt nur ein paar Schritte von diesem Aussichtspunkt entfernt direkt hinter mir und heißt natürlich »Bastei«.

BASTEI, ELBE SANDSTONE MOUNTAINS

It is really amazing how many Switzerlands there are – or how else would you call the plural of Switzerland? – besides the original one, how many, that is, north of Basel, Zurich and St. Gallen; for example »Saxon Switzerland« and, right next door in the Czech Republic, »Bohemian Switzerland«. There is even supposed to be one in Holstein and also in other flat regions where anything over 50 metres high is immediately dubbed a mountain.

Saxon Switzerland, however, got its name directly from two Swiss citizens, namely, from two artists from the Swiss Jura who came to study at the Dresden Art Academy in the 18th century. They often went on painting excursions into the Elbe Sandstone Mountains, which are less than 30 kilometres southeast of Dresden, where they immediately felt at home. The Grosser Zschirnstein is, after all, 560 metres high.

To the right and left of the Elbe, there are more than 1000 climbing peaks and 12,000 climbing paths that lead you to the top. But also for undemanding walkers and hikers like me, there are enough footpaths on which you can simply walk straight ahead.

The most famous cliff formation in the region is the Bastei (bastion), 194 metres above the Elbe and where I now stand, overlooking the river westwards. The town in the background on the riverbank, by the way, is Wehlen. The Bastei was indeed once part of a fortress, Fort Neurathen on the cliff; it served the famous painter Caspar David Friedrich as a motif when he painted »Felsenschlucht« in the early 19th century. And just as is proper for any genuine Switzerland, there is also a mountain hotel here. It lies just a few steps from this vantage point directly behind me and, as any good guess would tell you, it's called »Bastei«.

DRESDEN

Am 30. Oktober 2005 ist die rekonstruierte Dresdner Frauenkirche nach elf Jahren Bauzeit eingeweiht worden, und seitdem sieht die Silhouette der Altstadt weitgehend wieder so aus, wie sie der italienische Maler Bernardo Bellotto vor 250 Jahren gemalt hat. Die Semper-Oper gab es damals allerdings noch nicht, die kam erst gegen Ende des 19. Jahrhunderts dazu, und sie war das einzige Gebäude, von dem nach der Bombardierung im Februar 1945 wenigstens die Außenmauern stehen geblieben waren. Bis auf die Ruine der Frauenkirche sind alle anderen Trümmer nach dem Krieg weggeräumt worden.

Alles, was Dresden seit der Regierungszeit von August dem Starken im frühen 18. Jahrhundert so berühmt gemacht hatte, der Zwinger, das Schloss mit der Hofkirche, die Brühlschen Terrassen, das Albertinum und die Frauenkirche, war vollkommen zerstört und ist erst Jahrzehnte nach dem Zweiten Weltkrieg wieder aufgebaut worden. Das ist auch der Grund, warum die Altstadt allein nicht in die Unesco-Liste des Weltkulturerbes aufgenommen werden konnte, denn hier gibt es praktisch kein altes Gebäude mehr, fast alles stammt aus der Zeit nach 1945.

Aber als Teil der »Kulturlandschaft Dresdner Elbtal« gehört seit dem 24. Juni 2005 auch das neue »alte« barocke Zentrum zum Weltkulturerbe. Die Elbe schlängelt sich über 20 Kilometer vom Südosten zum Nordwesten durch die ganze Stadt.

Seit Jahrhunderten hat man den schönsten Blick auf Dresden vom rechten Elbufer aus. Ganz rechts die Semper-Oper, dann die Hofkirche und das Schloss, die Brühlschen Terrassen und links die Kuppel der Frauenkirche. Von dieser Seite, allerdings weiter elbeabwärts, nordwestlich der Augustusbrücke, hat auch schon Bellotto seine berühmte Ansicht gemalt.

DRESDEN

On October 30, 2005, the reconstructed Dresden Frauenkirche (Church of Our Lady) was inaugurated after eleven years of construction, and since then, the silhouette of the old city again looks more or less the way it did to the Italian painter Bernardo Bellotto when he painted it 250 years ago. However, the Semper Opera didn't exist then; it was not added till the end of the 19th century; and it was the one building whose outer walls, at least, were still standing after the bombardment in February 1945. Except for the ruins of the Frauenkirche, all the other rubble was cleared away after the war.

Everything that had made Dresden so famous since the administration of August the Strong in the early 18th century – the Zwinger, the castle with its Hofkirche (court church), the Brühl Terraces, the Albertinum and the Frauenkirche – was completely destroyed and not rebuilt till decades after World War II. That is also the reason the old city alone could never be put onto the Unesco cultural heritage list, for there is practically no old building left; almost everything stems from the time after 1945.

But since June 24, 2005, the new »old« Baroque centre is listed as a World Heritage Site, as part of the »cultural landscape of the Dresden Elbe Valley«. The Elbe winds its way over 20 kilometres through the whole city, from the southeast to the northwest.

For centuries, the best view of Dresden has been from the right bank of the Elbe. On the far right you see the Semper Opera, then the Hofkirche and the castle, the Brühl Terraces, and on the left the cupola of the Frauenkirche. It was from this side of the river – though further downstream, northwest of the Augustus Bridge – that Bellotto painted his famous view.

203

DU ALTER STAMM,
SEI STETS ERNEUT
IN EDLER FÜRSTEN
REIHE,
WIE ALLE ZEIT
DEIN VOLK DIR
WEIHT
DIE ALTE DEUTSCHE
TREUE.

FÜRSTENZUG, DRESDEN

102 Meter lang ist er, fast neuneinhalb Meter hoch, insgesamt 957 Quadratmeter groß, und er besteht aus 24.000 fugenlos gesetzten Meissener Porzellankacheln, jede 20,5 x 20,5 cm: der »Fürstenzug« in Dresden, das größte Porzellanbild der Welt. Der Maler Wilhelm Walter hatte es 1871 bis 1876 zunächst in Sgraffitotechnik auf die Wand gebracht, das war aber nicht wetterfest und ist deshalb von 1904 bis 1907 auf haltbare Kacheln übertragen worden; die haben selbst die Bombardierung von Dresden 1945 fast unbeschädigt überstanden.

35 sächsische Markgrafen, Kurfürsten und Könige reiten durch 800 Jahre Geschichte, der gesamte Stammbaum der Wettiner seit 1123: von Konrad dem Großen über Albrecht den Entarteten, Friedrich den Gebissenen, Albrecht den Beherzten, Georg den Bärtigen und August den Starken bis zu Georg. Als Georg König wurde, waren alle besonderen Merkmale offenbar schon längst vergeben, seit der Mitte des 16. Jahrhunderts wurden die Namen fast nur noch fortlaufend nummeriert. Im Zug fehlt nur der letzte sächsische König, Friedrich August III. Als das ursprüngliche Bild 1876 fertig wurde, war er noch ein Kind und konnte wahrscheinlich noch nicht reiten.

Neben den 35 Wettinern ziehen 58 Untertanen mit, Künstler, Studenten und Wissenschaftler, Soldaten, Bauern und Kinder, aber alle zu Fuß. Der Herr mit Hut ganz am Schluss ist der Maler Wilhelm Walter selbst.

Mit der »alten deutschen Treue« der Sachsen zu ihren Herrschern war es 1918 vorbei, die Monarchie wurde abgeschafft, Kaiser Wilhelm II. ging zum Holzhacken nach Holland, und seine daheim gebliebenen Könige hatten nichts mehr zu sagen. Höchstens noch Sätze wie den berühmten von Friedrich August III. bei der Abdankung: »Nu, dann machd eiern Dregg alleene.«

FÜRSTENZUG, DRESDEN

It is 102 metres long, almost nine and a half metres high, a total of 957 square metres in size and comprises of 24,000 contiguous Meissener porcelain tiles, each 20.5 x 20.5 cm – the »Fürstenzug« or Procession of the Princes in Dresden, the world's largest porcelain wall picture. The painter, Wilhelm Walter, had created the work between 1871 and 1876 using at first the technique of sgraffito, which turned out to be unsuitable because it was not weatherproof. The design was then transferred onto durable tiles from 1904 to 1907 and this version almost completely withstood the 1945 bombing of Dresden.

35 Saxon margraves, prince-electors and kings ride through 800 years of history, the complete family tree of the Wettin dynasty since 1123: from Konrad the Great by way of Albrecht the Degenerate, Friedrich the Bitten, Albrecht the Brave-Hearted, Georg the Bearded and August the Strong up to Georg. When Georg became king, almost all the adjectives designating special characteristics had long been used up, so that since the mid-16th century the names had almost all been merely numbered consecutively. The only one missing in the procession is the last Saxon king, Friedrich August III. When the original picture was finished in 1876, he was still a child and probably could not yet ride.

Along with the 35 rulers from the House of Wettin, 58 royal subjects, artists, students and scientists, soldiers, farmers and children follow along, but all on foot. The hatted gentleman at the end is the painter Wilhelm Walter himself.

In 1918, the Saxons' »old German loyalty« to their rulers had seen its day; the monarchy was done away with, Emperor Wilhelm II was in exile in Holland, occupied with chopping wood, and those kings that stayed home had nothing more to say. Except, at the most, a phrase like the famous one by Friedrich August III when he abdicated: »The dirty work is all yours.«

MOLKEREI PFUND, DRESDEN

»*Molkerei, Meierei,* Unternehmen zur Be- und Verarbeitung sowie zum Vertrieb von Milch und Milcherzeugnissen. Nach der Hauptbetriebsart unterscheidet man zw. Trink- und Werkmilch-M. (Buttereibetriebe, Hart-, Schnitt- und Weichkäsereien, Milchversandbetriebe). I. w. S. gehören zu den M. auch Dauermilch-, Schmelzkäse- und Caseinwerke.«

So steht's im Lexikon. Aber das hilft einem wenig, wenn man in der Dresdner Molkerei Pfund steht, dem »schönsten Milchladen der Welt«, egal ob man Milch, Butter oder Käse kaufen will. Unter mehr als 120 Käsesorten aus Rohmilch kann man hier wählen, und die Milch schmeckt so, wie ich sie noch von früher kenne. Das Geschäft ist rundum mit handbemalten Kacheln von Villeroy & Boch ausgekleidet, die alle aus dem 19. Jahrhundert stammen.

Die Molkerei Pfund gibt es seit 1892, und sie hat sich bis heute praktisch nicht verändert. Ihr Gründer Paul Gustav Leander Pfund war ein weitsichtiger Unternehmer, der aus der Milch alles machte, was man damals machen konnte: Sahne, Butter, Buttermilch, Käse, Joghurt, Kefir, Trocken- und Kondensmilch und sogar Seife.

Den größten Erfolg hatte Pfund mit der haltbaren Kondensmilch, für die die Molkerei bis zum Ersten Weltkrieg eine Weltmonopolstellung hatte. In den 30er Jahren des vergangenen Jahrhunderts haben die Pfund'schen Molkereien am Tag 60.000 Liter Milch verarbeitet. Den Krieg und sogar die Bombardierung von Dresden hat der Milchladen heil überstanden, aber nicht die sozialistische Planwirtschaft; in den 70er Jahren musste er schließen.

Schön, dass die neuen Inhaber 1995 den Mut hatten, den Laden in der Bautzener Straße wiederzueröffnen und an die großen alten Zeiten anzuknüpfen.

PFUND DAIRY, DRESDEN

»Dairy: A commercial establishment for processing and for selling milk and milk products. According to the main mode of operation, one differentiates between milk for drinking and for further processing (in butter dairies, hard, sliced and soft cheese dairies, milk shipment companies). Included are also works for the production of UHT milk, cheese spreads and casein.«

This is the way you'll find it stated in an encyclopaedia. All not very helpful when you're standing in Dresden's Molkerei Pfund, the »most beautiful milk shop in the world«, regardless of whether it's milk, butter or cheese that you want to buy. You can choose among 120 different cheeses made from unpasteurized milk, and here milk tastes the way it did in bygone days. The shop walls are lined in hand-painted Villeroy & Boch tiles, all from the 19th century.

The Pfund Dairy has been in business since 1892 and has practically remained unchanged over the years. Its founder, Gustav Leander Pfund, was a far sighted entrepreneur, who made everything out of milk that you could at the time: cream, butter, buttermilk, cheese, yoghurt, kefir, powdered and condensed milk, and even soap.

Pfund's greatest success was with long-life condensed milk, for which Pfund enjoyed a world monopoly up to World War I. In the 1930s, Pfund's dairy processed 60,000 litres of milk a day. The dairy shop survived the war and even the bombardment of Dresden intact, but not the socialist planned economy. It had to close in the 1970s.

It's good that the new owner had the courage in 1995 to re-open the shop on Bautzener Street and ring in the good old times once again.

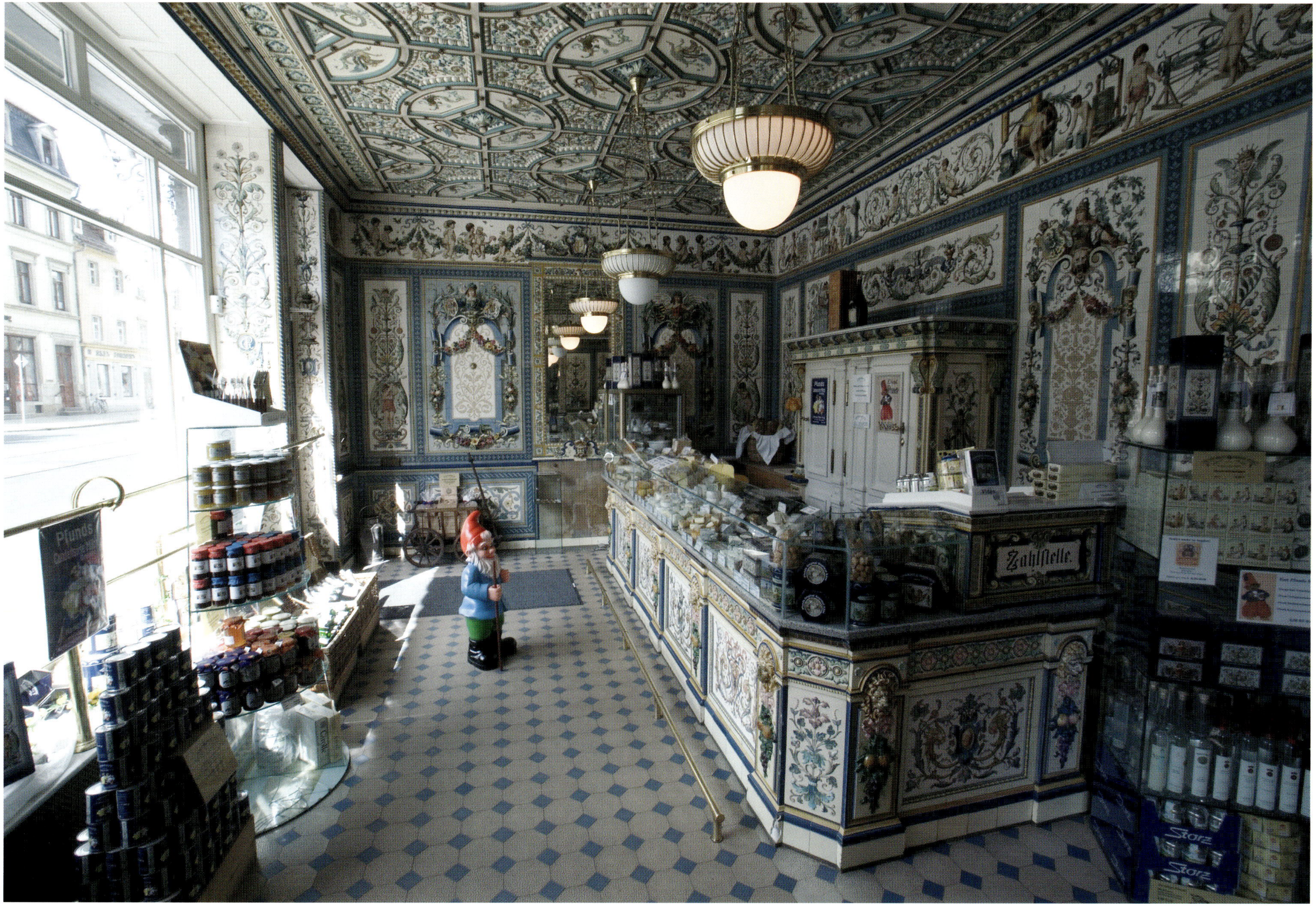
Pfunds
Zahlstelle.
Storz

»AUERBACHS KELLER«, LEIPZIG

Unter den zehn bekanntesten Lokalen der Welt sind zwei deutsche: das Hofbräuhaus in München auf Platz eins und Auerbachs Keller auf Platz fünf; das haben mal wieder die Amerikaner herausgefunden. Und jetzt frage ich mich: Ist Auerbachs Keller eigentlich so berühmt, weil Goethe dort den Mephisto mit dem Doktor Faust hat einkehren lassen, oder hat Mephisto Faust dorthin gebracht, weil man um Auerbachs Keller schon damals nicht herumkam?

Das Lokal gibt es unter diesem Namen seit dem Jahr 1530, und es war bald weit über Leipzig hinaus berühmt. Goethe hat hier oft gezecht, als er in Leipzig Jura studiert hat. Hier hat er womöglich auch zum ersten Mal von der Faustsage gehört und von dem sagenhaften Ritt auf dem Weinfass. Er spricht also aus Erfahrung, wenn er Mephisto zum sauertöpfischen Faust sagen lässt: »Ich muß dich nun vor allen Dingen / in lustige Gesellschaft bringen, / damit du siehst, wie leicht sichs leben läßt. / Dem Volke hier wird jeder Tag ein Fest.« Und bald darauf grölen die Studenten: »Uns ist ganz kannibalisch wohl / als wie fünfhundert Säuen.«

Das war den Leipzigern anscheinend aus der Seele gesprochen, denn wie es aussieht, haben sie ihren Wein besonders gerne hier getrunken: 1538 kam ein Drittel der städtischen Weinsteuer aus Auerbachs Keller.

Der erste Besitzer hieß eigentlich Heinrich Stromer. Er stammte aus Auerbach, einem kleinen Ort südlich von Bayreuth, und hat eines Tages den Namen seines Heimatortes angenommen. Er war unter anderem Leipziger Stadtrat, Medizinprofessor, Universitätsrektor und Leibarzt von Herzog Georg dem Bärtigen. Und er war ein Freund von Martin Luther. Außerdem soll er versucht haben, den berühmten Humanisten Erasmus von Rotterdam durch Fernbehandlung von einem Bandwurm zu kurieren.

»AUERBACH'S CELLAR«, LEIPZIG

Among the ten best-known taverns in the world, two are German: the Hofbräuhaus in Munich in first place and Auerbach's Keller in fifth. It was again the Americans who worked this out. And now I wonder: is Auerbach's Cellar so famous because the poet Goethe had Mephisto go there with Doctor Faust or did Mephisto take Faust there because Auerbach's Cellar, even at that time, could hardly be ignored?

The pub has existed under this name since the year 1530, and it was soon famous far beyond Leipzig. Goethe, in any case, knew of it and often went carousing there when he was a student of law in Leipzig. Here is where he possibly first heard of the Faust saga and the legendary ride on the flying wine barrel. He speaks from experience when he has Mephisto say to the down-in-the-mouth Faust: »Before all else I now must let you view / the doings of a jovial crew, / that you may see how lightly life can flow along / To this crowd every day's a feast and song.« Following which the students soon bellow out: »We feel as cannibalistically great / as would five hundred swine.«

This was apparently spoken straight from the hearts of the people of Leipzig, for it looks like they especially liked to drink their wine here: in 1538, one third of the city's wine taxes came from Auerbach's Cellar.

The first owner's name was actually Heinrich Stromer. He came from Auerbach, a village south of Bayreuth, and one day simply adopted the name of his birthplace. He was, among other things, a city councillor of Leipzig, a medical professor, university dean and the personal physician of Duke Georg the Bearded. And he was a friend of Martin Luther's. In addition, he was supposed to have attempted to cure the famous humanist Erasmus of Rotterdam of a tapeworm through distance healing.

209

KLEINGÄRTNERMUSEUM, LEIPZIG

Die Litfaßsäule, die Röntgenstrahlen, das Weckglas, der Nobelpreis, die Beringstraße, der Zeppelin, das Mausoleum, die Montgolfiere oder die Hubble-Konstante – alles Dinge, die nach ihren Erfindern oder Entdeckern heißen.

Und der Schrebergarten? – Nun, beim Schrebergarten liegt die Sache ein wenig anders. Ich hab' zwar bisher auch geglaubt, wie wahrscheinlich die meisten von euch, der Leipziger Arzt und Pädagoge Dr. Daniel Gottlob Moritz Schreber hätte diesen Garten erfunden, aber das ist ein Irrtum. Er ist nicht der Vater des Schrebergartens, sondern bloß, wenn ihr so wollt, der Schwiegervater.

1865, über drei Jahre nach Schrebers Tod, hat nämlich sein Schwiegersohn, der Schuldirektor Dr. Ernst Innocenz Hauschild, in Leipzig einen Verein gegründet und eine Turn- und Spielwiese angelegt, damit sich dort nach Schrebers Vorstellungen Kinder bewegen und austoben konnten; den hat er »Schreberplatz« genannt. In den Jahren danach haben die Vereinsmitglieder kleine Gärten angelegt, und die hießen dann natürlich »Schrebergärten«. Sie mussten allerdings 1875 einer Straße Platz machen, und der Verein ist auf ein neues Grundstück am Rande von Leipzig umgezogen.

Diese historische »Gartenanlage Dr. Schreber« gibt es heute noch, und sie steht schon lange unter Denkmalschutz. Im August 1996 ist dort das »Deutsche Museum der Kleingärtnerbewegung« eröffnet worden.

Ihr könnt euch sicher vorstellen, dass es mir hier gut gefallen hat. Abgesehen vom Vorgarten ist ja der Schrebergarten das wichtigste Siedlungsgebiet für meinesgleichen. Ich habe hier übrigens zum ersten Mal einen von uns sächsisch reden hören. Ich glaub', das meiste hab' ich verstanden, ei, verbibbsch.

ALLOTMENT GARDEN MUSEUM, LEIPZIG

The Litfass advertising pillar, roentgen or x-rays, the Weckglas or preserving jar, the Nobel Prize, the Bering Strait, the zeppelin, the mausoleum, the Montgolfière or Hubble's constant are all things that have been named after their inventor.

And the Schrebergarten or allotment garden? Well, in fact, things are a bit different with the Schreber garden. I had always believed up to now, probably like most of you, that the Leipzig doctor and pedagogue, Dr. Daniel Gottlob Moritz Schreber, had invented this type of garden, but that's a mistake. He is not the father of the allotment garden, but simply, if you will, its father-in-law.

In 1865, three years after Schreber's death, his son-in-law and a school headmaster, Dr. Ernst Innocenz Hauschild, founded a club in Leipzig and installed a gymnastics area and playground, so that – in accordance with Schreber's ideas – children could move and jump about, and this he called »Schreber Place«. In the following years, club members laid out small gardens, which were then naturally called »Schreber gardens«. However in 1875, these had to make way for a street, and the club moved to a new plot of land on the edge of Leipzig.

This historical »Dr. Schreber Garden Colony« is still there today, and has long been protected as a historic monument. In August 1996, the »German Museum of the Allotment Garden Movement« was opened.

You can imagine that I felt quite at home here. With the exception of the front garden, the allotment garden is the most important settlement area for my sort. By the way, for the first time I heard one of us speak Saxon. I think I understood most of it, for real.

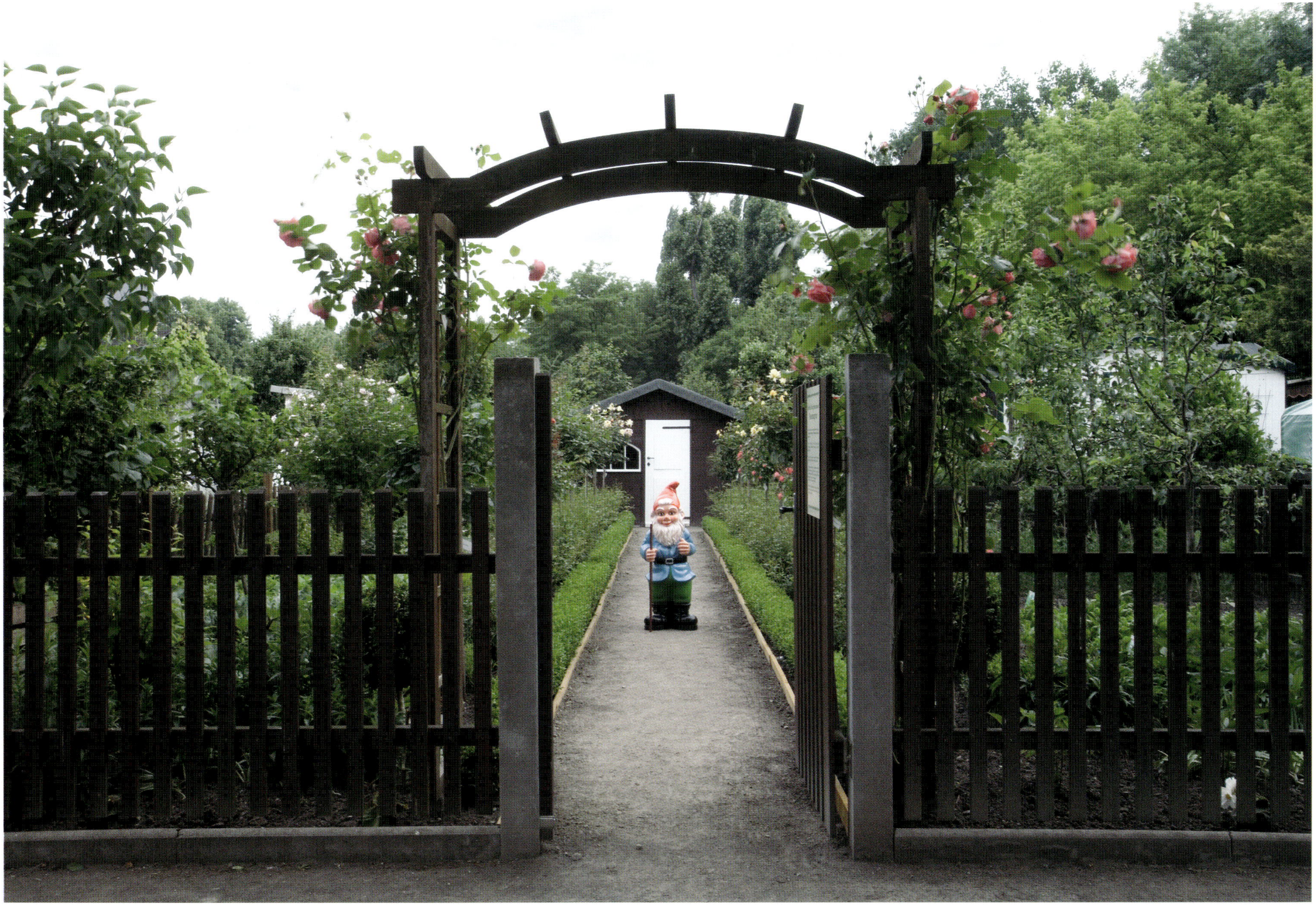

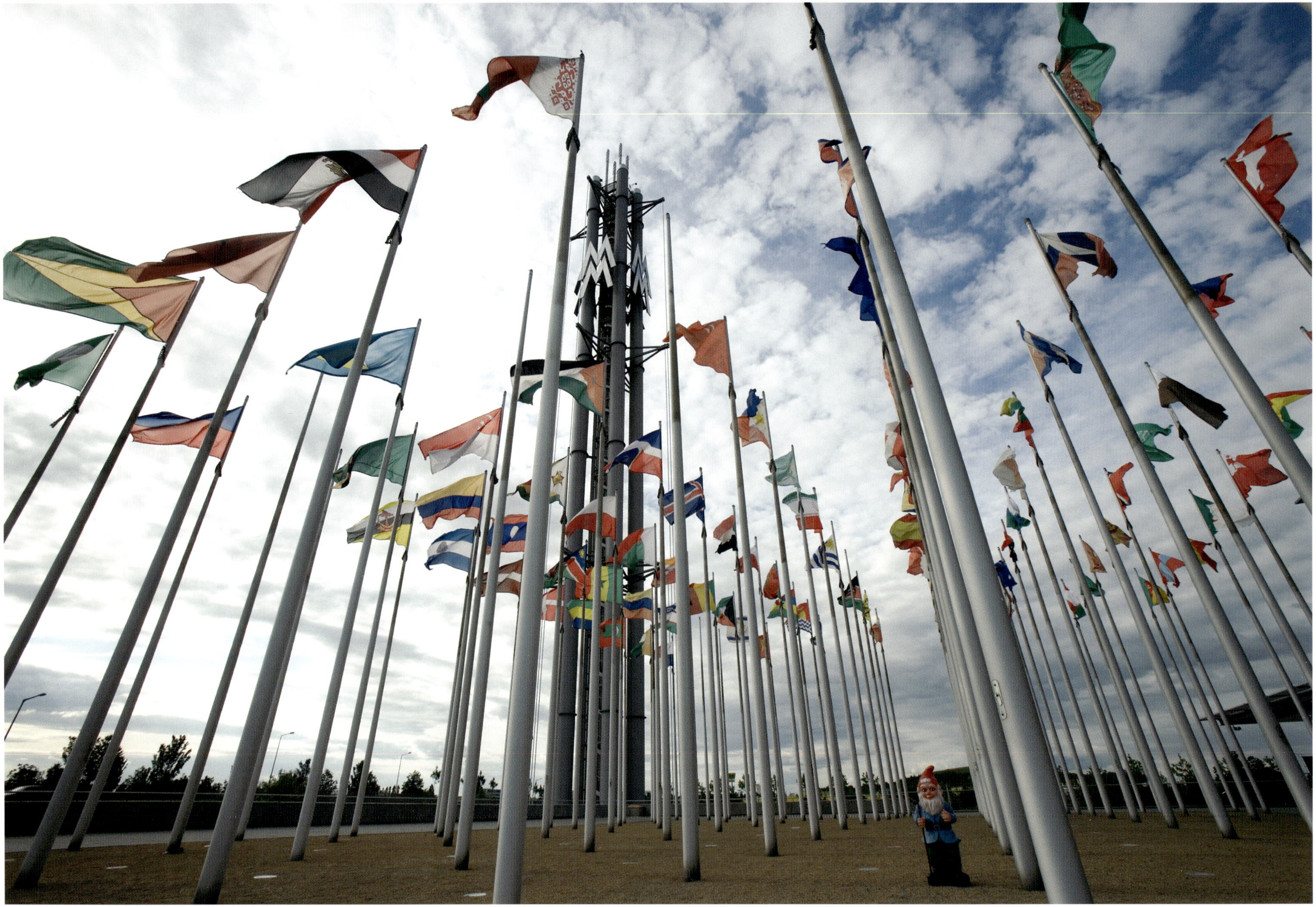

MESSE, LEIPZIG

Wer vor 800 oder 900 Jahren als Händler von Rom ins norwegische Bergen oder von Paris nach Nowgorod unterwegs war, kam mitten in Sachsen durch einen kleinen Ort namens Libzi. Hier kreuzten sich die beiden großen alten Handelswege, die »Via imperii« und die »Via regia«, und wie in solchen Fällen üblich, hat sich an dieser Kreuzung ein schnell wachsender Umschlagplatz entwickelt, mit allem, was dazugehört.

1165 bekam Libzi das Stadt- und das Marktrecht und 1268 das Messeprivileg. Händler richteten ihre Zwischenlager ein und Handelshäuser aus ganz Europa gründeten Niederlassungen. Seit dem Jahr 1507 durfte nach einem Dekret des Kaisers keine Stadt im Umkreis von 115 Kilometern eigene Lager halten. Kein Händler durfte die Stadt umgehen, jeder musste hier seine Waren wiegen lassen und verzollen und mindestens drei Tage zum Verkauf anbieten.

Aus Libzi war inzwischen Leipzig geworden. Kaiserliche Privilegien machten den Ort zu einem der wichtigsten Handelsplätze in Europa, und bis ins 20. Jahrhundert ist die Bedeutung von Leipzig als Messestadt immer weiter gewachsen. Erst der Zweite Weltkrieg hat das geändert: 1945 lagen die Messehallen zu 80 Prozent in Trümmern.

Erfahrung und Tradition waren den Leipzigern jedoch erhalten geblieben, und 1946 war schon wieder Messe. Aber da fing bereits der Kalte Krieg an. Leipzig lag östlich des Eisernen Vorhangs und wurde im Laufe der Jahrzehnte der wichtigste Ort für den Austausch zwischen Ost und West – nicht nur von Waren. Nach der Wiedervereinigung und dem Zusammenbruch des Ostblocks stand Leipzig plötzlich in Konkurrenz zu Hamburg, Köln oder München. Mit dem Bau des neuen Messegeländes knüpft Leipzig seit 1996 wieder an seine Geschichte als internationaler Messeplatz an.

TRADE FAIR, LEIPZIG

Any trader travelling about 800 or 900 years ago from Rome to the Norwegian Bergen or from Paris to Novgorod, would pass through a small town called Libzi in the middle of Saxony. It was here that both major trade routes crossed, the »Via Imperii« and the »Via Regia«, and, as was usual in such cases, a fast-growing trading centre developed, with everything that went with it.

In 1165, Libzi received a town charter and the right to hold a market and in 1268 trade-fair privileges. Merchants installed midway storehouses, and trading houses from all over Europe opened branches. Since 1507, according to an imperial decree, no other place within a 115-kilometre radius was allowed to maintain a warehouse. No trader was allowed to make a detour, but all were obliged to enter the city to have their goods weighed, to pay duty on them and to offer them for sale for at least three days.

In the meantime, Libzi had become Leipzig. Imperial privileges made it one of the most important trading centres in Europe. And the significance of Leipzig as a trade-fair city continued to grow into the 20th century. Not till World War II did this change: in 1945, 80 percent of the exhibition halls lay in ruins.

Experience and tradition, however, was still a feature of Leipzig. And in 1946, there was again a trade fair. However, the Cold War had just started and Leipzig lay to the east of the Iron Curtain. It thus, over the course of the next decades, turned into the most important centre for the exchange between East and West – and not only for commercial goods. After reunification and the breakdown of the East Block, Leipzig suddenly became a rival to Hamburg, Cologne and Munich. With the construction of its new trade fairgrounds, Leipzig has since 1996, once again linked up to its past as an international trade fair centre.

SCHLOSSKIRCHE, WITTENBERG

Genau hier soll am 31. Oktober 1517 ein 33-jähriger Augustinerpater ein Schriftstück mit 95 lateinischen Sätzen an die Kirchentür genagelt haben. So will es die Legende. Der Pater hieß Martin Luther, und er war an diesem Tag noch genauso katholisch wie die meisten Menschen in Europa. An so was wie die Reformation hat er damals nicht im Traum gedacht.

Die Kirchentür war eine Art Schwarzes Brett für die Universität, wo u. a. Disputationsthemen bekannt gegeben wurden. Etwas anderes hatte auch Luther zuerst nicht im Sinn, und schon gar nicht wollte er die Weltgeschichte verändern. »Aus Liebe zur Wahrheit«, das hatte er über seine Thesen geschrieben, »und in dem Bestreben, diese zu ergründen, soll in Wittenberg unter dem Vorsitz des ehrwürdigen Vaters Martin Luther, Magisters der freien Künste und der heiligen Theologie sowie deren ordentlicher Professor daselbst, über die folgenden Sätze disputiert werden.«

Luther nimmt sich in seiner Schrift den Ablasshandel vor. Der hatte damals ganz enorme Ausmaße angenommen, und Ablassprediger wie der Dominikaner Tetzel, eine Art Spendensammler für den Vatikan, verkündigten landauf, landab, jeder könnte sich mit ein paar Talern vom Fegefeuer freikaufen. Luther hatte aber erhebliche Zweifel, ob sich solche frommen Geschäfte mit dem vertrugen, was in der Bibel stand. Was später daraus wurde, ist ja bekannt.

Die alte Holztür gibt es schon lange nicht mehr, und die alte Kirche drum herum auch nicht. Sie ist zusammen mit dem Wittenberger Schloss im Siebenjährigen Krieg niedergebrannt. Heute könnte hier niemand mehr einen Nagel einschlagen, die Tür ist aus Bronze, und alle 95 Thesen stehen außen drauf, auf Lateinisch. Der preußische König Friedrich Wilhelm IV. hat sie der neu gebauten Kirche am 10. November 1858 zu Luthers 375. Geburtstag gestiftet.

CASTLE CHURCH, WITTENBERG

It is here exactly that a 33-year-old Augustinian monk wrote a list of 95 Latin Theses on official paper and supposedly nailed this to the church door. At least, that's the legend. The monk was Martin Luther, and on that day, he was just as Catholic as most of the people in Europe. And never in his wildest dreams was he thinking of a reformation.

The church door served as a kind of bulletin board that was used by the university to announce disputation themes, among other things. And it was nothing other than this that Luther at first had in mind, and he certainly never wanted to change world history. »Out of love for the truth,« he wrote above his theses, »and the desire to bring it to light, the following propositions will be discussed at Wittenberg, under the presidency of the Reverend Father Martin Luther, Master of Arts and of Sacred Theology, and Lecturer in Ordinary on the same at that place.«

In this paper Luther tackles the selling of indulgences, which at the time had snowballed to enormous proportions. Pardoners, such as the Dominican monk Tetzel – a sort of fundraiser for the Vatican – went from one end of the country to the other and proclaimed that, for a few thalers, anyone could buy himself release from the fires of purgatory. Luther, however, had serious doubts if such pious trade-offs were compatible with what the Bible said. And, as one says, the rest is history.

The old wooden door is long gone and the old church as well. It was burnt down together with the castle during the Seven Years' War. Today, no one could ever hammer a nail in it, for the door is made of bronze; and all 95 Theses are embossed on it in Latin. The Prussian King Friedrich Wilhelm IV donated it to the newly built church on November 10, 1858, to mark Luther's 375th birthday.

QUAE SACRORUM SEDES
EMENDATORUM BELLI
DIRUTA FLAMMIS III
ANNI X. FINE PROS-
PERE PERACTO NUNC
PULCHRIOR SURREXIT
SOLI DEO CONSECRA
TA VIII ID. AUG.

WÖRLITZER PARK, DESSAU

Fast 800 Jahre lang wusste kaum jemand etwas von dem kleinen Ort Wörlitz zwischen Dessau und Wittenberg – außer natürlich den Wörlitzern selber. Dann reiste der 23-jährige Fürst Leopold III. Friedrich Franz von Anhalt-Dessau 1763 nach England. Dort war er vor allen Dingen von den großzügigen Landschaftsgärten begeistert, die zwar künstlich angelegt waren, aber gar nicht so aussahen. So einen Garten wollte er auch haben.

Leopold Friedrich Franz war ein aufgeklärter Fürst. Er wollte die Ideen seiner Zeit – der »Aufklärung« – in seinem Fürstentum mit einem Reformprogramm verwirklichen, das alle Lebensbereiche erfasste. Nach seiner Rückkehr beschloss er, bei Wörlitz einen Garten nach englischem Vorbild anzulegen, in dem diese Ideen sichtbar werden sollten. Dazu holte er sich auf Reisen weitere Anregungen aus England, Holland, Frankreich, Italien und der Schweiz. So entstand der erste, größte und schönste Landschaftspark auf dem Kontinent, und er wurde zum Vorbild für viele andere, zum Beispiel auch für den Englischen Garten in München.

WÖRLITZ PARK, DESSAU

For almost 800 years hardly anyone ever heard anything about the small town of Wörlitz between Dessau and Wittenberg – except, of course, for the people of Wörlitz themselves. Then, in 1763, 23-year-old Prince Leopold III Friedrich Franz von Anhalt-Dessau travelled to England. There he was particularly taken with the grand and spacious landscaped gardens, which although artificially laid out, did not look so. And that's the kind of garden he wanted.

Leopold Friedrich Franz was an enlightened prince. He wanted the ideas of his time – that of the »Enlightenment« – to be realized in his principality through a reform programme that would take in all areas of life. After his return, he decided to design a garden near Wörlitz, modelled on English ones, where these ideas could be made visible. To do this, he collected further inspiration on other trips to England, Holland, France, Italy and Switzerland. Thus the first, the biggest and the most beautiful landscaped park on the continent came about, and it became a model for many others, for example, for the English Garden in Munich.

217

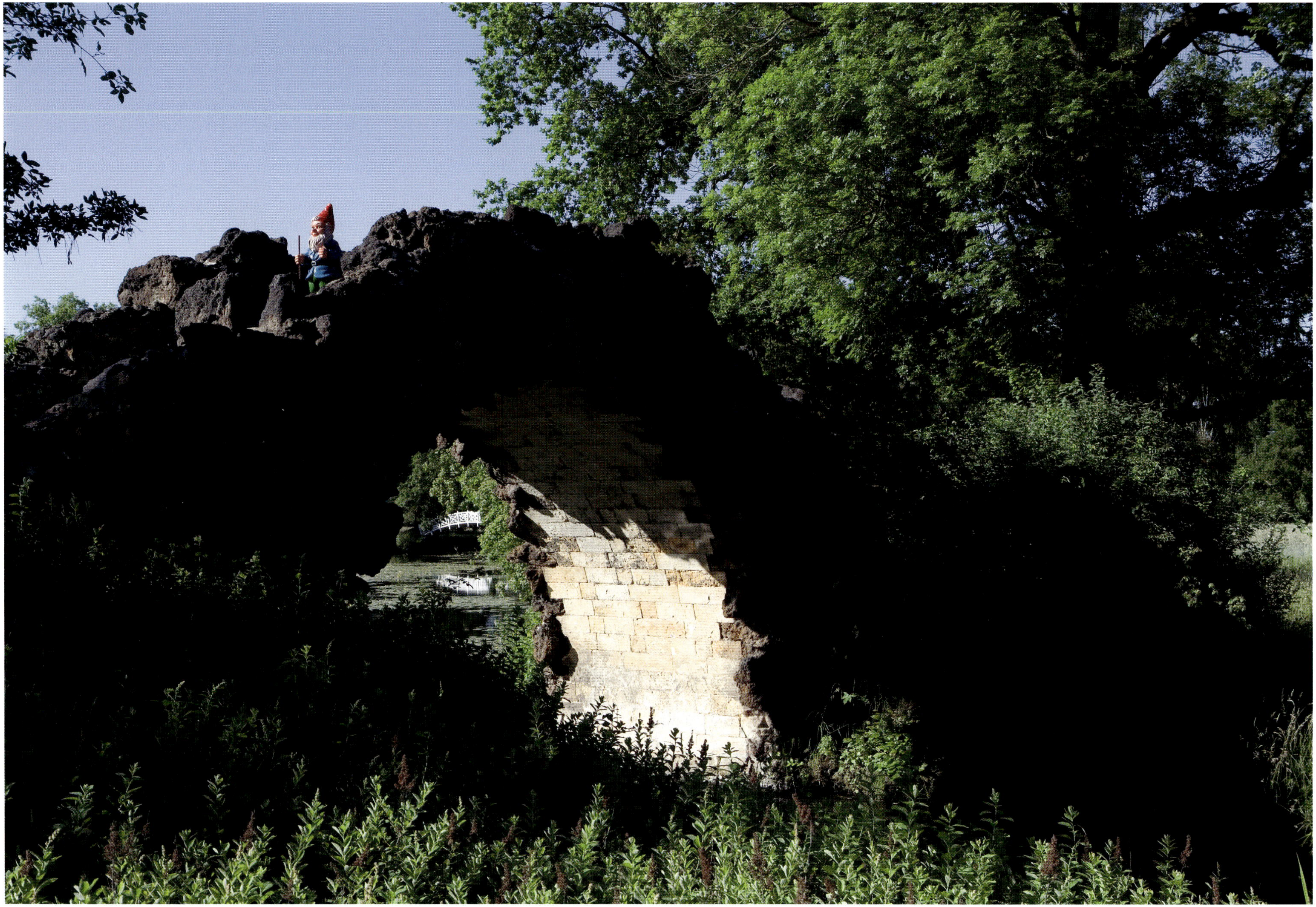

WÖRLITZER PARK, DESSAU

Einer der aufgeklärtesten Zeitgenossen von Fürst Leopold III. Friedrich Franz von Anhalt-Dessau, der neun Jahre jüngere Johann Wolfgang Goethe, schrieb 1778 nach einem Besuch in Wörlitz an Frau von Stein: »Hier ist's jetzt unendlich schön. Mich hat's gestern Abend, wie wir durch die Seen, Kanäle und Wäldchen schlichen, sehr gerührt, wie die Götter dem Fürsten erlaubt haben, einen Traum um sich herum zu schaffen. Es ist, wenn man so durchzieht, wie ein Märchen, das einem vorgetragen wird, und hat ganz den Charakter der elysischen Felder; in der sachtesten Mannigfaltigkeit fließt eins in das andere; keine Höhe zieht das Auge und das Verlangen auf einen einzigen Punkt; man streicht herum, ohne zu fragen, wo man ausgegangen ist und hinkommt. Das Buschwerk ist in seiner schönsten Jugend, und das Ganze hat die reinste Lieblichkeit.«

Genau 222 Jahre später hat die Unesco das Gartenreich in die »Weltkulturerbe«-Liste aufgenommen.

WÖRLITZ PARK, DESSAU

In 1778, after a visit to Wörlitz, one of the most enlightened contemporaries of Prince Leopold III Friedrich Franz von Anhalt-Dessau, namely Johann Wolfgang Goethe, nine years his junior, wrote to Frau von Stein the following: »Here it is now infinitely beautiful. Yesterday evening, as we slipped along the lakes, canals and woods, I was very touched by how the gods have allowed the Prince to create a dream to surround himself with. When you pass through it, it is like a fairy-tale that is being read aloud and has quite the character of the Elysian Fields; with the gentlest multiformity, one flows into the other; no high point draws eye and longing to a single point; you amble along without asking where you began nor will end. The shrubbery is in its loveliest youth, and the whole exudes the purest charm.«

Exactly 222 years later, Unesco declared this garden realm to be on the »world cultural heritage« list.

BAUHAUS, DESSAU

Lange Zeit hab' ich ja gedacht, ein Bauhaus ist ein Geschäft, wo man Zangen, Nägel, Akkuschrauber, Tapetenkleister, Spaten oder Blumendraht kaufen kann. Aber dann bin ich eines Tages nach Dessau in die Gropiusallee gekommen.

Hier steht das eigentliche, das richtige, das originale Bauhaus: das Gebäude nämlich, das der Architekt Walter Gropius 1925/26 für die Kunst-, Design- und Architekturschule gebaut hat. Sie musste nach Dessau umziehen, weil die Stadtväter von Weimar kein Geld mehr zur Verfügung stellen wollten.

Dort in Weimar hatte Walter Gropius 1919 das Bauhaus gegründet. Es war damals eine der ersten Hochschulen für Gestaltung und wurde bald die einflussreichste im 20. Jahrhundert. Viele bekannte Künstler, Designer und Architekten haben hier als Lehrer gearbeitet, und viele Studenten sind später bekannte Künstler, Designer oder Architekten geworden.

Der letzte Bauhaus-Direktor war von 1930 bis 1933 Ludwig Mies van der Rohe, der Architekt, der 35 Jahre später in Berlin die Neue Nationalgalerie gebaut hat. 1932 musste die Schule noch einmal umziehen, nach Berlin, und wurde auf Druck der Nationalsozialisten im Jahr darauf geschlossen. Viele der Lehrer sind nach Amerika gegangen und haben dort, zum Beispiel im »New Bauhaus« in Chicago, die Ideen von Weimar und Dessau weiterentwickelt.

Das Gebäude ist im Krieg schwer beschädigt worden. In den 50er und 60er Jahren hat man ein bisschen daran herumgebaut, damit man es wieder nutzen konnte. Knapp 30 Jahre später war eine weitere Restaurierung fällig, und jetzt sieht es endlich wieder so aus wie bei der Einweihung 80 Jahre zuvor.

BAUHAUS, DESSAU

For a long time I thought that a Bauhaus was a do-it-yourself shop where you buy pliers, nails, battery-operated screwdrivers, wallpaper paste, shovels or florist's wire. But then one day I arrived in Dessau in Gropiusallee.

Here stands the actual, the genuine, the original Bauhaus: that is to say the building that the architect, Walter Gropius, built in 1925/26 for the School of Art, Design and Architecture. It had to move to Dessau because Weimar's city fathers didn't want to give it any more financial backing.

It was there in Weimar that Walter Gropius had founded the Bauhaus in 1919. It was then one of the first institutions of higher education for design and was soon the most influential in the 20th century. Many well-known artists, designers and architects worked here as teachers and many of their students later became well-known as artists, designers or architects.

The last Bauhaus director, from 1930 to 1933, was Ludwig Mies van der Rohe, the architect who, 35 years later in Berlin, built the Neue Nationalgalerie. In 1932, the School again had to move, this time to Berlin, and was then – under pressure from the National Socialists – shut down the next year. Many of the teachers went to America and there, for instance in the »New Bauhaus« in Chicago, continued to develop the ideas of Weimar and Dessau.

The original building was severely damaged in the war. In the 1950s and '60s, it was renovated just enough so that it could be used again. Just short of thirty years later, further restoration was necessary, and finally now it looks like it did at its formal opening eighty years before.

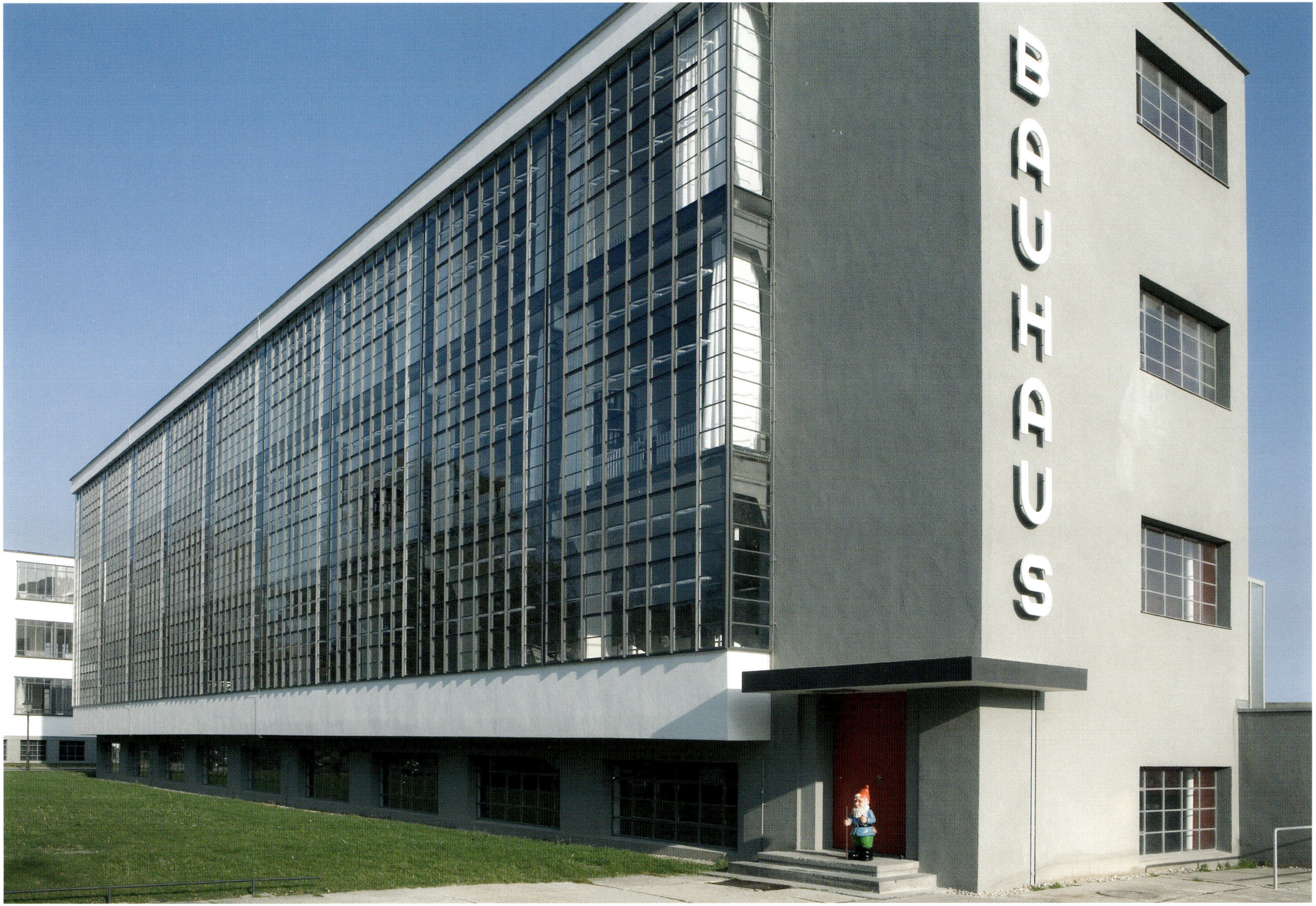
BAUHAUS

MARKTPLATZ, WERNIGERODE

Wernigerode liegt am nordöstlichen Rand des Harzes, ungefähr 60 Kilometer südlich von Wolfsburg. Ganz in der Nähe liegt der Brocken, der höchste Berg im Harz; bis dahin sind es nur zehn Kilometer Luftlinie, er ist von der Stadt aus gut zu sehen. Auf dem Brocken lässt Goethe im »Faust« die Walpurgisnacht spielen: »Die Hexen zu dem Brocken ziehn, / Die Stoppel ist gelb, die Saat ist grün. / Dort sammelt sich der große Hauf, / Herr Urian sitzt obenauf. / So geht es über Stein und Stock, / Es farzt die Hexe, es stinkt der Bock.« Die Idee mit dem Brocken ist Goethe vielleicht auf seiner Harzreise im Jahr 1777 gekommen, da war er auch in Wernigerode, und wie es scheint, hat es ihm hier gut gefallen.

Der Marktplatz von Wernigerode gehört zu den schönsten, die ich kenne. Er ist unter anderm wegen zweier Häuser berühmt: dem Rathaus, das mit den zwei Türmen hinter mir, und dem »Gothischen Haus« vom Ende des 15. Jahrhunderts, links von mir (von euch aus gesehen also rechts). Das Rathaus stammt ungefähr aus derselben Zeit, es ist aber im Jahr 1521 abgebrannt und wieder aufgebaut und 20 Jahre später noch einmal umgebaut worden; seitdem hat man es nicht mehr verändert.

MARKET PLACE, WERNIGERODE

Wernigerode lies on the northeast edge of the Harz Mountains, about 60 kilometres south of Wolfsburg. Nearby is the Brocken, the highest peak in the Harz; it is only 10 km away as the crow flies and can be seen very well from the town. It is on the Brocken that Walpurgis Night takes place in Goethe's Faust: »The witches t'ward the Brocken strain / When the stubble yellow, green the grain. / The rabble rushes – as 'tis meet – / To Sir Urian's lordly seat. O'er stick and stone we come, by jinks! / The witches fart, the he-goat stinks.« Goethe perhaps got his idea for the Brocken while on a trip to the Harz in 1777, when he was also in Wernigerode and seems to have liked it here.

Wernigerode's Market Place is one of the most beautiful I've ever seen. It is famous, among other things, for two of its houses: the Rathaus (town hall), which you can see behind me with its two towers, and the »Gothic House« which dates from the end of the 15th century, to the left of me (which is to the right of you). The Rathaus was built around the same time, but burned down in 1521 and was rebuilt. Meanwhile 20 years later, it was altered once again, but has remained unchanged ever since.

223

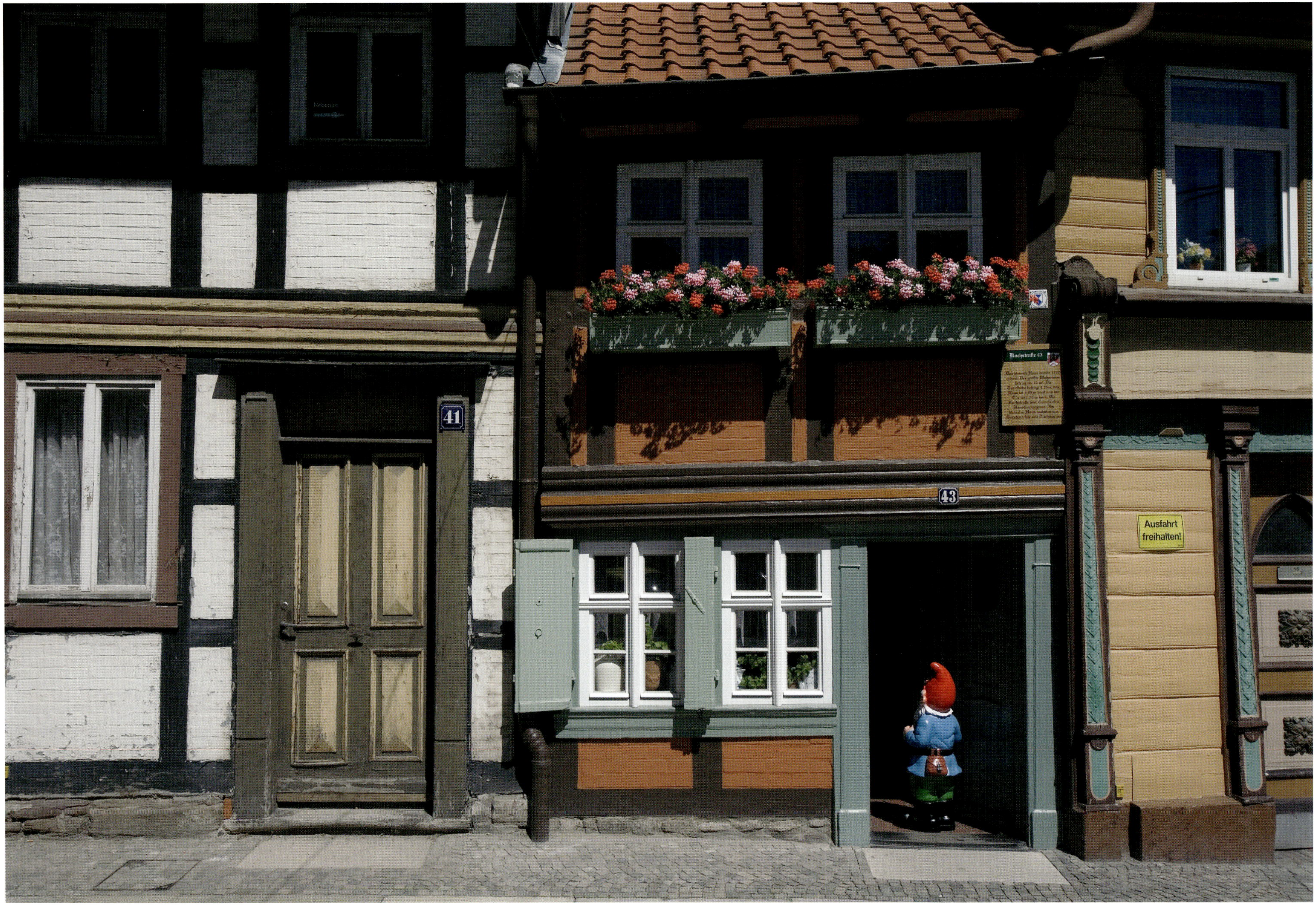
41
43
Ausfahrt
freihalten!

»KLEINSTES HAUS«, WERNIGERODE

Wernigerode hat neben dem Marktplatz, den alten Straßen und engen Gassen noch viele andere Sehenswürdigkeiten: das »Schiefe Haus« zum Beispiel, das »Krummelsche Haus«, das »Älteste Haus« oder die »Krellsche Schmiede«. Und auch ein Schloss gibt es hier. Das war früher der Sitz der Grafen zu Stolberg, die in dieser Gegend seit 1429 regiert haben, und es hat mich ein bisschen an Neuschwanstein erinnert.

Dann hab' ich aber noch ein Haus gefunden, in der Kochstraße, nicht weit vom Marktplatz, das gefällt mir ganz besonders gut. Es heißt einfach »Kleinstes Haus«, und damit ist auch schon alles gesagt. Es ist keine drei Meter breit und von der Straße bis zur Regenrinne nur vier Meter zwanzig hoch. Drin gibt's eine Stube, eine Küche und eine Schlafkammer, die Tür ist neunzig mal eins siebzig, für mich also völlig ausreichend; ihr müsst allerdings aufpassen und den Kopf einziehen.

Das Haus ist 1792 gebaut worden. Seit den 20er Jahren des letzten Jahrhunderts hat hier ein Oberpostschaffner mit seiner Frau und sieben Kindern gewohnt; das wäre selbst für unsereinen zu eng. 1976 ist die letzte Tochter des Schaffners gestorben und hat ihr Haus der Stadt vermacht. Seitdem ist hier ein Museum drin, in dem man erklärt bekommt, wie die Menschen früher in Häusern wie diesem gewohnt haben. Ich finde es sehr gemütlich, und ich glaube, hier würde ich mich wohl fühlen. Nur an das Plumpsklosett auf dem Hof müsste ich mich erst gewöhnen, aber das Haus ist ja sowieso nicht zu vermieten. Schade eigentlich.

»KLEINSTES HAUS«, WERNIGERODE

Wernigerode has, along with its Market Place, the old streets and narrow lanes, many other sightseeing attractions: the »Schiefe Haus« or crooked house, for example, the »Krummelsche Haus«, the »Älteste Haus« or oldest house, the »Krellsche Schmiede« or smithy. And there's also a castle. It used to be the seat of the counts zu Stolberg, a dynasty that has reigned in this region since 1429, and it reminded me a little of Neuschwanstein.

Then I found another house here in Kochstrasse, not far from the Market Place, which I especially took a fancy to. It is simply called »Kleinstes Haus« or smallest house, and that says it all. It is a bare three metres wide and, from the street up to the guttering, only four metres twenty high. Inside, there is one parlour, a kitchen and a bedroom. The front door is ninety centimetres wide by 1.70 metres high: therefore for me perfectly sufficient; you, though, have to watch out and keep your head down.

It was built in 1792. Since the 1920s, a post office official lived here with his wife and seven children; this would have been too tight a fit even for our sort. In 1976, the last daughter of the official died and left the house to the town. And ever since it has been a museum, in which it is explained how people used to live in houses like this one. I find it very cosy, and I think I would feel at home here. But I would first have to get used to the idea of an outdoor toilet in the backyard. But in any case, the house is not for rent. What a shame.

BUDDENBROOKHAUS, LÜBECK

Thomas Mann war 22 Jahre alt, als er anfing, seinen ersten Roman zu schreiben: die »Buddenbrooks«. Drei Jahre später, am 18. Juli 1900, war das Buch fertig, und ein Jahr darauf ist es in einer Auflage von 1000 Exemplaren erschienen. 1929 hat Thomas Mann dafür den Nobelpreis bekommen. Inzwischen hatte er zwar schon einiges mehr geschrieben – »Der Tod in Venedig« etwa oder »Der Zauberberg« –, aber noch im Jahr 1950 hat er notiert: »… manchmal geht mir auf, daß alles, was nach den ›Buddenbrooks‹ kam, im Grunde nur Nachspiel und anständiger Zeitvertreib war.«

Der Roman erzählt die Geschichte vom Verfall einer Lübecker Kaufmannsfamilie – Thomas Mann war Lübecker und stammte aus einer Kaufmannsfamilie –, und viele Episoden spielen in einem Haus, für das der Dichter das Haus seiner Großeltern zum Vorbild genommen hat, das »Buddenbrookhaus«, es steht heute noch in der Lübecker Mengstraße.

Das Gebäude ist im Zweiten Weltkrieg völlig zerstört worden, nur die Fassade stand noch, aber die Lübecker haben es wieder aufgebaut und für Thomas Mann und seinen Bruder Heinrich, ebenfalls ein berühmter Schriftsteller, ein Museum eingerichtet.

Ich stehe hier an einem Fenster des ehemaligen Musikzimmers in der Beletage, das hat der Dichter im Roman zum »Landschaftszimmer« gemacht.

1933, als die Nationalsozialisten an die Macht kamen, ist Thomas Mann mit seiner Familie emigriert, zunächst in die Schweiz, dann weiter nach Amerika. Als er nach dem Krieg wieder nach Europa zurückkehrte, hat er sich in Kilchberg bei Zürich niedergelassen und ist 1955 dort gestorben.

BUDDENBROOK HOUSE, LÜBECK

Thomas Mann was 22 years old when he began to write his first novel: the »Buddenbrooks«. Three years later, on July 18, 1900, the book was finished, and one year later it was published in an edition of 1000 copies. In 1929, Thomas Mann was awarded the Nobel Prize for it. In the meantime, he had gone on to write quite a bit more – »Death in Venice«, for instance, and »The Magic Mountain« – but in the year 1950 he noted: »… sometimes it dawns on me that everything that has followed ›Buddenbrooks‹ was in the end merely a sequel and a decent pastime.«

The novel tells the story of the decline and fall of a Lübeck merchant family – Thomas Mann was from Lübeck and came of a merchant family – and many episodes take place in a house, the model for which was the house of the author's grandparents, the »Buddenbrookhaus«. It still stands today in Lübeck's Mengstrasse.

The house was completely destroyed in World War II; only the façade was left standing. But the people of Lübeck rebuilt it and made it into a museum for Thomas Mann and his brother Heinrich, also a famous writer.

I am standing here on the first floor at the window of the former music room, which Thomas Mann in his novel turned into the »landscape-room«.

In 1933, when the Nazis came to power, Thomas Mann emigrated with his family first to Switzerland and then to America. When, after the war, he returned to Europe, he settled in Kilchberg, near Zurich and died there in 1955.

Anno Dominus providebit 1758

HELGOLAND

»Einigkeit und Recht und Freiheit / für das deutsche Vaterland! / danach laßt uns alle streben / brüderlich mit Herz und Hand! / Einigkeit und Recht und Freiheit / sind des Glückes Unterpfand; / blüh' im Glanze dieses Glückes, / blühe, deutsches Vaterland!«

Das ist die dritte Strophe des »Liedes der Deutschen«. Heinrich August Hoffmann von Fallersleben hat es 1841 auf Helgoland gedichtet; da gehörte die Insel seit 34 Jahren zu Großbritannien – davor war sie dänisch –, und Deutschland bestand aus rund 40 unabhängigen Kleinstaaten, dem »Deutschen Bund«. 1890 hat Kaiser Wilhelm II. den 1,7 Quadratkilometer großen Sandsteinfelsen gegen die tausendmal größere Insel Sansibar vor der Ostküste von Afrika eingetauscht.

55 Jahre später war Helgoland wieder britisches Hoheitsgebiet, und bis 1952, sieben Jahre nach dem Zweiten Weltkrieg, haben die Piloten der Royal Airforce hier das Bombenabwerfen geübt. Am 18. April 1947 ist die größte Explosion der Geschichte gezündet worden: 6700 Tonnen Sprengstoff. Damit wurden nicht nur die deutschen Marinebunker gesprengt, sondern auch die Südspitze der Insel. Am 1. März 1952 haben die Briten Helgoland wieder zurückgegeben.

Fast alles, was die Helgoländer zum Leben brauchen, kommt per Schiff vom 70 Kilometer entfernten Festland: Lebensmittel, Post, Brennstoff und vor allem 500.000 Touristen im Jahr. Die müssen aber häufig noch in die berühmten »Börteboote« umsteigen, eine Helgoländer Attraktion, die seit 1826 im Einsatz ist.

Kurz noch mal zurück zum »Lied der Deutschen«: Es ist 1922, auf die Melodie des »Kaiserquartetts« von Joseph Haydn, zur Nationalhymne erklärt worden, mit allen drei Strophen. Seit 1949 singen die Deutschen von ihrem Lied aber nur noch das letzte Drittel.

HELGOLAND

»Unity and right and freedom / For the German Fatherland; Let us all strive to this goal / Brotherly, with heart and hand. Unity and right and freedom / Are the pledge of fortune grand. Prosper in this fortune's glory, / Prosper German Fatherland.«

This is the third stanza of the German National Hymn. Heinrich August Hoffmann von Fallersleben wrote it in 1841 on Helgoland; at the time, the island had been British for 34 years – it was Danish before – and Germany was made up of around 40 independent small states called the Deutscher Bund. In 1890, Emperor Wilhelm II traded the 1.7 square kilometres of sandstone cliffs for the 1000 times larger island of Zanzibar off the east coast of Africa.

Fifty-five years later, Helgoland was again British territory, and up to 1952 – seven years after World War II – the pilots of the Royal Airforce practised bombing raids here. On April 18, 1947, the greatest explosion in history was detonated: 6700 tons of explosives. This not only destroyed the German navy bunker, but also the southern tip of the island. On March 1, 1952, the British returned Helgoland to Germany.

Almost everything the people of Helgoland need to live is brought to them by ship from the 70-kilometre-distant mainland: food, post, fuel and, above all, 500,000 tourists a year. However, they often have to transfer to the famous »Börte« boats, which are a Helgoland attraction and in operation since 1826.

But back briefly to the »German Hymn«. It was set to the melody of Joseph Haydn's Emperor Quartett and, in 1922, declared the National Anthem with all three stanzas. But since 1949, Germans have only sung the words to the last third of their hymn.

229

INSELBAHN DAGEBÜLL-LANGENESS

Früher hat Schleswig-Holstein einmal vollkommen anders ausgesehen als heute. Aber 1362 und 1634 gab es an der Nordseeküste gewaltige Sturmfluten, in denen große Teile des Festlands im Meer versunken sind. Übrig geblieben sind die Inseln Sylt, Föhr, Amrum, Pellworm, Nordstrand und – die Halligen. Halligen sind auch Inseln im Wattenmeer, kleinere allerdings, und das Besondere daran ist, dass sie keine Deiche haben, die sie gegen das Meer schützen. Wenn die Flut kommt, müssen sich die Bewohner oft in ihre Häuser zurückziehen. Und manchmal kommt die Flut ziemlich heftig, vor allem im Herbst und im Winter, dafür ist die Nordsee ja bekannt. Dann ist auf den Halligen 40- bis 50-mal »Land unter«.

Zehn Halligen gibt es heute insgesamt, fünf davon sind ständig bewohnt, die kleinste, Habel, ist 7, die größte, Langeneß, 956 Hektar groß. Es kommt auch vor, dass mehrere kleine Halligen im Lauf der Zeit durch Aufschwemmung wieder zu einer größeren zusammenwachsen; das ist bei Langeneß der Fall. Hier leben ungefähr 100 Menschen in 53 Haushalten auf 16 Warften. Warften sind vier bis fünf Meter hohe, künstlich aufgeschüttete Hügel, auf denen die Wohn- und Wirtschaftsgebäude stehen.

Langeneß ist mit dem Festland über eine Lorenbahn verbunden, die führt über die Hallig Oland nach Dagebüll. Aber nur bei Ebbe, bei Flut steht die ganze Strecke unter Wasser. Wenn die Bahn nicht fährt, kommt man auch mit dem Schiff nach Langeneß; bei der Rixwarft gibt's eine Anlegestelle.

Die Inselbahn ist nicht für den Personenverkehr vorgesehen, bei mir hat der Zugführer aber eine Ausnahme gemacht; hoffentlich bekommt er deswegen keine Schwierigkeiten.

ISLAND RAILWAY DAGEBÜLL-LANGENESS

A long time ago, Schleswig-Holstein used to look completely different from the way it does today. But in 1362 and 1634, violent storm tides battered the coast and large parts of the mainland sank into the sea. What remained are now the islands of Sylt, Föhr, Amrum, Pellworm, Nordstrand – and the Hallig Islands. The »Halligen« are also islands in the wadden sea, the coastal mud flats, but much smaller ones, and what's special about them is that they don't have dikes that could protect them from the sea. When high tide comes, the inhabitants often have to retreat to their houses. And sometimes the tide arrives pretty forcibly, especially in autumn and winter, which the North Sea is known for. Floods occur then 40 to 50 times on the Hallig Islands, announced in German as »land under (water)«.

There are today ten Hallig Islands in all, of which five are inhabited all year round. The smallest island, Habel, is 7 hectares in size, the biggest, Langeness, 956 hectares. It does happen that floods, over the course of the years, make one bigger island out of several small Hallig Islands. That is the case with Langeness. About 100 people in 53 households live here on 16 Warften, or mounds, raised artificially to a height of four-to-five metres, on which homes and outbuildings stand.

Langeness is linked to the mainland by freight wagon tracks that cross Hallig Oland Island to Dagebüll. But this only at low tide. At high tide, the entire stretch of tracks are under water. When the train isn't running, Langeness is reached by ship; Rixwarft has a landing stage.

The island railway is not meant to carry passengers, but the train driver made an exception for me. I hope he doesn't get into trouble for it.

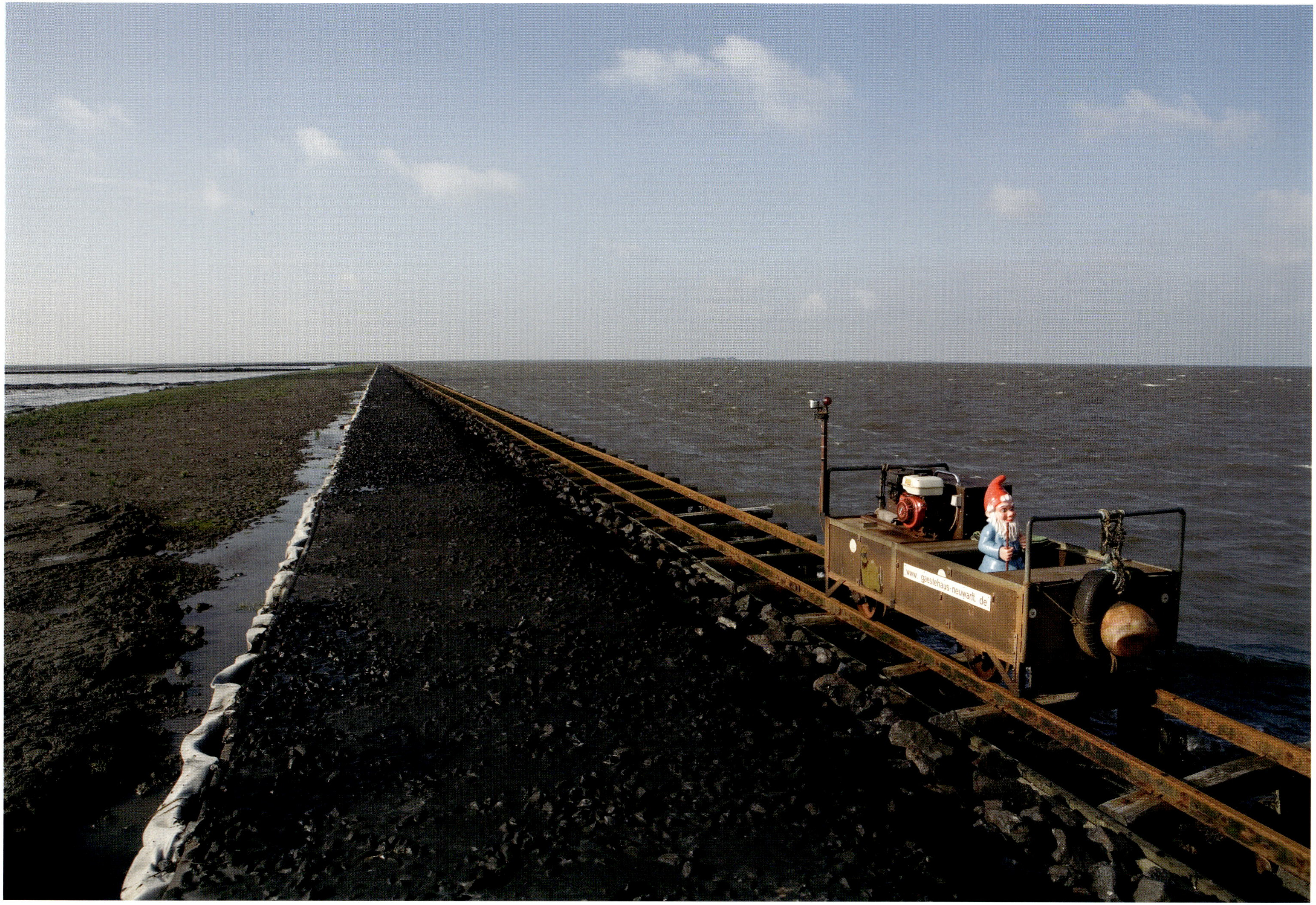
www. gaestehaus-neuwarft. de

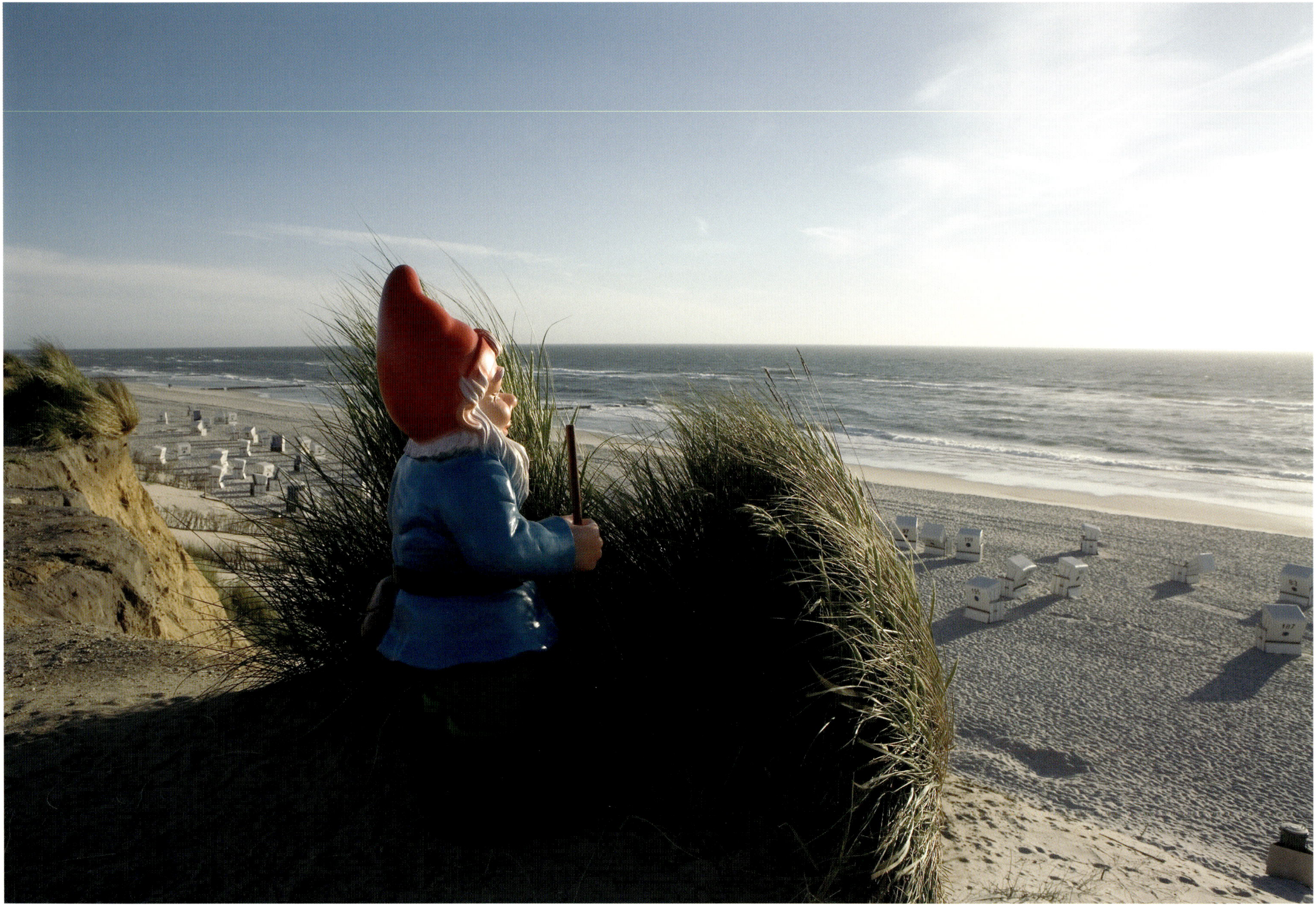

SYLT

Wisst ihr, was ein Charaktergras ist? Der Strandhafer, hinter dem ich hier stehe, ist zum Beispiel eins, und zwar ist er »charakteristisch für die Dünen an der Nord- und Ostseeküste«, so wie hier im Westen der Insel Sylt. Der Strandhafer muss ein sehr genügsames und zähes Gras sein, denn er wächst hauptsächlich im Sand, und die Küsten- und Inselbewohner pflanzen ihn an, damit das Meer den Strand nicht so schnell abnagt.

Sylt hat ungefähr 22.000 Einwohner und gut doppelt so viele Gästebetten. Außerdem stehen in der Hochsaison entlang der Westküste ungefähr 13.000 Strandkörbe. Zu den ständigen Bewohnern kommen noch mal gut 12.000 dazu, die auf der Insel eine Wohnung oder ein Haus haben, aber nur gelegentlich hierher kommen, im Urlaub, hauptsächlich im Sommer, oder am Wochenende – auf Sylt scheint die Sonne im Jahr 200 Stunden länger als in Hamburg.

Die Westküste ist ein 38 Kilometer langer Sandstrand, zwischen der Ostküste und dem Festland liegt das Wattenmeer; das kommt bei Ebbe fast vollständig aus dem Wasser. An der schmalsten Stelle, bei Rantum, liegen nur 360 Meter zwischen West- und Ostküste. Die größte Düne ist 52 Meter hoch, das ist in dieser Gegend schon so etwas wie ein Berg.

Bis zur großen Sturmflut, der »Manndränke« im Jahr 1362, gehörte Sylt, genauso wie die anderen Inseln und die Halligen, zum Festland. Seit 1927 gibt es über den Hindenburgdamm wieder eine feste Verbindung.

Sylt ist das nördlichste Stück von Deutschland. Das merkt man vor allem Mitte bis Ende Juni, dann dauern die Tage hier 17 Stunden. Rechnet man die zwei Stunden Dämmerung dazu, bleiben für die Nächte nur noch fünf Stunden, in denen es aber nie so richtig dunkel wird. Im Winter ist es dann allerdings genau andersrum.

SYLT

Do you know what character grass is? The beach grass, behind which I am standing, is one such grass. It is »characteristic for the dunes on the North and Baltic Sea coasts«, like here in the west of the island of Sylt. It must be very undemanding and hardy, for it grows mostly in sand, and the inhabitants of the coast and the islands plant it as a sandbinder to stabilize the beach against assaults from the sea.

Sylt has around 22,000 inhabitants and at least twice as many guest beds. In addition, during peak season, something like 13,000 wicker beach recliners dot the west coast. Along with the year-round inhabitants, there are over 12,000 people who keep a flat or a house on the island and only come over from time to time, chiefly on summer holidays or on the weekends. On Sylt, the sun shines 200 hours per year longer than in Hamburg.

The west coast has a 38 kilometre-long sandy beach, whereas between the east coast and the mainland lie the tidal flats that emerge almost completely from the water at low tide. At the most narrow point, near Rantum, there are only 360 metres of land between the west and the east coasts. The highest dune is 52 metres high, which in this region is actually something like a mountain.

Up until the year 1362, when the Great Manndränke storm tide hit, Sylt and all the other islands, including the Halligen, were part of the mainland. Since 1927, the Hindenburg Dike has again created a fixed link.

Sylt forms the most northern part of Germany. You notice this most distinctly from the middle to the end of June, when daylight lasts 17 hours. If you add the two hours for dawn and dusk, that leaves only five hours for the nights, which never do really get dark. In winter, however, it's the other way around.

GOETHES GARTENHAUS, WEIMAR

Am 22. April 1776 hat der sechsundzwanzigjährige, damals schon in ganz Europa berühmte Dichter Johann Wolfgang Goethe für 600 Taler den »Garten auf dem Horne samt dem darinnen befindlichen Gartenhause, nebst allem, was darinnen Erd-, Wand-, Band-, Nied- und Nagelfest ist«, gekauft. Aber eigentlich war es ein Geschenk des Herzogs Carl August, der den Dichter und vor allem den Juristen unbedingt in Weimar halten wollte und deshalb auch für die Renovierungsarbeiten aufkam. Goethe ist dadurch Bürger von Weimar geworden, und erst anschließend konnte ihn Carl August zum Geheimen Legationsrat im Dienst des Herzogtums Sachsen-Weimar-Eisenach ernennen; das war einer von den vielen Kleinstaaten, aus denen damals ganz Deutschland zum großen Teil bestand.

Im 16. Jahrhundert war dieses Haus am Hang des Flüsschens Ilm wahrscheinlich einmal ein Weinberghaus. Goethe hat es nach seinen Ansprüchen ausbauen lassen und sechs Jahre darin gewohnt. Für die Anlage des Parks hat er sich unter anderm das Gartenreich Wörlitz zum Vorbild genommen; er ist heute noch weitgehend in dem Zustand, wie Goethe ihn hinterlassen hat. Auch nach seinem Umzug in das Haus am Frauenplan mitten in Weimar hat sich der Dichter bis zu seinem Tod im Jahr 1832 immer wieder in sein »Gartenhaus« zurückgezogen.

Nur ein paar Schritte von Goethes Haus am Frauenplan entfernt steht das Deutsche Nationaltheater. Kurz nach dem Ersten Weltkrieg, im Februar 1919, ist hier die neu gewählte Nationalversammlung zusammengetreten; sie hatte den Auftrag, eine Verfassung auszuarbeiten. Die »Weimarer Verfassung« ist am 11. August verabschiedet worden. Aus diesem Grund hieß der erste demokratische Staat auf deutschem Boden »Weimarer Republik«. Bis zur Machtergreifung der Nationalsozialisten im Januar 1933 tagte sein Parlament im Berliner Reichstag.

GOETHE'S GARDEN HOUSE, WEIMAR

On April 22, 1776, the twenty-six-year-old poet Johann Wolfgang Goethe, at that time already famous in all of Europe, purchased for 600 Thaler the »garden on the Horne, including the garden house on it, along with everything that is fixed to ground and wall by string, rivet and nail.« But it was actually a donation by Duke Carl August, who definitely wanted to keep the poet, and above all the jurist, in Weimar and for that reason also paid for repairs and renovation. Goethe thus became a citizen of Weimar, it was then that Carl August could appoint him to the office of Privy Legation Councillor in the service of the Dukedom Saxon-Weimar-Eisenach. This was one of the many small states that made up the major part of Germany at the time.

In the 16th century, this house on a slope of the river Ilm was probably once part of a vineyard estate. Goethe had it converted to his specifications and lived there for six years. He modelled the layout of the park on, among other things, the garden realm of Wörlitz; and it is still today more or less in the same state as Goethe left it. Even after his move to the house on the Frauenplan in the middle of Weimar, and up to his death in the year 1832, the poet often retired to his »garden house«.

The German National Theatre is located only a few paces away from Goethe's house on the Frauenplan. Shortly after World War I, in February 1919, the newly elected National Assembly convened here; their mission was to work out a constitution. The »Weimarer Verfassung« was passed on August 11. For this reason, the first democratic state on German soil was called the Weimar Republic. Until the Nazis won power in January 1933, its parliament met in the Berlin Reichstag where they held their sessions.

235

DANKE!

Ich war auf meiner Reise quer durch Deutschland viele Monate unterwegs: mit dem Auto, dem Zug und dem Schiff; wenn's ging, bin ich gewandert, und einmal habe ich sogar in einem Flugzeug gesessen. Dabei habe ich unzählige Menschen kennen gelernt, die alle sehr hilfsbereit, freundlich und liebenswürdig zu mir waren, manchmal waren sie auch einfach neugierig. Viele von ihnen sind mir richtig ans Herz gewachsen, und manchmal kommt es mir so vor: ich ihnen auch. Ich würde gerne jeden einzelnen von ihnen nennen und eine Geschichte dazu erzählen, aber dafür würde der Platz nicht ausreichen. Und deswegen hier an alle, denen ich auf meiner Deutschlandtour begegnet bin und die sich an mich erinnern: Herzlichen Dank!

Ausdrücklich bedanken möchte ich mich bei meinen engsten Freunden, die mich mit vielen Tipps und Tricks, mit Rat und Tat unterstützt haben: beim Vorbereiten der Reisen und während der Reisen selbst, beim Fotografieren und beim Entziffern meiner Notizen, beim Aufbau und bei der Pflege meiner Website, beim Gestalten, Schreiben, Drucken und Verlegen dieses Buches. Danke also Alexander, Alexandra, Andrea, Andreas, Bernd, Charles, Dieter, Diethelm, Hans, Holger, Inge, Jeanne, June, Karl-Heinz, Marcel, Marion, Martina, Maximilian, Michael, Petra, Reinhard, Rulf, Thomas und Susanne. Ich liebe euch alle.

MY THANKS!

I have, for many months now, been on a trip right across Germany: by car, by train and by boat; when it worked out, I hiked, and I even once sat in an aeroplane. I came to meet a great deal of people this way, who were all very helpful, friendly and charming and who very kindly took care of me. I grew extremely fond of many of them, and sometimes it seemed to me that the feeling was mutual. I would very gladly mention all of them individually by name and tell the stories that go with them, but space doesn't allow it. So to all those I met on my tour of Germany and who remember me: my very warmest thanks!

I particularly want to thank my closest friends who supported me with tips and tricks of the trade, with verbal as well as hands-on advice, in preparing my trips and during the trips themselves, photographing and decoding my notes, in setting up and maintaining my website, in designing, writing, printing and publishing this book. Therefore, I thank Alexander, Alexandra, Andrea, Andreas, Bernd, Charles, Dieter, Diethelm, Hans, Holger, Inge, Jeanne, June, Karl-Heinz, Marcel, Marion, Martina, Maximilian, Michael, Petra, Reinhard, Rulf, Thomas and Susanne. I love you all.

© Concept, text, design and photographs: Mamywoto
www.mamywoto.com

Printed by:
druckpartner, Druck- und Medienhaus GmbH, Essen

Published by:
Nicolaische Verlagsbuchhandlung GmbH, Berlin

At www.nicolai-verlag.de you can subscribe to our
newsletter with information about our publishing
program and current titles.

© 2006 Nicolaische Verlagsbuchhandlung and Mamywoto

ISBN 13: 978-3-89479-295-4
ISBN 10:   3-89479-295-7

Printed in Germany

All rights reserved. No part of this book may be reproduced
or transmitted in any form or by any means, electronic or
mechanical, including photocopying, recording, storage in
an information retrieval system, or otherwise, without the
prior written permission of the author.
Contact: mamywoto@mamywoto.com